Vertical Take-Off Fighter Aircraft

CLASSIC
An imprint of
Ian Allan Publishing

By Bill Rose

First published 2013

ISBN 978 1 906537 39 5

Published by Classic Publishing
an imprint of Ian Allan Publishing Ltd, Hersham, Surrey KT12 4RG.

Printed in England

Visit the Ian Allan Publishing website at **www.ianallanpublishing.com**

FRONT COVER Lockheed-Martin F-35B Lightning II STOVL fighter (BF-02), undergoing low speed handling trials. *US Navy*

BACK COVER LEFT The Convair XFY-1 VTOL fighter prototype shortly after take-off. *US Navy*

BACK COVER RIGHT Preparing the SNECMA C.450 prototype for a VTOL test flight. *SNECMA*

PAGE 1 A Royal Navy Sea Harrier is prepared for flight in the early 1980s. *Bill Rose*

PAGE 2 The Lockheed XFV-1 VTOL prototype fighter in its transportation and elevation rig. *Lockheed*

Contents

Introduction

Until the arrival of fixed-wing aircraft, vertical take-off and landing (VTOL) was an accepted and uncomplicated feature of manned flight. The balloon or airship could operate from almost any site, whereas gliders and eventually powered aircraft required substantial areas of prepared space. As the size and weight of aircraft increased, so did take-off and landing requirements. This would lead to the establishment of permanent airfields with hard runways and all the necessary facilities. While the capability of fixed-wing aircraft developed rapidly, VTOL remained confined to lighter-than-air vehicles and eventually the helicopter. Designers continued to explore methods that would allow fixed-wing aircraft to take off and land in the shortest possible distance and many envisaged the progressive move towards high-speed civil and military aircraft able to operate from small, improvised sites and perhaps hover for short periods of time. Unfortunately, a lack of engine power and weight penalties would remain major stumbling blocks for several decades.

The advantage of combat aircraft with VTOL features has always been obvious, allowing operational flexibility and reduced vulnerability. Large airfields full of combat aircraft are first-strike targets and modern hardened aircraft shelters are vulnerable to attacks with the latest precision-guided weapons carrying conventional warheads. Furthermore, in a major conflict, an entire military base or large civil airport can be taken out with a single missile carrying a relatively low-yield nuclear warhead. Various types of VTOL aircraft are also well suited to the maritime environment, allowing deployment from carriers, larger warships, adapted commercial vessels and possibly borderline science fiction concepts such as submersible aircraft carriers, which have received serious consideration in the past.

The first vertical take-off (VTO) rocket fighter (the Bachem Ba 349 Natter) was developed and tested in Nazi Germany as a semi-expendable last-ditch weapon. This manned missile was deployed operationally during the final days of World War 2, but it never saw any action. Even if this aircraft (and similar weapons) had been

available in larger numbers a year earlier, it seems unlikely they would have made any difference to the outcome of World War 2. But the concept of a point defence daylight interceptor that could be deployed from dispersed sites would influence almost every postwar 'think-tank' concerned with air defence.

Subsequently, this led to various unusual proposals for high-performance manned interceptors, which in some cases reached the prototype stage. A number of offensive military roles can now be handled by helicopters, which have steadily improved in capability since World War 2. Nevertheless, the rotary-wing aircraft will never compete with a modern multi-role jet fighter in terms of speed, range, payload and low observability. It may also be stating the obvious, but in most respects a fixed-wing combat aircraft can never compete with a helicopter and it is not intended to. Building a VTOL, or short take-off and vertical landing (STOVL), capability into a fixed-wing combat aircraft has proved to be a major design challenge, requiring complex propulsion systems that introduce handling and reliability issues, while adding weight that limits range, performance and payload. To date, the only truly successful VTOL strike fighter has been the Harrier and when placed alongside a conventional contemporary combat aircraft such as the F-16 or MiG-29, the only advantage this aircraft possesses is its take-off and landing ability. In almost every other respect the cheaper alternatives are superior and much easier to fly. A full VTOL capability allows the use of improvised sites within city centres, forest clearings, or perhaps a desert location. However, taking off vertically with a full load is not a practical proposition and aircraft like the Harrier normally make a brief run to become airborne, so are more accurately classed as an STOVL type.

While Harriers have been prepared for emergency VTOL air defence operations, these aircraft were never intended for use in this manner and the extra power required for vertical lift-off uses a considerable amount of fuel and places significant restrictions on the aircraft's payload capability. This is one of the reasons why the Royal

Navy's ski ramp was employed to improve short rolling take-off performance on aircraft carriers. Land-based operations during conflicts have been more likely to take place (when necessary) from hastily prepared runways (as was demonstrated during the Falklands War), or using short sections of suitable roadway when available. The Harrier's Rolls-Royce Pegasus turbofan engine is this aircraft's most important feature and the use of vectorable thrust for lift and horizontal flight has set it aside from other STOVL designs.

A frequent shortcoming of many VTOL designs has been the need to carry extra engines for lift, as these become dead weight in horizontal flight. However, from the early 1950s to the mid-1960s, it looked as if VTOL was likely to become a standard feature for many new civil and military fixed-wing aircraft, with designers putting their faith in rapidly developing engine technology to provide the solution. In fact, the Harrier and Soviet Yak-38 are the only fixed-wing military VTOL aircraft to have entered service, with the Russian aircraft performing relatively poorly before it was withdrawn from use. The Harrier has remained operational with the British, Americans and several other nations, with numerous upgrades over the course of its life. It had quite a high accident rate and was expensive to operate and maintain, but has now been retired by the British, who plan to replace this unique aircraft with a version of the new Lockheed Martin F-35B Lightning stealth fighter.

It is hard to say what the future holds for manned combat aircraft with an STOVL or VTOL capability. At present, the controversial Lockheed Martin F-35B is the only new fighter that provides an STOVL capability. No comparable warplanes are known to be in development, although it is possible that China will field an STOVL fighter, possibly based on an advanced Yakovlev design.

It was never my intention to produce a catalogue of every known VTO, VTOL or STOVL fighter proposal and there may be some unusual designs missing from this book. One example would be flying disc fighter aircraft, but these can be found in my previous book *Flying Saucer Technology*, published by Midland in 2011. While I have included details of the Harrier and its engine, the Soviet Yakovlev VTOL designs and the Joint Strike Fighter (JSF) programme (leading to the F-35), I have not set out to provide highly detailed histories of these aircraft. Many excellent books are available that outline their development in considerable detail and it was my intention from the outset to concentrate on lesser-known types. From time to time this book strays a little from my original terms of reference, which were to produce a reasonably good outline of more obscure and sometimes previously classified VTOL fighters. After starting work, I decided to include a number of aircraft that were influential or related to VTOL aircraft, such as early VTO rocket fighters, rocket-launched conventional fighters or a few concepts with exceptional short take-off and landing (STOL) capabilities. I should add that there are always gaps in the histories of unusual military projects that were originally classified. When the details finally become public knowledge, much of the original documentation has often been disposed of or lost and the designers and engineers who worked on these projects have passed away.

Bill Rose
Norfolk
2013

Special Acknowledgements
Chris Gibson
Mike Pryce
Tony Buttler
Scott Lowther
Martin Müller
Alexi Malinovsky
Hans-Ulrich Willbold
John Luc Seligman

Chapter 1 1935-1945

Prior to World War 2, there were various attempts to develop a fixed-wing aircraft capable of taking off vertically or in an extremely short distance, but at that time the biggest problem for aeronautical engineers was engine power, which remained totally inadequate for this purpose. Some designers came closer than others in their quest for a short-take-off and landing (STOL) aircraft, but little progress was made, with the general focus of attention turning towards the helicopter and autogyro.

ABOVE A production Bachem Natter recovered by US forces. This example is in a fairly poor condition and appears to have a full load of air-to-air rockets in the nose. *US Army*

MAI Sokol (Falcon)

One of the earliest, well-considered attempts to design a VTOL fighter was undertaken from 1935 to 1936 by F. P. Kurochkin, a Russian aeronautical student attending the *Moskovskiy Aviatsionniy Institut* (MAI). His tutor, who encouraged and supervised this project, was Professor Boris Yuryev (1889-1957), who had been responsible for most of the early helicopter development in Russia. Kurochkin's proposal was for a compact one-man aircraft called the Falcon with tiltable propellers housed in wingtip nacelles. It would be powered by a 12Y Hispano-Suiza V-12 water-cooled engine with a quoted take-off output of 860hp (641kW). I have been unable to locate the specific variant of this engine, but it is likely that a Klimov licence-built unit, similar to the 12Ydrs, was intended. This engine was mounted in the rear of the fuselage behind the cockpit and shaft-coupled to each propeller nacelle. The forward-mounted three-blade propellers would have an overall radius of 13.1ft (4m). In addition, a third two-blade propeller unit with a radius of 6.5ft (2m) was positioned in a slot at the rear of the fuselage and directly coupled to the engine via a clutch and gearbox. An engine-cooling radiator would be placed in the nose of the aircraft with the option to adjust airflow depending on conditions.

The Falcon's overall length was 24ft (7.53m), with a wingspan of 19ft (5.80m) and an estimated take-off weight of 4,078lb (1,850kg). Maximum horizontal speed was expected to be 327mph (527km/h) although the range is unknown. The initial suggestion for armament was a single machine gun ahead of the cockpit. VTOL operations would be undertaken with a substantial section of the wing and both engines turned upwards by 90°. The landing gear comprised a tailskid and a

LEFT A scale model of Kurochkin's VTOL Falcon fighter, with the wings tilted upwards to show VTOL operation. *Bill Rose collection*

BELOW A three-view drawing of the VTOL fighter designed in the mid-1930s by F. P. Kurochkin, an aeronautical student attending the Moskovskiy Aviatsionniy Institut (MAI). *Bill Rose*

single retractable wheel below the central fuselage section. Small outrigger wheels would be fitted to the rear of the engine nacelles. This layout, combined with propeller size, indicates that Kurochkin had no intention of providing a horizontal take-off and landing capability. In October 1936, Professor B. Yuryev arranged for a model of the aircraft to be wind tunnel tested and available documentation suggests these trials provided some promising results. Nevertheless, the design was regarded as too much of a technical challenge to build and it was finally abandoned, which was undoubtedly the right decision at that time. In comparison, the controversial V-22 Osprey tiltrotor transporter, built by Bell Helicopter Textron and Boeing Helicopters, entered service relatively recently, having taken several decades and billions of dollars to fully develop.

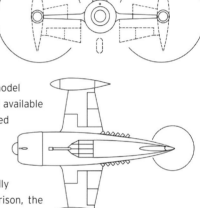

Muck VTOL Concept

ABOVE Otto Muck, engineer, designer and author. *Via Bill Rose*

Another interesting 1930s concept was a VTOL tailsitter, designed and patented by Austrian-born Dipl.Ing Otto Heinrich Muck (1892-1956), who lived in the small southern German town of Uffing, close to Munich. On 10 September 1938, Muck applied for a patent and this was published on 22 October 1942 (Ref: 728526). Muck applied for a second patent on 1 November 1938 and this was published on 19 November 1941 (Ref: 714001). These documents appear to have remained secret for the duration of the war. Muck was a highly qualified design engineer, who held a string of patents dating back to the mid-1920s. He had served as a pilot during World War 1 and became involved with an Austrian military aircraft project during the 1920s. By the late 1930s, Muck was employed by Siemens to conduct research into electromagnetic railguns. During World War 2, he specialised in projectile design (possibly as part of the

railgun project), working for much of this period at the Peenemünde rocket-testing centre in Northern Germany.

The surviving technical details for Muck's first tailsitter are very brief and rather vague, although the aircraft appears to have been designed as a single seater. It utilised a large fixed wing and was fitted with contra-rotating propeller blades of equal span that would counteract any torque problems. Muck believed these large propellers were necessary to generate sufficient lift for VTOL. They would be driven by an unspecified internal combustion engine located ahead of the centrally positioned cockpit. The tail section was fitted with cruciform fins and presumably control surfaces, with each fin having a nacelle to contain a hydraulic landing leg. One other unusual and seemingly rather dubious feature was a section of the rear fuselage that would telescope inwards on landing to reduce the overall length of the

ABOVE These sketchy details show the overall appearance of Otto Muck's first VTOL aircraft design. *German Patent Office*

RIGHT The second VTOL tailsitter design produced by Otto Muck in the late 1930s. *German Patent Office*

aircraft, making it more stable, while acting as a dampener. No details of the anticipated powerplant are mentioned, or any other specifications, such as dimensions, weights or performance. Muck appears to have intended this aircraft to function as a fighter, probably equipped with synchronised forward-firing machine guns.

The second proposal shows a winged tailsitter with a tail section that expands outwards into four separate legs to support the aircraft on the ground. Short fins are attached to the tail sections and each would be equipped with a small wheel. This version of the tailsitter utilised propeller blades with a significantly larger radius than the wingspan. Although interesting designs, Muck's complex proposals failed to generate significant interest within the *Reichsluftfahrtministerium* (RLM – Wartime German Air Ministry) and they remained unknown until relatively recently. However, the overall concept is believed to have inspired development of the more advanced Focke-Wulf Triebflügel, which is discussed in a later section of this chapter.

After the war, Muck worked as an engineering consultant for various companies and continued to patent designs. One of his last projects was a book about the legendary island of Atlantis but soon after its completion he was killed in a car crash.

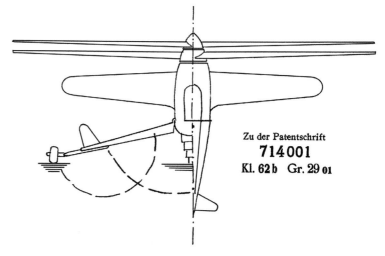

Zu der Patentschrift
714001
Kl. 62b Gr. 29 01

Leonard VTOL Fighter

Another interesting series of VTOL designs to emerge during the immediate prewar years were produced by American engineer Lloyd Hugo Leonard. He submitted detailed proposals for a rather unusual and advanced VTOL tailsitter to the US Army Air Corps and the Navy in mid-1939. At this time, Leonard was working as an engineer for the National Advisory Committee for Aeronautics (NACA – the forerunner of NASA) at Langley Field, Virginia. Leonard's name appeared on various NACA scientific reports until the mid-1950s, although his background is rather obscure and what I have learnt remains unverified, so this information is not included.

Leonard's first VTOL concept, which he described as a 'helicopter-type aircraft', was intended to be a fighter. The anticipated method of propulsion was a 1,000hp (745kW) Pratt & Whitney twin-radial engine, driving contra-rotating, twin-bladed sets of propellers with a radius of 40ft (12.1m). Leonard suggested that a single set of blades was possible, although he preferred contra-propellers, as this would eliminate torque. He also believed that in the event of an engine failure, the aircraft could descend without power, relying on the

rotation of these sizeable blades to permit an emergency vertical landing. Air for cooling the engine would be drawn in via the central section of the forward spinner, exiting from just behind the second set of propellers. Leonard claimed a maximum speed at sea level of 428mph (688km/h), reaching about 500mph (800km/h) at 20,000ft (6,096m) and a climb rate of 3,750ft/min (1,143m/min), with a ceiling in excess of 40,000ft (12,192m). On paper, this seemed possible when allowing for the aircraft's estimated overall weight of 5,000lb (2,268kg) and very clean aerodynamic lines. In practice, it looks as if he was being rather optimistic. This torpedo-shaped aircraft had a length of 25ft (7.3m) and a fuselage diameter of 46in (1.16m), with a wingspan of 20ft (6m). The pilot would sit directly behind the propeller/engine section, in a cockpit covered by upper and lower bubble canopies and fitted with clear side panels. In addition, his seat was designed to swivel through 90º during transition from vertical take-off to level flight to provide adequate visibility at all times.

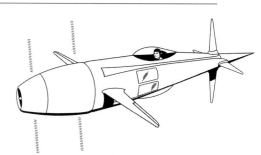

ABOVE Drawing based on original artwork showing the appearance of Leonard's initial design for a manned VTOL aircraft. *Bill Rose*

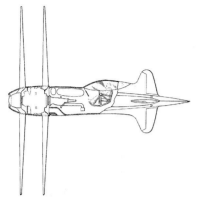

LEFT This cross-section of a Leonard aircraft proposal shows some of the layout details that could be found in the improved version of his initial VTOL fighter design. *US Patent Office*

RIGHT Leonard's VTOL fighter design showing the landing leg arrangement. *US Patent Office*

Leonard proposed rather a complex undercarriage for the aircraft, which comprised four legs that opened outwards from the fuselage, each containing a small, dampened wheel. One interesting feature was a central tail probe used for landings. On contact with the ground this would release the four legs, which would swing outwards and lock into position. Drawings of Leonard's first VTOL concept show control surfaces on the wings and although the early illustrations are somewhat unclear, it seems likely that Leonard intended to utilise the four small tail fins for more than just directional stability. The first proposal shows insufficient space for weapons, which would presumably take the form of forward-firing machine guns. This is probably the only type of armamant that could be carried by this design. There was also limited space for fuel storage, creating significant restrictions on flight duration.

Leonard then reworked the design, increasing the weight to 8,000lb (3,628kg) and making a series of changes and improvements. This was a subject of a second US Patent (Ref: 2387762), which he applied for on 25 January 1941 and was published on 30 October 1945. Broadly similar to the initial design, it was fitted with larger tail fins, each with a control surface, and there were significant cockpit alterations. Leonard retained the swivelling pilot's seat, but abandoned the lower canopy and large side windows. While no alternative is shown, Leonard must have envisaged some means for the pilot to observe his surroundings during take-off and landing. On the other hand, it is possible that he simply decided not to tilt the seat forward by more than about 45º. There is no indication of how Leonard proposed to arm this aircraft, but it seems fair to assume that it would have taken the form of two or four forward-firing machine guns. Leonard estimated that this aircraft would be capable of 399mph (642km/h) at sea level and 485mph (780km/h) at an altitude of 20,000ft (6,096m). Like the first design, this aircraft was expected to make the transition from vertical to horizontal flight in less than 3.5 seconds.

Leonard produced a third helicopter-type aircraft design, which he submitted to the military for consideration. This futuristic teardrop-shaped concept

RIGHT Leonard's surprisingly futuristic teardrop-shaped design for a VTOL helicopter-type aircraft. Relocating the engine and propeller blades allowed excellent visibility from the forward-positioned cockpit, which in this illustration provided accommodation for two in side-by-side positions that swivelled during VTOL operations. A one-man proposal for this type of aircraft was submitted to the US military in 1939, but it was rejected, probably on the grounds of being too unusual and presenting numerous technical challenges to develop and build. *US Patent Office*

differed considerably from the earlier proposals. The cockpit was moved to the front of the aircraft and the engine and propeller blades were now centrally positioned. The new arrangement provided excellent visibility for the pilot and a development of this aircraft allowed a second crew member in a side-by-side position. The seating was contained within a swivelling framework, providing 90º of tilt for VTOL operations. The original powerplant would be used, driving smaller propellers with a radius of 28ft (8.5m). The overall length of this aircraft was 26.5ft (8m). Leonard decided to position narrow wings with control surfaces behind the propeller/engine section and these would be equipped with control surfaces, having an overall span of 24ft (7.3m). The slightly enhanced version of this particular design was fitted with four forward-positioned fins with small control surfaces, presumably to improve stability.

The Materials Division of the US Army Air Corps at Wright field formally received Leonard's proposals, with an assessment being conducted by Paul H. Kemmer, who headed the Aircraft Laboratory. He concluded that numerous technical issues would need to be resolved before such an aircraft could be built and Kemmer's final report must have been very disappointing to the designer. Much the same response appears to have been

BELOW This sectional drawing of a Leonard VTOL design shows how he intended to use an internal combustion engine to deliver air and fuel to the tip-mounted combustion jets. Some elements of this concept do not appear to have been considered in sufficient detail to be workable. *US Patent Office*

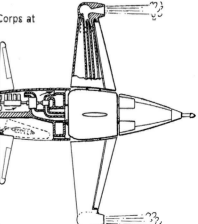

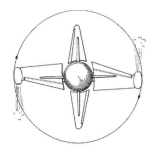

LEFT This Leonard helicopter-type aircraft concept from 1943 is propelled by two large rotors with jet (or rocket) engines at each tip. The design has rear-mounted fins and control surfaces in a section of fuselage that fully opens for landing. *US Patent Office*

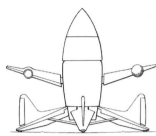

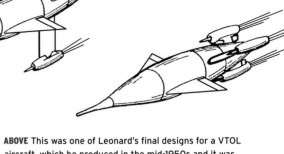

forthcoming from the US Navy, who dismissed Leonard's proposals as being over-optimistic and technically too demanding.

These seem to have been reasonably fair comments as many of Leonard's claims were based on the application of unproven methods and his performance estimates seem very over-optimistic. Despite these rejections, Leonard went on to file further patents for similar VTOL concepts. One design used jet/ramjet engines mounted on a single set of four propeller blades, while there was a similar arrangement using small propellers. Eventually, in the mid-1950s, he produced a revised proposal for an aircraft with podded jet engines at the tips of three rotors that folded back in flight. Nothing came from any of this work, although Leonard almost certainly built and tested small models

ABOVE This was one of Leonard's final designs for a VTOL aircraft, which he produced in the mid-1950s and it was powered by a turbojet or ramjet in a nacelle at each rotor tip. In level flight, the rotor would slow to a fixed position with the engines facing rearward. It would then be possible to swing the rotor blades rearward to improve performance and allow supersonic speed. *Leonard/Bill Rose*

and probably undertook wind tunnel tests while working for NACA, Langley. Whether or not any of his designs might have flown remains hard to say, but Leonard's VTOL designs were extremely futuristic and many features would prove influential.

Bell VTOL Fighter

Arthur Middleton Young (1905–1995) was another exceptionally talented designer, engineer and creative thinker. Today, he is remembered by the aeronautical community as the inventor of the Bell helicopter. As a child, he was known to his family as an 'expert gadgeteer' and, having graduated in mathematics from Princeton University in 1927, Young began to work privately on various inventions and, specifically, designs for helicopters. By the early 1930s, Young had built a working helicopter model that attracted the attention of Lawrence Bell, who had a long track record in the aviation industry and had just founded the Bell Aircraft Corporation in Buffalo, New York. Bell was on the lookout for innovative technology for his new company and immediately reached a financial agreement with Young to continue work on helicopter development. Having moved to Buffalo, he developed the rotor stabiliser bar (flybar) and completed a one-man tailless VTOL aircraft design, which made considerable use of features normally applied to a helicopter. It seems that this aircraft was conceived as a fighter from the outset and Young assigned this design to the Bell Aircraft Corporation, who applied for a US Patent on 8 January 1941. It remained undisclosed until the end of World War 2, being finally published on 14 August 1945 (Ref: 2382460).

The proposed aircraft was a single-seat tailsitter, although it was effectively completely tailless, with only

the engine and landing gear occupying a short section of fuselage behind the cockpit. The aircraft would be equipped with fairly conventional wings fitted with ailerons. Propulsion would be achieved by two sets of contra-rotating two-blade propellers, which operated in a fairly unorthodox manner, drawing on Young's experience with helicopter development. Aside from counteracting torque, the operation of the propellers was quite complex, with the forward rotor designed to alter its inclination in any direction and provide flight control, while the rear unit would only be capable of changes in pitch. The aircraft would rest on the ground supported by three hydraulically dampened landing legs fitted with wheels. These would be extended outwards and downwards during rest and would fully retract during flight to avoid drag.

Power was provided by an unspecified air-cooled radial engine. This would be located directly behind the cockpit and coupled to a gearbox and the propellers by a long driveshaft that would be positioned between the pilot's legs. The engine would be cooled by air drawn in via an inlet below the cockpit, with Young suggesting the option of ducting it from slots in the wings. The air used for cooling would then be expelled from the tail of the aircraft, possibly

BELOW Arthur Young's VTOL fighter design, produced in 1941 while he was working for the Bell Aircraft Corporation. This concept remained secret until the end of World War 2. *US Patent Office*

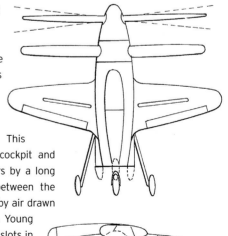

provide extra visibility during lift-off and once transition to horizontal flight had taken place, the pilot's seat would swivel forward through 90°.

Young was convinced that, in an emergency, the aircraft could use auto-rotation to undertake a hard landing, but like all the previous designs it would be difficult for the pilot to escape from the aircraft during flight and there was no provision for ejection. There are no details currently available that show proposed dimensions, weights or estimated performance. It seems likely that Bell approached the military with this design, but there are no documents currently available that show any serious interest being taken.

The design eventually re-emerged in the March 1948 issue of *Mechanix Illustrated* magazine as a short feature called 'Convertible Jet Helicopter' by Gilbert Paust.

The content was actually a little misleading as the aircraft was not jet powered or a radical new design as Paust claimed. Illustrations showed it in a civil role as a two-seat delivery aircraft for the US Mail, but everything suggests that Young envisaged this as a single-seat highly manoeuvrable fighter from the outset and the idea of this concept being used as a mail plane was unrealistic.

LEFT This drawing based on the Bell VTOL fighter appeared in the March 1948 issue of *Mechanix Illustrated* and accompanied an article by Gilbert Paust called 'Convertible Jet Helicopter'. Paust adapted the aircraft to the peacetime role of delivering mail, although it would have been unsuitable in many respects, not least the lack of cargo space. *Reproduced with the permission of Charles Shopsin of modernmechanix.com*

with the assistance of a fan coupled to the engine, and exhaust gas from the engine would be ducted into the flow from a manifold system. The overall outflow was expected to provide a small amount of additional thrust. Prior to take-off, the pilot would gain entry to the cockpit via a fuselage hatch next to the wing. There would be a glass panel directly opposite the cockpit canopy to

Supermarine VTOL Fighter

Almost nothing is known about Supermarine's wartime proposal for a VTOL fighter, which appeared as a drawing on a company document with the reference Technical Office Report No 4040 of 26 February 1944. That said, a number of deductions can be drawn from the information available. This one-man tailsitter was designed with a torpedo-shaped fuselage supported on four tail fins. Each would be equipped with a nacelle at the tip containing a landing leg and wheel. The centrally located wing had a leading edge sweep of approximately 12°, utilising ailerons, and there were large pods at each tip, located just beyond the radius of the propellers. Each would contain two cannons of an unspecified calibre.

Engine radiators were located in units on the underside of each wing and the engine was positioned at the centre of the aircraft between the wings, with short exhaust ports on each side. Suitable engines that come to mind might have been the experimental high-powered

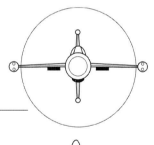

24-cylinder Rolls-Royce Eagle or a late version of the Napier Sabre. This would be shaft-coupled to the forward contra-rotating propellers, via a gearbox arrangement. The exact number of blades chosen for this aircraft remains unknown and although there have been claims that the assembly would have used two sets of four blades, this remains unconfirmed. No dimensions, weights or claims for performance are quoted and it is not known if the designers considered a swivelling seat for the pilot. Although it was an interesting concept, the Supermarine VTOL fighter does not appear to have progressed much further than the drawing board, and perhaps the rapid progress being made with turbojets had some bearing on the issue?

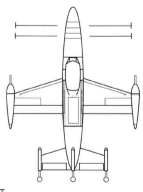

RIGHT The general appearance of Supermarine's wartime VTOL fighter concept. Relatively little is currently known about this impressive tailsitter. *Bill Rose*

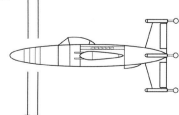

Vertical Take-Off Interceptors

The famous German scientist Wernher von Braun (1912-1977) produced the first known design for a rocket-powered vertical take-off (VTO) interceptor in the late 1930s. It would climb rapidly to intercept enemy bombers and return to base after completing its mission, making a glide landing. The initial proposal had an overall length of 28ft (8.5m), a wingspan of 30ft (9.15m) and a gross weight of approximately 11,200lb (5,080kg). The liquid-fuel rocket engine was designed by von Braun and would produce an estimated take-off thrust of 22,400lb (99.6kN). With an impressive rate of climb calculated at 50 seconds to 25,000ft (7,620m), von Braun suggested that it might be necessary to throttle back to avoid encountering the anticipated sound barrier. Having reached its cruising altitude, a second 1,700lb (7.56kN) thrust chamber would be used to provide a speed of 430mph (692km/h), with an anticipated ceiling of about 35,000ft (10,668m). Armed with four machine guns, the aircraft would be directed to its target by ground controllers, eventually assisted with radar.

After 15 minutes, the fuel would be exhausted and the aircraft would glide back to base, landing on a retractable skid. Wind tunnel models of the aircraft were tested and von Braun sought the assistance of Dr Helmut von Zborowski (1905-1969) at the BMW Bramo facility in Berlin-Spandau to improve the rocket engine. Plans for this VTO interceptor were finally submitted to the RLM on 6 July 1939, although the idea of developing such an aircraft generated relatively little interest within Luftwaffe circles. Germany had robust air defences and there was simply no perceived need for such an aircraft. Nevertheless, Heinkel and GerhardFieselerWerke both expressed interest in the project, which kept it alive and led to some further development, although the RLM finally decided to scrap the programme in mid-1941. There was still no significant requirement for a VTO design, although the Luftwaffe was committed to the Me163B rocket interceptor. While von Braun's concept seemed to be at an end, some further studies were undertaken by Dr Erich Bachem (1906-1960) who was responsible for development of the Fieseler Fi103 flying bomb at the Peenemünde rocket site. He produced two different VTO rocket-powered interceptor proposals, which both carried the reference Fi166.

Bachem's first design was a two-stage system, utilising a modified A5 rocket as the launch vehicle and a twin-turbojet-powered fighter based on a Bf109 airframe. This concept did not make a great deal of progress and he then reverted to a simpler design that was closer to the original von Braun aircraft. This was powered by a single rocket engine, providing a maximum speed of 515mph (829km/h) and a 45-minute

endurance. Nothing came of Bachem's ideas and they were shelved. In early 1942, Bachem left Fieseler to establish Bachem Werke, which would manufacture spares and components for fighter aircraft. When the war began to turn against Germany, air defence became increasingly important and the RLM issued a requirement for a lower cost alternative to the Me163B rocket fighter. A hastily arranged design contest was undertaken, with the RLM finally choosing the near-vertically launched Heinkel P.1077 Julia over a rival Junkers proposal known as the EF 127 Walli.

Although Heinkel started work on its project almost immediately, this did not deter Dr Bachem from submitting a new design to the RLM.

It utilised many features developed for the later Fi-166 and further ideas suggested by his friend von Braun. The new semi-expendable interceptor called the Natter (Adder) was powered by a single liquid fuel Walter HWK 109-509A rocket engine of 3,750lb (16.6kN) thrust that had also been chosen for the Heinkel P.1077 and Junkers EF 127. In addition, there were four strap-on solid-fuel booster rockets, which would be jettisoned about 10 seconds after launch. Like the Julia, this interceptor was mainly constructed from cheap, easy-to-fabricate wooden components that could be manufactured at dispersed sites by semi-skilled workers using basic hand tools. Bachem estimated that one complete aircraft would take about 1,000 man-hours of labour, although he hoped it might be possible to reduce this to 600 man-hours.

The Natter was a semi-disposable weapon system capable of being deployed at improvised sites. It utilised an automated launch procedure and radio guidance, which suggests that a relatively inexperienced pilot

TOP Von Braun's 1939 design for a rocket-powered interceptor. This concept underwent a steady amount of refinement, but it was generally regarded as being superfluous to requirements and technically too far ahead of its time to warrant development.

CENTRE The Heinkel P.1077 Julia rocket interceptor. Selected for development in 1944, this aircraft was largely pushed aside by the Bachem Natter (Adder).

BOTTOM The Natter was a low-cost semi-expendable manned missile using the same engine and boosters as the Heinkel. It remains hard to say which of these aircraft would have been more dangerous to fly, but both were born out of desperation. These three drawings are roughly to scale. *All Bill Rose*

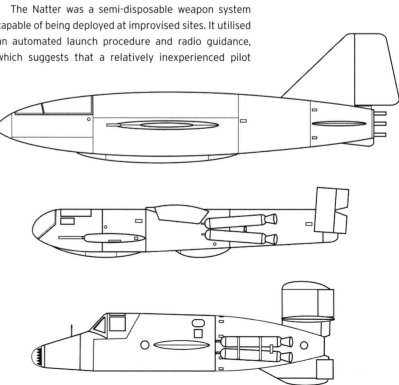

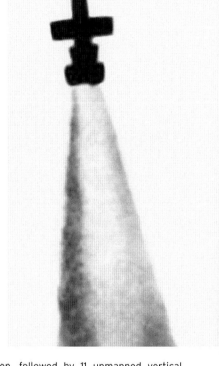

could fly the interceptor. When launched, Bachem's interceptor would rapidly climb towards the enemy bombers at a speed of 30,000ft (9,144m) per minute. Maximum speed would be in the region of 560mph (900km/h) with a ceiling in excess of 50,000ft (15,240m), but it had a somewhat restricted range of approximately 37 miles (59km). Once the pilot came within target range, he would fire a salvo of 24 Föhn (Storm) 73mm unguided air-to-air rockets, or alternatively 33 R4M 55mm folding fin rockets. These were contained in the nose section. The rocket motor's fuel would then be exhausted and the pilot would bale out. The front section of the aircraft would eventually crash, while the valuable engine would descend by parachute and be recovered by a ground crew for reuse. The entire mission would have lasted no more than a matter of minutes.

Although the RLM initially rejected Bachem's proposal on the grounds that Heinkel had been awarded the rocket interceptor contract and its aircraft was fully reusable, there was a change of mind when Heinrich Himmler became involved. It is not entirely clear how Bachem managed to gain his support, but nobody was going to argue with the head of the dreaded SS. As a consequence, Himmler immediately ordered the construction of 150 interceptors, to be paid for by the SS, and another 50 aircraft would follow for the Luftwaffe. Heinkel was relegated into second place, although development of the P.1077 continued, while Bachem put the finishing touches to his initial prototype. The vertically launched interceptor measured 18.75ft (5.7m) in length, with a wingspan of 11.8ft (3.60m) and a height of 7.3ft (2.25m). Fully loaded with boosters attached, the Natter weighed 4,850lb (2,200kg).

Models of the Natter were wind tunnel tested at Braunschweig to Mach .95 and the first prototype airframes were assembled at Bachem's Waldsee factory in the Black Forest. The first unpowered, manned test flight took place on 14 December 1944 at Neuberg on the Danube, when the third prototype was towed behind a Heinkel He-111 to an altitude of 18,000ft (5,500m) and released. This trial went well and the escape procedure proved satisfactory. Several further manned flights

TOP LEFT This illustration is believed to be based on a photograph of the Heinkel Julia mock-up built at the Vienna works. *Bill Rose collection*

CENTRE An unmanned Bachem Natter is prepared for a test launch and this example was just a shell powered by the four Schmidding boosters. *Bill Rose collection*

RIGHT This photograph shows one of the Natter test models just seconds after launch. *Bill Rose collection*

were undertaken, followed by 11 unmanned vertical launches using the solid-fuel booster rockets, which began on 22 December 1944. Early prototypes were referred to as the Ba20 and pre-production models received the designation Ba349A. There was now significant pressure to bring the Natter into operational service as quickly as possible, with the RLM becoming increasingly concerned that the USAAF was about to start using high-altitude B-29 bombers in Europe.

The first rocket-powered, manned test flight was undertaken on 1 March 1945 by Bachem's test pilot Lothar Siebert (1922-1945), a highly qualified flyer who had previously been assigned to the secretive special operations unit KG200. But soon after launch, disaster struck and he was killed. The brief inquiry into this accident concluded that the cockpit canopy became detached and he was rendered unconscious, losing control of the aircraft. In fact, the truth was somewhat different and a problem with one of the booster rockets was identified as the cause. Siebert had apparently tried to bale out, but failed, and the Natter climbed in a high arc then headed straight down at full speed, possibly breaking the sound barrier. The aircraft hit the ground about 4.3 miles (7km) from the launch site, resulting in a substantial explosion that left a large crater 16ft (5m) deep. Very little of Siebert's body was recovered from the crash site.

Clearly the Natter was an extremely risky machine to fly and the previous unmanned test that took place on 26 February 1945 had ended with the aircraft blowing up a few seconds after launch. Nevertheless,

the SS intended to have this project in operation as soon as possible and the review panel were simply ordered to conceal the true details of this accident and cause no noticeable delay. Possibly as many as six or seven further manned VTO flights were undertaken and then ten Ba 349A Natters were deployed for operational use at Kirchheim on Teck during April 1945. However, the arrival of American ground forces in the area led the crews to destroy all ten aircraft, preventing them from falling into enemy hands. By now, Bachem had made some modifications to the Natter, resulting in an improved rate of climb, higher maximum speed of 630mph (1,013km/h) and slightly better range. This version was called the Ba 349B and it was already in production, following one test flight. There was a further proposal to alter the armament to 24 Föhn 73mm unguided air-to-air rockets and two 30mm MK 108 cannons, which might have also been recoverable.

The Bachem Ba 349C was the final, little-known version of this design. It was intended for launch from a short rail mounted on the back of a truck, but the Ba 349C never progressed beyond a proposal. These rocket-powered interceptors were little more than manned missiles and incapable of making a controlled vertical landing. However, this aircraft and several related designs proved very influential with postwar aeronautical designers and military planners. The Ba 349B would generate various attempts to develop VTOL tailsitters, rocket fighters and zero-length launch (shortened to ZEL) aircraft, resulting in trials of actual hardware.

Although the Bachem Natter was selected in 1944 as the RLM's low-cost, point defence VTO rocket interceptor, work on the Heinkel P.1077 Julia continued at the company's Vienna works. By late 1944, engineers had completed a mock-up of the Julia and Heinkel had started production of components for the first batch of aircraft. Then almost everything at the factory was destroyed during a bombing raid, although Heinkel's engineers managed to resume work on the Julia project and when Soviet forces finally overran the factory in 1945, two prototypes were nearing completion. The Heinkel Julia was slightly more refined in design than the Natter. It used the same engine and booster system, but would glide back to base, landing on skids. The first version carried the pilot in a prone position, but the cockpit was later modified to a more conventional design with an upright seat. This was known as Julia II. There was a further proposal to equip this small aircraft with an inexpensive pulsejet engine and this version was called Romeo.

Heinkel Wespe

While the Julia was undergoing development, another relatively sophisticated VTOL interceptor was being designed by Heinkel at Vienna, called the Wespe (Wasp). The engineers responsible for this unusual project were Dr-Ing Kurt Reiniger and Dr-Ing Gerhard Schulz, who literally started with a blank sheet of paper when they set out to design a fully reusable VTOL interceptor that could be operated from improvised sites. Unlike Julia, this aircraft would be a tailsitter drawing on ideas produced by Otto Muck and Werner E. Herrmann (1916–2004), a projectile specialist also working at Peenemünde, who is generally acknowledged as the inventor of the modern ring (or annular) wing design. This wartime innovation was initially intended to enhance the performance of bombs and Herrmann was later employed by Lockheed in California, where he continued to refine the concept.

Reiniger and Schulz decided to power this tailsitter with a Daimler-Benz DB-109-021 turboprop (based on the Heinkel HeS011 turbojet), which was under development as an alternative engine for the Arado Ar 234 and Messerschmitt Me 262 jets. The anticipated performance of this engine is quoted by several sources as 2,000hp (1,491kW), but this remains unconfirmed. The engine would be positioned in the rear fuselage section of the tailsitter and it would drive a centrally located six-blade propeller, enclosed in a circular shroud. It is not known if this would have led to possible issues related to torque. Jet exhaust would leave the aircraft from a central tail outlet, providing additional thrust. The forward section of the fuselage housed the pilot in an upright position. It is not known if an ejector seat was planned, although leaving the aircraft in an emergency might have been

BELOW Heinkel's imaginative Wespe (Wasp) VTOL tailsitter. *Bill Rose*

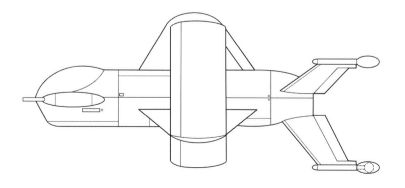

hazardous. Air for the engine would be drawn through an inlet and duct below the cockpit and two forward-firing 30mm MK108 cannon were positioned on each side of the cockpit in a similar configuration to the Julia rocket interceptor.

The wing was a hybrid design, divided between the annular wing enclosing the propeller blades and additional short wings with small control surfaces. On the ground, the aircraft rested on three swept tail fins.

Each was fitted with a landing leg and wheel that would be retracted and enclosed by a pod during flight. There was also a control surface on each fin. The Wespe was specifically designed to operate from dispersed sites and defend high-value targets against the next generation of high-flying USAAF bombers. Most of the design work was completed by February 1945, but was then abandoned in favour of an alternative, somewhat similar, design that had been in parallel development.

Heinkel Lerche (Lark)

The Heinkel Lerche (Lark) was a design study initiated in late 1944 by Reiniger and Schulz as a VTOL ground-attack aircraft. Although comparable to the Wespe in appearance, it differed considerably on closer inspection. This VTOL design was larger, heavier and used a completely different propulsion system driving centrally located contra-rotating propellers. As priorities shifted, it was decided to drop the ground-attack version and develop the Lerche as an interceptor. Now called the Lerche II, this proposal was more aerodynamic than the Wespe and used a less complex propulsion system.

Power for the six blades of the centrally located contra-rotating propeller assembly would be provided by two separate Daimler DB605D 12-cylinder inverted-V piston engines, located in fuselage sections forward and aft of the annular wing. Take-off output for this engine is quoted as 1,775hp (1,324kW) and the DB605 series of engines were mass-produced throughout the war, mainly for Messerschmitt fighters. This type of proven propulsion made the Lerche a more realistic proposition than the Wespe, with the main area of concern being the power transmission to the variable-pitch 13ft (4m) diameter propellers, housed within the annular wing. In theory, these substantial blades would produce no torque, but it seems unlikely that the behaviour of this system was clearly understood. In level flight, the annular wing surrounding the propeller generated most of the lift and this took the Lerche into largely uncharted territory.

The torpedo-shaped fuselage carried the pilot in a prone position at the nose, surrounded by a conformal canopy offering excellent forward and sideways visibility. For VTOL operations this configuration had obvious advantages. However, there are no clear indications that armour was planned to protect the pilot during combat and there was no obvious or easy way to bale out. Other experimental aircraft using a prone layout have shown that pilot safety is hard to achieve and the position of the propeller blades suggests that leaving the aircraft in an emergency was probably not possible. Like the Wespe, this aircraft would stand upright on three rather inadequate-looking

tail fins, fitted with a dampened landing leg and wheel at each tip. The fins were also equipped with control surfaces. Some details of the design such as flight control and features like engine breathing, cooling and exhaust are rather unclear.

There is no information that shows how the original ground-attack version might have been armed. It is possible that large-calibre cannons were envisaged. The proposed armament for the interceptor was two 30mm MK 108 cannons mounted on each side of the cockpit. It might also have been possible to carry two air-to-air missiles, or rockets on the outer wing surfaces. It is hard to guess how well the Lerche might have performed. The ability to operate from a small forest clearing or urban environment was the only real selling point for this design and the aircraft had little else in its favour. If the war had lasted longer and the Lerche had progressed to the hardware stage, this design might have proved dangerous to fly, ineffective as an interceptor and prone to serious landing accidents.

The initial plans for the Lerche II were completed by the beginning of March 1945, but by this time resources were running out and it was clear that the war in Europe was drawing to a close, which meant that the project would never progress any further. However, the idea did not completely die and during the 1950s a team of German engineers based in France revived some elements of the project. This would lead to the construction and flight-testing of the SNECMA C.450 Coléoptère, discussed in a later chapter.

BELOW The Heinkel Lerche, developed as a successor to the Wespe, using more readily available propulsion technology. *Bill Rose*

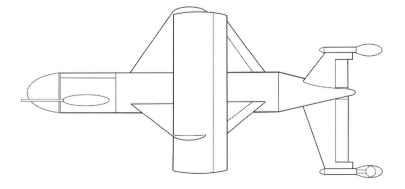

Focke-Wulf Triebflügel

Unquestionably the most interesting VTOL concept to emerge during World War 2 was the Focke-Wulf Triebflügel (Thrust Wing) designed by Heinz von Halem in autumn 1944. It was conceived to fulfil the same role as the Wespe and Lerche, acting as an interceptor that could operate from improvised sites close to high-value targets. The inspiration for this unusual concept is far from clear-cut, as this design seems to have emerged from a combination of ideas. The basic VTOL tailsitter was probably inspired by Otto Muck's design, while some of the more complex groundwork can be attributed to work carried out by Professor Erich von Holst (1908-1962) and Dr Dietrich Küchemann (1911-1976). They experimented with flapping wing aircraft in the late 1930s at Göttingen Technical University and this led to the demonstration of a small model called Libelle (Dragonfly) in Breslau during 1940. However, the Triebflügel only became a viable proposition due to advances made in ramjet engine technology. This seemingly uncomplicated type of propulsion can be traced back to the French inventor René Lorin (1877-1933) who produced the first design for a ramjet in 1908. The idea was further developed in the 1930s by the German rocket engineer Hellmuth Walter (1900-1980) and organisations such as BMW, Junkers and the research centre operated by Dr Eugen Sänger (1905-1964).

In 1939, Friedrich von Doblhoff (1916-2000), who ran a small aviation development company called Wiener Neustadt Flugzeugwerke (WNF) located in Vienna, came up with the idea of mounting small Lorin units at the tips of helicopter blades to provide torque free rotation. This proposal eventually generated interest within the RLM, which funded a helicopter development project in 1942. Four tip-powered prototypes were built and test flown by the end of the war, proving this system viable. While WNF was starting work on its first helicopter, Dr Otto Ernst Pabst who headed Focke-Wulf's Gas Dynamics Department at Bad Eilsen, was considering ramjets for various applications and initiated a programme to produce a small engine suitable for the proposed Triebflügel. Whether there was any direct contact between Pabst and von Doblhoff remains unknown, but it seems possible.

The compact ramjet engine designed by Pabst with the assistance of his colleague Dr Theodor Zobel was 4.6ft (1.4m) in length, with a diameter of 2.3ft (0.7m). The ramjet would operate at Mach 0.85, producing a thrust of 1,845lb (8.2kN). A ramjet cannot operate at low speeds and in this particular application the rotors would need to be spun up

The impressive Focke-Wulf Triebflügel. Although never built, this innovative design would prove very influential, especially with Pentagon staff. *Bill Rose*

first. The Pabst engine was lightweight, relatively simple in construction and could run on various different fuels. Some accounts suggest that Dr Heinz von Halem was an engineering consultant brought in during 1944 to take charge of the Triebflügel project at Bad Eilsen. It is possible that the company already employed him, but it was not possible to verify this detail at the time of writing. It is certainly clear that by March 1944 there had been considerable progress with development of the ramjet engine. Tests had been conducted and Pabst was confidently predicting that the technology would function at altitudes of almost 60,000ft (18,000m) and run on low-cost fuels.

The torpedo-shaped Triebflügel was 30ft (9.1m) in length and would stand on its four tail fins and a central tailwheel. The aircraft lacked conventional wings, which were replaced by three substantial, variable-pitch rotor blades. These were positioned mid-fuselage at the centre of gravity, with an overall radius of 35.5ft (10.8m). A ramjet unit was located at each tip, with fuel being channelled along the length of each blade from the central hub by centrifugal force. There would be no torque generated by this propulsion system. However, ramjets only function when a significant speed has been reached and initiating this propulsion system required the use of small liquid-fuel rocket engines made by Walter. These booster units would be an integral feature of each ramjet unit, individually delivering 660lb (2.93kN) thrust. Strap-on units would not have been an option for this system. When the rotor tips reached sufficient speed, the ramjets would become functional and the aircraft would be ready to take off vertically like a helicopter. As the rotor's pitch was adjusted, the aircraft would lift off. The rotational speed was fixed at 220rpm in level flight and the whole assembly was

Testing Pabst ramjet technology, which was intended for eventual use with the Focke-Wulf Triebflügel. *Bill Rose collection*

designed to tilt during flight. Landing was essentially a reverse of take-off and transition to level flight, but potentially quite dangerous.

The forward location of the pressurised cockpit would have provided good visibility in horizontal flight, but the pilot's seat was fixed in position, making downward sight a major issue. Whether this aircraft was equipped with an ejector seat is unknown, but the Triebflügel really needed one. In flight, the Triebflügel would alter direction by use of the control surfaces in its four tail fins. The fins would assist with stability and house most of the aircraft's landing gear. This comprised a single dampened wheel in the tail that would normally be covered by a shroud during flight and would take most of the force during a touchdown. In addition, each fin would carry a hydraulic strut with a smaller wheel at its tip, which would also be housed in a nacelle during flight.

The idea of moving these four struts outwards from the fins to improve stability was also considered, despite adding further mechanical complexity to the design.

The estimated maximum speed is widely quoted at 620mph (997km/h) at sea level, with a ceiling of 45,000ft (13,716m). Both these figures are probably a little over-optimistic. The Triebflügel would be armed with forward-firing cannons in the nose section. These were expected to be two 30mm MK 103s, each with 100 rounds, and two 20mm MG 151/20s, each with 250 rounds. There was no scope to carry any external stores on this aircraft.

From its inception, the Triebflügel's purpose was to act as a high-performance point defence interceptor, operating from improvised sites close to strategic targets. Potential problems with the design were numerous and it is hardly surprising that work on the Triebflügel was abandoned in early 1945. Nevertheless, by this time the small ramjet was known to be viable and models of the Triebflügel had been windtunnel tested, showing promising results. That said, this aircraft was probably always an unrealistic proposal, being mechanically complex, using new and largely unproven technology and requiring the best pilots, who would be risking their lives with every flight. The Triebflügel would have been expensive to build, perhaps less effective as an interceptor than the low-cost Bachem Ba349 Natter and probably very troublesome to operate. There would have been issues with high levels of sound produced by the ramjets, vibration concerns and perhaps much higher fuel consumption than anticipated. Landings would have been a nightmare for the pilots, even with various aids and cockpit modifications. On the other hand, this design made quite an impression on Allied specialists who examined the proposals in considerable detail. In the early 1950s, ramjet-driven rotors were developed and proven with the Hiller Hornet, although results were very disappointing. That aside, interest in the Triebflügel led to a whole series of postwar VTOL tailsitter designs that in some cases reached the flight-testing stage.

Rheinmetall-Borsig VTO Interceptor

Another German concept for a target defence interceptor that emerged in the final days of the Third Reich was produced by Rheinmetall-Borsig. This large company is now best remembered as the manufacturer of armoured vehicles, artillery, the advanced MG 42 machine gun and various surface-to-surface and surface-to-air missiles. By 1945, German aircraft manufacturers were turning their attention to VTO and VTOL interceptors that could operate from improvised sites to counter Allied bombers. As a consequence, designers at Rheinmetall-Borsig's missile section began to consider the possibility of a manned VTO interceptor. It would be constructed from the cheapest possible materials, powered by a single BMW or Junkers turbojet and capable of vertical launch and horizontal landing.

The concept they produced was extremely basic, very functional and rather ugly in appearance, supported on the ground in a vertical position by three large tail fins. The turbojet would be carried in a nacelle on the outside of the fuselage, opposite the cockpit. Three small control fins would be attached to

the aircraft near the nose and there would be two fixed struts with wheels in tandem position to facilitate horizontal landing, probably used in association with skids fitted below the wingtips. Armament remains unclear, but it is thought that two 30mm MK 108 cannons would have been chosen. Nothing is known about the method envisaged for transporting the aircraft by road, although this would require the removal of the wings. Performance is unknown, but it seems unlikely that the aircraft would have achieved vertical take-off without the assistance of rocket boosters. Like many other last-ditch German World War 2 military projects, nothing came of this proposal.

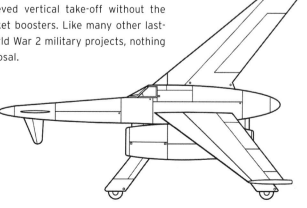

The Rheinmetall-Borsig VTO interceptor, designed during the closing days of World War 2. *Bill Rose*

Golovin's Army Support Fighter

The Russian Golovin IVS (*Istrebitel Voyskovogo Soprovozhdeniya* – Army Support Fighter) falls into a unique category. This design had an overall length of 9.85ft (3m) and probably qualifies as the smallest rocket-powered fighter ever conceived. Soviet Aircraft Engineer Lev Grigorevich Golovin developed the IVS in 1941 and this diminutive interceptor was intended to ram enemy bombers. It remains unclear if the pilot stood much chance of survival and the idea won little support from the Commission who studied it. Golovin immediately revised his design, making a number of changes, which included a 20mm ShVAK cannon, with 20 rounds of ammunition. The pilot would control the aircraft from a prone position and was partly protected from enemy fire by an armoured nose cone. Most of the aircraft was built from wood and the life expectancy of this aircraft is unknown, but was probably quite short. The original proposal utilised a single solid-fuel rocket motor, but this was replaced by a more sophisticated liquid-fuel rocket engine. The IVS would be transported on the back of a truck and launched from the vehicle with a 20ft (6m) rail, elevated to about 40°. A Dushkin rocket engine producing 660lb (2.93kN) powered the aircraft and this would be supplemented for the first 6 seconds after lift-off by a solid-fuel booster rocket, providing an additional 2,249lb (10kN) of thrust. This combination would accelerate the aircraft to approximately 528mph (850km/h) before the exhausted booster was jettisoned. It was hoped that the pilot's prone position would counteract the massive acceleration in the initial stages of flight.

The expected maximum speed was in the region of 650mph (146km/h), with a ceiling of approximately 25,000ft (7,620m), and it was anticipated that the IVS would have two brief opportunities to attack an enemy aircraft before its fuel was exhausted. Then the aircraft would glide back to a location near the launch site,

deploying an 818ft² (76m²) braking parachute at 1,000ft (305m) altitude and touching down on a skid lowered from the aircraft's underside. The truck would then drive to the landing site and recover the IVS, using a winch to lift it on the launch rail. A three-man crew would be responsible for all parts of this operation and they comprised the pilot, a mechanic and the truck driver. Enough ammunition, replacement parachutes, fuel and boosters would be carried for four or five flights. Golovin also suggested carrying these fighters beneath the wing of a large bomber and believed they could reach altitudes of 50,000ft (15,240m). Another version of the design was produced for naval applications, called the ISF (*Istrebitel Soprovozhdeniya Flota* – Navy Support Fighter). It has not been possible to find a great deal of information on this proposal, but it appears that the pilot would bale out after completing his mission and then be recovered from the sea. Some drawings show a version of the fighter with the pilot seated in an upright position and what appear to be fuel tanks directly ahead of the instrument panel. I cannot imagine a worse place to locate a large tank of something like nitric acid!

Golovin worked on the IVS project until 1944, but finally abandoned the idea after a third official rejection. It seemed that the Army considered anti-aircraft artillery to be a more effective method of defence. However, Golovin's work was recognised as innovative and after the war he completed a doctorate in engineering and became director of *Opytnoe Konstructorskoe Byuro* (Experimental Design Bureau) No 464 (OKB-464), working on the development of surface-to-air missiles. Golovin was eventually assigned to Russia's space programme, becoming involved with the Soyuz spacecraft project.

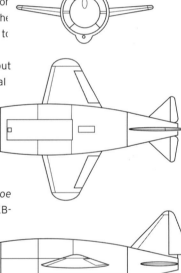

BELOW General appearance of Lev Golovin's ultra-compact, rocket-powered area defence interceptor, conceived during World War 2, but never built. *Bill Rose*

Shulikov VTOL Fighters

The last series of VTOL aircraft to be discussed in this chapter were conceived by the Russian designer Konstantin Vladimirovich Shulikov (original name Pelenberg.1911–). Shulikov graduated from the Moscow Aviation Institute with a degree in mechanical engineering in 1939. He then joined the Mikoyan Design Office, which became OKB-155 during World War 2. One of Shulikov's first wartime tasks was to assist with a development programme for the MiG-1 and MiG-3, which apparently involved regular trips to Air Force units on the Western Front. One of his initial design jobs involved the development of equipment to manufacture flexible fuel tanks and in late 1942 he began work on ideas for a

fighter aircraft in his spare time. By early 1943 he had completed initial proposals for a twin-boom fighter aircraft using a rear-mounted pusher configuration set of contra-props. It has not been possible to locate any detailed information for this aircraft, but it appears to be roughly in the same class as a Lockheed P-38 Lightning. The cockpit for the pilot would have provided good forward visibility, the aircraft sat on a fairly high tricycle undercarriage and armament would have comprised four cannons or machine guns mounted in the forward section of the fuselage. The unspecified engine was located behind the fuselage and connected to the propeller unit via a gearbox and driveshaft. Shulikov chose contra-rotating propellers to eliminate torque and these appear to be of a three-blade type.

The propeller assembly was one of the most important features of this design, as it was intended to swivel downwards through 90° until it was in a horizontal position below the centre of the aircraft. Shulikov hoped this would generate sufficient lift to provide VTOL performance, although he would later come to realise that this aspiration was somewhat unrealistic with prevailing engine technology. Apparently, Mikoyan was impressed with Shulikov's proposal, although this design failed to progress beyond the paperwork stage. Nevertheless, some of the innovative features would reappear in the future, such as variable-geometry wings and methods of assisting STOL. When the war ended, Shulikov was involved with the evaluation of captured German technology and development of Russia's first jet fighter. He also spent part of his time teaching at the MAI.

Shulikov maintained his personal interest in VTOL aircraft and began to consider a twin-boom fighter similar to his wartime VTOL proposal, but powered by a single jet engine, with an innovative idea for directing the exhaust flow downwards. In later years, vectored thrust would be developed much further, eventually leading to engines like the Pegasus, which powered the Harrier. OKB-155's main focus of attention was now the MiG-15 jet fighter and during 1946 the British Labour Government, in its infinite wisdom, approved the export of 40 Rolls-Royce Nene centrifugal-flow turbojet engines to the Soviet Union. At that time, the Nene was the best turbojet in production and it was ideal for Russia's new fighter. As a consequence, high priority was given to back-engineering this British engine and a large team was assembled to duplicate the technology. Within months they had produced a crude copy called the RD-45, although there were serious metallurgical issues which needed to be addressed.

These problems were eventually resolved and the Russian Nene copy entered mass production as the slightly modified Klimov VK-1. This engine made the MiG-15 a formidable warplane and Shulikov immediately recognised the turbojet's potential for use in the VTOL fighter he was designing. Shulikov had now developed a one-man, single-tailed jet fighter proposal with a nose intake for the forward-mounted Klimov VK-1 jet engine. This would be positioned with a rearward tilt downwards of 10-15° and connected to a duct system. It would then channel exhaust gas through four nozzles that would be directed downwards during take-off/landing and via ducts in the wings to centrally placed stabilising fans. In level flight the main nozzles would be (electrically) directed rearwards and the secondary outlets blocked.

The dimensions of this design put it roughly in the same category as other early prototype Soviet jet fighters such as the Lavochkin La-150 or MiG-9, but with a smaller wingspan. Untypically, the undercarriage comprised of two forward retractable main wheels and a tailwheel. The location of the engine meant that the cockpit was positioned roughly at the centre of the aircraft and Shulikov added a single forward-firing cannon, which might have been a Nudelman 37mm. Mikoyan continued to unofficially support him and suggested that Shulikov should patent his work. He also arranged for

ABOVE Konstantin Vladimirovich Shulikov, who produced a string of original aviation designs including variable-geometry wings and vectored jet exhaust. *Bill Rose collection*

LEFT Original artwork depicting the Shulikov VTOL flat riser lifting off under jet power. *Bill Rose collection*

BELOW This drawing shows the general arrangement of the original Shulikov twin-boom VTOL fighter concept. *Bill Rose*

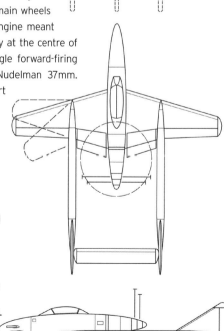

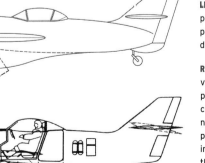

LEFT Engine and duct position for Shulikov's postwar VTOL jet fighter design. *Bill Rose*

RIGHT This is the improved version of Shulikov's postwar VTOL jet fighter concept. It featured a number of changes and perhaps the most obvious immediate difference is the tricycle undercarriage. *Bill Rose collection*

an official assessment of the VTOL design to establish if there was any possibility of securing state funding for a development project. This took place in January 1947, with the Commission expressing considerable interest in the idea, but declining to go beyond recommending further studies.

Further refinements to the design took place, including better aerodynamics, the use of a tricycle undercarriage and a number of changes to the ducting within the wings, which now supplied simpler nozzles at the wingtips. This feature appears to have undergone many revisions, finally leading to another patent being issued, although this work remained classified. It seems probable that models were built and perhaps some wind tunnel testing undertaken, but no details are currently available.

In 1951 Shulikov left MiG and worked in several other state-run aircraft facilities, eventually arriving at Lavochkin, where he developed missile guidance systems. Throughout the 1950s Shulikov continued to privately develop and refine his ideas for a VTOL fighter and although these designs were never built, they proved highly influential and many of the technical features would be utilised in later Soviet VTOL aircraft. Shulikov was officially acknowledged as the inventor of the rotary jet nozzle in the mid-1960s, although by this time the technology had been fully developed by the British. In 1976, Shulikov moved to Molniya, becoming involved with development of the Buran space shuttle, and he was still undertaking design work in the late 1990s.

Shavrov's High-Speed VTOL Fighter

Soon after the end of World War 2, the well-known Russian aircraft designer Vadim Borisovich Shavrov (1898-1976) turned his attention to the development of a *Vysoko-Skorostnoy Istrebitel* (VSI – High-Speed Fighter) with a VTOL capability.

Powered by two RD-45/Klimov VK-1 turbojets (an unauthorised copy of the Rolls-Royce Nene) mounted in wingtip nacelles, these units would swivel to allow vertical take-off. Most of this design work took place from 1946 to 1947 and Shavrov anticipated a maximum level speed of 932mph (1,500km/h), which was clearly rather unrealistic. In retrospect, it becomes obvious that the design was seriously flawed, although the same concept would be developed and proven viable some years later in the US and West Germany.

No dimensions or weights are available for the VSI-VTOL, but it seems very likely that armament would have taken the form of cannons. Models of the design were built and wind tunnel tests may have been carried out, but nothing came of this project.

LEFT A model of the advanced VSI high-performance VTOL fighter, designed by V. B. Shavrov in the USSR during 1946–1947. Powered by two RD-45/Klimov VK-1 turbojets (an unauthorised copy of the Rolls-Royce Nene), the available reference material indicates an expected maximum speed of 932mph (1,500km/h), which seems rather unrealistic. *Bill Rose collection*

Chapter One: Aircraft Details

MAI Sokol (Falcon)
Crew: 1
Wingspan: 19ft (5.8m)
Wing Area: 100ft^2 (9.3m^2)
Length: 24.7ft (7.53m)
Height: N/A
Propeller Diameter: 13.1ft (4m)
Take-off Weight: 4,078lb (1,850kg)
Maximum Speed: 327mph (527km/h)
Ceiling: N/A
Range: N/A
Powerplant: 1 x Hispano Suiza 12Y (probably a Klimov M-100 copy), liquid-cooled V-12 engine, rated at 860hp (641.3kW) take-off power
Armament: One unspecified forward-firing machine gun or cannon

Muck VTOL Concept
Crew: 1
Wingspan: N/A
Length: N/A
Weight: N/A
Maximum Speed: N/A
Powerplant: N/A

Leonard VTOL Fighter (Initial Design)
Crew: 1
Wingspan: 20ft (6m)
Propeller Diameter: 40ft (12.1m)
Wing Area (Including Fuselage Section: 25ft^2 (2.32m^2)
Length: 25ft (7.62m)
Tail Fin Span: 8ft (2.43m)

Fuselage Maximum Diameter: 3.8ft (1.16m)
Gross Weight: 5,000lb (2,268kg)
Maximum Speed: 428mph (688km/h) at sea level; 500mph (800km/h) at 20,000ft (6,096m)
Rate of Climb: 3,750ft/min (1,143m/min)
Ceiling: In excess of 40,000ft (12,192m)
Range: N/A
Powerplant: 1 x P&W 1,000hp (745kW) double-row radial engine
Armament: Unknown

Bell VTOL Fighter
Crew: 1
Wingspan: N/A
Length: N/A

Gross Weight: N/A
Maximum Speed: N/A
Ceiling: N/A
Range: N/A
Powerplant: An unspecified air-cooled radial engine
Armament: N/A

Supermarine 4040
Crew: 1
Wingspan: N/A
Length: N/A
Gross Weight: N/A
Maximum Speed: N/A
Ceiling: N/A
Range: N/A
Powerplant: A high-performance liquid-cooled engine in the Napier Sabre class
Armament: 4 x unspecified cannons in wingtip pods

Von Braun Rocket Interceptor I
Crew: 1
Wingspan: 30ft (9.14m)
Length: 28ft (8.5m)
Gross Weight: 11,200lb (5,080kg)
Maximum Speed (Level flight using cruise chamber): 429mph (690km/h)
Ceiling: 35,000ft+ (10,668m+) estimated
Rate of Climb: 50 seconds to 25,000ft (7,620m)
Operational Endurance on cruise chamber: About 15 minutes
Powerplant: 1 x von Braun designed liquid-fuel (nitric acid/visol) rocket motor providing 22,400lb (99.6kN) thrust Cruise chamber providing 1,700lb (7.56kN) thrust
Armament: 4 x machine guns

Heinkel P.1077 Julia
Crew: 1
Wingspan: 15.1ft (4.6m)
Wing Area: 77.5ft² (7.2m²)
Sweep (leading edge): 6°
Length: 22.3ft (6.8m)
Height: N/A
Take-off Weight: 3,950lb (1,791kg)
Maximum Speed: 610mph (980km/h)
Ceiling: 45,000ft (13,716m) estimated
Range: 40 miles (64km) approx
Powerplant: 1 x Walter HWK 109-509A-2 rocket engine, producing 3,750lb (16.6kN) thrust; 4 x Schmidding 109-553 boosters, each providing an additional 1,100lb (4.89kN) thrust. Alternatively: 2 x Schmidding SG34 solid-fuel boosters, each producing 2,204lb (9.8kN) thrust for 10 seconds
Armament: 2 x MK 108 30mm cannons

Bachem Ba 349A Natter (Adder)
Crew: 1
Length: 18.75ft (5.7m)
Wingspan: 11.8ft (3.60m)

Wing Area: 29.6ft² (2.75m²)
Height: 7.3ft (2.25m).
Gross Weight: 4,850lb (2,200kg)
Maximum Speed: 560mph (900km/h)
Rate of Climb: 30,000ft (9,144m) per minute
Ceiling: 52,000ft (15,849m)
Range: 37 miles (59km)
Powerplant: 1 x Walter HWK 109-509A rocket engine, producing 3,750lb (16.6kN) thrust. 4 x Schmidding 109-553 boosters, each providing an additional 1,100lb (4.89kN) thrust for 10 seconds. Alternatively: 2 x Schmidding SG34 solid-fuel boosters, each producing 2,204lb (9.8kN) thrust for 10 seconds
Armament: 24 Föhn (Storm) 73mm unguided air-to-air rockets, or alternatively 33 R4M 55mm folding fin rockets

Heinkel Wespe (Wasp)
Crew: 1
Wingspan: 16.4ft (5m)
Length: 20.3ft (6.20m)
Gross Weight: 4,850lb (2,200kg) approx
Maximum Speed: 497mph (800km/h) at 20,000ft (6,096m)
Ceiling: 40,000ft (12,192m) estimated
Range: 403 miles (650km) estimated
Powerplant: 1 x Daimler-Benz DB-109-021 turboprop engine (based on the Heinkel HeS 011 turbojet) producing an estimated 2,000hp (1,491kW)
Armament: 2 x MK 108 30mm cannon

Heinkel Lerche II
Crew: 1
Wingspan: 14.9ft (4.55m)
Length: 32.8ft (10m) (wheels included)
Wing Area: 129ft² (12.00m²)
Fuselage Width: 4.1ft (1.25m)
Propeller Diameter: 13.1ft (4m)
Empty Weight: 9,920lb (4,500kg)
Gross Weight: 12,345lb (5,600kg)
Maximum Speed: 497mph (800km/h)
Ceiling: 47,000ft (14,325m)
Range: 75 miles (120km)
Powerplant: 2 x DB605D liquid-cooled supercharged, inverted V-12 engines, each rated at 2,000hp (1,491kW)
Armament: 2 x 30mm MK 108 cannons

Focke-Wulf Triebflügel
Crew: 1
Rotor Span: 35.5ft (10.8m)
Length: 30ft (9m)
Empty Weight: 7,056lb (3,200kg)
Gross Weight: 11,400lb (5,175kg)
Maximum Speed (sea level): 620mph (997km/h)
Ceiling: 45,000ft (13,716m) estimated
Range: Approx 400 miles (643km) at sea level and 1,500 miles (2,414km) at high altitude
Powerplant: 3 x Pabst ramjets, each with an

approximate rating of 1,800lb (8kN) thrust; 3 x integral Walter liquid-fuel rockets delivering 660lb (2.93kN) thrust during start-up
Armament: 2 x MK 103 30mm cannons with 100 rounds of ammunition and 2 x MG 151 20mm cannons with 250 rounds of ammunition

Rheinmetall-Borsig VTO Interceptor
Crew: 1
Wingspan: N/A
Length: N/A
Gross Weight: N/A
Maximum Speed: 500mph (800km/h). Speculative
Ceiling: N/A
Range: N/A
Powerplant: 1 x unspecified turbojet engine; solid-fuel boosters for VTO
Armament: 2 x 30mm MK 108 cannons

Golovin IVS
Crew: 1
Wingspan: 5.75ft (1.75m)
Wing Area: 10.76ft² (1m²)
Length: 9.85ft (3m)
Height: 3.45ft (1.05m)
Launch Weight: 550-660lb (250-300kg)
Fuel Weight: 110lb (50kg)
Maximum Speed: 658mph (1,060km/h)
Rate of Climb: About 50,000ft/min (15,240m/min)
Ceiling: 25,000ft (7,620m)
Powerplant: 1 x Dushkin rocket engine fuelled with kerosene and nitric acid, providing 660lb (2.93kN) thrust; 1 x solid-fuel booster rocket, providing 2,249lb (10kN) of thrust for 6 seconds
Armament: 1 x 20mm ShVAK cannon with 20 rounds
Landing Equipment: 1 x 818ft² (76m²) parachute and retractable skid (not used on the proposed Naval version.)

Shulikov VTOL Jet Fighter Version 1
Crew: 1
Wingspan: 23ft (7m)
Length: 30.8ft (9.4m)
Height: N/A
Empty Weight: Estimated 4,500-5,500lb (2,041-2,495kg)
Gross Weight: N/A
Maximum Speed: Estimated 550mph (885km/h)
Ceiling: Estimated 45,000ft (13,716m)
Range: N/A
Powerplant: 1 x adapted RD-45/Klimov VK-1 (unauthorised copy of Rolls-Royce Nene) centrifugal-flow turbojet with a thrust of 5,955lb (26.5kN)
Armament: one (unspecified) cannon starboard side of nose; possibly an N37

Chapter 2 Postwar Fighters

When the European conflict ended in May 1945, large quantities of German military hardware fell into Allied hands. Special intelligence units had already been prepared to secure advanced technology and some of the aviation and weapon projects they uncovered came as quite a surprise. Within the mountain of data were details of vertical take-off rocket-powered interceptors, supersonic combat aircraft and cutting-edge concepts like the Focke-Wulf Triebflügel VTOL fighter. This design was based on unproven technology and duplication would have presented major challenges, but the overall idea of a VTOL tailsitter that could operate from an improvised site or the deck of a warship generated considerable interest within US military circles.

Many advances in aviation had been made during the war, but the Triebflügel was pointing towards a major improvement in flexibility and perhaps a move away from the established need to cluster important assets in one relatively small area. With the atomic bomb a reality and the likelihood of Soviet Russia developing this technology in the near term, it seemed possible that even the biggest airfield with hardened shelters could be taken out with a single weapon. Furthermore, should it eventually become possible to reduce the size and weight of an atom bomb to that of the warhead carried by a V-2 type rocket, this would make the situation even more problematic. The US Navy was also very interested in the idea of a VTOL fighter powered by turboprop or turbojet that could operate from aircraft carriers and smaller platforms on warships, suitable merchant vessels, or perhaps a highly modified submarine.

By 1946, the USAAF and US Navy had jointly entered into informal discussions with various aircraft contractors, which quickly led to requests for preliminary studies under a joint-services umbrella programme known as Project Hummingbird.

ABOVE The first Ryan X-13 is prepared for transportation by road from Ryan's San Diego plant to Edwards AFB. Some parts of the aircraft needed to be removed for the journey and a conventional temporary undercarriage was fitted before leaving. The markings on the wheels and tail fin are to aid photography during testing. *Ryan*

Ryan Jet-Powered VTOL Designs

In January 1947, the Ryan Aeronautical Company of San Diego, California, (later Teledyne-Ryan and eventually a part of Northrop Grumman) responded to the Pentagon's requirement for a prototype jet-powered, single-seat VTOL fighter. Company President Tubal 'Claude' Ryan (1898-1982) was convinced that his engineers could develop and build this type of aircraft within a reasonable timeframe for an acceptable price. Ryan's chief designer Benjamin Tyler Salmon (1911-1992) had already produced an initial concept, which was given the company reference Model 38-1. Salmon decided at the outset to use the Rolls-Royce Nene or General Electric/Allison J33-GE-25 turbojet, which were both in the 5,000lb (22.2kN) thrust class. However, with a gross weight of 7,700lb (3,492kg), the Model 38-1 would have a problem with the thrust/weight ratio during take-off. To work around the problem, Salmon added four rocket assisted take-off (RATO) units, although this would become unnecessary as engine performance improved. During February 1947, the Model 38 had evolved into two new proposals, which were the Model 38-2 with an X-shaped tail and tip-mounted jets, followed by Model 38-3, with a four-finned tail.

The US Navy now assumed primary responsibility for the Ryan proposal (over the USAF) and in April 1947 it awarded a $50,000 contract to the company for further development, with the aim of finally constructing two prototypes. Ryan immediately started work on a remote-controlled test rig, which used an Allison J33 engine. Over the coming years this was progressively upgraded, eventually being fitted with a cockpit formed from part of a surplus B-47 external tank that allowed hands-on experience for Ryan's test pilot. Wind tunnel trials using models also took place, with an estimated 80 different configurations being studied. By autumn 1951, Salmon had designed a somewhat larger, delta-winged weaponised version of the aircraft weighing 17,500lb (7,937kg). The exact designation for this version remains unclear at the present time, as available documentation simply refers to it as the Ryan Model 38.

Propulsion would be provided by a new experimental General Electric XJ53-GE-X10 turbojet, which was expected to produce 21,000lb (93.4kN) thrust without the use of an afterburner and had been designed to power the next generation of supersonic fighters. Claude Ryan proposed the construction of a prototype to the Navy, but it was immediately concerned about the aircraft's significant increase in weight and reliance on a new, cutting-edge engine that remained unproven and was primarily intended for use by the USAF.

Ryan's production version of the Model 38 would be armed with four 20mm cannons and possibly air-to-air

guided missiles when available. It would have a full VTOL capability and utilised a number of unusual features that included a vectorable exhaust outlet, providing low-speed pitch and yaw control, plus ducts feeding engine compressor air to outlets in the wings for low-speed roll control. It seems fair to assume that an ejection seat would have been fitted and this was intended to swivel, making VTOL operations easier. Salmon was convinced that this aircraft would be capable of meeting all the performance predictions with relative ease. No performance details are available, but the design was expected to be capable of high-subsonic speed, with a ceiling of around 50,000ft (15,240m).

Nevertheless, towards the end of 1951, the Navy decided not to fund any further development of this proposal. The judgement appears to have involved cost, performance of the aircraft and, above all, concerns about the engine, which had only run for the first time in March 1951 and showed no signs of being available in the short term. This encouraged Ryan to completely revise the design and propose a prototype with an alternative engine, but it was not enough to regain full support from the Navy, which had largely lost interest in the project and intended to cut its funding. Ryan's VTOL concept might have ended at this point, but the USAF agreed to continue with sponsorship of the project, although it specified a redesign of the proposed prototype, which included the use of a new engine.

This revision would be known by the company reference Model 69 and the USAF finally decided to issue a further study contract (AF33[600]-25895) followed by a formal contract in 1954 to construct a mock-up and two experimental aircraft (54-1619 and 54-1620). However, rather confusingly, this project received USAF designations that included WS-603A, WS-1227 and WS-693A.

The aircraft was finally called the X-13 Vertijet and in appearance was closely based on the test-rig assembly. The X-13 was very compact with a high-mounted delta

TOP The Allison J33-powered test rig built at Ryan for VTOL testing during the early stages of the X-13 project. *Ryan*

BOTTOM Ryan's test rig equipped with wings and a cockpit with its shell fabricated from a surplus B-47 fuel tank. *Ryan*

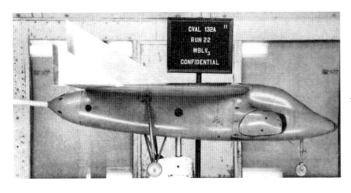

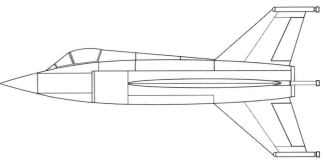

ABOVE One of many different wind tunnel models tested during the X-13 programme. *Ryan*

ABOVE RIGHT The general appearance of Ryan's first proposal for a VTOL fighter referred to as the Model 38. *Bill Rose*

wing, small wingtip stabilisers and a substantial tailfin. The pilot was positioned immediately ahead of the engine, with air inlets on each side of the fuselage below the rear of the canopy. The airframe was mainly built from aluminium, with newly available titanium being used in some key areas. Overall dimensions for the X-13 were a length of 23.4ft (7.13m), with a wingspan of 21ft (6.4m), making it little bigger than the main section used in the test rig. The forward-positioned cockpit was fairly cramped, although allowance was made to tilt the seat forward when the aircraft was in a vertical position.

The new engine, specified by the USAF, was a non-afterburning Rolls-Royce Avon RA.28-49 axial-flow gas turbine, capable of providing 10,000lb (44.4kN) static thrust. This provided a good thrust/weight ratio, when allowing for a gross weight of 7,300lb (3,311kg). The engine exhaust would be directable to control pitch and yaw, with a reaction control system to provide stability and roll control. A single fuel tank carried 271 (US) gallons (1,025 litres) of JP-4 fuel and this provided the aircraft with an estimated 167-mile (268km) range. The maximum level speed was about 483mph (777km/h), with a service ceiling of 30,000ft (9,144m), although neither appears to have been tested. For an

experimental proof-of-concept VTOL jet aircraft, the level of performance was more than adequate, but, depending on how the trials progressed, Ryan had already drawn up new plans for a follow-on experimental fighter. This would be closer to the weaponised Model 38 and powered by an afterburning Avon, which raised the possibility of supersonic performance in level flight.

Assembly of the first X-13 began in early 1954 and it was completed by autumn 1955. At around the same time, former Korean War combat pilot and aeronautical engineer Willis Louis 'Lou' Everett (1924-1965) was hired by Ryan to participate in the X-13 Vertijet programme. This brought Ryan's X-13 flight team up to three pilots, including Ryan's Chief Engineer Pete Girard (1918-2011) and William 'Bill' T. Immenschuh (1917-1997), who designed the XFR-1 Fireball with Ben Salmon during World War 2. The first X-13 (54-1619) flew at Edwards AFB on 10 December 1955, piloted by Girard. It was simply a brief horizontal flight to prove airworthiness, using an improvised, fixed tricycle undercarriage. The flight lasted for 7 minutes, during which time a number of control issues became apparent. Although unwelcome, the problems, which concerned roll and yaw, were successfully addressed during the following two weeks and trials resumed.

Testing quickly progressed to flight transitions and brief periods of hover. The tricycle undercarriage was then replaced with a tail-mounted framework fitted with dampened wheels that would allow short VTOL trials. This apparatus was soon referred to as the Roller Skate by ground crew. However, this added considerable weight to the aircraft and it was necessary to remove many components to compensate, which even included the cockpit canopy and control surfaces. On 28 May 1956, Pete Girard completed the first X-13 vertical take-off and landing using the Roller Skate.

The second X-13 aircraft (54-1620) had now been completed at San Diego and benefited from various generally minor improvements, but the only obvious difference was an alteration to the cockpit canopy, which improved the pilot's visibility while the aircraft was in an upright position. In spring 1956, it was shipped on a trailer to Edwards AFB and fitted with a fixed-position tricycle undercarriage to allow conventional take-offs and landings. Like the earlier X-13, some basic testing

RIGHT An engineer adjusts a scale model of the Ryan X-13 VTOL test vehicle at NACA Langley in March 1956. *NASA*

BELOW Side view of the second Ryan X-13 prototype showing the modified cockpit canopy. *Bill Rose*

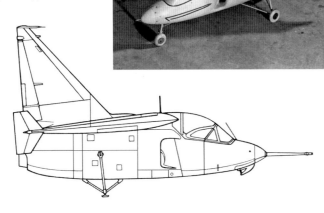

was considered necessary to ensure there were no issues that needed attention before VTOL trials began. No problems arose and the aircraft was then fitted with the necessary attachment gear that would allow it to operate from a special handling assembly called the 'pogo rig'. This required an attachment hook beneath the nose of the X-13 in the position previously occupied by the nosewheel strut. The hook engaged with a small trapeze unit when the aircraft was at rest. Two dampened struts below the fuselage replaced the rear undercarriage struts to act as stabilisers. The final arrangement for this launch and recovery system would utilise a trailer specially built by Fruehauf Trailer Company that could be operated from any suitable area. The trailer would first need to be made stable, then the pogo assembly with the aircraft could be raised hydraulically into a vertical position and the X-13 would be ready for launch.

Because the aircraft did not have an undercarriage system allowing it to take off and land in an upright position from a flat surface, it was referred to as vertical attitude take-off and landing (VATOL) design as opposed to a tailsitter. On 28 November 1956, the aircraft, flown by Girard (with the conventional undercarriage refitted), made a perfect transition from level flight to hover at an altitude of 6,000ft (1,828m) and then returned to level flight, which was another first for the programme. This was followed on 11 April 1957 by a vertical take-off from the support trailer, transition to horizontal flight and a vertical return to the pogo rig.

LEFT The first Ryan X-13 which was configured for VTOL testing is moved into position with a crane. *Ryan*

The biggest demonstration of the X-13 took place in July 1957, after the second X-13 had been shipped to the Pentagon in Washington DC via the Panama Canal aboard USS *Young America*. A substantial team from Ryan was flown from San Diego to Washington DC, including all three test pilots. Several short flights were made at Andrews AFB and then the aircraft was set up on its trailer by the Pentagon on 30 July 1957. About 3,000 officials and members of the media were present when Girard made a single demonstration flight lasting 7 minutes. It was well received and generated considerable public interest. By this time, Ryan had completed a number of separate USAF studies that began with a supersonic VTOL daylight interceptor and stretched to a dispersed site fighter-bomber. (This project is discussed in the next chapter.)

BELOW The X-13 is demonstrated to a large group of officials at Washington DC. Please note, there is a lamppost directly in front of the trailer, which is not a feature of this equipment! *Ryan*

The company was hoping to secure a development contract from the USAF and perhaps generate Navy interest in this work. Unfortunately, official enthusiasm for this type of VTOL aircraft had declined, with the realisation that there might be better ways of achieving a VTOL capability that offered improved handling and superior performance. Having spent $9.4 million on the X-13, the USAF decided to cut its losses and terminate the project in early 1958. It is generally accepted that Ryan handled this project well. There were no serious incidents and all targets were met, with the pilots adjusting relatively easily to VTOL operations. Nevertheless, the X-13 programme was at an end and the first aircraft (54-1619) was passed to the Smithsonian National Air and Space Museum in Washington DC. It is currently on loan to the San Diego Air and Space Museum. The second X-13 (54-1620) was presented to the National Museum of the USAF at Wright-Patterson AFB, where it is currently on display.

RIGHT X-13 (54-1620) in free hover during a brief trial using the trailer. *Ryan*

BELOW The second Ryan X-13 prototype (54-1620) on public display at Wright-Patterson AFB. *USAF*

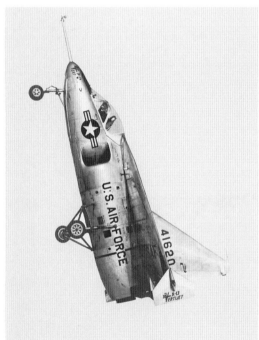

TOP The first X-13, minus normal horizontal control surfaces, cockpit canopy and other minor components considered unnecessary for VTO trials when using the tubular test rig. Weight reduction was essential to compensate for the rig's added mass. *Ryan*

ABOVE The second X-13 fitted with its temporary tricycle undercarriage demonstrates an ability to hover on jet power. This photograph shows the modified cockpit canopy that provided a better view for the pilot in an upright position. The winglets were fitted to the outer wings as a method of improving stability during VTOL operations and they proved highly effective at low speeds. *Ryan*

Turboprop Tailsitters

Two further aircraft originated from the Pentagon's postwar VTOL programme and both were tailsitting fighters, powered by turboprops. The US Navy was eager to encourage development of this particular type of VTOL aircraft, but it remains unclear why it proceeded. It is understandable that it would consider all possible alternatives, but turboprop power was now an unrealistic proposition for any fighter and it is tempting to think that it simply had too much money to spend on new projects. Nevertheless, in the late 1940s, NACA Langley began a programme of testing wind tunnel models of VTOL tailsitter aircraft that would be equipped with forward-mounted contra-rotating propellers. At least one small straight-winged model with 5hp (3.73kW) electric propulsion was tested using two sets of four-blade propellers and these trials were sufficiently encouraging to convince the Navy to commission the development of at least one prototype.

In 1948, the Navy issued requests to various contractors for an experimental turboprop-powered VTOL tailsitter aircraft capable of operating from small platforms on ships. The requirement continued to evolve and in 1950 Operational Specification 122 (OS-122) requested a research aircraft that could be developed into a ship-based VTOL convoy escort fighter. A number of designs were submitted by Lockheed, Northrop, Goodyear, Martin and Convair, which were similarly specified and could undoubtedly have all been built and flown. But, the final selection was narrowed down to the Convair and Lockheed proposals. The Convair aircraft was considered to be the best design, with the lowest estimated development cost. Lockheed's aircraft came a close second and both companies were at locations that suited the US Navy.

RIGHT A VTOL tailsitter model with electrically powered contra-rotating propellers, tested at NACA Langley during the late 1940s. *NASA*

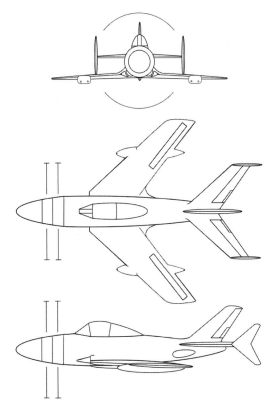

LEFT Based directly on original material, this drawing shows the overall appearance of Martin's Model 262 proposal for a Navy VTOL fighter. The undercarriage is not obvious, although it is possible that legs might have been fitted to the tail fins, perhaps with an additional retractable strut on the underside of the rear fuselage. *Bill Rose*

RIGHT Northrop's N-63 VTOL fighter proposal. Although this aircraft possessed a few unusual design features, there seems little doubt that it could have been built and would have flown as well as the Convair or Lockheed aircraft. *Bill Rose*

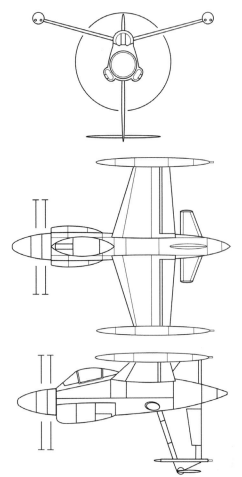

Convair XFY-1

On 31 March 1951, the Navy issued Convair with a contract to build three prototypes and serial numbers were issued (138648, 138649 and 138650). Convair's VTOL fighter had been given the company reference Model 5, but now received the official designation XFY-1 and, later, the semi-official name 'Pogo'. Initially, a number of scale models were built in association with NACA Langley and these were wind tunnel tested with electrically driven three- and four-blade contra props.

The XFY-1 was a single-seat VTOL tailsitter, with a substantial delta wing and two large tail fins that provided the necessary support in an upright position.

Apparently, it was necessary to trim down the ventral fin's size, as this created handling problems on the ground. Dampened struts with small wheels were positioned at the tips of the wings and tailplanes. In the event of an emergency horizontal landing proving necessary, the ventral tail fin could be jettisoned by

means of explosive bolts. What seems to have been dismissed were the two sets of 16ft (4.87m) diameter contra-rotating three-blade propellers at the nose of the aircraft that would have made an emergency landing extremely hazardous.

Contra-rotating blades were chosen from the outset to eliminate torque problems and without this feature the aircraft would probably have been uncontrollable at low speeds. The propulsion unit chosen for the XFY-1 was an Allison XT40-A-6 engine producing 5,850hp (4,362kW), which was based on two coupled T38 turboprops. Air intakes for the engine were located at the wing roots, with an engine exhaust outlet in the tail. The propulsion system was seen as an interim measure until a more powerful YT40-A-14 engine became available from Allison. The cockpit was reasonably well positioned for horizontal flight, but less than satisfactory during VTOL operations. Mounted on a gimballed assembly, the ejector seat swivelled forward

BELOW The Convair XFY-1 'Pogo' is moved on a transportation trailer. *Convair*

by 45° when the aircraft was upright and although an improvement on a fixed assembly, it was far from ideal. The cockpit canopy slid backwards and this was generally left open during VTOL tests to improve visibility. A further complication for the pilot was entry and exit, which required a special trolley with a ladder. Using this was always rather unsatisfactory. The XFY-1 had an overall length of 34.95ft (10.6m), a wingspan of 27.66ft (7.86m) and a horizontal height of 22.1ft (6.73m). Dimensions were an important part of the specification as the XFY-1 was intended for maritime operations, with limiting hangar storage requirements. Proposed armament for a fully developed version would be either four 20mm cannons or two separate packs of 2.75in (70mm) folding fin rockets. Either system would be carried in the large wingtip pods.

Estimated performance with the upgraded powerplant suggested a maximum speed of 610mph (981km/h) at 15,000ft (4,572m), which seems slightly optimistic. The anticipated ceiling was 43,700ft (13,319m) and endurance would be one hour, operating at an altitude of 35,000ft (10,669m). Take-off weight was calculated at 16,250lb (7,370kg) and this would require full engine power. Once in the air, the XFY-1 would climb to a safe height vertically and gradually nose forward to become horizontal. After completion of the mission, the aircraft would return to the landing pad and pitch up into a vertical position and carefully reduce power during the final descent. This would undoubtedly have been the most dangerous part of the flight. The Navy ordered three aircraft, but only one became airworthy. The first prototype (138648) was partly assembled and used for engine trials and it is the author's understanding that the third aircraft (138650) was used for destructive stress tests. This left the second aircraft (138649), which had been fully

ABOVE Convair XFY-1 prototype VTOL fighter with engine running and the ground crew moving the gantry into position. *Convair*

RIGHT The Convair XFY-1 undergoing tethered hangar tests. *US Navy*

completed by the start of 1954.

This prototype was then transported to the Moffett Field Naval Air Station near San Francisco, where engine and brief lift-off trials were undertaken within a huge hangar, originally designed to house blimps. The aircraft was tethered to a support structure in the building's roof and the first test was undertaken on 29 April 1954, with Convair's test pilot James 'Skeets' Coleman (1918–) at the controls. Things generally went well and several lift-offs were completed, although the environment proved rather unsuitable due to extreme levels of noise being generated and problems with the downwash creating clouds of dust. The XFY-1 made its first brief (outside) free flight on 1 August 1954 and was then shipped to Naval Auxiliary Air Station Brown Field at San Diego, where Coleman made the first lift-off, transition to level flight and vertical landing on 2 November 1954. This 20-minute flight was the first successful VTOL flight in history (excluding helicopters) and, as a result, Coleman was awarded the Harmon Aviation Trophy. (Its most distinguished recipients have been the crew of Apollo 11.)

By this time, serious design problems were becoming apparent, with the ability to land safely now a prime issue. Visibility from the cockpit during descent was very poor and the pilot's workload considerable. Although Coleman was always assisted by observers on the ground during test flights, estimating the rate of descent and position were based on guesswork until a radar altimeter was fitted in the port pod and connected to a small traffic-light system in the cockpit.

Nevertheless, Coleman was a highly qualified test pilot and it was recognised that there would be major problems for even a good fighter pilot making vertical landings on ships, especially in poor conditions. Furthermore, there were increasing problems with engine reliability and alarm bells must have sounded when pieces of metal began to appear in the gearbox oil. By spring 1955, the Navy was aware that the XFY-1 was dead-end technology that would be unable to match the performance of anticipated near-future Soviet fighters and bombers. It would be costly and difficult to operate and potentially as dangerous as the Bachem Natter for the pilots.

On 19 May 1955, another test pilot, John Knebel, attempted to fly the XFY-1 at Lindbergh Field, having declined to undertake any acclimatisation lift-offs with the tethered rig. This nearly ended in disaster, with Knebel almost losing control of the aircraft, and it was the last time he was allowed to fly the XFY-1. In May 1956, the Navy moved the tethered rig from Moffett Field to Brown Field and two new pilots were prepared to begin training with the aircraft.

Coleman made one more flight in the XFY-1 on 16 June 1955 and then on 1 August 1956 the Navy pulled the plug on the project. It was probably not an unexpected development and should have happened much earlier. Several years later the XFY-1 was transported to NAS Norfolk, Virginia, where it was used as a gate guardian, and in 1973 the aircraft was passed to the National Air and Space Museum in Washington DC. At the time of writing, it is in storage at the Smithsonian's NASM Garber Storage Facility, Silver Hill, Maryland.

ABOVE Convair Test pilot James 'Skeets' Coleman, who flew the XFY-1 and made the first complete (non-helicopter) VTOL flight in history, winning him the Harmon Trophy. *Convair*

BOTTOM LEFT A staged photograph, showing the pilot being assisted into the cockpit. By all accounts, a rather awkward undertaking! *Convair*

BOTTOM RIGHT This photograph shows the Convair XFY-1 elevated to 45° on its transportation unit. *US Navy*

TOP LEFT Seen from below, the Convair XFY-1 climbs into the sky. *US Navy*

TOP RIGHT The Convair XFY-1 in horizontal flight. *US Navy*

LEFT The Convair XFY-1 shortly after take-off. The pilot can be seen in the forward tilted position and during these trials, it was normal practice to leave the cockpit canopy open. *US Navy*

BOTTOM RIGHT The Convair XFY-1 photographed from a chase plane while passing over countryside. *US Navy*

Lockheed XFV-1

ABOVE A scale model of Lockheed's proposal for a VTOL turboprop fighter. *Lockheed Martin*

Lockheed responded to the US Navy's OS-122 request for an experimental VTOL tailsitter fighter with a design that closely rivalled the XFY-1. It used the same engine, gearbox and propeller set as the Convair design, carried the same armament and delivered approximately the same level of performance. Art Flock, assisted by Clarence 'Kelly' Johnson (1910–1990), undertook most of the initial design work for this aircraft. The project reference was L-200, which included a number of variants with swept wings and canard layouts. The Model L-200-1 was finally selected for development, briefly being known as the Model 081-40-01. Several small models were built, followed by a one-quarter-sized scale model with contra-rotating propellers driven by two powerful electric motors. Wind tunnel tests were conducted at NACA Langley and the results were good enough to secure the design as an alternative to the Convair XFY-1.

Subsequently, the official designation XFO-1 was applied and finally changed to XFV-1, with a Navy contract being issued on 19 April 1951 for the construction of two XFV-1 prototypes, which were issued with the serial numbers 138657 and 138658, plus a (generally unacknowledged) static test article and a mock-up. The XFV-1's fuselage was torpedo shaped, with two straight wings carrying large pods at

the tips and four tail fins, with dampened struts and wheels that would normally support the aircraft in a vertical position. An Allison XT40-A-6 turboprop provided propulsion and it was virtually identical to that used in the Convair aircraft, with exhaust ducted through a port on the lower rear fuselage. It was planned to replace this engine with the more powerful YT40-A-14 when it became available.

Like Convair's XFY-1, the engine was shaft-coupled via a substantial gearbox to a set of 16ft (4.87m) diameter Curtiss-Wright 'Turboelectric' contra-rotating three-blade propellers. Ahead of this assembly, in the spinner fairing, was sufficient room to accommodate a gun-aiming radar unit that was planned for the production FV-2 aircraft. Maximum take-off weight was 16,220lb (7,357kg) allowing an approximate power/weight ratio of 1.2 to 1. However, maximum performance with the replacement Allison YT40-A-14 engine was estimated as 580mph (933km/h), with a ceiling of 43,000ft (13,100m) and a combat radius of 500 miles (804km). Situated just behind the propellers, and between the engine air intakes, was the pressurised cockpit. This position offered a reasonably good view for the pilot in horizontal flight, but suffered the same visibility problems as the Convair design during VTOL operations. To improve matters, the Lockheed design also used a 45° forward-swivelling ejector seat. Nevertheless, like the Convair VTOL fighter, there was also the issue of gaining entry to the cockpit when the aircraft was vertical and a special trolley with ladder had to be fabricated for this purpose. The Lockheed XFV-1 was slightly larger than Convair's design, measuring 36.8ft (11.2m) in length, with a wingspan (including pods) of 30.9ft (9.4m) and a wing area of 246ft² (22.8m²). Should the design have proved successful, the XFV-1 was to be followed by the FV-2 (Model 181-43-02), which would have been powered by the Allison T54-A-16 turboprop engine, fitted with a radar system and have a bulletproof windshield. It was expected to be armed with four 20mm cannons or alternatively two separate packs of 2.75in (70mm) rockets carried in the wingtip pods.

The first prototype XFV-1 (138657) was completed at Burbank in spring 1953 and after testing had been completed it was transported to Edwards AFB. However, it was decided that the XT40-A-6 engine was on the borderline of providing sufficient power for vertical operations and it would be wiser to fit a temporary fixed-position undercarriage and undertake horizontal tests while waiting for the more powerful YT40-A-14 unit. The undercarriage was actually quite crude, comprising two forward wheels supported by four struts and downward-facing wheels on the two lower tail fins.

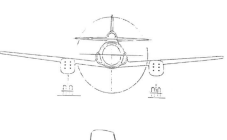

LEFT An original Lockheed drawing showing the L-200-1 design that would form the basis of the XFV-1 turboprop VTOL fighter project. *Lockheed*

RIGHT This illustration shows a Lockheed fighter design (L-210-2) based on the XFV-1 VTOL aircraft, but configured for normal horizontal take-off and landing. *Lockheed*

BELOW Two Lockheed drawings that show proposed VTOL fighter designs that were considered during the early stages of the XFV-1 project. *Lockheed*

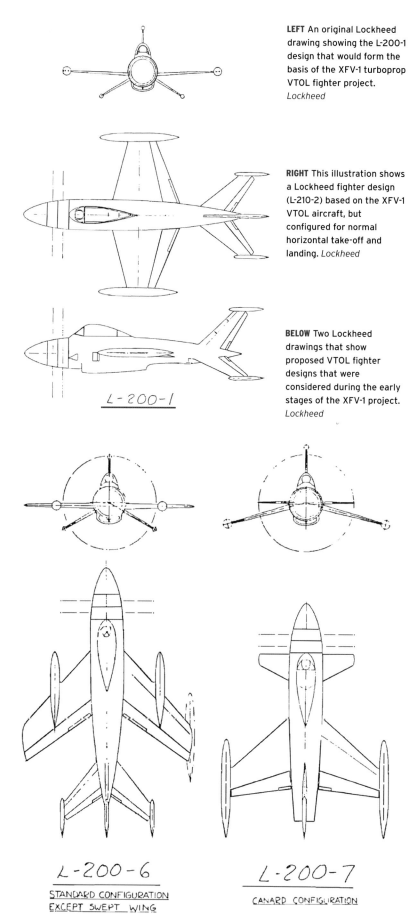

L-200-1

L-200-6
STANDARD CONFIGURATION
EXCEPT SWEPT WING

L-200-7
CANARD CONFIGURATION

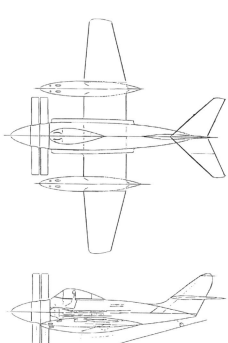

L-210-2

In addition to this, a special ground-handling rig was produced that would allow the aircraft (minus undercarriage) to be moved easily in a horizontal position and tilted upright for take-off. It was now late November 1953 and the XFV-1 was ready to begin ground tests and taxiing trials. At the controls, was Lockheed's test pilot Herman 'Fish' Salmon (1913–1980), who would soon have the aircraft unofficially named after him. On 23 December 1953, during a fast taxiing run, Salmon inadvertently left the ground for a few seconds, making this the first unofficial flight. Nevertheless, the engine had not been flight rated and the XFV-1 would not be recorded as having flown until 16 June 1954. Salmon then undertook a series of brief flights, conducting propeller vibration tests and eventually making several transitions from horizontal to vertical flight. Apparently, the aircraft was quite difficult to control in this position.

Problems with engine reliability and control of the contra-props continued into 1955 and there was no sign of the replacement engine, with Allison running into serious technical problems during its development. On 15 March 1955, Salmon made the last of 22 flights in the XFV-1 at Edwards AFB. The aircraft had never actually

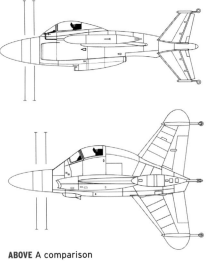

ABOVE A comparison between the Lockheed XFV-1 (upper) and Convair XFY-1 (lower) VTOL prototype fighters. *Bill Rose*

ABOVE Rear view of the XFV-1, showing the temporary undercarriage fitted to allow horizontal flight-testing. *Lockheed*

LEFT Underside view of the XFV-1. *Lockheed*

BELOW A full-sized mock-up of the Lockheed XFV-1 VTOL fighter, showing the proposed forward-facing radar installation in the aircraft's nose, access panels open and ejector ports in the wingtip pods for spent cartridge casings. *Lockheed Martin*

made a vertical take-off or landing. The Navy had already advised Lockheed that the aircraft was likely to remain experimental and would not be developed into a combat aircraft. Three months later, it cancelled the Lockheed and Convair tailsitters.

Much was wrong with these ill-conceived aircraft. The engine was simply not right and Allison's attempt to marry two T38 engines with a single gearbox had been a recipe for disaster from the outset. Handling the turboprop tailsitters during VTOL operations was extremely difficult and it should be remembered that the pilots who flew these prototypes were amongst the best in the business. An aircraft of this type could only be operated from a ship in the most favourable circumstances and even with most of the bugs ironed out, the probability of accidents was very high. Furthermore a turboprop fighter would be no match for a supersonic MiG and there was very little scope to upgrade either the Convair or Lockheed aircraft in any way.

Following cancellation, the first Lockheed XFV-1 (138657) was transported to Hiller Helicopters at Palo Alto, California, where its engine was used for ground tests. The aircraft was eventually presented to the San Diego Aerospace Museum. The second XFV-1 (138658) was largely completed but never flew and resided as a gate guardian at NAS Los Alamitos for many years. It was finally moved to the Naval Aviation Museum at Pensacola, Florida, where it is currently on display. As for the third test example, it has not been possible to verify if this was fully assembled, but it seems unlikely. While this should have been the end of any American ambitions to develop a VTOL tailsitting interceptor, there were a number of other projects already under way, which will be discussed in the next chapter.

RIGHT The XFV-1 is positioned by its transportation rig and the pilot's gantry is in place. *Lockheed*

FAR RIGHT A staged picture, showing the Lockheed XFV-1 to good effect. In fact, the aircraft never made a vertical take-off or landing. *Lockheed*

BELOW The XFV-1 makes a high-speed taxiing run at Edwards AFB. *Lockheed*

LEFT The XFV-1 skims above the ground during take-off. *Lockheed*

ABOVE The transportation rig used to raise the XFV-1 into a position suitable for VTOL operations. *Lockheed*

ABOVE A rare colour image of the XFV-1 in flight. *US Navy*

BELOW The XFV-1 making a conventional test flight above California. The fixed undercarriage limited performance considerably. *US Navy*

Soviet Developments

During the immediate postwar years, the Russians showed relatively limited interest in VTOL combat aircraft projects. Their overriding priority was the development of affordable, rugged and capable supersonic fighters that could match the more refined Western designs, plus long-range nuclear bombers. A few relatively obscure VTOL design studies were undertaken during the immediate postwar years and one of them started out in 1946 as a theoretical project at the Zhukovsky Military Engineering Air Academy. F. P. Kurochkin and V. N. Tironom were responsible for this tailsitter concept, with considerable assistance from Professor Boris Yuryev.

The aircraft was given the designation KIT-1 (almost certainly based on the names of the designers) and their concept comprised a fairly conventional fuselage section with an overall length of 22.1ft (6.75m), a delta wing with a span of 26.25ft (8m), plus large dorsal and ventral tail fins. Supporting dampeners and small wheels were fitted to housings at the wingtips and tail fin tips, allowing the aircraft to stand in a vertical position. The aircraft was powered by a centrally positioned Klimov VK-108 liquid-cooled V-12 piston engine producing 1,850hp (1,379kW), which was shaft-coupled via a gearbox to the forward propeller assembly. This comprised two contra-rotating blade assemblies of different size. The forward blades had a diameter of 11.8ft (3.6m) and were intended to propel the aircraft in level flight. The two much larger blades positioned directly behind had a 26.25ft (8m) radius and were intended to provide the necessary lift during take-off and landing. The plan was to de-clutch these after transition to level flight and place them in a horizontally parked position, where they would act as canard stabilisers. Control surfaces were located in the tail fins and wings, with entry into the cockpit via a side door. Armament for the fighter was to be a single 37mm cannon with 120 rounds and there might have been the possibility of adding one or two additional forward-firing guns, but the option of carrying external stores was not available.

At some point in the development of this project it was realised that the large delta wing was unnecessary and there was potential for performance improvement by replacement with a new profile having a span of approximately 11ft (3.35m).

The significantly reduced chord also meant that wingtip landing struts would need considerable extension while the aircraft was standing on the ground. Given the designation KIT-2, it was decided to upgrade the propeller

system with a contra-rotating set of three-blade propellers in the nose with a radius of 9ft (2.8m), followed by a larger secondary twin-blade unit with an estimated overall diameter of 16.4ft (5m). Some documentation suggests the possibility of increasing the length of these blades during take-off and landing.

Like the first design, this larger propeller would be stopped during horizontal flight to act as a forward stabiliser. KIT-1 had been expected to have a maximum level speed of 497mph (800km/h) and the designers now anticipated an increase to 570mph (920km/h). Both figures (taken from Russian sources) would appear somewhat over-optimistic, especially when drawing comparisons with the sleek Yak-3 fighters tested with VK-108 engines. One of these managed to reach 463mph (745km/h) at 20,639ft (6,290m) before experiencing engine overheating problems.

KIT-2 had an estimated take-off weight of 6,613lb (3,000kg), which meant that the aircraft would initially operate at the limit of its power-to-weight ratio. For this reason, it was decided to add several solid-fuel booster rockets until a more powerful engine became available. There is no evidence to show that KIT-1 or KIT-2 ever progressed much further than small models and wind tunnel tests.

LEFT General appearance of the Soviet KIT-1 VTOL fighter. *Bill Rose*

RIGHT General appearance of the Soviet KIT-2 VTOL fighter. *Bill Rose*

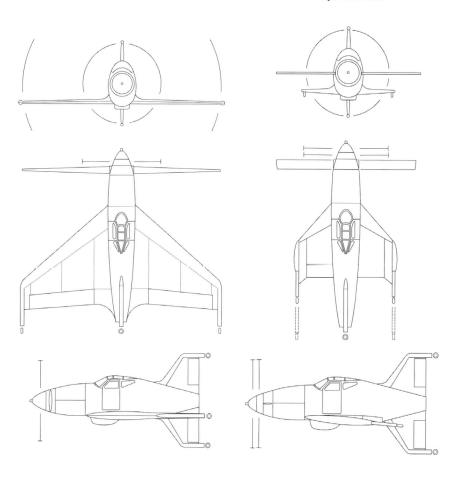

Fairey VTO Projects

Soon after World War 2 ended, Fairey Aviation began to receive substantial amounts of German aviation research material. In addition to this, Reimar Horten (1915-1994), who worked at the forefront of flying wing design, was briefly associated with Fairey during this period, although it is said that company staff refused to work with him and, as a consequence, Horten returned to Germany. The company was especially interested in Germany's rocket-powered point defence fighters such as the Bachem Ba 349 and wartime experience with delta wings, pioneered by Alexander Lippisch. The careful study of this research documentation quickly encouraged Fairey's chief designer Herbert Eugene Chaplin (1896-1979) to begin work on a twin, jet-engined flying wing concept known as Type K. Perhaps not surprisingly, this design had the hallmarks of being influenced by Horten.

The Type K aircraft was a tailless swept-wing design, powered by two side-by-side Rolls-Royce AJ.65s (the proposed Avon), with air drawn from two nose inlets. Take-off weight was set at 13,500lb (6,123kg) and the Type K had an estimated maximum speed of 650mph (1,046km/h) at sea level. Armament was expected to be two 30mm cannons. The Ministry of Supply (MoS) was approached to fund further development of this aircraft in mid-1946, but the design failed to generate sufficient interest as a fighter for the RAF. However, the Type K was also configured as a naval VTO interceptor and some details of the concept can be seen in a UK Patent (Ref: 733770) that Fairey applied for in June 1946. Chaplin must have anticipated an improvement in engine thrust, or the use of rocket booster assistance, to make vertical take-offs possible.

The drawings show a compact, swept-wing fighter, which would be tilted over the side of an aircraft carrier for vertical launch. Chaplin designed the forward-located cockpit to swivel up to 90° when the aircraft was in an upright position for VTO. There is nothing in this documentation to explain how the aircraft lands back on the carrier and it does not appear to use a conventional undercarriage. But a second UK Patent (Ref: 761230), applied for in May 1952, shows a similar aircraft in slightly more detail, now equipped with a rather complicated retractable skid undercarriage.

This could be used to raise the aircraft into an upright position for vertical take-offs and landings, or to make horizontal take-offs and landings from a land site. VTOL would be undertaken with the cockpit swivelled forward to aid visibility. In addition, Chaplin suggested the use of a large landing mat arrangement at the stern of a ship to capture a returning aircraft. The exact origin of this idea is unclear as it appears directly connected to flexible carrier decks which were experimented with at Royal Aircraft Establishment (RAE) Farnborough as early as

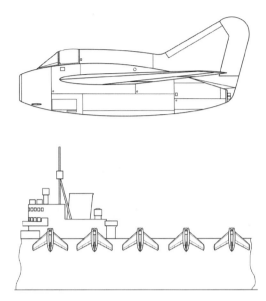

TOP An early Chaplin design for a VTO fighter based on the Type K proposal. *Bill Rose*

BOTTOM Herbert Chaplin's VTO flying wing fighters mounted on the sides of a carrier and ready for launch. *Herbert Chaplin/Restoration Bill Rose*

1947. The RAE then undertook trials with its chief test pilot Captain Eric Melrose 'Winkle' Brown (1919-) on HMS *Warrior* and the system worked, but was not judged to be a great success. At around the same time, Fairey was informally discussing ideas with the MoS for a VTO interceptor that could be launched from a mobile ramp, rather like the proposed Bachem Ba 349C. The one-man Fairey aircraft would be powered by a single jet engine, with the addition of expendable solid-fuel booster rockets for take-off. Once its mission was completed, the aircraft would return to a suitable area near the launch site to make a conventional horizontal landing.

Fairey generated sufficient interest to secure an MoS contract for rocket-launched, radio-controlled models and this soon progressed to Specification E.10/47 (OR.252) for an option on three small delta-winged, manned prototypes. While the design of an experimental manned VTO prototype progressed, a series of small rocket-powered models were built at Heston and they were generally referred to as the Fairey-Heston VTOs (or sometimes Fairey-Heston Deltas). With a similar appearance to the manned proposal, the delta-winged model had a 48° leading edge and a 7ft (2.13m) span. Propulsion was provided by an RAE-developed and Fairey-manufactured liquid-fuel Beta-1 rocket engine that employed two 900lb (4kN) thrust chambers. Liquid fuel for the Beta-1 engine was normally exhausted after one minute. The model was also fitted with two jettisonable solid-fuel rocket boosters, each providing an additional 600lb (2.66kN) of thrust during launch. The model was equipped with elevons and a tail rudder, with an autopilot controlling pitch and yaw and telemetry relayed to the ground.

The first flight test of a Fairey-Heston VTO

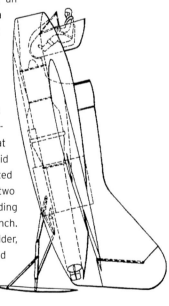

BELOW An early Fairey VTO fighter proposal showing the retractable undercarriage system in upright launch position and cockpit fully swivelled forward. *Fairey*

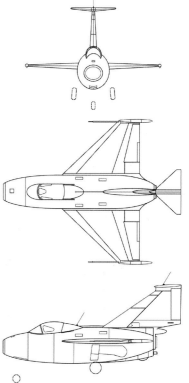

ABOVE The FD.1 during a test flight.
Fairey/Bill Rose

RIGHT Three-view drawing of the FD.1. *Bill Rose*

took place from a ship anchored in Cardigan Bay during 1949 and further trials followed at Woomera, Australia, which continued until 1953. It is also worth noting that many aspects of this work were classified as top secret. The design of the prototype fighter had now evolved considerably from Chaplin's early VTO jet fighter and it was initially known as the Fairey Type R. It had clipped delta wings with a span of 15.33ft (4.67m), an overall length of 28.67ft (8.73m) and was fitted with a nose inlet for the single turbojet. As the design continued to evolve, these dimensions changed slightly, with completion at Fairey's Stockport facility in early 1950. The prototype now received the company designation FD.1 and was assigned the serial number VX350.

The wingspan was now increased to 19.5ft (5.94m), with fixed leading-edge slats and the aircraft's length was reduced to 26.25ft (8m). It was powered by a single Rolls-Royce Derwent 8 turbojet, providing 3,600lb (16kN) of static thrust. With a gross weight of 6,800lb (3,084kg), this was expected to allow a maximum level speed of 628mph (1,010km/h) at altitude. Elevons and a large rudder provided flight control and, after initial tests, a delta-shaped tailplane was added to the top of the tail fin. FD.1 was prepared to receive the modifications that would allow it to be ramp launched, but the aircraft was also fitted with a conventional, fully retractable tricycle undercarriage. Some taxing tests were undertaken at Manchester's Ringway Airport and then it was partly disassembled and moved to RAF Boscombe Down by road.

In March 1951, the FD.1 made its first flight, with Fairey's test pilot Group Captain R. Gordon Slade at the controls. There were some control issues and it was soon realised that although the tailplane counteracted pitching problems, it also generated a good deal of unwanted drag, limiting the aircraft's maximum speed to about 345mph (555km/h). The idea of a ramp-launched fighter had now been officially dropped, although the FD.1 continued to be flown as a research aircraft. In September 1951, the FD.1 was damaged in a landing accident and, while repairs took place, it was decided to remove the leading-edge slats and wingtip-positioned anti-spin parachutes.

Flying resumed in May 1953, but the FD.1 remained a demanding aircraft to control and the project was finally cancelled. By this time, the option to build second and third FD.1 prototypes (VX357 and VX364) had been abandoned. The FD.1, which pre-dated the American X-13 by several years, cannot be regarded as a great success. After the programme was scrapped, the airframe was sent to the Shoeburyness, Essex Weapons Range, where it was used for target practice and ultimately destroyed. Some relatively low-level UK interest in VTOL fighters persisted and Herbert Chaplin moved on to design the record-breaking supersonic Fairey FD.2, before leaving the company in 1957.

BELOW One of the Fairey-Heston rocket-powered VTO models is test launched at Woomera, Australia. *Fairey*

Chapter Two: Aircraft Details

Ryan Model 38 VTOL Fighter
Crew: 1
Wingspan: 25ft (7.62m) approx
Wing Area: N/A
Sweep (leading edge): 30°
Length: 35ft (10.6m) approx
Height: N/A
Empty Weight: N/A
Gross Weight: 17,500lb (7,937kg)
Maximum Speed: High subsonic
Ceiling: 50,000ft (15,240m) estimated
Range: N/A
Powerplant: 1 x experimental General Electric
   XJ53-GE-X10 turbojet, expected to deliver
   21,000lb (93.4kN) thrust without the use of
   an afterburner
Armament: 4 x 20mm cannons. 2 x air-to-air
   Missiles, when available

Ryan X-13
Crew: 1
Wingspan: 21ft (6.4m)
Wing Area: 191ft² (17.74m²)
Wing Loading: 35.2lb/ft²
Sweep (leading edge): 30°
Length: 23.4ft (7.13m)
Height: 15.16ft (4.62m)
Empty Weight: 5,335lb (2,420kg)
Gross Weight: 7,300lb (3,311kg)
Maximum Speed: 483mph (777km/h)
Ceiling: 30,000ft (9,144m) estimated
Range: 167 miles (268km)
Powerplant: 1 x non-afterburning Rolls-Royce
   Avon RA.28-49 axial-flow gas turbine,
   capable of providing 10,000lb (44.4kN)
   static thrust
Armament: None

Convair XFY-1 Pogo
Crew: 1
Length: 34.95ft (10.6m)
Wingspan: 27.66ft (8.4m)
Wing Area: 355ft² (32.98m²)
Sweep (leading edge): 53°
Horizontal Height: 22.1ft (6.73m)
Empty Weight: 11,760lb (5,334kg)
Gross Weight: 16,250lb (7,370kg)
Maximum Speed (XT40-A-16): 610mph
   (981km/h) at 15,000ft (4,572m)
Maximum Speed: 474mph (762km/h) at sea
   level
Initial Rate of Climb: 10,500ft (3,200m)/min
Ceiling: 43,700ft (13,319m)
Range: 402 miles (650km)
Endurance: One hour, operating at an altitude
   of 35,000ft (10,669m)
Powerplant: 1 x Allison YT40-A-6 turboprop,
   rated at 5,850hp (4,362kW)
Armament: 4 x 20mm cannon or 48 x 2+
   (70mm) FFARs

Lockheed XFV-1 Salmon
Crew: 1
Wingspan (including pods): 30.9ft (9.4m)
Wing Area: 246ft² (22.9m²)
Sweep (leading edge): 17°
Length: 36.8ft (11.2m)
Height: N/A
Empty Weight: 11,600lb (5,260kg)
Gross Weight: 16,220lb (7,357kg)
Maximum Speed: 580mph (933km/h) at
   15,000ft (4,572m)
Cruising Speed: 410mph (660km/h)
Ceiling: 43,000ft (13,100m) estimated
Initial Rate of Climb: 10,800ft (3,292m)/
   minute
Endurance: 80 minutes at 35,000ft (10,668m)
Powerplant: 1 x Allison YT40-A-6 turboprop,
   rated at 5,850hp (4,362kW)
Armament: 4 x 20mm cannons or 48 x 2¾
   (70mm) FFARs in the wingtip pods

Martin Model 262 (Anticipated Future Designation XFM-1)
Crew: 1
Wingspan: 31.5ft (9.6m)
Wing Area: N/A
Sweep (leading edge): 50° estimated
Length: 44.66ft (13.6m)
Height: N/A
Empty Weight: 11-12,000lb (5,000-5,440kg)
Gross Weight: 15-16,000lb (6,800-7,250kg)
Maximum Speed: 550-575mph
   (885-925km/h) approx
Ceiling: 40,000ft+ (12,192m+) estimated
Combat Radius: 490 miles (790km) approx
Powerplant: 1 x Allison YT40-A-6 turboprop,
   rated at 5,850hp (4,362kW)
Armament: 4 x 20mm cannons, or possibly
   FFARs

Northrop N-63
Crew: 1
Wingspan: 30.2ft (9.2m)
Wing Area: 250ft² (23.3m²)
Sweep (leading edge): 17.5° estimated
Prop Blade Diameter: 15.5ft (4.72m)
Length: 36.7ft (11.1m)
Height: 20.4ft (6.23m)
Empty Weight: 11-12,000lb (5,000-5,440kg)
   approx
Gross Weight: 15,454lb (7,010kg)
Maximum Speed: 608mph (978km/h)
Ceiling: 47,000ft (14,325m) estimated
Combat Radius: 490 miles (790km) approx
Powerplant: 1 x Allison XT40-A-8, producing
   6,832hp (5,089kW)
Armament: 4 x 20mm cannons or FFAR
   rockets

KIT-1 and -2 VTOL
Crew: 1
Wingspan: KIT-1: 26.25ft (8m); KIT-2: 11ft
   (3.35m)
Wing Area: N/A
Sweep (leading edge): KIT-1: 41°; KIT-2: 45°
Length: 22.1ft (6.75m)
Empty Weight: N/A
Take-off Weight (KIT-2): 6,613lb (3,000kg)
Maximum Speed: KIT-1: 497mph (800km/h);.
   KIT-2: 570mph (920km/h)
Ceiling: KIT-1: 30,000ft (9,144m) estimated
Range: N/A
Endurance: 1.5 hours
Powerplant: Klimov VK-108 liquid-cooled V-12
   piston engine producing 1,850hp (1,379kW)
Armament: 1 x 37mm cannon with 120 rounds

Fairey VTO Flying Wing (Type K Configuration)
Crew: 1
Wingspan: N/A
Wing Area: N/A
Sweep (leading edge): 41.5° estimated
Length: N/A
Height: N/A
Empty Weight: N/A
Gross Weight: 13,500lb (6,123kg)
Estimated Maximum Speed (sea level):
   650mph (1,046km/h)
Ceiling: N/A
Range: N/A
Powerplant: 2 x Rolls-Royce AJ.65s (the
   proposed Avon), each producing 6,500lb
   (29kN) of static thrust
Armament: 2 x 30mm cannons

Fairey FD.1
Crew: 1
Wingspan: 19.5ft (5.94m). Initial Type R
   specification: 15.33ft (4.67m)
Wing Area: N/A
Sweep (leading edge): 47.5°
Length: 26.25ft (8m). Initial Type R
   specification: 28.67ft (8.73m)
Height: 19.5ft (5.94m)
Empty Weight: N/A
Gross Weight: 6,800lb (3,084kg)
Estimated Maximum Speed: 628mph
   (1,010km/h)
Practical Maximum Speed: 345mph
   (555km/h)
Ceiling: N/A
Range: N/A
Powerplant: 1 x Rolls-Royce Derwent 8
   turbojet, providing 3,600lb (16kN) static
   thrust
Armament: None

Chapter 3 Advanced Tailsitters

When initial trials of the Convair and Lockheed tailsitters began, interest in this type of aircraft was already in decline. Military planners began to realise that, although VTOL was highly desirable, the tailsitter provided it in a second-rate form. Tailsitters were dangerous to operate and, once airborne, existing designs were hopelessly inadequate. That aside, a second generation of tailsitters (or VATOLs) were already in development and these designs were conceived as supersonic successors to the turboprop aircraft. Developed for naval and land use, they were expected to enter service during the 1960s.

ABOVE The SNECMA C.450 Coléoptère on its transport trailer, which is braced in a static position. *SNECMA*

Convair Supersonic VTOL Studies 1953-1954

In December 1953, Convair received a classified $75,000 contract (AF33(616)-2313) from the USAF's Wright Air Development Center to study a lightweight supersonic tailsitter over a six-month period. This project would draw on work taking place to develop a conventional supersonic delta-winged fighter. The USAF issued similar classified contracts to three other aviation contractors (Lockheed, Temco and Ryan Aeronautical) and held discussions with North American Aviation, who declined to participate, but finally conducted a sponsored VTOL fighter-bomber study in 1955. Each USAF contract was tailored to include specific individual features and, in Convair's case, it was asked to determine if its existing 60° delta wing was suitable for a VTOL combat aircraft.

The USAF considered a thrust/weight (T/W) of 1.1 as a good starting point for its requirement, suggesting the Allison J71-A (Series 600-B30) turbojet with a gas coupled turbofan unit. This proposed version of the J71 was expected to deliver a maximum thrust of 26,600lb (118kN) using an afterburner, although it was recognised that additional rocket boosters might be required to launch the aircraft in hot conditions or at higher altitudes. Take-off weight was set at a maximum of 23,000lb (10,432kg) with supersonic speed available in level flight and an operational radius of approximately 288 miles (463km). Therefore, it seems reasonable to deduce that an intercept mission would have been relatively brief and the aircraft was considered little more than a manned missile, rather like the wartime Bachem Natter.

Convair considered a number of different designs, all using the same basic wing planform and a modified NACA 0005-63 section, but varying in area. One of the first concepts to emerge featured a fuselage containing little more than the jet engine with a nose intake and

unguided rockets carried in retracted forward-located packs. The aircraft would stand upright on the ground, supported by four dampened struts in wing nacelles and two tail fins. The cockpit would be located in a large pod attached to the upper tail fin, with the pilot in a prone position. A revision of this design placed this cockpit at the front of the aircraft, largely surrounded by the engine inlet. While technically interesting, this idea proved impractical and it was decided to use a normal forward-positioned cockpit, with a swivelling ejector seat to improve visibility during VTOL operations. This was designed to move through 40°, with ejection possible with the seat tipped fully forward. From this position, the pilot would be able to see the wingtip landing gear.

Most of the original drawings show a fairly typical cockpit canopy design, as opposed to the V-shaped, reflection-reducing windshield used for the Convair F-102. In addition, a large air inlet for the turbofan was placed directly below the cockpit, a ventral pod housed the aircraft's cannon and a landing strut, and the wing position was revised. This design was known as Configuration IVa. Having decided this was the best option for further development, Convair applied to the Wright Air Development Center for an extension to the study contract, which was granted on 1 May 1954. Support was already forthcoming from NACA Langley, which undertook model tests, concluding that the design was reasonably sound, with hovering and transition to level flight being unlikely to present any major problems. However, there were some initial concerns about the aircraft's directional stability, which Convair considered fixable. One other known variant of the Configuration IV design was fitted with small delta-shaped canard fins on each side of the cockpit and this is thought to have directly resulted from the work

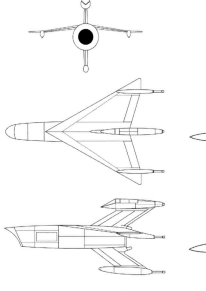
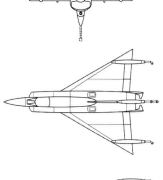
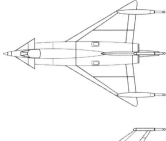
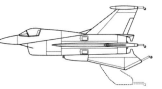
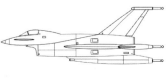

LEFT This unusual-looking 1950s Convair proposal for a supersonic delta-winged VTOL interceptor carried the pilot within a fin-mounted pod in a prone position. *Bill Rose*

CENTRE Convair Configuration IVa delta-winged VTOL interceptor. *Bill Rose*

RIGHT A canard version of Convair's supersonic tailsitter interceptor. *Bill Rose*

undertaken at NACA Langley, although these changes appear to have proven unnecessary.

Convair investigated several systems for low-speed control, such as wingtip thrusters, using air bled from the engine compressor. The exhaust nozzle area could be adjusted for lift-off and normal flight and Convair considered the possibility of using vanes in the exhaust flow to control roll, pitch and yaw, perhaps eliminating the need for wingtip thrusters. During horizontal flight, the aircraft would utilise elevons and a rudder. Most of the airframe would be built from aluminium alloy, with specialised high-temperature materials used wherever necessary, and the fuselage was designed to achieve optimal aerodynamic performance using 'area rule'.

Convair was reluctant to fit a ventral fin to the fighter, which would have increased drag at substantial speed and would have needed to be detached before attempting an emergency horizontal crash landing. However, a lower fin would have improved some handling characteristics and more importantly allowed the aircraft to land in a more stable manner. Occupying the same area was a large fairing, enclosing a 20mm rotary cannon and ammunition in the forward section and a dampened strut at the rear. As an improvement, Convair's designers decided to make this strut flip out for landing, which would increase stability on the ground. The unit would also be surrounded by a fairing,

creating some of the properties of a ventral fin. Each dampened strut was fitted with a small wheel, although this would have been less than satisfactory when used at some improvised sites. In addition, the amount of strut extension could be adjusted, allowing tilt up to 5°, which might prove useful when taking off in windy conditions or on uneven ground. Wind tunnel testing of models showed stability up to Mach 2.85, although the use of a large air inlet for the J71's turbofan was found to cause pitch and yaw problems at low speeds.

Part of the problem with this VTOL concept was the USAF's engine choice and although the Allison J71 was an improvement on earlier engines, it was soon outclassed by models from other manufacturers. With a take-off weight of around 23,000lb (10,432kg), Convair concluded that the engine performance was inadequate for the aircraft and a more powerful turbojet was required with at least 35,000lb (155kN) static thrust. This relatively brief study failed to address a number of important issues, such as the close vicinity of the exhaust to the ground, potential undercarriage problems and a range of ground handling and transportation requirements.

However, despite being a fairly complex design, Convair completed its report with the promise of being able to meet or surpass the original requirement if a decision was taken to proceed to a prototype.

Lockheed Supersonic VTOL Designs

In 1954, Lockheed Aircraft received a USAF contract for the study of a supersonic VTOL tailsitter that would last one year. (The initial contract for the CL-295-1 was AFI8(500)-123P and this was followed by AFI8(600)-1232 for the CL-295-4.) The basic requirements were the same as those issued to Convair, Temco and Ryan for a daylight high-performance interceptor, but with more flexibility in engine choice and the option of using a Ryan-style cable-hanging system or self-raising landing gear. Lockheed had already conducted some studies into the possibility of building a jet-powered VTOL tailsitter and believed that the best approach was to keep things as simple as possible. The company reference for this project was CL-295 and the starting point was a lightweight aircraft closely based on the F-104A Starfighter, which was a VATOL concept, operating from an upright position, supported at rest by a retractable hook on the forward underside of the aircraft. Powered by a proposed Wright TJC32C4 turbojet, this was considered the most suitable engine available when the project started.

Designated as CL-295-1, this design quickly gave way to the CL-295-3, which made use of an experimental General Electric X-84 jet engine with afterburner, providing a slightly improved thrust/weight ratio. There

would be sufficient fuel carried to allow an intercept mission with a 230-mile (370km) combat radius and the re-engined CL-295-3 was expected to provide a maximum speed of Mach 2.2 at 35,000ft (10,668m). The CL-295-3 was fitted with inlets for the engine on each side of the fuselage and stubby wings, rather like the F-104A although some 5% thicker. Similarities also included ailerons, a rudder and an all-moving tailplane for conventional flight. However, it was felt necessary to fit a lower, all-moving control surface below the rear fuselage section, which was one-third the size of the

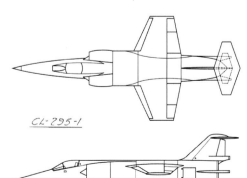

RIGHT This study known as CL-295-1 began life as little more than an upended F-104A Starfighter that would be adapted to provide a VTOL capability. However, as the design rapidly evolved, it began to differ considerably from the Starfighter. The CL-295-1 would utilise a launch support system similar to that developed for the Ryan VTOL fighter proposals, it would be equipped with an exhaust flow control system, reaction jets and a secondary stabilising fin for VTOL. *Bill Rose*

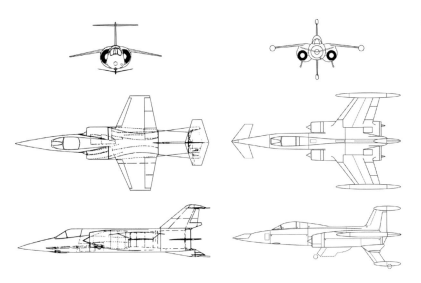

LEFT The relatively compact Lockheed CL-295-3 VTOL tailsitter interceptor, clearly derived from the F-104 Starfighter. *Pete Clukey Lockheed Martin/Bill Rose*

RIGHT The twin-engined Lockheed CL-295-4 VTOL fighter, equipped with self-erecting undercarriage. *Bill Rose*

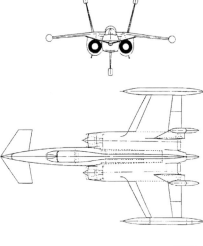

CL-349-17

LEFT Lockheed's CL-349-17, self-erecting VTOL fighter. Direct comparisons show this design to be identical in all respects to the twin-engined CL-295-2 and the reasons for altering the designation are unknown. *Pete Clukey Lockheed Martin/Bill Rose*

upper tailplane. The reason for this unusual arrangement was to counteract pitching moments.

For low-speed pitch and yaw control during VTOL operations, the aircraft was equipped with an exhaust deflection system comprising four tail-mounted vanes. Made from Inconel X, they would be cooled by air bleed from the engine compressor that was channelled through the blade root and exited from the trailing edge. The vanes would be retracted from the exhaust flow once the aircraft achieved conventional flight. Lockheed also decided to use compressor-bleed air at the wingtips for low-speed roll control.

Although the aircraft would be manually controlled by the pilot at low speeds, Lockheed's designers considered it important to reduce the workload by as much as possible and proposed a programmed autopilot, which would improve safety and lower fuel consumption. Both the CL-295-1 and CL-295-3 would be built mainly from aluminium alloy and there was no conventional undercarriage, so horizontal landing was not an option. Whether or not Lockheed considered the consequences of making a crash landing are unknown, but the lower tail fin might have been made jettisonable for such an emergency. The cockpit was fully pressurised, with emergency downward ejection and

the ability to tilt the seat forward by 22.5° during VTOL operations as a means of improving the pilot's visibility. Armament for the single-engined VTOL interceptor was a General Electric TE-171-E3 (later M61) Vulcan 20mm six-barrelled Gatling-type cannon with 800 rounds of ammunition. This was specified by the USAF for all designs considered during these studies and there are no indications that any other types of weapons like air-to-air missiles were considered.

The single-engined CL-295 (-1/3) VATOL would attach to an upright launch platform in a similar manner to the Ryan X-13 and a transportation rig was envisaged for horizontal ground handling. A somewhat different design for a self-erecting VTOL interceptor was developed in parallel. Designated as the CL-295-4, this proposal utilised two General Electric X-84 turbofans and was supported in an upright position by two tail fins and two wingtip nacelles. Soon after the CL-295 study began, General Electric disclosed that its high-performance afterburning J79 turbojet had been successfully tested and Lockheed decided it was ideal for the project, offering an improved lift capability. As a consequence, the CL-295-4 was modified to take this engine, becoming (a little confusingly) the CL-295-2. To supplement the jet engine(s) on all proposed VTOL versions (when operating in difficult conditions), Lockheed allowed for the attachment of four solid-fuel rocket boosters, with each providing a thrust of 1,000lb (4.48kN) for 30 seconds, duration.

Like the CL-295-4, the CL-295-2 utilised a canard layout to lower the centre of gravity and allow wingtip nacelles for ground-support purposes. But an increase of weight due to the different engines altered the centre of gravity and led to a revision of the wing profile and twin dorsal tail fins to maintain stability. This meant there were now five undercarriage points on the aircraft. Otherwise, the handling remained largely unchanged and maximum performance matched the single-engine proposal with an estimated maximum speed of Mach 2.2 at 35,000ft (10,668m) being available. Constructionally, the airframe would be largely made from aluminium alloy and this aircraft would use the same pressurised cockpit as the single-engine design. In addition, the method of control during VTOL operations also used vanes in the exhaust flows of both engines to control pitch and yaw, with wingtip compressed air nozzles to handle roll at low speed. A major feature of the twin-engined design was the self-erecting undercarriage, which added considerable weight to the aircraft and dictated the use of two engines. Both the CL-295-4 and CL-295-2 used the same system, which worked in the same manner for both designs.

From a horizontal transport and maintenance position, the aircraft could be raised to stand vertically on its dampened struts, which would be equipped with small temperature-resistant, swivelling wheels. These appear to retract during flight. The folding ventral fin unit was used to lift the aircraft into position. It would move across the ground using a wheel controlled by an internal gear-driven block and tackle system driven by a 5hp (3.7kW) hydraulic motor that was powered by a ground service unit. The time allowed to erect the aircraft was two minutes. Lowering the aircraft was an unpowered operation that utilised the same hydraulic release principle found in a car jack.

Many variations of the two original designs for the study were produced, although most of the original documentation has been lost or destroyed. However, it was possible to find the design for a single-engined fighter with the reference CL-295-68, which retained the overall appearance of an F-104A but was fitted with a ventral engine intake. The wings were moved as far backwards as possible and the overall span (including wingtip fuel tanks) was approximately 25ft (7.62m), with an estimated area of 220ft^2 (20.4m^2). The aircraft had a length of approximately 45ft (13.7m) and a cruciform of swept tailfins provided tip-mounted supports for the aircraft in a vertical position. Power for the CL-295-68 would be provided by an afterburning Wright J67 turbojet (based on the Bristol Olympus), with low-speed vane control in the exhaust flow.

Possibly the final design in this series was given the reference CL-295-77. It was a twin-engined aircraft, powered by GE X-84 turbofans mounted in wingtip nacelles. As expected, this version used vanes in the exhaust flow and compressed air nozzles in the wingtips for low-speed vertical control, with normal control surfaces for horizontal flight. Aside from the rearrangement of engines, the canard CL-295-77 was similar to the other twin-engined Lockheed VTOL

interceptors in terms of features, weight and performance. The overall length was slightly shorter at 38ft (11.6m), with a wingspan (including engine nacelles) of approximately 25ft (7.62m). Details revealed in available company documentation show provision for a radar system and the expectation that these aircraft would carry Sidewinder air-to-air Missiles (AAM).

Lockheed considered the twin-engined canard VTOL fighter to be the best option and believed there were no serious technical issues to prevent a prototype being built. Models were wind tunnel tested, but no details remain to show the results. Nevertheless, there are several issues that failed to be addressed during this study and similar concerns appear to have been glossed over by other contractors working on VTOL projects. For example, engine failure or loss of control while the aircraft was in a vertical position would have left the pilot no option aside from ejection. Combat damage might also have prevented a vertical landing and it is unclear if a horizontal landing was possible.

Another obvious problem with the Lockheed designs was the close proximity of the engine exhaust to the ground. The effects of this, perhaps in conjunction with solid-fuel jettisonable rockets during lift-off, do not appear to have been explored.

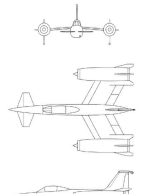

TOP Another Lockheed VTOL tailsitter design. The CL-295-77 has its twin engines contained in wingtip nacelles, which also function as part of the undercarriage system. *Bill Rose*

BOTTOM One of the later Lockheed designs produced during the VTOL tailsitting fighter series developed during the 1950s. Few details of this concept, designated CL-295-68, have survived. *Bill Rose*

Temco Model 39 VTOL Tailsitter

The third aviation company to undertake a supersonic tailsitter design study for the USAF was Temco, which received a six-month contract (AF33(616)-2314) in September 1953. The Temco Aircraft Corporation, located in Dallas, Texas, was a major subcontractor for specialised military aircraft components and eventually became part of the Ling-Temco-Vought group. The main stipulation of this USAF contract for a supersonic VTOL fighter study was the use of an afterburning Allison J71-A (Series 600-B30) turbojet with a gas coupled turbofan unit. A second requirement was the need for this aircraft to operate from an improvised site, surrounded by 50ft (15.2m) obstacles, with winds up to 20kt (37km/h). The USAF also instructed Temco to consider the possibility of a tailsitter that carried the pilot in a prone position, with the intention of making VTOL operations simpler and safer.

Temco allocated the company reference Model 39 to this project and almost immediately dismissed the idea of a prone position for the pilot as too complex to be resolved in a six-month period. Consequently, it settled on a forward-positioned conventional cockpit with a swivelling seat for use during VTOL operations and emergency upward ejection. The first layout was for a canard configuration, but Temco's designers finally dropped this idea, choosing a wing with a leading edge sweep of 57.6°. This was moved rearward to achieve a desirable centre of gravity and for undercarriage considerations. To improve the aircraft's stall characteristics during transition, an extension was located on the outer 50% of the leading edge and it is possible that NACA Langley established this need during wind tunnel tests of models. In addition, two substantial stabilising fins were located in dorsal and ventral positions at the rear of the fuselage.

Temco's designers then decided on a maximum take-off weight of 21,000lb (9,525kg) to maintain a superior thrust/weight ratio, although this limited the combat radius to 88 miles (141km), which seems to have been a rather unsatisfactory decision, taking into account the original USAF requirement. It was also concluded that rocket-assisted take-off would be required in a hot climate or at high altitudes. The undercarriage was formed from four dampened struts in nacelles at the wingtips and on each tail fin. Wheels, when needed for ground handling, appear to have been considered an optional extra.

The Model 39's airframe would be built mainly from aluminium alloy, with steel and other high-strength materials in some key areas. The engine inlet was located on the underside of the fuselage below the cockpit, with the fuselage diameter directly related to the size of the J71-A engine and cooling requirements. No consideration seems to have been given to aerodynamic 'area-ruling' during the design of the Model 39, which looks like a major oversight. The pressurised cockpit contained a swivelling ejector seat to provide an improved rearward view for the pilot during low-speed vertical flight. The instrument panel would also move in relation to the seat position. However, the ejection mechanism was disabled while the aircraft was in an upright position, which would have raised major safety concerns and is unlikely to have been accepted by the USAF.

The chosen method of controlling the aircraft in low-speed vertical flight was by means of exhaust-deflecting vanes and Temco believed that it would be possible to manufacture these from enamel-coated high-temperature steel and avoid the need for complicated air cooling, while leaving them locked in position during conventional flight. In common with the other VTOL designs produced during these USAF-sponsored studies, there would be reaction jets at the wingtips, using air taken from the engine's compressor stage. In normal flight, the aircraft would be directed by

hydraulically operated elevons and rudders. There was nothing particularly unusual about the way these surfaces were controlled by the pilot. However, the stick functioned differently during low-speed vertical flight and transitions while connected to the vanes. Lateral movements controlled yaw as opposed to roll, which was now produced by twisting the stick. This system would have presented problems and is unlikely to have been accepted for use with a prototype. Other features of interest were the large dorsal speed brakes and the ability to jettison most of the lower fin in the event of attempting an emergency horizontal landing. Armament was specified by the USAF as a 20mm cannon with 800 rounds and this would have been located in the forward fuselage near the cockpit. There would also be provision for radar equipment in the nose, although no details of this are available. Maximum speed at altitude was estimated to be in the region of Mach 1.6-2, with a ceiling in excess of 50,000ft (15,240m). At the end of its study, Temco concluded that the J71-A turbofan chosen by the Air Force was unsuitable for this type of aircraft, and suggested that a more advanced engine would provide better flight performance and an increased combat radius. That said, it also concluded that a prototype could be built using the Allison J71-A turbofan.

It is hard to determine why Convair's heavier Configuration IVa tailsitter was expected to provide a significantly greater combat radius than the Temco Model 39. Temco also allocated little, if any, time to considering ground handling, transportation or maintenance requirements and the Model 39 study does appear to have been somewhat rushed. One problem that seems to have been overlooked by Convair, Lockheed and Temco when designing these tailsitters was the effect of a powerful engine exhaust on the ground from a relatively close distance. At improvised sites, some surfaces would melt, others might catch fire and debris would be thrown into the air, producing a dangerous situation for the ground crew and a possibility of damaging the aircraft.

ABOVE General appearance of the Temco Model 39 supersonic VTOL interceptor. *Bill Rose*

Ryan Advanced VTOL Studies

When Ryan Aeronautical received a USAF contract (AF18(600)-1157) to explore the design of a supersonic VTOL fighter in early 1954, it was already well ahead of the game. The company had been interested in developing just such an aircraft since the late 1940s and was responsible for the X-13 VTOL project. The short-term design study discussed here, was for a VATOL daylight tailsitting fighter that received the company designation Model 84. Ryan's design team, working under Ben Salmon, was able to draw on a substantial amount of research for the Model 38 and the

X-13, deciding from the outset that a hook-suspended aircraft was preferable to a freestanding tailsitter. This type of design had many clear advantages that included the lowest possible weights, aerodynamic cleanness and relatively easy transportation and ground-handling features. It would also be possible to have effective control of jet blast and avoidance of recirculation problems due to the launch equipment design.

The starting point for the Model 84's propulsion system was a single Pratt & Whitney J75 afterburning turbojet, which was still in development and had an anticipated static thrust of 23,500lb (104kN). It was then decided that two side-by-side General Electric J79-GE1 afterburning turbojets, each providing an estimated 14,350lb (63.3kN) of static thrust, were more suitable and provided a better combat radius. Like the J75, this engine was also in the development stage. In total, 14 different single- and twin-engine configurations were considered. In addition to this, Ryan also examined the possibility of a modified version of the Model 84 (Model 84F-7), which was able to use the General Electric X-84 and X-301 turbofan engines. This showed the potential for improved performance, although these engines were not expected to become available until the early 1960s. As a result of this, Ryan decided that the J79 was the obvious choice of engine if the USAF decided to go ahead with full development of the aircraft in 1955, with expectations of service entry by 1961. Ryan also had the most advanced method of thrust deflection, using vectoring engine nozzles, and this idea for controlling pitch, yaw and roll at low speeds was very much ahead of its time.

The proposed aircraft had some similarities in overall appearance to the French Mirage IIIA and the Convair F-102A. It was designed around a delta wing and single tail fin, with engine inlets on each side of the forward fuselage. The pressurised cockpit was fitted with a swivelling ejector seat similar to that found on the X-13. There was no undercarriage as such, but the aircraft would be fitted with a retractable hook on the underside of the forward fuselage. The study was duly presented to the USAF, which seems to have considered it to be the best proposal and, although there does not appear to have been a clear-cut plan to progress to a development programme, Ryan was advised that the Model 84 had been well received and its fighter was the preferred design. As a direct result of the feedback received from the Wright Air Development Center, a decision was taken by Claude Ryan to fund a more detailed study of an improved supersonic VTOL fighter, which would be paid for by the company. Work on a new aircraft began in 1955 and the chosen design received the company designation Model 112. It was very similar in appearance to the Model 84 and would be powered by two J79-GE-2A/B turbojets. The study continued until 1956 and attracted USAF interest, alongside the X-13 programme, which was progressing fairly well.

This led to the USAF deciding to fund continuation of the design study (Contract: AF 18(600)-1641), with a revised version of the aircraft becoming Model 115 and more emphasis on the nuclear strike role. The reason for the gaps in company references at this point are not entirely clear, but it is believed that the US Navy was approached to consider a version of the Model 112 and, as a consequence, two modified versions of the aircraft were proposed (Model 113 and 114). Again, the Model 115 was very similar in appearance to the previous delta-winged

Ryan VATOL fighters, but with various enhancements. The exact details of the proposed armament for this entire series of Ryan VTOL designs are somewhat unclear, but it seems likely that the USAF originally specified a 20mm cannon with 800 rounds for the Model 84. Whether this was included in the later designs is unclear. Documentation indicates a ventral bay that would allow the carriage of a free-fall tactical nuclear weapon, with anticipated dimensions of no more than 18in (0.45m) by 60in (1.52m). The carriage of external stores was also examined, but no details are available.

The Ryan Model 115 series was eventually stretched by approximately 6ft (1.82m) to accommodate (amongst other things) a larger bay housing a single tactical nuclear weapon, or four Sidewinder/Falcon AAMs. The final version (Model 115C) was substantially altered to meet revised USAF requirements that included greater range and increased flexibility. Much of the airframe would be built from stainless steel as opposed to aluminium or magnesium alloy, with Ryan believing it was a more suitable material to handle aerodynamic and engine heating issues. Area rule was applied to the fuselage and the notched delta wing was essentially the same as chosen for previous models.

Air inlets for the engines were changed from semi-circular to circular and an anticipated small improvement in turbojet performance suggested a maximum speed of Mach 2.5, with a ceiling of at least 65,000ft (19,812m). Although the J79 was the engine chosen for this aircraft, Ryan believed that a further version of the aircraft might benefit from high-performance turbofan engines when the technology had matured. As with earlier versions of this design, the option to use strap-on solid-fuel rockets during launch was retained. Several alternative methods of boosting take-off performance were considered such as water injection and the brief use of exotic fuels, but rockets were considered the most satisfactory.

LEFT With a relatively conventional appearance, the Ryan Model 115 VTOL interceptor was well received in official circles and the design underwent extensive development, with wind tunnel testing in model form. *Bill Rose*

RIGHT The Ryan Model 115C was the final design in this series. Slightly stretched in length, this aircraft would have been capable of VTOL operations and conventional take-offs and landings. The USAF appears to have been very impressed with this proposal and undertook extensive costing for development, manufacture and deployment to Europe. *Bill Rose*

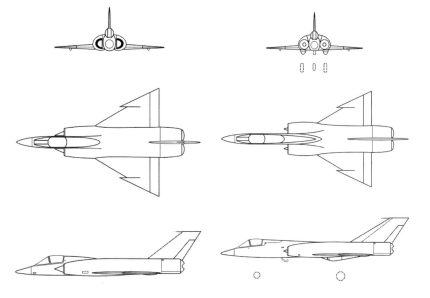

The final incarnation of this aircraft design was intended to accommodate an optional tricycle undercarriage and a braking parachute, which allowed conventional take-offs and landings from a runway, or a vertical take-off and horizontal landing. This would add an additional 12% to the aircraft's empty weight, although the undercarriage could be fitted or removed in the field if only the attachment hook was required. With the undercarriage in place, it improved ground handling and allowed the aircraft to taxi onto the VTOL support unit, which incorporated a blast deflector. An all-weather capability was envisaged for the Model 115C, with intercept radar, advanced infrared tracking, inertial navigation and perhaps eventually automated take-off and landing. Three principal missions were considered for the Model 115C, operating from improvised sites. These were a (relatively) long-range strike of 500 miles (925km) delivering one free-fall tactical nuclear weapon, which would mostly be undertaken at high subsonic speed; a second shorter nuclear strike, partly at supersonic speed with a maximum range of 280 miles (518km); and the third was interception of enemy aircraft at supersonic speed using air-to-air missiles.

Aside from the relatively impressive level of performance promised by the most advanced Ryan VTOL fighter-bomber, a major factor in encouraging the USAF to continue funding this study were the estimates for operational costs. These would be at least 24% cheaper than any of the tailsitters proposed by the other contractors in this series of studies. The Model 115C study was completed in 1957 and submitted to the USAF at about the same time as Ryan successfully demonstrated the X-13 to officials at the Pentagon in Washington DC. Claude Ryan must have felt reasonably hopeful that this would lead directly to a development contract for the Model 115C. The design appears to have been well considered, with potential for upgrades, and the company was confident that a prototype would perform as anticipated. However, by this time the USAF had largely decided that there was no real future for the VATOL configuration and horizontal flat risers were the way forward.

Perhaps with the exception of the least favoured Temco concept, all of these more advanced tailsitters and hanging designs could have been built and flown, but there were many technical problems which lacked solutions. The aircraft all stood relatively tall on the ground (or support system) and presented themselves as easy targets for the enemy. Engine failure during ascent, transition or landing would probably prove catastrophic and landing away from the launch site might not have been easy or even possible with some designs. Indeed, this problem was noted during initial development of the Ryan Model 84. In the case of a tailsitter making a successful emergency vertical landing, it would be necessary for the pilot to make an escape to the ground, probably using some sort of compact ladder or abseiling gear from a considerable height. This might not be so easy in a hostile environment when the aircraft was damaged, on fire, or in danger of imminent attack. All the designers must have considered these possibilities, with each aircraft being potentially dangerous to operate.

Unusual US Naval VTOL Concepts

The postwar years gave birth to many bizarre US military aerospace projects that in most cases were unaffordable, far beyond the technical capabilities of the time, dangerous or just plain crazy. They included various forms of nuclear propulsion for aircraft, missiles and spaceships, giant airborne aircraft carriers, supersonic flying disc fighters, secret fortresses on the Moon and submersible aircraft carriers. Many postwar US 'black' projects costing billions of dollars were undertaken. Some went no further than studies, while others were tested. The details of many classified programmes remain secret and, decades later, the value of this work is impossible to determine.

In the case of submarine aircraft carriers, this idea was first tested on a small scale during World War 1, and Germany considered the possibility of launching cruise missiles and rockets from submarines during World War 2. By the 1950s the US Navy was operating submarines capable of carrying surface-launched Regulus I missiles and it occurred to staff in the Office of Naval Research (ONR) that it would be possible to substitute these fighter-sized, rail-launched weapons with an air defence or attack aircraft. Douglas Aircraft was approached to study this idea and Ed Heinemann, who was the company's senior designer, proposed a small catapult-launched jet aircraft that could be stowed (in folded condition) within a Regulus hangar. His concept received the company designation Model 640 and it would be capable of carrying a single nuclear weapon in the strike role.

The aircraft would return to the carrier after its mission and land in the sea by the submarine for recovery using a crane. An alternative study proposed the construction of a submarine capable of carrying three modified Convair F2Y Sea Dart fighters within a hangar area inside the hull. These would be launched using a 170ft (51m) rail mounted on the rear deck area. Returning aircraft would put down on the sea and be lifted back on the submarine by a crane. Nothing came of either study, although the idea continued to generate

interest and after the larger Regulus II missile had been developed there were further proposals to modify submarines carrying this weapon for aircraft use. Perhaps there was some sense to this thinking. The move towards submerged strategic missiles had been initiated in 1956 under the Polaris Project and it would rapidly replace vulnerable surface-launched missiles, making the Regulus obsolete. The option of a fighter might give Regulus submarines a new lease of life. Subsequently, Boeing in Wichita, Kansas, was commissioned by the ONR in late 1957 or early 1958 to undertake a feasibility study involving the carriage of an effective fighter aircraft onboard a Regulus submarine such as the USS *Grayback* or USS *Halibut*.

Boeing selected the Grumman F11F fighter as a suitable candidate for development and added a compact, jet-powered, recoverable vertical launch platform. This is said to have been an idea proposed by the ONR, but it appears to be an adaptation of a patented design (Ref: 3058691) produced by German scientists working for the French aviation organisation *Société Nationale d'Études et de Construction de Moteurs d'Aviation* (SNECMA) during the mid-1950s. The Boeing version of this vertical launch unit was called the Flying Carpet and consisted of little more than two turbojet engines and fuel, encased in an aerodynamic housing. Apparently, this unit would return to the carrier after separating from the fighter, making a controlled cable capture similar to that employed by the X-13. On completion of its mission the Grumman Tiger would also return to the carrier, making a similar cable-supported vertical landing. The kind of mission intended for this fighter is unclear, but its main roles would probably be the interception of hostile aircraft, reconnaissance, or the delivery of a single tactical nuclear weapon in a pre-emptive strike.

The Grumman Tiger would have been extensively modified for this role, requiring a major redesign. The undercarriage would be removed, vertical landing components installed and sections of the airframe strengthened. Low-speed controls would be required, including a thrust vectoring system and wingtip reaction controls. In addition, to this, the cockpit would need to be redesigned with a swivelling ejection seat to improve visibility during landing. The wings and fins would fold to reduce storage space to the minimum and I suspect the Boeing designers would have wanted this aircraft built to Super Tiger specification with the superior General Electric J79-GE-3A turbojet engine.

BELOW A Regulus II missile is prepared for a simulated launch from USS *Grayback* (SSG-574) during an exercise in 1960. This submarine system was seriously considered for adaptation to a manned VTOL strike fighter. *US Navy*

ABOVE A Grumman F11F Tiger in flight. This aircraft was selected by Boeing for redevelopment as a special operations fighter, capable of being carried by a submersible carrier. *Grumman/Bill Rose*

BELOW Folding system for the Grumman F11F VTOL design and Boeing Flying Carpet launcher, allowing storage in a submersible pressurised hangar. *Bill Rose*

span of 21.1ft (6.43m). The height of the aircraft was 19.5ft (5.9m). Maximum speed would exceed Mach 3, although the usefulness of this performance is hard to determine. Propulsion would be provided by a single Wright SE-105 turbojet producing 23,000lb (102kN) thrust at sea level. It has not been possible to find any information on this engine, which appears to have been little more than a proposal or experimental design. No details exist of the aircraft's range or weapons carried, which would be located in an internal bay. In this respect, it is likely that the aircraft would have had the same capability as Ryan's Model 115C. Take-off would involve the use of a reusable Flying Carpet launcher and the aircraft would return to the submarine after its mission, using the cable and hook system to land on the submarine.

Many details of this study are unclear due to lack of documentation, but it is known that other aircraft were considered and it has been suggested to the author by a source within the US Navy that these may have included an adapted Vought Crusader and a version of the Ryan VTOL supersonic fighter developed for use by the USAF. Boeing at Wichita, Kansas, continued to work on this project, developing plans for an advanced nuclear-powered submarine-carrier with the company reference AN-1, which would carry eight vertically launched Mach 3 fighters. This would have been a vessel of substantial size, with a projected surface displacement of 9,260 tons (8,400 metric tonnes) and 14,700 tons (13,335 metric tonnes) submerged, and a length of almost 500ft (152m). Original Boeing documentation for AN-1 shows a design with two large integral pressurised hangars located in the forward section of the hull. Each of these would accommodate four Mach 3 fighters, each fitted with a Flying Carpet. A second submarine-carrier design with the reference AN-2 would carry the aircraft in a row of forward-positioned vertical storage tubes. In this case the pilot would enter the aircraft before it was raised to a position above the deck for vertical launch. After completing a mission and recovery, the aircraft would be lowered back into the storage tube before the pilot left the aircraft.

There may have been several options considered for these two submarine carriers and it is possible that adapted F11F Tigers would initially be carried until the advanced Mach 3 fighter became available. It has also been suggested by several sources that disposable solid-fuel boosters might have been used to launch the aircraft. With a significantly higher price tag than a Polaris submarine and some major technical challenges, the US Navy soon dropped the idea of a submersible aircraft carrier. This was an intriguing concept, but it remains hard to see any real advantages to the idea. Even before the era of submerged missile launching, the ability to carry fighter aircraft on a submarine had limited value. The Flying Carpet may have had some

TOP The USS *Grayback* (SSG-574) at sea, showing storage facilities considered suitable for a supersonic VTOL strike fighter. *US Navy*

BOTTOM A Regulus I missile is launched from the USS *Halibut* (SSG-587) submarine during trials. *US Navy*

For this reason, I suggest a maximum speed in clean condition that was closer to Mach 2 and a ceiling of at least 60,000ft (18,288m). Weapons for an intercept mission would be Sidewinder AAMs and there would be provision for an underwing tactical nuclear weapon or possibly anti-shipping rockets or additional fuel tanks. There may also have been the option of a daylight photo-reconnaissance pack that could fit into a section of the fuselage. All this amounts to a completely new combat aircraft! It is said that modifying USS *Grayback* to accept the Grumman F11F aircraft and Flying Carpet unit would take six to eight months. This may be so, but the development of a suitable strike fighter would have undoubtedly taken several years.

Having conceived this submarine aircraft system, Boeing then moved on to a next-generation combat aircraft that seemed to bear some similarities to the North American SM-64 Navaho ramjet-powered cruise missile and perhaps the Boeing Bomarc surface-to-air missile. It remains a little unclear if there was a proposal to use this aircraft on converted Regulus submarines or more advanced vessels. The two hangars of a Regulus submarine such as the USS *Grayback* were about 80ft (24.38m) long and able to contain four Regulus 1 missiles or two Regulus II missiles, so it would have been possible to house one of the more advanced aircraft and several specifically configured Flying Carpets.

Boeing's dart-shaped, one-man, canard fighter was 70ft (21.3m) in length, with highly swept wings that had a useful applications, but why make life difficult when you can use throwaway rocket boosters for launching the aircraft? Recovery in wartime conditions would add to the time a submarine remained a vulnerable surface target. In the case of the Regulus missiles, these used solid-fuel boosters and the impressive Vought Regulus II was a long-range, supersonic, fire-and-forget weapon with a high-yield thermonuclear warhead that allowed the submarine to dive soon after launch. Then there is the issue of the cable landing system, undertaken without the benefit of present-day computer technology. In poor weather and a choppy sea, this sounds like a nightmare scenario for the pilot. Finally, the proposal to develop a Mach 3 fighter also appears pointless and may have been put forward simply to impress officials.

For anyone interested in reading detailed information on the topic of submarine aircraft carriers, I would recommend Scott Lowther's excellent Aerospace Projects Review, Volume 1, number 6. Contact details can easily be located on the Internet.

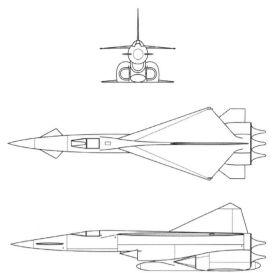

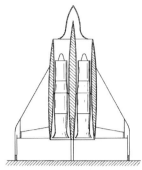

ABOVE General appearance of Boeing's Mach 3 VTOL strike fighter designed for use with submersible aircraft carriers. *Bill Rose*

ABOVE This is the VTOL lift vehicle designed by SNECMA engineers during the 1950s. It is almost certain that Boeing took this invention and developed it for use with its submarine-launched fighter project. The lift vehicle was given the name Flying Carpet by Boeing. *SNECMA*

Zborowski's Flying Beetle

Many of France's most important postwar military aviation programmes were based on captured German research material or developed with the assistance of German scientists and engineers. One particularly notable group of German scientists was the *Bureau Technique Zborowski* (BTZ), headed by the former Austrian SS Lieutenant Dr Helmut von Zborowski. He was a leading expert in jet and rocket propulsion, a personal friend of the rocket pioneer Wernher von Braun and a recipient of the Knight's Cross, presented by Hitler for services to the Reich. Zborowski joined BMW in Munich during 1934 and rapidly ascended through the company ranks. By the outbreak of war, he was the director of BMW Bramo's advanced ramjet and rocket development section at Berlin-Spandau, where he participated in development of various advanced systems. These included the Walter rocket engine for Messerschmitt's Me163B interceptor, a simplified replacement for the V-2 missile, possibly the development of an advanced radial-flow gas turbine (RFGT), and research into ramjets.

In 1944 the BMW Bramo section was moved from Berlin to Bruckmühl near Rosenheim and, after Germany's defeat, Zborowski was detained by US Intelligence and interned at Prisoner of War Camp 317 near Göttingen. Soon after this he was released into French custody and taken to a château near Paris with many of his colleagues including Eugen and Irene Sänger, who developed the first designs for a workable spaceplane. Zborowski then struck some kind of deal with the French and in 1947 he travelled to Bonn and

recruited a number of Germany's top aviation experts. His group now included Professor Heinrich Hertel (1902-1982), who headed development at Junkers, and the highly respected aerodynamicist Dr Wilhelm Seibold. Drawing on the expertise of his colleagues and research material that remained hidden from the Allies, Zborowski produced a series of designs for annular (or ring) winged VTOL aircraft. There are one or two early examples of experimental annular-winged designs but this concept seems to have originated in 1942 and can be credited to Werner Herrmann, who worked on missile development at Peenemünde (and later found employment with Lockheed's Skunk Works). His aim was to increase the range of glide bombs with a small annular wing. The new designs produced by Zborowski were very sophisticated and perhaps a generation ahead of wartime proposals for VTOL interceptors such as the Heinkel Lerche. Zborowski now met with senior officials from the nationally owned French engine manufacturer SNECMA and sold them the rights to these designs in exchange for an undisclosed sum and retention of his team as technical specialists.

During 1950, Zborowski opened an office at Brunoy near Paris and moved his family into the former home of artist André Dunoyer de Segonzac at nearby Boussy St Antoine. The BTZ consultancy was now ready for business and the full transfer of the designs would be completed by the following year. SNECMA had been the Gnome et Rhône engine manufacturer originally founded in 1915. The company continued to operate

BELOW One of Zborowski's early proposals for a VTOL fighter, known as the Bruche (Beetle). His team assigned the name of a beetle to each VTOL concept it produced, usually reflecting the aircraft's overall shape. The Bruche is a clear ancestor of later SNECMA designs. *SNECMA*

ABOVE Zborowski completed this design in 1955, which was used to outline his ideas for a rocket-boosted escape capsule, primarily intended for use with VTOL strike fighters and ground-attack aircraft using an annular wing. *US Patent Office*

LEFT Test pilot Auguste Morel prepares to board the second Atar Volant (Flying Atar) experimental VTOL vehicle. *SNECMA*

CENTRE SNECMA's CP.400-P.2 experimental VTOL vehicle in free flight with the company's test pilot Auguste Morel at the controls. It was similar to the first prototype, but fitted with an ejector seat, flight controls and instruments. *SNECMA*

RIGHT The Atar Volant (Flying Atar) experimental VTOL vehicles. In this posed photograph test pilot Auguste Morel is seated in the CP.400-P.2, nearest to the camera. The unmanned CP.400-P.1 is directly behind. *SNECMA*

under this name until 1945, although it effectively became a subsidiary of BMW during World War 2. Having become SNECMA in May 1945, the company remained heavily reliant on German expertise for its new turbojet programme and had started to develop the *Atelier Technique Aéronautique Rickenbach* (Atar) jet engines, which were a continuation of BMW's wartime designs. In 1945, BMW's chief designer (for the turbojet division) Dr Hermann Östrich was detained by US military officials at Stassfurt and sent to England. Soon after this Östrich and a number of his colleagues were approached by members of the French Secret Service with an offer that was too good to refuse. As a consequence, the Atar Company was set up at Rickenbach and Atar turbojets produced by SNECMA became vital to the postwar French aviation industry. This situation obviously suited Zborowski well, as there were large numbers of German engineers and technicians employed by SNECMA in all departments.

The aircraft designs that Zborowski sold to SNECMA were significantly more advanced than any German wartime concepts and SNECMA immediately recognised their potential for military and perhaps civil use. Although Professor Heinrich Hertel decided to return to Germany, BTZ continued to develop advanced and innovative designs for annular-winged VTOL combat aircraft. SNECMA now arranged for models of the BTZ aircraft to be tested in the wind tunnel at Cannes and the results were sufficiently encouraging to green light the project in late 1952.

As each new BTZ concept appeared, Zborowski assigned the name of a beetle to it, reflecting the aircraft's overall shape. This included the Bruche (Beetle), which was a compact supersonic VTOL ground-attack aircraft, the Hannerton (Cockchafer

beetle), which was a single-seat VTOL utility plane driven by two enclosed contra-rotating propellers and the Lucane (Stag beetle) VTOL light transport aircraft which used swivelling ducted fan propulsion. SNECMA was committed to proceeding with development of the VTOL proposal and tests started in 1952 using a modified de Havilland Vampire to validate the idea of controlling flight direction with high-velocity jets of compressor-bleed air, directed into the aircraft engine's exhaust. A substantial number of German engineers and scientists occupied management positions within SNECMA and former Junkers development engineer Gerhard Eggers (1912–1998) headed the VTOL project. He was unquestionably the most capable person for this task and was also responsible for designing the Flying Carpet VTOL launch system adopted by Boeing. Under his direction, a vertical test rig was constructed, which supported a small Ecrevisse pulsejet producing 99lb (044kN) thrust. This was remotely controlled with a joystick, and an electrically powered gyroscope was fitted to simulate the presence of a turbojet engine.

The first successful test was completed on 31 March 1954 and the results convinced SNECMA's board to proceed with construction of a proof-of-concept prototype test vehicle called the CP.400-P.1 Atar Volant (Flying Atar). This vehicle was little more than a slightly modified Atar D jet engine providing 6,400lb (28.4kN) thrust, which was contained in an upright cylindrical housing supported by four legs extending from the base, each fitted with a castor wheel. Remotely controlled, the CP.400-P.1 was suspended beneath a substantial steel support structure with a height of 115ft (35m). Remote controlled testing began on 22 September 1956 and approximately 250 very brief tethered flights followed.

By this time, the *Bundesministerium der Verteidigung* (BMVg: West Germany's Ministry of Defence) was taking a keen interest in the SNECMA VTOL project and it began to provide additional funding

for research and development. A decision had been taken to re-equip the Luftwaffe with the Lockheed F-104 Starfighter, but there was a desire to eventually replace this with a V/STOL interceptor and strike aircraft that could operate from improvised sites. The requirement for this combat aircraft was known as VJ (Vertikal Jäger – VTOL Fighter) 101 and the Luftwaffe expected a maximum speed of Mach 2.5, a ceiling of 72,000ft (22,000m) and an operational range of at least 310 miles (500km). Nevertheless, West Germany's aviation industry was still recovering from World War 2. Its best scientists and engineers were working for foreign contractors and many of the companies had been forced to diversify into less demanding fields and were manufacturing goods for domestic consumption. However, the government encouraged the four major West German aviation companies to begin studies of future V/STOL fighters, with incentives to collaborate with SNECMA and draw on the expertise of BTZ. This led to a number of unusual designs that would steadily evolve into flat risers during the coming decade and help to revive Germany's aviation industry. With substantial financial support from the West German government, SNECMA wasted no time in pushing forward with the VTOL project and a new test platform was built, called the CP.400-P.2. The most obvious difference was the attachment of a fairly basic set of controls at the top of the vehicle and an ejector seat for a pilot, allowing manned untethered flights. A cockpit might be stretching the description a little too far! The Atar DV engine also differed slightly, with a number of small modifications and slightly more thrust. Fuel capacity of 158 gallons (600 litres) allowed a few minutes of flight, the exhaust vectoring system controlled pitch and yaw, a reaction control handled roll, while an automatic stabilisation system kept the CP.400-P.2 upright.

The first tethered flight was made on 30 March 1957 and SNECMA's test pilot Auguste Morel undertook the first free flight on 14 May 1957. Few problems arose and as a result of this it was decided to publicly demonstrate the CP.400-P.2 in free vertical flight at the Paris (Le Bourget) Air Show on 1 and 2 June 1957. By the following year a further version called the CP.400-P.3 was completed. This was fitted with a swivelling ejector seat and inlets for the turbojet on either side of the cockpit area. But there were concerns that this arrangement might hamper the engine's ability to provide adequate thrust in certain descent conditions, so a decision was taken to test the new vehicle in a horizontal position, mounted on a carriage towed by a diesel-electric locomotive. While these rather unorthodox trials took place, models of several advanced ring-wing designs were being wind tunnel tested. This was followed by the construction of a full-sized mock-up of a VTOL prototype, which in turn led to Nord Aviation at

Châtillon-sous-Bagneux being contracted to build a flying aircraft in mid-1958.

The new aircraft received the SNECMA designation C.450-01 and Zborowski chose the name Coléoptère (Flying Beetle) for this prototype. To transport the aircraft in a horizontal position, a special cradle was fitted to a flatbed trailer and there was an erecting mechanism to raise the aircraft into a vertical lift-off position. The Coléoptère was completed by the following year and delivered to SNECMA at Melun-Villaroche. It bore little resemblance to the previous test vehicles and much of the exterior was taken up by the annular wing surrounding much of the fuselage. The undercarriage comprised four, equally dispersed shock-absorbing legs, each fitted with a small castoring wheel to aid ground handling. Most of the aircraft was built from aluminium alloy, with steel in some areas where extra strength was required. The fully enclosed cockpit was fitted with an ejector seat capable of swivelling through 55° in about four seconds and there were transparent panels to improve the pilot's view when the aircraft was vertical. Some external details varied after delivery, with the aircraft sometimes being equipped with a nose probe and carrying the letter Y on the forward fuselage. (X and Y letters have often been used as a prefix for aircraft designations to show their experimental nature and the Coléoptère may have received this marking before inspection by dignitaries or for a photo-shoot.)

The Coléoptère had a length of 26.3ft (8.03m), an overall width of 14.8ft (4.50m) and a total wing area of 304.6ft^2 (28.3m^2). Zborowski theorised that without engine power, the aircraft should be able to glide for some distance, although a horizontal hard landing was not possible and in an emergency the only option for the pilot was ejection. The aircraft's gross weight was 6,613lb (3,000kg), of which 1,545lb (700kg) was taken up by fuel. This would allow a 25-minute endurance, with a theoretical maximum speed of 500mph (804km/h). Power was provided by an Atar 101 E-5V gas turbine delivering a maximum of 7,700lb (34.2kN) static thrust. As with the previous test vehicles, this engine was modified in several ways for sustained vertical use. The alterations included a vertical control system and a rearrangement of bearing lubrication requirements. At low speed, exhaust vectoring provided pitch and yaw control, thrust would maintain height and reaction jets

ABOVE The manned SNECMA CP.400-P.2 VTOL test vehicle undertakes an untethered flight. None of these trial flights lasted for more than a few minutes, but they were sufficient to prove the viability of the complex control system. *SNECMA*

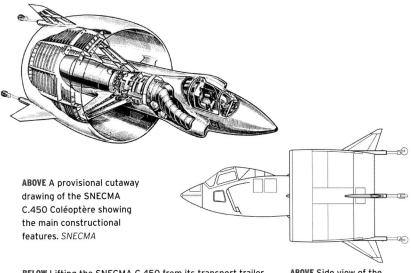

ABOVE A provisional cutaway drawing of the SNECMA C.450 Coléoptère showing the main constructional features. *SNECMA*

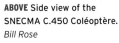

BELOW Lifting the SNECMA C.450 from its transport trailer to an upright position in preparation for a VTOL test flight. *SNECMA*

ABOVE Side view of the SNECMA C.450 Coléoptère. *Bill Rose*

ABOVE This photograph shows the SNECMA Coléoptère being prepared for a test flight at Melun-Villaroche, with the service gantry in place. Note the nose probe and letter Y on the forward fuselage denoting the experimental nature of the aircraft. *SNECMA*

BELOW The SNECMA C.450 fitted with nose probe hovers in the air, with test pilot Auguste Morel at the controls. *SNECMA*

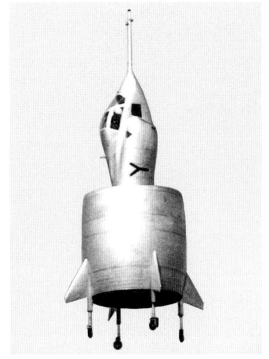

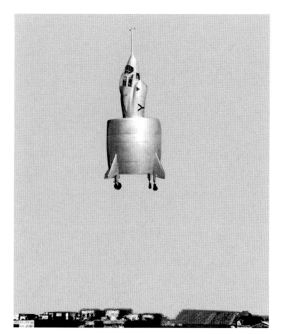

on the outer surface of the ring wing regulated roll. At higher speed in normal flight four fins acted as control surfaces. There were also small fins fitted to the nose of the aircraft to assist with flight transition but these appear to have been a later addition.

Development of more advanced versions of the Coléoptère was already under way and it was hoped to replace the C.450 with a pre-production supersonic VTOL fighter powered by a SNECMA TF104 (modified P&W TF30) supplemented by ramjet propulsion. This Coléoptère was given the code name AP.507 and it was to have an overall length of 36ft (11.0m) and an annular wing with an 8.75ft (2.7m) diameter. Maximum speed was estimated at Mach 3, with a ceiling of 80,000ft (24,384m), and the armament would be two or possibly four air-to-air missiles mounted outside the wing. One major advantage the ring wing possessed was its ability to make very sharp turns, giving it a significant advantage in a close-range engagement. BTZ is thought to have offered a broadly similar version of this design to West Germany's Luftwaffe, but the proposal did not progress very far as West German companies were now deeply involved in alternative BTZ/SNECMA research projects.

Another design directly based on the C.450 Coléoptère was a high-performance subsonic ground-attack aircraft, designated AP.503. Powered by an afterburning Atar 101 G-32 turbojet, it would have a range of up to 434 miles (700km). Stores would be carried on the lower external side of the annular wing, probably comprising free-fall bombs or rocket packs. On 17 April 1959, the C.450 Coléoptère flown by test pilot Auguste Morel undertook its first tethered hover at Melun-Villaroche and soon after this, on 3 May 1959, the first free hover took place, which lasted several minutes. The ninth flight took place on 25 July 1959

and Morel climbed to an altitude of 2,000ft (609m) and made a transition to about 35° before returning to the vertical position. He then began to descend, but the aircraft became unstable and Morel was unable to maintain control. Although he had dropped to 150ft (45m), Morel's only option was to eject. The C.450 continued to pitch and roll for several seconds, before smashing into the ground. Morel was seriously injured when his parachute failed to fully deploy and the aircraft was completely destroyed. The exact cause of the accident remains unclear. SNECMA executives met the following day and it was decided to scrap the project. The technology was considered dangerous, the publicity from the accident was damaging and the military potential of the aircraft was rapidly dwindling. It was a substantial setback for SNECMA and especially BTZ, which lost several important members of staff to West German companies in the following weeks.

Some years earlier Dr Hertel parted company with Zborowski and returned to West Germany, where he accepted an academic post at the Berlin Technical University. At around the time when SNECMA abandoned the Coléoptère project, Hertel joined Focke-Wulf in Bremen. Major changes were taking place within the German aviation industry and Hertel took charge of a design group working on a joint Focke-Wulf SNECMA VTOL fighter project. Several BTZ engineers and designers then joined his team, which appears to have been more than just a coincidence. Focke-Wulf had been working since 1957 on a VTOL tailsitting fighter with a self-erecting undercarriage that would lift it into

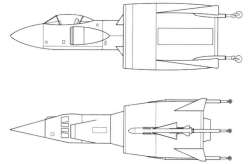

LEFT One of many SNECMA concepts for an alternative VTOL design to the Coléoptère series. The influence of early postwar American research is clearly evident. *SNECMA*

RIGHT An unidentified SNECMA VTOL tailsitter design, possibly developed from research undertaken with a West German aircraft company. The propulsion system is unclear, but there would almost certainly need to be a turbojet in the fuselage capable of exhaust vectoring during VTOL operations. No air inlet for the engine is evident! The wingtip nacelles may contain either turbojets or ramjets. *SNECMA*

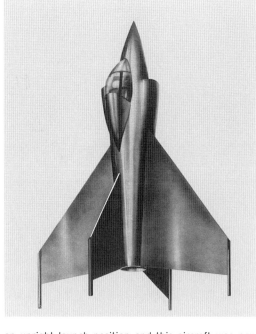

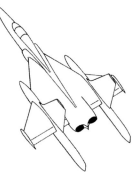

ABOVE The SNECMA AP.519, which might be considered a French version of the proposed Fw 860 VTOL interceptor. *SNECMA*

RIGHT Developed in parallel to SNECMA's AP.519 project, the Focke-Wulf Fw 860 was similar in terms of performance. It used an unusual undercarriage that was designed to allow taxiing in a horizontal position and upright take-off and landing. It is not clear if conventional rolling take-offs were considered as an option. The aircraft's forward fuselage section containing the cockpit remained level with the ground during VTOL operations, which generated increased mechanical complexity but maintained good downward visibility for the pilot. *Bill Rose*

an upright launch position and this aircraft was now designated as the Fw 860. It shared many similarities with a French VTOL fighter and many models of these designs are thought to have been wind tunnel tested at the same time. The Fw 860 would be powered by two Pratt & Whitney JTF10 turbojets providing Mach 2.5 performance and a ceiling of 65,000ft (19,812m). The wingspan was 21.3ft (6.48m), with a length of 35.4ft (10.8m) and a quoted take-off weight of 16,448lb (7,640kg). The initial choice of weapons was either a single cannon or two AAMs and the operational range was expected to be 288 miles (463km). An unusual feature of this design and the similarly specified SNECMA AP.519 was the folding undercarriage. This could be raised to allow vertical take-offs, or used to make conventional rolling take-offs and landings. While the majority of tailsitters used a swivelling ejector seat to improve visibility for the pilot during VTOL operations, Focke-Wulf went one step further, designing the entire forward nose section to drop forward and remain horizontal. It is not clear if the AP.519 would also have utilised this feature.

Messerschmitt was another West German company that drew heavily on the same research, leading to a single-engined supersonic VTOL fighter with the reference Me X1-21. Fitted with a large tail fin, and two small forward canard fins ahead of the substantial air intakes on each side of the tiltable cockpit section, this design appears to have used a similar undercarriage to the Fw 860 and the AP.519. Development of the Fw 860, the Messerschmitt Me X1-21 and the SNECMA AP.519 continued into 1960, but the Luftwaffe showed little enthusiasm for the concepts and the AP.519 was rejected by the *Armée de l'Air* (French Air Force), which had selected the Dassault Mirage 111V for its next

fighter. The AP.519 proved to be the last VTOL fighter project that SNECMA would work on, although the Germans now reviewed their future needs and continued to fund the development of a different type of VTOL aircraft.

One other unusual German VTOL tailsitter fighter that is thought to have involved BTZ was the Heinkel He 231, designed by Dr. Siegfried Günter (1899–1969), who rejoined the company in 1957 after working on the MiG-15 fighter in the Soviet Union. Looking like a small spaceship with an overall length of 33.75ft (10.3m), the He 231 was fitted with four large triangular wings that contained the landing gear. A single afterburning General Electric J85 turbojet provided propulsion, with

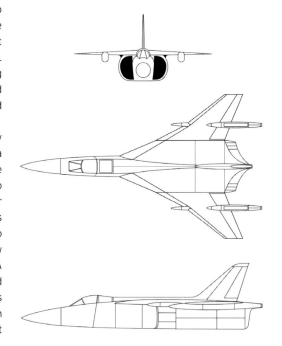

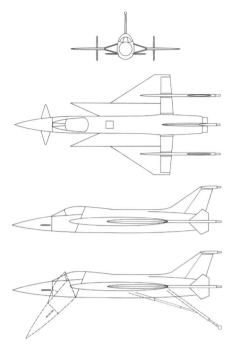

LEFT The Messerschmitt Me X1-21 was a single-engined canard VTOL fighter concept, using similar design features to the Fw 860 that included a forward-tilting cockpit section designed to alleviate visibility problems for the pilot during take-off and landing. *Bill Rose*

RIGHT Looking as if it belonged in a sci-fi comic strip, the VTOL Heinkel He 231 VTOL interceptor was designed for high-performance target defence. The project appears to have been abandoned before it progressed much further than the drawing board, being replaced by a VTOL flat riser with exactly the same designation. *Bill Rose*

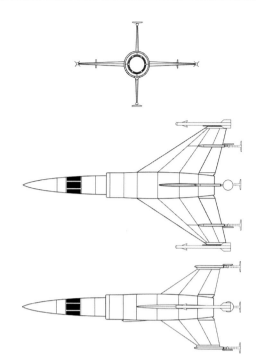

a ramjet option, and the pilot would fly this aircraft in a prone position. Quoted performance suggests a maximum speed of about Mach 2.5, a ceiling of 65,000ft (19,812m) and a combat radius of 310 miles (500km). Armament comprised a single Oerlikon 25mm cannon (under development at that time), and/or air-to-air missiles, using an alternative wing design. Wind tunnel testing of models took place, but the technically complex design was abandoned in favour of an entirely different flat riser, rather confusingly also designated He 231.

Another West German concept based on the unmanned CP.400-P.1 Atar Volant (Flying Atar) and the C.450 Coléoptère was a small, unmanned VTOL fighter developed by Bölkow designated P.110.01. Very compact in size, this ambitious delta-winged aircraft was intended to meet the VJ 101 requirement. The P.110 was powered by a single Bristol Orpheus 12 engine producing a maximum thrust of 6,800lb (30kN). The overall length of the initial version was approximately 13.4ft (4.09m), with a wingspan of about 10.9ft (3.32m) and a quoted weight of 8,650lb (3,923kg). The aircraft was supported on the ground by fully retractable, dampened landing legs and it was armed with two heat-seeking Sidewinder missiles. However, there were serious issues with weight and the control systems. Several different engine configurations were considered but the P.110 was simply much too ambitious and an unmanned VTOL interceptor of this type belonged to the 21st century, not the late 1950s. As a consequence Bölkow abandoned the P.110 and eventually accepted a role in the development of VTOL projects being undertaken by Messerschmitt and Heinkel. SNECMA and BTZ had worked on VTOL tailsitters for almost a decade, producing proposals for combat aircraft,

BELOW The futuristic Heinkel He 231 interceptor depicted in this artwork never progressed beyond the concept stage and was soon replaced by a more conventional proposal. *Bill Rose*

various guided missiles and utility aircraft for the civilian market. It is hard to say if it was just the C.450 Coléoptère accident that brought this programme to a halt, or the fact that there was a growing realisation that the VTOL tailsitter had too many drawbacks for manned use.

In 1960, Convair studied designs for a new Close Air Support (CAS) aircraft, producing the Model 49, which resembled the Coléoptère. It flew a small proof-of-concept demonstrator, but the Model 49 was abandoned in favour of advanced attack helicopters. The company also developed several annular-winged drones, intended mainly for surveillance operations. This project was also cancelled, although the annular wing has reappeared in more recent Unmanned Aerial Vehicles (UAVs). BTZ continued to work for French and West German aviation companies such as Heinkel, which was developing VTOL fighter proposals such as the revised He 231 for West Germany's Luftwaffe. The consultancy finally closed when Zborowski died on 16 November 1969 at Brunoy and the C.400-P.2 ended up on display at the Le Bourget Air Museum.

RIGHT The Bölkow P.110.01 was a very compact, unmanned VTOL interceptor based on work undertaken by BTZ and SNECMA. Armed with two Sidewinder missiles, this remote-controlled fighter was technically too ambitious for the time and met with swift cancellation. *Bölkow*

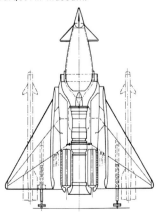

Payen Pa-59 Aldebaran VTOL Tailsitter

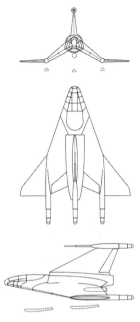

ABOVE Payen produced many unusual designs and this VTOL interceptor was no exception. It does not appear to have progressed much further than an early concept. *Bill Rose*

Nicolas Roland Payen (1914-2004) was a French engineer, now remembered in aviation circles for creating unusual, often rather quirky aircraft, typically with a rear-mounted delta wing and forward canard fins. From about 1930 onwards he designed hundreds of different aircraft, which were often regarded as rather futuristic, although few progressed beyond the drawing board. In May 1954, Payen began to take an interest in VTOL and started work on a small lightweight turbojet-powered tailsitter. This would draw on his company's experience with the diminutive experimental Pa.49A jet aircraft, which was completed in 1953. Some official government funding had been forthcoming and test flights of the modified aircraft (now called Pa.49B 'Katy') were continuing, with Payen hoping this project might lead to the development of a larger jet fighter for the *Armée de l'Air*. The new tailsitter was designated Pa.59 and given the name Aldebaran, probably chosen to associate its spaceship appearance with a celestial object. The P.59 would be another compact aircraft, with a length of 20.3ft (6.2m) and a 17ft (5.2m) wingspan. The aircraft stood upright for launch, supported by three dampened struts, each fitted with a castor wheel to facilitate easy ground handling. The pilot would be contained within a forward pressurised cockpit with a fully glazed nose. A prone position would be necessary (in line with the fuselage), permitting good visibility during take-off and allowing improved streamlining. However, there are no indications of any ejector system or an easy way to leave the aircraft in an emergency. Entry to the cockpit would be from an upper fuselage hatch and directly behind this was the dorsal engine inlet.

Formed from a double delta, the primary wing had a 70° leading edge sweep, with the secondary outer section reducing to 50°. The main section of wing also had a considerable anhedral angle, which seems to have been used for purposes concerning the upright undercarriage positioning. In addition to this support system, the Pa.59 would have been equipped with three deployable landing skids to allow the aircraft to put down on suitable surfaces, such as grass. Take-offs using the skids (possibly with detachable wheels) may also have been considered. The PA.59 would be powered by a compact Turboméca Gabizo turbojet, which was chosen by Payen before it had undergone any initial testing. Details of the installation are sketchy, but the use of an afterburner would have been essential and this provided a maximum thrust of about 3,350lb (14.9kN). In addition, there are references to the use of at least one strap-on solid-fuel booster to assist launch. Payen visualised this aircraft as an interceptor with Mach 1 performance and equipped with two 30mm DEFA cannons or unguided air-to-air rockets. Although the design is visually pleasing, there would have been serious problems translating such a concept into hardware that was safe to fly and provided the kind of performance that Payen envisaged. The Pa.59 Aldebaran still generates considerable interest with model makers, but never progressed much further than the elementary design stage.

SFECMAS 1500 VTOL Tailsitter

The available documentation for this French tailsitter design often describes it as a VTOL interceptor directly based on the Nord Griffon 1500-01, which was a prototype delta-winged supersonic fighter. The Griffon was conceived in the late 1940s at the *Arsenal de l'Aéronautique* who became the *Société Française d'Etude et de Construction de Matériels Aéronautiques Spéciaux* (SFECMAS) in 1953. The VTOL interceptor came about during this period and was developed by a design team headed by Claude Flamand (1912-1986). I should just add that SFECMAS was absorbed by the *Société Nationale de Constructions Aéronautiques du Nord* (SNCAN) in December 1954 and Nord Aviation in 1958. This can make designations a little confusing at times. While the VTOL design appeared visually similar to the Griffon 1500-01, the two aircraft were significantly different and it was not just a matter of simply upending the Griffon, fitting a new undercarriage and adapting it to the VTOL role. The proposed VTOL interceptor was shorter than the Griffon 1500-01, with an overall length

of 36ft (11m) as opposed to 47.73ft (14.54m) and it would have been somewhat lighter than the conventional prototype, with an anticipated take-off weight of 11,023lb (5,000kg), compared to 14,872lb (6,745kg). The wing profile also differed considerably, with the canard fins positioned further forward.

During VTOL operations, deflector plates in the engine's exhaust stream would control the aircraft.

BELOW The Nord Griffon 1500-01 supersonic fighter. Although the SFECMAS VTOL fighter proposal shows family similarities to this aircraft, the design was significantly different. *Nord Aviation*

There would also be an air-bleed reaction control system, with nozzles at the wingtips and near the nose. In normal flight a system of conventional control surfaces would be used. If this aircraft had progressed to the construction stage it would have required a powerful afterburning turbojet in the class of a General Electric J79 to provide an adequate thrust-to-weight ratio and perhaps solid-fuel boosters to assist take-off. A ventral air inlet was located below the cockpit in a similar position to the conventional Griffon. Various performance estimates have been suggested from Mach 1+ to Mach 2 in clean condition. However, it was recognised that finding a suitable engine was a real problem, which proved to be a major stumbling block for progress with the design.

On the ground the VTOL fighter would be supported by three dampened struts contained in nacelles at the wingtips and the dorsal fin. The wings may have been given an anhedral angle simply to increase the undercarriage span and improve stability in an upright position. The cockpit appears superior to the Griffon 1500-01 and 02 prototypes, with better horizontal visibility, although the position of the canard fins may have caused some problems and it should be noted that these were located just behind the cockpit on the Griffon 1500-01/02. The VTOL would have been equipped with an ejector seat and it seems highly probable that it would swivel to improve the pilot's visibility during vertical take-off and landing. Unlike many other tailsitters, it may have been possible to make an emergency hard landing on an appropriate surface, although such an undertaking would have still been very risky. Constructionally, the aircraft would be fabricated from aluminium alloy, with stronger (or heat resistant) materials where necessary.

The aircraft was only intended to operate as an interceptor based at improvised sites and armament would comprise of two air-to-air missiles. Nothing is known about proposed ground-handling equipment, but presumably the aircraft would be transportable in a horizontal position using some kind of specially designed trailer. With problems finding the right kind of engine, an apparent lack of official interest, numerous unanswered technical problems and the probability of high development costs, the project seems to have been completely abandoned in 1955 or 1956.

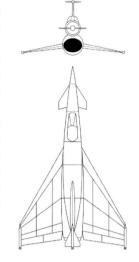

RIGHT Sharing some general similarities with the prototype Nord 1500 Griffon supersonic fighter, the SFECMAS VTOL project was abandoned, primarily due to the lack of a suitable engine and anticipated high development costs. *Bill Rose*

Avro VTOL Tailsitters

The VTOL tailsitter seems to have generated relatively little interest in postwar Britain, although Avro UK undertook several studies in the early 1950s, probably as an alternative to work being undertaken by its Canadian subsidiary on a disc-shaped VTOL fighter. (See the author's previous book, *Flying Saucer Technology*, published by Midland in 2011.)

The UK project was assigned the reference P.724 and it led to two (known) designs powered by advanced afterburning turbojets that were still in the development stage. Work on the rather unattractive-looking P.724 began in early 1953. Flown from a prone position within the lower forward fuselage section, the P.724 looks as if it had been accidentally turned upside down. It is hard to visualise how the pilot might easily escape from the aircraft in an emergency, unless there was a plan to make the cockpit section detachable. On the ground, the P.724 would have been supported in a vertical position by a shock-absorbing leg carried in the single tail fin and two legs, which retracted into fairings along the wing roots. This was a daylight interceptor guided to its target by ground control and there was no provision for an onboard radar system. Armament is not specified, but it seems likely that two missiles would have been carried, probably on wingtip launch rails. Power was to be provided by a single Rolls-Royce axial-flow turbojet engine, fed from a nose intake. The RB.106 was still in early development, but appeared to be a very promising engine, with an anticipated static thrust of 15,000lb (66kN), rising to 21,800lb (97kN) with afterburner.

Technically, this was a sophisticated engine, with the afterburner forming an integral feature of the design. However, as a consequence of the UK's stance on future fighter development, the RB.106 was cancelled in 1957, although it appears that much of the technology found its way into the Orenda Iroquois engine developed for the Avro-Canada CF-105 Arrow. The P.724 would have been controlled at low speed using a system similar to several other VTOL tailsitters that employed vanes in the exhaust stream and compressor-bleed air channelled to the wingtips. In normal flight, elevons and a rudder would be used. The Avro P.724 had an overall length of 32.5ft (9.9m) and its wingspan was 16ft (4.87m). The exact take-off weight is unclear, but it is believed to have been in the region of 18,000-20,000lb (8,164-9,071kg). Mach 2 performance at altitude was anticipated, with a ceiling of about 60,000ft (18,288m).

Nevertheless, the thrust-to-weight ratio was a matter of considerable concern and this design would have required rocket boosters to assist launches.

BELOW Version one of the rather unattractive Avro P.724 VTOL interceptor shown in this drawing was abandoned when it was realised that a single engine provided insufficient power for reliable VTOL operations. *Avro*

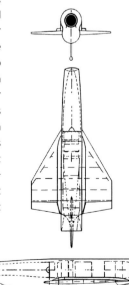

This led to a swift rethink and a decision was taken to scrap the design and start again with a twin-engined configuration, although the same project reference was retained. The new design was totally different, using two side-by-side afterburning RB.106 engines, a delta wing with a 60° leading edge and a single tail fin with a nacelle to accommodate a dampened undercarriage strut. The overall length of the second P.724 was 37ft (11.2m), with a wingspan of 24ft (7.3m). Air intakes for the engines were positioned alongside the pressurised cockpit section, which accommodated the pilot in a prone position. As with the previous design, there appears to be no obvious provision for ejection or easy escape in the event of an emergency. The undercarriage arrangement was essentially the same as that found on the earlier single-engine design, comprising the tail fin strut and two fully retractable shock-absorbing legs carried in nacelles below the wing roots. Take-off weight was estimated at about 24,500lb (11,113kg), which included 8,000lb (3,628kg) of fuel carried in the wings and central tanks. With two high-performance engines, any initial concerns about VTOL performance were overcome.

Calculations indicated that the twin-engined P.724 would be capable of Mach 2.5, with a service ceiling of 60,000ft+ (18,288m+). It was planned to install airborne radar, or make provision for this in the future, and the aircraft was to be armed with two Blue Jay (later called Firestreak) heat-seeking air-to-air missiles mounted on wingtip launch rails. By June 1953, several P.724 models had been tested in Avro UK's wind tunnel, although this project seems to have been little more than a design study undertaken to compete with the exotic Project Y interceptor under development at Avro-Canada. As such, the P.724 was regarded as a less complex alternative, with some potential if VTOL tailsitters created an unexpected surge of official UK interest. This never came about and the Avro P.724 was moved to the back burner and eventually forgotten about.

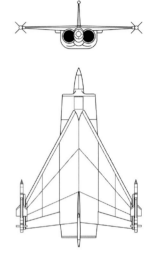

RIGHT Avro's twin-engined version of the P.724 VTOL interceptor, possibly developed to the stage of models being wind tunnel tested. It was regarded as an alternative to the Project Y fighter project being undertaken by the company's Canadian subsidiary. *Bill Rose*

Sukhoi Shkval (Squall) 1A

In early 1963, a team of 10 graduate engineers from the Moscow Aviation Institute (MAI) were given the opportunity to develop a series of proposals for military aircraft at the Sukhoi OKB. Heading this team as the main designer and group organiser was Rollan Martirosov, and the principal objective was to develop proposals for a supersonic VTOL fighter. Other members of the group who would go on to secure important positions in Russian aviation were A. I. Blinov and L. I. Andrianov. The design this group settled on was a fuselage that might almost be described as a shortened MiG-25, fitted with cruciform wings at the tail and two forward canard fins just behind the air inlets. This tailsitter was given the name Shkval (Squall) 1A and a number of models were built and wind tunnel tested at TsAGI (Central Aerohydrodynamic Institute – Russia's equivalent to NACA/NASA). This resulted in two very similar configurations that differed in the position of the forward fins. The full-sized aircraft would be supported on dampened struts housed in nacelles at the tip of each wing and it is unclear if castors would be fitted to facilitate easy ground handling.

The overall length of the Shkval 1A was to be approximately 49ft (15m), with an estimated wingspan of 19ft (5.8m). Two unspecified afterburning Tumansky turbojet engines provided propulsion and, at a guess, the Tumansky R-13 engine may have been the design group's starting point. It appears that it was intended to

LEFT This original Soviet drawing shows the VTOL Squall interceptor in flight. *Unknown*

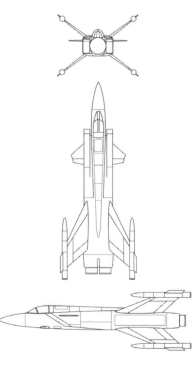

RIGHT Developed by a team of 10 engineering graduates working at the Sukhoi OKB in the early 1960s, this VTOL interceptor called the Squall progressed to wind tunnel testing and the construction of a cockpit section for demonstration purposes. Although the project was well received, it failed to attract official funding for further development. *Bill Rose*

use air directed into the exhaust stream of each engine outlet and air bleed from the compressors to provide low-speed flight control during VTOL operations. Available Russian documentation seems to suggest that the development of a fully automated low-speed control system was anticipated. Armament for this aircraft would be a single cannon carried in the fuselage and there is no mention of missiles. To improve the pilot's visibility during take-offs and landings, the pilot's ejector seat would swivel forward. This led to further official funding which allowed the construction of a full-sized mock-up of the Shkval's cockpit and forward fuselage section. The role envisaged for this aircraft is far from clear. The Soviets had proven their ability to

shoot down high-altitude American spy planes using surface-to-air missiles and a complicated supersonic VTOL fighter with limited range would seem to have limited use.

The six-month project concluded in August 1963 and Pavel Sukhoi undertook an initial assessment. Subsequently, there was a formal visit from the First Secretary of the Central Committee Sergey Pavlov, accompanied by his technical advisor Henry Vasilivich Novozhilov from the Ilyushin OKB. Martirosov was then requested to submit plans for official evaluation, but it was decided that the Shkval 1A would be impractical to build and fulfilled no immediate air defence requirement.

Zero-Length Launch (ZEL) Fighters

I was undecided about including this section on zero-length launch (ZEL or sometimes ZELL) fighters developed during the 1950s, as they were not VTO aircraft. In fact, all the aircraft discussed in this final section were modified versions of conventional jet fighters. However, they performed almost the same function as VTO fighters and ZEL was repeatedly proven viable in trials and could have been used operationally. From the NATO viewpoint, all military airfields in Europe were first-strike targets that would have been wiped off the map in a major war, so there was much to be gained from the dispersal of adapted combat aircraft to improvised sites.

A ZEL fighter cost a good deal less to produce than a complex VTOL strike fighter and it could be delivered on a trailer to any suitable site, for air defence or to undertake a nuclear strike. The only real issue with this

plan was finding a return location for the fighter, as the pilot would need to make a conventional horizontal landing. In a major European conflict, the Luftwaffe already intended to use various stretches of autobahns as emergency runways and the Nazis had undertaken this during World War 2. In more recent years, NATO C-130 transports, German F-104A Starfighters, RAF and USAF combat aircraft have all landed and been refuelled on sections of these roads. So it seems probable that any Luftwaffe ZEL strike fighters would return to an emergency landing stretch on an autobahn as the first option, perhaps with carefully selected civil airfields as secondary choices.

Although some heavily laden bombers had been assisted during take-off with solid-fuel booster rockets during World War 2, the zero-length launch & mat landing (ZELMAL) concept surfaced in the early 1950s as a USAF

LEFT A modified F-84G touches down on the specially fabricated landing mat. *USAF*

TOP The first F-100D (56-2904) modified for ZEL trials is mounted on its trailer, awaiting launch at Edwards AFB. After several successful tests, this aircraft was written off when the booster failed to separate. *USAF*

BOTTOM F-100D Super Sabre (56-2904) makes a rocket-assisted launch with Major Robert F. Titus at the controls. The port wing was retouched to remove the dummy nuclear bomb carried, making this image suitable for public release in the 1950s. *National Museum of the US Air Force*

project designed to facilitate fighter operations from improvised sites, primarily in Europe. The Glenn L. Martin Company was chosen to develop the ZELMAL system at Edwards AFB, because of its experience with the Matador missile, which was ramp launched with the assistance of a solid-fuel booster rocket.

The ZELMAL system would allow a conventional fighter to be launched from a Matador ramp with a rocket booster and it would return to the same site and land on a special inflatable mat. This mat was custom manufactured by Goodyear and it measured 800ft x 80ft x 3ft (244m x 24.5m x 0.91m). It was transported to the landing site by two trucks and an arrestor cable was positioned at one end of the mat and caught by a tailhook on the aircraft, causing the fighter to put down on the air-filled mat without the use of an undercarriage. This system appears to have been inspired by Herbert Chaplin's design for a landing net proposed in 1952 as a means of capturing returning VTO fighters on the rear of a ship. The fighter chosen for the ZELMAT experiments was a straight-winged Republic F-84G Thunderjet, which required various modest modifications. Work on the project proceeded fairly quickly and the first unmanned aircraft to be launched from the northeast shoreline of Rogers Dry Lake was a salvaged F-84G. This took place on 15 December 1953 and it seems probable that the F-84G was simply allowed to crash in the desert.

The first manned launch of a modified F-84G was made on 5 January 1954 and Martin's test pilot Robert Turner was at the controls. The take-off was apparently no worse than a catapult launch from the deck of an aircraft carrier and Turner made a conventional runway landing. After some problems with the inflatable mat it was returned to Goodyear for repairs and modifications, which delayed the first mat landing trial until the summer. On 2 June 1954, Robert Turner made the first touchdown and things went disastrously wrong. The aircraft's arrestor gear ripped a huge hole in the mat and the Thunderjet was badly damaged and had to be scrapped. As another consequence of this controlled crash landing, Turner was injured and was unable to fly for many months.

Two more landings on the mat were made by test pilot George Rodney, who suffered a lasting neck injury. While it had been possible to make some improvements and not rupture the mat, it was clear that this part of the concept was seriously flawed and it was abandoned. However, the USAF remained interested in the idea of rocket-launched fighters and trials continued, with the second F-84G making conventional runway landings. The USAF put ZEL on the back burner for a while and then took another look at the idea, deciding that a more capable aircraft could use the same system to deliver a nuclear strike from a dispersed hardened shelter away from any airfield.

In 1956, the USAF decided that a ZEL-adapted North American F-100D Super Sabre was the ideal combat aircraft to deliver a nuclear weapon from a dispersed hardened shelter away from any first- strike target. Subsequently, a contract revision was undertaken, with North American Aviation, on 12 October 1956, to modify the last batch of F-100D aircraft on order to undertake ZEL launches.

Furthermore, it was agreed that two company-owned F-100Ds (56-2904 and 56-2947) would be loaned to the USAF for ZEL tests before this work commenced. The only immediate problem was weight as the F-100D was almost twice as heavy as the F-84G and increased booster performance was required. To meet this need, North American's Rocketdyne Division developed and manufactured a solid-fuel rocket booster that would generate a massive thrust of 130,000lb (578kN), lasting for four seconds, and this unit would be attached to the lower rear of the fuselage. When the booster detached, the F-100D would have attained a speed of about 300mph (482km/h) and an altitude of 400ft (121m). The first launch test took place on 12 December 1957 and a simulated aircraft was used with the same mass as an F-100D.

Four similar launches followed and then a manned flight was undertaken on 26 March 1958, using aircraft No 56-2904, with test pilot Al Blackburn at the controls. Blackburn started the engine, went to full afterburner

and ignited the booster. He lifted off in a cloud of smoke, the aircraft climbed away and minutes later, Blackburn returned to make a routine landing. Unfortunately, the second test flight was not so successful. The booster failed to separate, Blackburn was unable to control the aircraft and had to eject. The aircraft came down in the desert and was destroyed. It was immediately obvious that the explosive bolts had failed to shear and as a result the system was extensively modified. F-100D No 56-2947 was now put into service for ZEL tests and a further 14 flights took place, lasting up to October 1958. Several pilots undertook these trials and there were no further incidents, with the system operating well on each occasion. Some of the final launches were made carrying underwing fuel tanks and dummy nuclear weapons. When official photographs of these trials were released to the public, the bombs were carefully airbrushed out.

A handful of further tests were then undertaken at Holloman AFB, New Mexico, from a hardened shelter and the last of these took place on 26 August 1959. Modifications were made to all F-100Ds on order so they could be used for ZEL operations, but a lack of enthusiasm lingered within the USAF and plans for deployment remained on hold. Several other fighters were considered for ZEL modification, including versions of the cancelled Avro-Canada CF-105 Arrow and proposed North American F-108 Rapier. The Luftwaffe also liked the idea of applying ZEL to some of its Lockheed F-104G Starfighters, which would be used to undertake nuclear strike missions from dispersed sites in the event of an all-out war with the Soviet Union.

Lockheed was approached by the West Germans to conduct experiments, launching an F-104G with the same type of Rocketdyne solid-fuel booster tested with the F-100D. It was then agreed in 1963 that Lockheed would modify the third F-104G Starfighter built for German use (DA+102 assigned to JBG 31) and ZEL testing would take place at Edwards AFB. Lockheed's test pilot Ed Brown was assigned to undertake a series of flights and it was essentially a rerun of the F-100D project with a different aircraft. These classified trials proceeded well and without incident. The F-104G was finally returned to the Luftwaffe and two further Starfighters (DB+127 and DB+128) were adapted for ZEL. Test launches took place during 1966 at Lechfeld, Germany (which was the home of JBG 32), but the system was finally abandoned. There were major security concerns about the transportation of nuclear weapons by road through rural locations and the ZEL aircraft concept would soon be replaced by the use of very accurate battlefield missiles fitted with nuclear warheads.

As a footnote to this section, the Luftwaffe also participated with the US Marine Corps in a special development project called Short Airfield for Tactical Support (SATS). This was a series of experiments to establish if an F-104G could be launched in a very short distance from a ground shelter using a catapult system and eventually retrieved at the same location using arrestor gear. Three Luftwaffe F-104Gs (Werk-Nr. 8007, 2080 and 9005) were modified for these trials and several hundred take-offs and landings were made at the Naval Air Test Facility at Lakehurst, New Jersey, between 1964 and 1965. The project was not a resounding success and SATS was abandoned soon after the trials ended.

ABOVE An adapted Lockheed F-104G Starfighter (DA+102) belonging to the Luftwaffe is test launched at Edwards AFB, using a Rocketdyne solid-fuel booster. These ZEL trials were undertaken by Lockheed's test pilot Ed Brown and all took place without incident. *Lockheed*

Russian ZEL

The closest the Russians came to producing a fighter capable of operating from an improvised site during the 1950s was a ZEL adaptation of the supersonic MiG-19, a fighter generally regarded as a counterpart to the USAF's F-100. That said, the MiG would be used for forward air defence and not strike missions. The Mikoyan-Gurevich (MiG) Design Bureau began work on this project in April 1955. Designated as the SM-30, this modified version of the aircraft was launched from a ramp on a trailer, set from 15° to 30°. The aircraft was fitted with a PRD-22 solid-fuel booster that provided about 130,000lb (578kN) of thrust for 2.5 seconds and produced massive acceleration, peaking at about 4.5g. For this reason, the main changes to the aircraft were reinforced sections of the airframe and a modified headrest for the pilot to prevent whiplash.

The first test was conducted with an unmanned, remote-controlled SM-30 in autumn 1956. Things went well, although the launcher was damaged and a series of modifications were required. On 13 April 1957, test pilot Georgy Mikhailovich Shiyanov (1910–1995) undertook the first manned launch, having rehearsed the flight on a specially built catapult simulator. The guide rails were raised to an angle of 15° and Shiyanov started both engines, throttling up to full afterburner thrust. Then he ignited the boosters. This was enough to shear the bolts holding

the aircraft in place and the MiG shot into the sky, leaving a huge cloud of dust behind. This first test went without a hitch, but there were problems attempting to land the aircraft in very short distances on rough strips. Like the original American ZELMAT concept, minimum-distance touchdowns near the launch site were a feature of the original proposal. A larger braking parachute was required, plus improved brakes and an arrestor hook to connect with a steel landing cable. The system would theoretically allow the fighter to put down in a distance of about 400ft (122m), but it is known that a number of significant technical difficulties were encountered. The seventh flight was undertaken by Sergei Nikolayevich Anokhin (1910–1986), who was another highly respected test pilot and, this time the aircraft carried full underwing fuel tanks. One more test launch was made by Shiyanov and then the MiG and its support equipment were moved to the Air Force's Scientific Testing Institute (NII VVS).

A further 11 launches were undertaken by several different pilots and at some point the system was demonstrated to Marshal Georgy Zhukov (1896–1974), who reacted favourably to the ZEL MiG. The Soviet Air Force finally abandoned this concept when transportable surface-to-air missiles became available to provide adequate forward defence.

BELOW A modified MiG-19, designated SM-30 is shown on its mobile launch ramp. The first manned take-off was undertaken by Georgy Shiyanov in April 1957 and although these trials proved successful, attempting to land in extremely short distances near the launch site was very difficult. This had been specified in the original terms of reference and the requirement proved unrealistic. The Russians aimed to provide air defence from an improvised forward position, but the concept became redundant when mobile surface-to-air missiles reached operational status. *Bill Rose collection*

Chapter Three: Aircraft Details

Convair VTOL Configuration IVa
Crew: 1
Wingspan: 32.75ft (9.98m)
Sweep (leading edge): 60°
Wing Area: 459ft² (42.6m²)
Length: 45.5ft (13.86m)
Empty Weight: 16,050lb (7,280kg)
Combat Weight: 20,834lb (9,450kg)
Maximum Speed: Mach 1 at sea level; Mach 2 at 35,000ft (10,668m)
Ceiling: 65,500ft (19,964m)
Combat Radius: 287 miles (460km)
Powerplant: 1 x afterburning Allison J71 (B30) with turbofan unit, producing a maximum thrust of 25,568lb (113.7kN)
Armament: 1 x General Electric TE-171-E3 (later M61) Vulcan 20mm six-barrelled Gatling-type cannon, with 800 rounds

Convair Configuration IV Canard Version (Ref: SD-54-09001)
Crew: 1
Wingspan: 34.5ft (10.5m)
Length: 42.5ft (12.95m)
Empty Weight: 16-17,500lb (7,257-7,711kg) approx
Combat Weight: 20-21,000lb (9,071-9,525kg) approx
Maximum Speed: Mach 2
Ceiling: 60,000ft+ (18,288m+)
Powerplant: 1 x afterburning Allison J71 (B30) with turbofan unit, producing a maximum thrust of 25,568lb (113.7kN)
Armament: 1 x General Electric TE-171-E3 (later M61) Vulcan 20mm six-barrelled Gatling-type cannon, with 800 rounds

Lockheed CL-295-1
Crew: 1
Wingspan: 22.9ft (6.97m)
Wing Area: 210ft² (19.5m²)
Length: 50ft (15.24m)
Empty Weight: 12,905lb (5,853kg)
Gross Weight: 18,767lb (8,512kg)
Maximum Speed: Mach 2.09
Ceiling: 60,000ft (19,288m)
Combat Radius: 402 miles (647km) approx
Powerplant: Wright TJC32C4 turbojet with a maximum thrust of 24,000lb (106.75kN)
Armament: 1 x General Electric TE-171-E3 (later M61) Vulcan 20mm six-barrelled Gatling-type cannon, with 800 rounds

Lockheed CL-295-3 (Based on the CL-295-1)
Crew: 1
Wingspan: 20.9ft (6.3m)
Wing Area: 175ft² (16.25m²)
Length: 45.33ft (13.8m)
Height: N/A
Empty Weight: 9,527lb (4,321kg)

Gross Weight: 14,940lb (6,776.6kg)
Maximum Speed: Mach 2
Ceiling: 60,000ft (19,288m)
Range: 402 miles (647km) approx
Powerplant: 1 x General electric GE X-84 afterburning turbofan, rated at 20,100lb (89.4kN) thrust
Armament: 1 x General Electric TE-171-E3 (later M61) Vulcan 20mm six-barrelled Gatling-type cannon, with 800 rounds

Lockheed CL-295-4
Crew: 1
Wingspan: 23.33ft (7.11m)
Wing Area: 190ft² (17.6m²)
Sweep (leading edge): 40° estimated
Length: 42.5ft (12.95m)
Empty Weight: 12,030lb (5,457kg)
Gross Weight: 18,308lb (8,304kg)
Maximum Speed: Mach 2.2
Ceiling: 60,000ft (18,288m)
Combat Radius: 402 miles (647km) approx
Powerplant: 2 x afterburning General Electric GE X-84 turbofan engines, each producing an estimated maximum thrust of 20,100lb (89.4kN)
Armament: 1 x General Electric TE-171-E3 (later M61) Vulcan 20mm six-barrelled Gatling-type cannon, with 800 rounds

Lockheed CL-295-2 (Based on the CL-295-4)
Crew: 1
Wingspan: 28.6ft (8.71m)
Wing Area: 297ft² (27.5m²)
Sweep (leading edge): 28° estimated
Length: 44.66ft (13.6m)
Empty Weight: 18,110lb (8,214.5kg)
Gross Weight: 25,795lb (11,700kg)
Maximum Speed: Mach 2.3
Ceiling: 62,000ft (18,897m)
Combat Radius: 402 miles (647km) approx
Powerplant: 2 x General Electric J79-X207 turbojets, initially each rated at 15,000lb (66.7kN) thrust
Armament: 1 x General Electric TE-171-E3 (later M61) Vulcan 20mm six-barrelled Gatling-type cannon, with 800 rounds; air-to-air missiles

Temco Model 39
Crew: 1
Wingspan: 32ft (9.75m)
Wing Area: 320ft² (29.7m²)
Sweep (leading edge): 57.6°
Length: 51.3ft (15.6m)
Empty Weight: 14,831lb (6,727kg)
Combat Weight: 19,450lb (8,822kg)
Maximum Speed: Mach 1 at sea level; Mach 2 at altitude
Maximum Rate of Climb: 35,000ft/min

(10,668m/min)
Ceiling: 60,000ft (18,288m)
Combat Radius: 88.6 miles (141km)
Powerplant: Afterburning Allison J71 (B30) with turbofan unit, producing a maximum thrust of 25,568lb (113.7kN)
Armament: 1 x General Electric TE-171-E3 (later M61) Vulcan 20mm six-barrelled Gatling-type cannon, with 800 rounds

Ryan 84 Model 84F-7
Crew: 1
Wingspan: 36ft (10.97m)
Wing Area: N/A
Sweep (leading edge): 60°
Length: 55.5ft (16.91m)
Height (horizontal attitude): 14.9ft (4.54m)
Empty Weight: 21,000lb (9,525kg)
Gross Weight: 29,000lb (13,154kg)
Maximum Speed: Mach 2.5
Ceiling: 70,600ft (21,518m) estimated
Combat Radius: 600 miles (965km)
Powerplant: 2 x General Electric X-301 afterburning turbofan engines, with an anticipated maximum thrust for each engine in excess of 20,000lb (89kN)
Armament: 1 x 20mm Gatling-type gun with 800 rounds of ammunition; air-to-air missiles or one free-fall nuclear weapon

Ryan 112
Crew: 1
Wingspan: 31.1ft (9.47m)
Wing Area: 420ft² (39m²)
Sweep (leading edge): 60°
Length: 55.5ft (16.91m)
Height (horizontal attitude): 12.66ft (3.86m)
Empty Weight: 16,523lb (7,495kg)
Gross Weight: 26,727lb (12,123kg)
Maximum Speed: Mach 2
Ceiling: 65,000ft (19,812m) estimated
Range: N/A
Powerplant: 2 x J79-GE-2A/B engines, each producing a maximum thrust of 17,000lb (75.6kN) at sea level
Armament: 1 x 20mm Gatling-type gun with 800 rounds of ammunition; air-to-air missiles or one free-fall nuclear weapon

Ryan 115
Crew: 1
Wingspan: 31.1ft (9.47m)
Wing Area: 420ft² (39m²)
Sweep (leading edge): 60°
Length: 55.5ft (16.91m)
Height (horizontal attitude): 12.66ft (3.85m)
Empty Weight: 16,471lb (7,462kg)
Gross Weight: 28,914lb (13,115kg)
Maximum Speed: Mach 2.2
Ceiling: 67,000ft (20,421m) estimated
Combat Radius: 400 miles (643km) estimated

Powerplant: 2 x J79-GE-X207A engines, each producing an estimated maximum thrust of 18,000lb (80kN) at sea level

Armament: 1 x 20mm Gatling-type gun with 800 rounds of ammunition; air-to-air missiles or one free-fall nuclear weapon

Ryan 115C

Crew: 1
Wingspan: 31.1ft (9.47m)
Wing Area: 420ft² (39m²)
Sweep (leading edge): 60°
Length: 61.16ft (18.64m)
Height (horizontal attitude): 13.75ft (4.1m)
Empty Weight: 17,685lb (8,021kg)
Gross Weight: 33,737lb (15,302kg)
Maximum Speed: Mach 2.5
Ceiling: 65,000ft (19,812m) estimated
Range: 517 miles (832km) depending on mission
Powerplant: 2 x J79-GE-X207A engines, each producing an estimated maximum thrust of 18,000lb (80kN) at sea level
Armament: 4 x air-to-air missiles, or one free-fall nuclear weapon, carried internally; probably other external options

Boeing Modified Grumman F11F VTOL Fighter (to Super Tiger Spec)

Crew: 1
Wingspan: 31.66ft (9.65m)
Wing Area: 250ft² (23.25m²)
Length: 48.75ft (14.85m)
Height: N/A
Empty Weight: 13,810lb (6,277kg)
Maximum Take-off Weight (not including carpet): 26,086lb (11,833kg)
Maximum Speed: Mach 2.04
Ceiling: 59,000ft (17,983m)
Range: 750 miles (1,207km) estimated
Powerplant: 1 x General Electric J79-GE-3A afterburning turbojet, providing a maximum thrust of 17,000lb (75.6kN)
Armament: 4 x 20mm Colt Mk 12 cannon with 125 rounds per gun; provision to carry AIM-9 Sidewinder air-to-air missiles, drop tanks, reconnaissance pod or a single free-fall nuclear weapon

Boeing Flying Carpet for F11F

Crew: None. Remote Control
Wingspan: 18.5ft (5.6m)
Length (stabilising fin deployed): 22ft (6.7m)
Height: 7ft (2.1m)
Weight: N/A
Powerplant: 2 x unspecified turbojets

Boeing Mach 3 VTOL Attack Fighter

Crew: 1
Wingspan: 21.1ft (6.43m)
Wing Area: 400ft² (37.16m²)
Sweep (leading edge): 70°

Length: 70ft (21.3m)
Height: 19.5ft (5.9m)
Empty Weight: 15,380lb (6,976kg)
Gross Weight: 32,630lb (14,800kg)
JP5 Fuel Weight: 15,750lb (7,144kg)
Maximum Speed: Mach 3
Ceiling: 60,000ft+ (18,288m+) estimated
Range: N/A
Powerplant: 1 x Wright SE-105 turbojet producing 23,000lb (102kN) static thrust at sea level
Armament: 2 x Sidewinder AAMs and 2 Sparrow AAMs; possibly anti-shipping missiles, or one free-fall tactical nuclear weapon
Maximum Weapons Weight: 1,500lb (680kg)

Boeing Flying Carpet for Mach 3 Attack Fighter

Wingspan: 20.5ft (6.25m)
Length: 36ft (10.9m)
Height: 19.5ft (5.94m)
Empty Weight: 11,000lb (4,989kg)
Gross Weight: 14,000lb (6,350kg)
JP5 Fuel Weight: 3,000lb (1,360kg)
Maximum Speed: N/A
Powerplant: 2 x Wright SE-105 turbojets, each producing 23,000lb (102kN) static thrust

SNECMA C.450

Crew: 1
Overall Width: 14.8ft (4.5m)
Total Wing Area: 304.6ft² (28.3m²)
Planform Wing Area: 97ft² (9m²)
Length: 26.3ft (8.03m)
Overall Height (horizontal attitude): 14.8ft (4.5m)
Empty Weight: 4,870lb (2,209kg)
Gross Weight 6,615lb (3,000kg)
Maximum Design Speed: 500mph (804km/h)
Ceiling: N/A
Endurance: 25min
Engine: 1 x Atar 101 E-5V turbojet, producing 7,700lb (34.2kN) of static thrust
Armament: None

BZT/SNECMA Bruche Variant 1

Crew: 1
Overall Width: 8.5ft (2.6m)
Overall Length: 27.5ft (6.36m)
Weight: N/A
Maximum Speed: Mach 1.2
Ceiling: 55,000ft (16,764m) estimated
Powerplant: 1 x Atar 101 G-32 afterburning turbojet, producing a maximum thrust of 9,260lb (41kN); ramjet supplement for cruise
Armament: Stores carried on the lower external wing surface; possibly an internal cannon

SNECMA AP.503 (Ground-Attack Aircraft)

Crew: 1
Maximum Diameter: 8.6ft (2.62m)
Wing Area: N/A
Length: 29.2ft (8.9m)
Empty Weight: 4,542lb (2,060kg)
Gross Weight: 8,989lb (3,760kg)
Maximum Speed: Mach 0.96
Ceiling: 49,000ft (14,935m) estimated
Range: 186 miles (300km) at sea level; 434 miles (700km) at 20,000ft (6,000m) altitude
Powerplant: 1 x Atar 101 G-32 afterburning turbojet, producing a maximum thrust of 9,260lb (41kN)
Armament: Unspecified external stores

SNECMA AP.507

Crew: 1
Maximum Diameter: 8.9ft (2.7m)
Wing Area: N/A
Finspan: 12.1ft (3.7m)
Length: 36.2ft (11.02m)
Empty Weight: 8,719lb (3,955kg)
Gross Weight: 17,637lb (8,000kg)
Maximum Speed: Mach 3
Ceiling: 65,000ft (19,812m)
Range: 559 miles (900km) with external drop tanks
Powerplant: Unspecified turbojet/ramjet
Armament: 2 (possibly 4) air-to-air missiles

SNECMA AP.519

Crew: 1
Wingspan: 22ft (6.7m) estimated
Length: 35ft (10.6m) estimated
Empty Weight: 10,000lb (4,536kg)
Maximum Take-off Weight: 16,579lb (7,520kg)
Maximum Speed: Mach 2.3
Ceiling: 60,000ft+ (18,288m+) estimated
Operational Radius: 287 miles (461km)
Powerplant: 2 x (SNECMA-licensed) Pratt & Whitney JTF10 (TF30) afterburning turbojets, each producing a maximum thrust of 10,360lb (46kN)
Armament: Air-to-air missiles, air-to-surface missiles, or bombs

Heinkel He231 Tailsitter

Crew: 1
Span: 19.6ft (6m)
Sweep (leading edge-wings and fins): 58°
Length: 35.4ft (10.3m)
Empty Weight: 10,140lb (4,600kg)
Maximum Take-off Weight: 16,534lb (7,500kg)
Maximum Speed: Mach 2.5
Ceiling: 65,000ft (19,812km)
Radius of Action: 310 miles (500km)
Powerplant: 1 x General Electric J85 afterburning turbojet, plus ramjet option
Armament: 1 x 25mm Oerlikon cannon and two air-to-air missiles

Payen Pa.59 Aldebaran
Crew: 1
Wingspan: 17ft (5.2m)
Wing Area: 125ft² (11.6m²)
Sweep (leading edge): Primary 70°;
  Secondary: 50°
Length: 20.3ft (6.2m)
Height: 9.2ft (2.8m)
Empty Weight: 1,941lb (880kg)
Maximum VTO Weight: 3,000lb (1,360kg)
Maximum Speed: Mach 1
Ceiling: N/A
Endurance: N/A
Powerplant: 1 x Turboméca Gabizo turbojet,
  producing 2,426lb (10.79kN) static thrust
  and approximately 3,350lb (14.9kN) with
  afterburner; in addition, one or possibly two
  solid-fuel rocket boosters might be
  necessary to assist vertical take-offs
Armament: 2 x 30mm DEFA cannon or
  air-to-air rockets

Nord 1500 VTOL
Crew: 1
Wingspan: 21.5ft (6.55m)
Wing Area: 25m² (269ft²)
Sweep (leading edge): 60°
Length: 36ft (11m)
Height: 10.8ft (3.29m)
Total Weight: 11,023lb (5,000kg)
Powerplant: 1 x Atar 101 E-3 turbojet with
  afterburner producing a thrust of 7,710lb
  (34.3kN)
Maximum Speed: Mach 1.8
Ceiling: N/A
Range: N/A
Armament: Air-to-air missiles

Avro P.724 Single-Engine
Crew: 1
Wingspan: 16ft (4.87m)
Wing Area: 192ft² (17.8m²)
Length: 32.5ft (9.9m)
Take-off Weight: 18,000-20,000lb (8,164-
  9,071kg) estimated
Maximum Speed: Mach 2 at altitude
Ceiling: 60,000ft (18,288m) approx
Powerplant: 1 x Rolls-Royce RB.106 with an
  anticipated static thrust of 15,000lb (66kN),
  rising to 21,800lb (97kN) with afterburner
Armament: 2 x air-to-air missiles

Avro P.724 Twin-Engine
Crew: 1
Wingspan: 24ft (7.3m)
Wing Area: 375ft² (34.8m²)
Sweep (leading edge): 60°
Length: 37ft (11.2m)
Take-off Weight: 24,500lb (11,113kg) approx

Maximum Speed: Mach 2.5
Ceiling: 60,000ft+ (18,288m+)
Powerplant: 2 x Rolls-Royce RB.106, each with
  an anticipated static thrust of 15,000lb
  (66kN), rising to 21,800lb (97kN) with
  afterburner
Armament: 2 x Blue Jay (later called
  Firestreak) heat-seeking air-to-air missiles

MAI/Sukhoi Shkval (Squall) 1A VTOL
Crew: 1
Wingspan: 19ft (5.79m)
Wing Area: N/A
Length: 49ft (14.9m)
Empty Weight: N/A
Gross Weight: N/A
Maximum Speed: Mach 2+ at altitude
Ceiling: 60,000ft (18,288m) estimated
Range: N/A
Powerplant: 2 x unspecified afterburning
  Tumansky turbojets
Armament: Single cannon

F-84G Thunderjet ZELMAL
Crew: 1
Wingspan: 36.4ft (11.10m)
Wing Area: 260ft² (24m²)
Wing Loading: 70lb/ft² (342kg/m²)
Length: 38.08ft (11.60m)
Height: 12.58ft (3.84m)
Empty Weight: 11,470lb (5,200kg)
Maximum Take-off Weight: 23,340lb
  (10,585kg)
Maximum Speed: 622mph (1,000km/h)
Ceiling: 40,500ft (12,350m)
Range: 1,000 miles (1,609km)
Powerplant: 1 x Allison J35-A-29 turbojet
  producing 5,560lb (24.89kN) thrust
Booster: Aerojet General, jettisonable
  solid-fuel rocket, producing 55,000lb
  (244.6kN) of thrust for 2 seconds.
Armament: Not fitted to test aircraft

F-100D ZEL
Crew: 1
Wingspan: 38.75ft (11.81m)
Wing Area: 400ft² (37.1m²)
Length: 50ft (15.2m)
Height: 16.22ft (4.95m)
Empty Weight: 21,000lb (9,500kg)
Maximum Take-off Weight: 34,832lb
  (15,800kg)
Maximum Speed: Mach 1.13 at sea level
  (clean); Mach 1.3 at 36,000ft (10,973m)
  (clean)
Ceiling: 50,000ft (15,000m)
Normal Range: 534 miles (859km)
Maximum Range: 1,995 miles (3,210km)
Powerplant: 1 x Pratt & Whitney J57-P-21/21A

turbojet, producing 10,200lb (45.3kN) dry
  thrust and 16,000lb (71kN) thrust with
  afterburning
Booster: 1 x Rocketdyne solid-fuel rocket
  motor delivering a thrust of 130,000lb
  (578kN) for 4 seconds
Armament: 4 x 20mm Pontiac M-39 cannons;
  underwing pylons for drop tanks, air-to-air
  missiles or several types of free-fall nuclear
  weapons

Lockheed F-104G Starfighter ZEL
Crew: 1
Wingspan: 21.75ft (6.63m)
Wing Area: 196ft² (18.2m²)
Length: 54.66ft (16.66m)
Height: 13.4ft (4.09m)
Empty Weight: 13,995lb (6,350kg)
Maximum Take-off Weight: 29,040lb (13,170kg)
Maximum Speed: 1,328mph (2,137km/h) at
  35,000ft (10,668m)
Ceiling: 58,000ft (17,675m)
Range (without drop tanks): 1,080 miles
  (1,740km); with 4 tanks: 1,630 miles
  (2,623km)
Powerplant: 1 x J79-GE-11A afterburning
  turbojet engine, producing 10,000lb
  (44.5kN) dry thrust and 15,600lb (70.28kN)
  thrust with afterburning
Booster: 1 x Rocketdyne solid-fuel rocket
  motor delivering 130,000lb (578kN) thrust
  for 4 seconds
Armament: One 20mm M61A1 cannon with
  725 rounds and 2 air-to-air missiles, or one
  US-provided free-fall nuclear bomb

Mikoyan MiG-19S ZEL
Crew: 1
Wingspan: 30.16ft (9.2m)
Wing Area: 269.1ft² (25m²)
Length: 48.8ft (14.9m)
Height: 12.75ft (3.88m)
Empty Weight: 12,700lb (5,760kg)
Maximum Take-off Weight: 22,000lb
  (10,000kg)
Maximum Speed (at altitude): 955mph
  (1,536km/h)
Ceiling: 58,725feet (17,900m)
Combat radius: 425 miles (685km) with drop
  tanks
Powerplant: 2 x Tumansky RD-9B
  afterburning turbojet engines, each
  providing a maximum thrust of 7,178lb
  (31.9kN)
Booster: PRD-22 solid-fuel rocket unit,
  producing about 130,000lb (578kN) thrust
  for 2.5 seconds
Armament: 3 x NR-30 30mm cannon

Chapter 4 Postwar Flat Risers

In the immediate postwar years, the tailsitter was the favoured design for a VTOL fighter, with thinking heavily influenced by wartime German research. Within a short period of time it became obvious that although the tailsitter was a relatively straightforward design (putting some technical issues aside), it had major disadvantages. On land, an aircraft standing in an upright launch position was vulnerable to attack and at sea, there were major safety concerns about landing vertically on a carrier in difficult conditions.

VTOL (or VATOL) was a popular concept with military planners, but this type of aircraft seemed to have a limited future and many designers began to consider alternatives, such as the flat riser, so named because it would be able to take off and land while remaining in a horizontal position. Such an aircraft would also have the ability to operate in a conventional manner using a runway, making it a more attractive proposition. The problems were propulsion, mechanical complexity and weight, which all came together to make the flat riser a substantial design challenge. For example, it would be possible to use secondary engines for lift, but these became dead weight once the fighter was airborne.

Furthermore, the amount of additional fuel required to make vertical take-offs and landings would seriously restrict range and this remains a limiting factor for VTOL aircraft. That said, the quest to develop a multi-role fighter-bomber with flat-rising capabilities would lead to some ingenious methods of propulsion and eventually a number of attempts to develop existing combat aircraft into VTOL versions.

ABOVE This full-sized engineering model of the proposed VJ 101B-0004 was built by Messerschmitt AG at Augsburg. Various experiments were undertaken to establish lift flow and the operation of control systems using compressed air. *EADS Corporate Heritage*

Bell VTOL Fighter Designs

By the start of the postwar period, Bell Aircraft had established itself as a leading developer of advanced, experimental military aircraft. With official interest in VTOL fighters gathering momentum, Bell's chief engineer Robert J. Woods turned his attention to the design of a flat riser that would be powered by two turbojets carried in swivelling wingtip nacelles in a similar fashion to the Shavrov VSI design. The idea seemed viable, but Woods recognised the limitations of jet engine power and knew it would be necessary to supplement them during take-off with two solid-fuel rocket boosters.

In 1951, the proposal was assigned the company reference D-109-I and the following year a design based on this work was submitted to the US Patent Office (Ref: 170393). D-109-I was a relatively compact aircraft with a length of 47.1ft (14.35m) and an overall wingspan of 31.8ft (9.69m). Two Allison J33-A-16 turbojets, each having an approximate rating of 4,000lb (17.8kN), provided the lift and would be used in level flight. However, even with rocket assistance adding another 6,500lb (28.9kN) of thrust, this seems inadequate for anything more than a very short rolling take-off when allowing for a gross weight of 19,640lb (8,912kg). Woods estimated that D-109 would have a maximum speed of around 650mph at 30,000ft (1,046km/h at 9,144m) and a ceiling of 54,400ft (16,581m), with an expected rate of climb at sea level of 19,150ft/min (5,836m/min). The aircraft would be fitted with two retractable skids, presumably as a weight limitation measure, and armed with four cannon positioned in the forward fuselage.

A more advanced version would be fitted with Allison turbofan engines when they became available and this was to be known as D-109-II. It is unclear if the D-109 progressed to the stage of being wind tunnel tested in model form, but the concept went no further, at least not at that time. That aside, some of the initial estimates for performance seem rather optimistic and D-109 is unlikely to have provided proper VTOL performance. However, Woods would eventually review the D-109 and develop it into a significantly more advanced proposal, which is discussed shortly. The D-109 was one of many advanced studies undertaken by Bell during the early 1950s and the company was working on various classified projects that included a high-altitude spy plane known as the X-16. This twin-engined aircraft was completed as a mock-up and production was about to start, with 28 on order for the USAF. Even the official serial numbers had been assigned, but aggressive lobbying by Lockheed resulted in the project being scrapped in favour of the U-2.

Aerodynamicist Frank W. Kux (1916-1991) was the principal designer of the Bell X-16 and he also developed an early VTOL flat riser concept that would steadily evolve during the remainder of the 1950s. His initial proposal led to a company project, designated as Model D-139, which used a complex ducted exhaust lift system known as the 'Vertiburner'. During VTOL operations, the rear exhaust port for the single afterburning Pratt & Whitney J75 turbojet would close and the gas would be diverted into six separate nozzles, each fitted with a form of afterburner. Positioned along the underside of fuselage, these units could be directed downwards, or turned up to 45° rearwards. Much of the aircraft would be occupied by the very complex propulsion system and this created undercarriage problems, with a decision being taken to house the tailwheels in nacelles on the rear fins and use a retractable twin nosewheel. But the propulsion system was an engineering nightmare and it was finally deemed unworkable. Despite this, Bell believed the overall concept had considerable potential and replaced the 'Vertiburner' system with two J79-GE-2 turbojets for horizontal flight and nine modified J85-GE-1 engines in upright position between them. This new horizontal lift system was called the 'Verti-Pack'. In addition, each main engine was equipped with a thrust diverter positioned between the engine and afterburner to improve the aircraft's balance during hover, and low-speed control was

LEFT The appearance of the Bell D-109 VTOL would closely resemble this illustration used for an early US Patent application. *US Patent Office*

CENTRE A fairly basic three-view drawing representing the Bell D-139 used for patent documentation. *US Patent Office*

RIGHT Early artwork for Bell's D-139 VTOL fighter proposal. *US Patent Office*

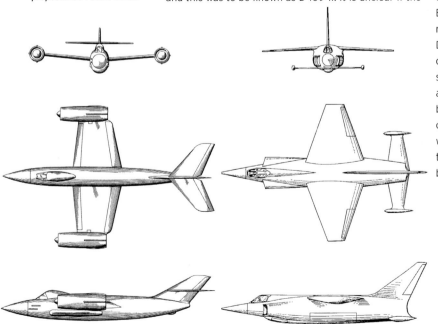

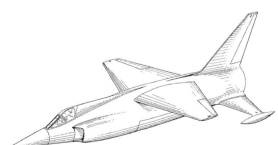

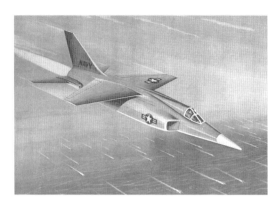

provided by air bled from the compressor stages and channelled to nozzles at the fore and aft of the fuselage and wingtips.

This aircraft was now renamed as the Model D-188. Several alternative engine layouts were considered, although it is hard to be specific about designations, as some confusion exists with Bell's paperwork references. A similar problem can be found with classified Avro-Canada and USAF documentation from the same period and it is possible that the details of some secret projects were made intentionally misleading for perceived security reasons. In 1955, Bell submitted initial plans for its D-188 VTOL fighter to the US Navy Bureau of Aeronautics (BuAer) and by June 1956 the company had developed this proposal for a formal US Navy VTOL fighter requirement known (in slightly shortened terms) as Type Specification For VTOL Jet Fighter, Number 140 (TS-140). The Bell D-188 would operate from aircraft carriers, warships and land bases, with significantly better performance than the D-139.

In October 1956, a series of 1/56-size scale models were wind tunnel testing at the MIT Naval Supersonic Laboratory at speeds up to Mach 2.25. This led to several minor design changes that reduced drag and improved stability.

Using the proposed J79-GE-2 engines, it was estimated that the prototype would be able to attain a maximum speed of Mach 2.02 at an altitude in excess of 25,000ft (7,620m), with a ceiling of about 57,000ft (17,373m). The production version would be equipped with more advanced afterburning J79-GE-X207 turbojets for normal flight, making it slightly faster, with a maximum speed of about Mach 2.2. The ceiling would also increase to about 60,000ft (18,288m). Missing from currently available documentation are any estimates for range, which may have been played down, as they probably were not too encouraging.

The prototype was expected to weigh about 22,011lb (9,984kg) empty, with a gross figure of approximately 32,414lb (14,702kg). Estimates for the production model indicated an empty weight of 23,021lb (10,442kg) and a gross weight of 34,164lb (15496kg). The D-188 would use aluminium alloy for most parts of the airframe and more specialised 7075-T6 aluminium alloy for the wings. The wingspan of the Bell D-188 was 33ft (10m) and overall length was about 61ft (18.6m), so in overall terms of size, weight and appearance, the D-188 was fairly similar to the D-139.

Armament considered for the production aircraft included a 20mm Gatling gun, four (proposed) folding fin Sidewinder AAMs carried internally in a retractable pack, free-fall bombs or 72 x 2in (50.8mm) rockets. An

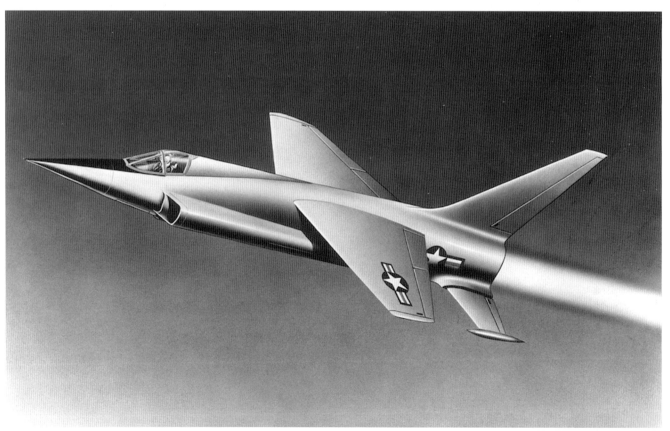

LEFT The Bell D-139 VTOL fighter makes a vertical lift-off from a remote mountain site. *Bell Aircraft Corporation*

BELOW Simulated artwork showing an operational Bell D-188 VTOL fighter belonging to the US Navy in flight. *Bill Rose*

LEFT A metal scale model of a Bell D-188 undergoing wind tunnel trials. *US Navy*

AN/APS-67 radar unit and AFCS EX-16 fire control system would be fitted. Bell suggested that the D-188 had considerable potential for future upgrades and believed that an all-weather capability would be attainable without too much difficulty. A development period of 31 months was quoted in company literature to reach the prototype testing stage.

However, Bell failed to generate sufficient interest in this design, possibly due to concerns about the aircraft's ability to compete with a conventional design, the overall mechanical complexity and the cost of development. This might have been the end of Bell's attempts to produce a VTOL fighter-bomber for the US Navy, and possibly the USAF, but an alternative project based on the original D-109 was already under way. Earlier in 1954, Bell allocated $100,000 of company money to fund development of an experimental proof-of-concept aircraft called the 65 Air Test Vehicle (ATV). It was a conglomeration of different parts, assembled around a Schweizer sailplane. The wings were taken from a surplus Cessna 170 monoplane and two Fairchild J44 turbojets, each providing 1,000lb (4.44kN) of thrust, were mounted on each side of the fuselage at the centre of gravity. They were contained in nacelles that could turn through 90°, providing upward lift and horizontal propulsion. A Turbomeca Palouste turbo-compressor was used to provide controlling jets of air at the wingtips and tail, and the aircraft was supported on the ground by a fixed Bell 47 landing gear.

After prolonged ground tests the 65 ATV made its first trial flight on 16 November 1954 and demonstrated that the propulsion system was viable. A total of 20 flights were conducted over the next year and then the project ended, with the 65 ATV being donated to the Smithsonian National Air and Space Museum. Although the D-188 had been rejected, Bell believed its alternative system had been proven viable and, in 1956, began development of a new high-altitude VTOL fighter, confusingly designated Model D-188A. Bell considered a number of different engine layouts and wing profiles, but finally settled on Configuration No 2.

This design featured a long area-ruled fuselage with the cockpit moved well forward to provide good visibility. The short wings were fitted with nacelles at the tips, containing two afterburning J85-GE-5 turbojets, each rated at a maximum thrust of 3,850lb (17.1kN). These engines provided two-thirds of the aircraft's propulsion in level flight and, like the 65 ATV, they swivelled downwards to produce lift during VTOL operations. A further two non-afterburning engines used for lift would be carried in vertical positions within the fuselage area just behind the cockpit (shutdown in normal flight) and two horizontal afterburning J85-GE-5 engines were located in the rear fuselage section. These would be equipped with exhaust diverters, positioned between the turbojet and afterburner of each engine to direct exhaust gas downwards and balance lift during VTOL operations. It was also thought that the J83 engine undergoing development would perform equally well in place of the J85. Low-speed control would take the form of an air bleed system, drawing on the fuselage engine compressors, with nozzles at each end of the aircraft. In normal flight, conventional control surfaces would take over. The overall length of the aircraft was set at 54.9ft (16.7m), with a fairly short wingspan of 23.66ft (7.2m). Aluminium alloy was proposed for use in many parts of the airframe, although recently available titanium was selected for some sections requiring extra strength or improved heat resistance.

The weights for the Configuration 2 aircraft quoted by Bell in 1957 are slightly higher than initially anticipated. Empty, the D-188A was expected to be 12,805lb (5,808kg), with a variety of weights permissible under operational conditions. Allowing for a vertical take-off and supersonic intercept at 60,000ft (18,288m), the gross weight would be 22,670lb (10,282kg). This would also apply to a vertical take-off and subsonic attack. However, by making a rolling take-off and vertical landing on return, the D-188A's gross weight could be increased to 28,000lb (12,700kg) for an attack mission, possibly carrying a single tactical nuclear weapon. Endurance and range would depend

BELOW Bell's Model 65 Air Test Vehicle (ATV) was built from an assortment of surplus components during the mid-1950s to demonstrate that it would be possible to fly a VTOL fighter using turbojets that swivelled for lift and horizontal flight. The aircraft completed 20 largely successful flights proving the technology and was finally donated to the Smithsonian National Air and Space Museum. *Bell Aircraft Corporation*

on the type of take-off and landing selected and the mission chosen. A Configuration 2, D-188A VTO supersonic intercept at 60,000ft (18,288m) would permit 2 minutes of combat and an operational radius of 270 miles (500km). In-flight refuelling was proposed to extend range. Operating at gross weight, the D-188A would have a hover ceiling of about 4,900ft (1493m), which could theoretically be raised to 20,000ft (9,096m) with a reduced payload.

Various armament possibilities were considered and the D-188A would have carried up to four 20mm cannon, or alternatively, a single Gatling-type gun. An internal weapons bay would accommodate four specially modified Sidewinder air-to-air missiles, two Bullpup air-to-surface missiles or a pack of 70mm rockets. Other possibilities include underwing air-to-surface missiles, free-fall bombs up to 4,000lb (1,800kg), or a single tactical nuclear weapon.

The D-188A continued to generate considerable interest within the upper ranks of the US Navy and, in June 1957, Bell began the next phase of this project, having received a six-month contract from the Navy and additional funding. Bell now completed a series of engineering reports and construction began on a full-sized mock-up of the aircraft. At the same time wind tunnel testing continued with different sized models at Naval Air Station Point Mugu.

Bell also approached the USAF during this period, submitting proposals for a modified version of the D-188A for consideration in the Air Force's SR-141 competition. As a consequence, the Navy and USAF met to discuss the possibility of undertaking a jointly funded development project for a broadly similar VTOL fighter-bomber. An agreement was reached, although the Navy's specialists were already raising serious concerns about performance and the aircraft's mechanical complexity.

However, the USN and USAF continued to show interest in the D-188A, with a formal inspection of the mock-up taking place at Bell Aircraft Corporation's Wheatfield plant in early January 1958. Also attending the inspection and a detailed presentation of the project were officials from the US Army and Marine Corps. In what appears to have been an attempt to move things forward and gain further official support for the project, Bell unofficially began to apply the USAF fighter designation XF-109A to the D-188A. This had already been considered for the McDonnell F-101B Voodoo, a development of the Convair F-106, and possibly the Ryan Model 115 VTOL fighter, although it remained unused. The US Navy designation XF3L-1 was also unofficially attached to the D-188A by Bell.

The company is understood to have approached the USAF a few weeks after the mock-up was first displayed, requesting that the designation XF-109 should be assigned to the aircraft. This was rejected, although,

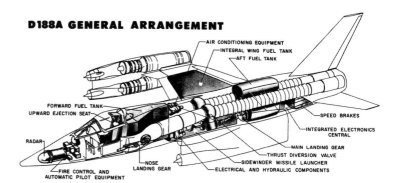

D188A GENERAL ARRANGEMENT

rather curiously, the USAF serial numbers 59-2109 and 60-2715 appear to have been allocated for use with two possible prototypes, suggesting that the USAF had indicated a willingness to progress much further. Yet another company designation that appeared was the Model 2000 and there were now two slightly different models being proposed for the USN and USAF. Development of the D-188A slowed during 1958, although the designation XF-109A appears to have stuck and it was regularly appearing in documentation. In early 1959, a joint services review of the project took place and the Navy decided to call it a day and cancel any further funding. Bell had now turned its attention towards the USAF, hoping to encourage it to continue supporting the project. There was certainly considerable interest within senior Air Force circles at this time, with Convair being selected to participate in production of the aircraft.

The original mock-up had now been partly rebuilt, with a broader rear fuselage and changes to the tailplane. The mock-up was painted in USAF markings and carried the official designation 92109 on its tail fin. It seems inconceivable that Bell would have done this without USAF approval and there must be another side to this story which remains untold at present. NASA Langley Research Center conducted further

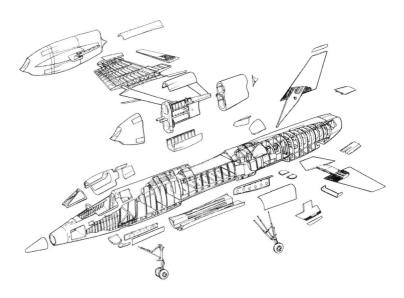

TOP Cutaway illustration showing the principal features of the Bell D-188A VTOL fighter. *US Navy*

BOTTOM The Bell D-188A in disassembled form, showing all its structural components. *Bell Aircraft Corporation*

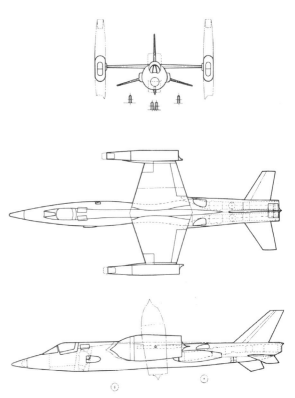

ABOVE Artwork showing the Bell D-188A as it might have appeared in operational use by the US Navy. *Bell Aircraft Corporation*

BELOW A US Navy Bell D-188A VTOL fighter hovers above the ground. *Bill Rose*

RIGHT This three-view drawing of the Bell D-188A shows how it might have appeared in its US Navy multi-role form. *US Navy*

LEFT A company promotional photograph of the Bell D-188A VTOL fighter mock-up in US Navy form. *Bell Aircraft Corporation*

BELOW This photograph of the Bell D-188A VTOL fighter mock-up shows the main engines positioned for horizontal flight. *US Navy*

tests of 1/8 scale D-188A models in the Free Spinning Tunnel and Full Scale Tunnel, but development of the D-188A remained in a state of stagnation for another year. Then the mock-up was revealed to the public as the anticipated XF-109A fighter, but the project went no further and was abandoned in early 1961 when the USAF reached the same conclusions as the USN about mechanical complexity and cost. There seems little doubt that the D-188A would have flown and West German designers took the same approach as Bell during the 1960s, building two experimental prototypes (the VJ 101C), which were similar to the D-188A and reached the flight-testing phase. However, the D-188A was a very complex piece of machinery, requiring constant and exacting maintenance. It would have taken substantial funding to develop into an operational combat aircraft and performance was always questionable, with obvious issues concerning range and payload.

LEFT In this photograph, the Bell D-188A mock-up is shown with its main engines turned into the vertical position, required for VTOL operations. *US Navy*

TOP One of many models of the Bell D-188A, Configuration 1, which were wind tunnel tested at the Naval Air Missile Test Center, Point Mugu, California. During this particular series of trials, the engine nacelles were shifted slightly rearward. *US Navy*

BOTTOM This wind tunnel model of the Bell D-188A Configuration 1 design was fitted with end plates. *US Navy*

TOP This underside view of a Bell D-188A Configuration 1 model shows simulated split-flap control and the engine nacelles in a forward position. *US Navy*

BOTTOM Scale-size, windtunnel all-metal model of the proposed Bell D-188A Configuration 1 VTOL fighter, fitted with end plates. On this occasion, fins were attached. *US Navy*

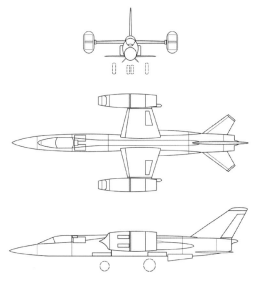

RIGHT This three-view drawing shows the Bell D-188A as it was intended for the USAF. Some minor details differ from the US Navy proposal. *Bill Rose*

BELOW This mock-up of the Bell D-188A was specifically produced to show the proposed aircraft in a USAF form, complete with the serial number, which appears to have been allocated to an anticipated prototype. *USAF*

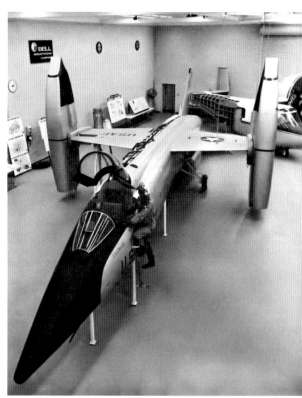

ABOVE This forward view of the Bell D-188A mock-up was clearly used for company promotion purposes, showing a pilot preparing to enter the cockpit and both engine nacelles tilted upright for vertical lift-off. *Bell Aircraft Corporation*

Avro's TS-140 VTOL Submission

After the US Navy issued TS-140 to aircraft contractors in 1956, Avro-Canada, based at Malton, Ontario, responded with a VTOL fighter design that has remained largely unknown. The company was already engaged in the top secret development of a disc-shaped supersonic VTOL interceptor for the USAF and a long-range, high-performance fighter for the RCAF, so this supersonic VTOL daylight fighter with a flat rising capability was well within its capabilities. The company designation for this proposal remains unknown, but the rather unusual-looking concept comprised of a conventional fuselage with an overall length of 50ft (15.24m) and canard wings with large engine nacelles at the tips. The front set of wings were noticeably anhedral and the larger rear wings dihedral, producing an unusual X-shaped configuration when viewed from the front. The overall wingspan was set at 25.25ft (7.6m), making it easy to stow in an aircraft carrier's hangar deck. Each engine nacelle would contain a Canadian-built version of the Bristol Orpheus turbojet, with a fairly straightforward deflector built into the engine's exhaust system, directing gas downward during VTOL operations. It was hoped to use an automated control system during take-off, hover, transition to and from level flight, or landings.

One of the principal reasons for the X-wing configuration was to separate the exhaust streams in level flight and reduce the possibility of gas ingestion by the rear engines. Afterburning was considered unnecessary to achieve the performance requirements. During normal flight, ailerons on each set of wings and a large tail rudder would control the aircraft. The wings and most of the airframe would be fabricated from

24ST aluminium alloy and the aircraft would have an empty weight of 11,250lb (5,102kg) and a gross weight of 16,250lb (7,370kg). This would allow adequate power for VTOL operations in all conditions and a maximum speed of Mach 1.75 at altitude, which might have increased to Mach 2 with improved engines. Nearly all the aircraft's fuel would be carried in four cells located along the central section of the fuselage, with a weapons bay below, permitting the carriage of four proposed folding fin versions of the Sidewinder AAM in a retractable unit, spin-stabilised rockets or a daylight photo-reconnaissance pack. The pressurised cockpit

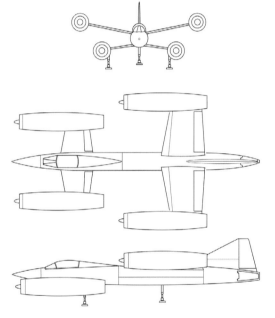

LEFT A three-view drawing of Avro-Canada's VTOL fighter designed in the mid-1950s. *Bill Rose*

BELOW Avro-Canada's proposed VTOL interceptor for the US Navy. *Avro-Canada/Bill Rose*

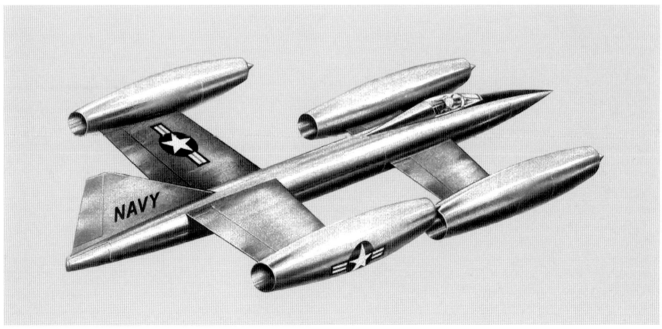

was positioned well forward, providing excellent
visibility for the pilot and an AN/APS-67 search radar
system would be installed in the nose section. In-flight
refuelling was considered a necessity from the outset,
as the main limitation of this and most other VTOL
aircraft was range.

The aircraft would be fitted with a very simple
retractable undercarriage comprising three dampened

struts. Because there would be no wheels fitted, special
wheeled units and a tender vehicle would be required
for ground handling. However, it was believed that in an
emergency the fighter would be capable of surviving a
horizontal crash landing at a speed of almost 200mph
(320km/h) without destroying the aircraft. That aside,
there seems to have been no potential for development
as a land-based aircraft.

Avro-Canada built at least one 1/7-sized scale model
of the VTOL fighter and advised the US Navy that,
following a one-year engineering study, it would take
three years to complete a flying test rig. Although a
little quirky in appearance, the Avro-Canada VTOL
fighter had the advantage of being mechanically less
complex than any of the Bell designs. It is impossible to
say with any certainty if this proposal could have
become an effective combat aircraft, although the US
Navy rejected it in favour of a US proposal.

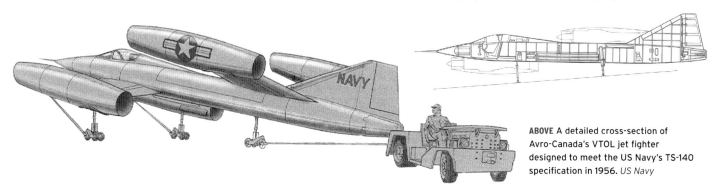

Sud Est X-115

During the 1950s, designers working for Sud Est
(which became Sud Aviation in 1957) proposed the
development of a compact, single-seat lightweight
VTOL fighter. Several sources indicate that Project X-115
was intended to rival the West German VJ101C VTOL
fighter, but the French concept appeared several years
before the VJ 101C and had little in common with it,
apart from some features of the main propulsion
system. X-155 was to have an overall length of 37.4ft
(11.4m) and would be powered by two SNECMA R.105
turbojets in wingtip nacelles. These would swivel
downwards by about 45° to provide lift. There was an
expectation that X-115 would be capable of full VTOL
and able to attain a maximum speed of about Mach 1.6
at altitude. Straight flat wings were positioned at the
centre of the fuselage supporting the engine nacelles
and the tail was highly swept. The aircraft's fully
retractable undercarriage would comprise a single
forward strut fitted with two wheels and a single
tailwheel, which seems to have been quite substantial.
This arrangement would lift the front of the aircraft by
10°, providing adequate clearance for the engine
exhausts. In addition, there would be small outrigger

wheels carried in each engine nacelle to ensure
stability on the ground. The proposed engines
were newly developed afterburning versions of
the SNECMA R.105 Vesta turbojet, expected to
produce a maximum thrust of 4,000-5,000lb
(17.8-22.2kN) thrust. Some drawings suggest that
exhaust vanes were contemplated for low-speed
control. Nothing is known about anticipated
payload or armament. X-115 was an interesting
design, although performance expectations
appear to be rather optimistic. It
seems unlikely that an aircraft built
to this design would be capable of
more than STOL performance and VTOL seems
unrealistic, along with the suggested supersonic
maximum speed.

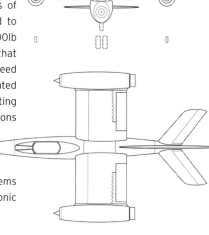

West Germany's VTOL Fighter-Bomber Projects

West Germany joined NATO in 1955, although the country remained reliant on the supply of military aircraft (or components for assembly) from overseas contractors. The Luftwaffe was planning to re-equip with the supersonic Lockheed F-104G Starfighter, but consideration was already being given to a follow-on aircraft, which would ideally be built by West German contractors. This led to the principal West German aircraft companies becoming involved with the French engine manufacturer SNECMA in an attempt to develop a VTOL interceptor that would meet the Luftwaffe's VJ 101 requirement. Unfortunately, the SNECMA programme failed to generate adequate official French interest and following the destruction of the C.450 Coléoptère, West German participation with SNECMA came to an end. The Luftwaffe's needs were shifting, although a V/STOL strike fighter was considered essential for the future defence of Northern Europe in a confrontation with Soviet and Warsaw Pact forces. Some technical expertise had been gained by West German contractors during the French-German VTOL fighter project, although tailsitters were no longer considered viable. Consequently, the Federal Government decided that the leading contractors,

which were Bölkow, Messerschmitt and Heinkel, should work together for the national good and examine the feasibility of developing an advanced VTOL flat riser to meet Germany's future fighter requirements.

West Germany's government also used the fighter project to begin a process of rationalising and strengthening the German aircraft industry through a series of mergers and takeovers. This began in February 1959, when Messerschmitt, Bölkow and Heinkel were encouraged to form a consortium called *Entwicklungsring-Süd* (Southern Development Circle: EWR-Süd). The aim was to pool ideas for a flat riser, high-altitude supersonic fighter, with a multi-role capability that would eventually replace the American F-104G. In addition, a separate West German project would begin in 1962 to produce a VTOL strike fighter that was capable of replacing the Fiat G.91. Changes to NATO strategy, recommending a more flexible non-nuclear response, made this an attractive proposition. Development was undertaken by a northern consortium known as *Vereinigte Flugtechnische Werke* (VFW – United Aircraft Technical Works), formed from designers and engineers working for Focke-Wulf, Heinkel and Weser.

EWR Supersonic VTOL Fighter

When the SNECMA VTOL fighter project came to an end, Heinkel was already working on an alternative to its supersonic He 231 VTOL tailsitter. Confusingly, Heinkel decided to use the same designation for the new fighter concept, which was a totally different flat riser, also capable of horizontal take-offs and landings.

The new He 231 VTOL was a relatively lightweight compact fighter designed with a full VTOL capability powered by two General Electric J85 turbojets positioned at the front of the aircraft and two J85 engines directly behind in the rear fuselage section. The exhausts for the forward engines were located on the central underside section of the fuselage and all four engine exhausts would be fitted with rotating nozzles to direct the gasses downward by as much as 80° during take-off, hover and landing. The dimensions and weight were almost the same as the He 231 tailsitter, with an overall wingspan of 20.33ft (6.2m), a length of 33.8ft (10.3m) and a gross take-off weight of 16,534lb (7,500kg). The main wing was positioned at the rear of the fuselage with a sweep of 45° and air intakes for the rear engines placed in the roots. A small set of canards were positioned towards the front of the fuselage and these had an estimated sweep of 60°. The pressurised cockpit was positioned at the centre of the

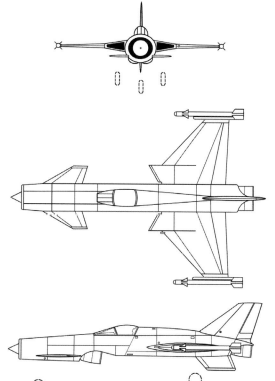

LEFT Heinkel's early attempts to replace the He 231 tailsitter resulted in this unusual canard flat riser. It progressed no further than the design stage. Confusingly, Heinkel designated this concept as the He 231 and then used it for the next proposal, which was equally different. *Bill Rose*

LEFT For no obvious reason, Heinkel applied the reference He 231 to this design, which had been used for two earlier and very different VTOL concepts. However, as the VTOL fighter project progressed it became known as the VJ 101A. The aircraft would have been powered by six turbojets in swivelling nacelles that would be used for VTOL operations. *Bill Rose*

RIGHT A slightly reconfigured version of the Heinkel VJ 101A proposal, with several obvious aerodynamic differences. *Bill Rose*

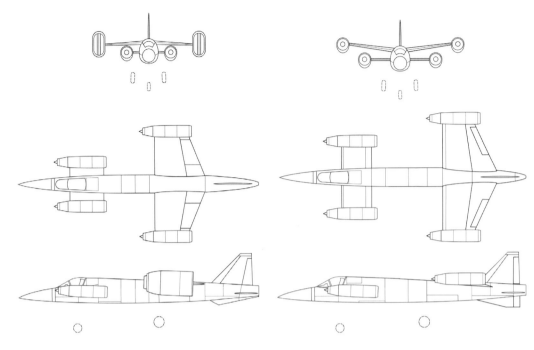

BELOW One of several VTOL flat riser concepts designed by Messerschmitt in the late 1950s. Relatively compact and conventional in appearance, this fighter received the company designation VJ 101B-002 and was powered by two afterburning turbojets and an additional lift engine for VTOL operations. *Bill Rose*

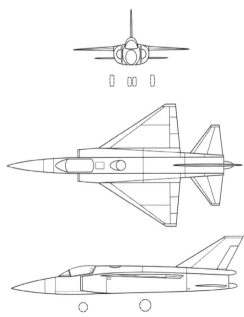

aircraft, in a less than ideal location, due to the engine positioning. A reasonably conventional tricycle undercarriage was proposed and this would allow horizontal take-offs and landings. There is no available description of low-speed flight control systems, but it is likely that air bleed to strategically placed nozzles was envisaged. In normal flight, the fighter would use control surfaces in the wings, movement of the canards and the tail rudder. Heinkel designers also felt it was necessary to fit a small fin below the tail, probably indicating wind tunnel testing of models was undertaken to provide initial data on the design. The aircraft would be armed with a single wing-mounted 25mm Oerlikon cannon and there would be the option of carrying two air-to-air missiles on wingtip launch rails.

There were many potential problems with this design and it is hard to envisage the engines providing adequate thrust to meet performance requirements, despite this being a lightweight design. The cockpit was not well placed and controlling acoustic levels and vibration would have probably been a major issue. Furthermore, the nosewheel would sit between two engine exhausts while retracted and this was probably undesirable. However, it appears that the various shortcomings became apparently almost immediately and this first attempt to design a flat riser was abandoned. Heinkel

engineers then completely revised their concept, producing an aircraft that showed many obvious improvements and looked rather like a combination of the Avro-Canada TS-140 submission and the Bell D-188A.

Once more, Heinkel decided to designate this aircraft as He 231, which seems to make no sense, but must have been done for some reason. The new proposal for the VJ 101 requirement was a canard design with four engines in wingtip nacelles designed to rotate for VTOL operations. At this stage a number of variants were studied, with different length wings and alternative engine layouts. The design was significantly better than the previous concept, with the cockpit now moved to a forward position. The aircraft would be equipped with a tricycle undercarriage allowing horizontal take-offs and landings and Heinkel envisaged stores being carried below the forward canard section or under the main wing. Available documentation indicates that much the same formula for size and weight was used for this third He 231 incarnation. The design was subsequently referred to as the VJ 101A1, with different suffixes for the variants, ie VJ 101A1-A8.

Messerschmitt had also been working on a VTOL interceptor, which was given the company designation P1227 and the official reference VJ 101B. This VTOL flat riser was relatively conventional in appearance, with a centrally located delta wing, tailplane and fin. Various engine layouts were examined, with the first design featuring four horizontal engines for normal flight, with a fairly complex exhaust diversion system for VTOL operations and one or two forward-located lift engines. All variants placed the cockpit in a forward position, with the engine air intakes either alongside or just behind. A somewhat smaller twin-engined proposal would be powered by two RB.145 afterburning turbojets for normal flight, with the exhaust being ducted downwards for VTOL. An RB.108 jet engine was vertically positioned inside the fuselage behind the cockpit to balance lift. Once the EWR-Süd consortium had been formed in early 1959 there was strong government encouragement for the three different design groups to work together and Heinkel's long-standing Chief Engineer Karl Schwärzler (1901–1974) was appointed as project director.

Heinkel and Messerschmitt had been working on very different proposals, but this was less of a problem for Bölkow, which had taken a very different approach to the others with its advanced unmanned fighter proposal and was willing to start from scratch. Each proposal had merits and disadvantages, but after some months of discussion and negotiation Heinkel agreed to scrap its canard arrangement and Messerschmitt accepted the idea of using engines in wingtip nacelles for lift and normal flight. The new EWR-Süd development group had largely reached an agreement on retention of the best ideas, with Bölkow's technicians largely taking responsibility for the avionics and control systems. The new combat aircraft would be known as the VJ 101C and the preliminary design met with immediate government approval, leading to EWR-Süd receiving a formal contract to proceed during December 1959.

It was now agreed that in addition to the development of a new design suitable for future Luftwaffe needs there would be an extensive research programme that would involve wind tunnel trials, the construction of a ground test rig and a more sophisticated rig capable of untethered manned flight. This would be followed by the construction of two experimental prototypes (X-1 and X-2, which received the serial numbers: D9517 and D9518). The EWR-Süd team had now completed its initial aircraft design, with a fuselage bearing some resemblance to a Starfighter that was equipped with two large twin-engined nacelles at each wingtip. These would rotate for VTOL and there would be provision for the carriage of stores beneath the wings. This design was followed by a change to the wing profile and side-by-side engine pods were considered. It was also accepted that two vertically positioned turbojets were be required behind the cockpit to balance the aircraft at low

ABOVE Part of the full-sized, mainly wooden, mock-up of the VJ 101C completed by mid-1960. *EADS Corporate Heritage*

BELOW An early proposal for the EWR VJ 101C VTOL fighter, drawing on work already undertaken by each design team in the consortium. The main engines are attached to tiltable wing tips and two lift engines would be positioned behind the cockpit area to provide balance during VTOL. *Bill Rose*

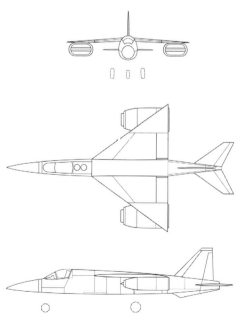

speed. A number of specialist foreign contractors were brought in, with the biggest being Rolls-Royce, who would provide the RB.145 turbojets. These would be developed in association with MAN Turbomotoren and Rolls-Royce would manufacture the engine nacelles for both prototypes and undertake related research at the company's Flight Development Establishment. Another notable company working on the project was Minneapolis-Honeywell in the US, which designed the stabilising control system, followed by several smaller UK companies such as Dowty Rotol, which supplied the hydraulic-powered flight controls. In total, about 20 well-known British, American and French aviation contractors were involved with the VJ 101C.

Construction of a wooden mock-up had been completed by the summer of 1960 and work on the X-1 airframe was starting at Messerschmitt AG's plant in Augsburg. When largely complete, this would be transported by road to Manching, where the undercarriage, wings and engines would be fitted. At the same time a fairly basic manned test rig was built to gain basic experience of VTOL control. Given the name Wippe (See-Saw), this assembly comprised a horizontal beam attached by pivot to a rigid support at one end and with a vertically positioned Rolls-Royce RB.108 turbojet and a simple cockpit at the other. The beam would allow considerable movement and the purpose of the apparatus was to simulate hovering under power and refine methods of pitch and roll control.

Tests involving the Wippe were successfully completed at Manching (the Bundeswehr Flight Test Centre, near Munich), before the end of 1960, having yielded considerable data. Construction of a more advanced hover rig known as the Schwebegestell (Hovering Bedstead) was already under way and it was ready for captive trials by May 1961. This apparatus was built from an open tubular steel framework, which had an overall length of approximately 35ft (10.6m) and a width of about 33ft (10m). It simulated the fighter's airframe and wings, with approximately the same undercarriage and cockpit positions. Three Rolls-Royce

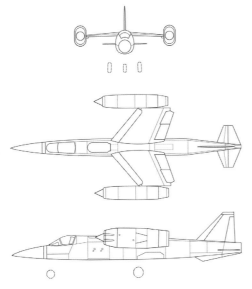

RB.108 turbojets were installed in the positions that would be occupied by the fighter's engines and the wingtip RB.108s would be able to rotate by plus or minus 6° from the vertical position to control yaw. After a series of initial tethered tests had been undertaken, the first free flight took place on 21 March 1962. The Schwebegestell was flown by George L. Bright (1925–1997), an experienced American test pilot, who had been hired by EWR as the project's senior pilot. A flight would have a maximum endurance of about 10 minutes and several German, British and US pilots also flew the rig. Good progress was made, with relatively few problems arising, and the rig was finally flown with a cloth covering to simulate a fuselage skin. In this condition, the machine performed well in wet and cold conditions.

The VJ 101C X-I prototype was largely completed by the end of 1962 and following trials mounted on a telescopic pylon X-1 undertook its first free-flight hover at Manching airfield, near Munich, on 10 April 1963, with George Bright at the controls. All initial hover flights were made with the undercarriage in a fixed position and the engine inlets were fitted with special screens to prevent ingestion of unwanted debris and other matter. On 20 September 1963, the first transition from hover

to horizontal flight took place and during the following year virtually all requirements were met. The VJ 101C X-1 was now making routine flights, normally accompanied by an Ex-Luftwaffe Canadair CL-13B Sabre chase plane, or a Fouga CM-170 Magister used for aerial photography. On 29 July 1964, X-1 became the world's first VTOL aircraft to achieve supersonic speed, reaching just over Mach 1 in a shallow dive. This was repeated on two or three subsequent occasions, with the VJ 101C finally attaining Mach 1.08 in level flight.

It is also worth mentioning that around this time the US Department of Defense came close to contracting EWR-Süd to provide four VJ 101C aircraft to the USAF/NASA for high-performance VTOL research. The aircraft would have been re-engined with more powerful General Electric GE1-J1B turbofans. This proposal was finally rejected on the advice of NASA for technical reasons. However, the VJ 101C project ran into serious difficulties on 14 September 1964 during a routine X-1 test flight involving a horizontal runway take-off. Bright had just left the ground when the aircraft suddenly began to roll uncontrollably. His only option was to eject from about 10ft (3m) above the ground, which led to Bright sustaining fairly serious injuries. The aircraft was a write-off and an investigation later determined that a malfunction occurred with the roll-rate gyro, which had been incorrectly installed. The incident was filmed and photographed, but it was decided at a government level that images of the accident should not be made public.

The second VJ 101C, X-2, was equipped with afterburning RB.145 engines, designed to provide supersonic performance in level flight, although this aircraft made its initial hovering free flight on 12 June 1965 without the use of afterburners. This would have to wait until trials had been completed using the telescopic pylon, with the first afterburner lift-off taking place on 10 October 1965. Results were rather unsatisfactory, with the realisation that using afterburners for take-offs could damage runways and create an unacceptable build-up of heat below the aircraft, causing a range of different, potentially

RIGHT Construction of the VJ 101C X-1 fuselage, at Messerschmitt AG. *EADS Corporate Heritage*

LEFT The first VJ 101C fuselage is moved by road from the Messerschmitt factory at Augsburg to Manching for final assembly and testing. *EADS Corporate Heritage*

LEFT Mounted on the telescopic pylon, X-1 is prepared for static engine testing in cold winter conditions. The fuselage air inlet section is protected with a cover to prevent the ingestion of damaging debris. *EADS Corporate Heritage*

LEFT Just prior to its first flight, the EWR VJ 101 X-1 was equipped with temporary stabilising braces. *EADS Corporate Heritage*

RIGHT The completed EWR VJ 101C X-1 prototype. *Based on an original EWR image*

BELOW The EWR VJ 101C X-1 during an early test flight. *EADS/Bill Rose*

dangerous problems. In addition, there were issues of exhaust recirculation. This led to various procedural revisions and a decision not to use afterburners in these circumstances. Increased weights requiring greater engine performance would require short rolling take-offs, with the engine nacelles inclined to 70°.

Ideas for arming a production version of the aircraft were now being discussed and it seems that the options included an internal 25mm cannon, underwing air-to-air missiles, and the possibility of carrying a single tactical nuclear weapon below the centre of the fuselage. Testing the X-2 continued until 1967, when X-2 made a very hard landing after engine problems caused by ingestion of exhaust gasses after lift-off. There was damage to the undercarriage and aluminium alloy airframe, but the X-2 was repaired and trials resumed.

Aside from this, the programme proceeded without any serious incidents and in addition to horizontal take-offs and landings, X-2 completed 45 hover flights, using afterburners on 38 occasions, made 9 transitions and attained a maximum speed of Mach 1.14.

Two further prototypes were considered but never built. The X-3 was a two-seater and the X-4 seems to have been intended for weapons trials. The project came to an end in 1971, by which time the Luftwaffe had re-evaluated its needs, moving on from the original VTOL requirement. X-2 was finally presented to the Deutsches Museum at Schleissheim near Munich, where it is currently on display.

A new fighter design to supersede the EWR-Süd VJ 101C, known as the VJ 101D, was first discussed some 10 years earlier during a contest known as the NATO Basic Military Requirement 3 (NBMR-3). This concept seems to have been regarded by many observers during that period as simply a refined production version of the VJ 101C, although the VJ 101D was a very different multi-role strike fighter. Having more in common with designs like the French Balzac, Short PD.56 and Fiat G.95, it was clear that EWR-Süd's designers recognised from an early stage that the VJ 101C had very limited scope for development and would be incapable of meeting future NATO requirements. Larger and heavier than the VJ 101C, the VJ 101D (known within EWR-Süd as Dora) would be powered by two Rolls-Royce/MAN RB.153-61 afterburning turbofans for horizontal flight and VTOL operations. A deflector unit would be fitted immediately after each engine to channel the exhaust downward during take-off, hover and landing. In addition, five vertically positioned Rolls-Royce RB.162-31 engines would be positioned in the forward fuselage section behind the cockpit area, providing additional lift during VTOL.

The VJ 101D would be equipped with a conventional tricycle undercarriage allowing runway take-offs and

landings and there would be sufficient space available to carry an additional crew member if this was considered desirable. With a maximum speed in excess of Mach 2, the VJ 101D would be capable of operating as a high-altitude interceptor armed with at least four air-to-air missiles. It would also be able to undertake reconnaissance missions and tactical nuclear strikes. It is unknown if any other weapons were considered, such as conventional bombs or air-to-surface missiles. According to some sources, the West German government seriously considered the funding of two prototypes, but seems to have had second thoughts after reviewing the subsonic VAK 191B VTOL strike fighter project, which appeared more promising.

Interestingly, EWR-Süd had already proposed the development of a smaller-sized variant of the VJ 101D for the VAK 191 competition, which received the reference VAK 191C, before it was rejected. The VJ 101D failed to progress much further than wind tunnel tests of models and some engineering work on the proposed propulsion system, although there was one further series of two-seat designs known as the VJ 101E. The first VJ 101E concept featured a similar wing and tailplane layout to the VJ 101D, although the fuselage was widened to accept four forward-located swivelling lift jets that would lie in a horizontal position during normal flight. Two powerful afterburning turbofans with vectored thrust units would provide the propulsion in normal flight and during VTOL. A further proposal was a variable-geometry version of the VJ 101E, which was clearly linked to another project being undertaken by EWR-Süd.

This programme was intended to develop a very complex VTOL strike fighter with variable-geometry wings, known as the Advanced V/STOL Tactical Fighter Weapons System (AVS). Development began in early 1964 (at the latest) and involved Boeing and Fairchild Hiller Republic Aviation. West Germany was still considering a high-performance VTOL successor for the F-104G and there was general USAF interest in the AVS. Some sources have suggested that the AVS project was undertaken separately from the VJ 101C/D, but there are indications that both programmes were quite closely interlinked and versions of the VJ 101E were at least in part designed by Boeing engineers who had been assigned to work with EWR-Süd's design team at Munich.

The AVS was a large, variable-geometry (swing-wing) supersonic two-man fighter, bearing some resemblance to the Grumman F-14A Tomcat naval fighter and various proposals for the TFX fighter competition, which led to the F-111. Engine thrust from the two main turbofan engines would be vectored downwards for VTOL and this would be balanced by the use of four vertically positioned lift engines that would swing out from the fuselage, just behind the cockpit area. Several different arrangements were considered, with the support structure usually being integrated with an opening door. Air inlets for the main engines were located above the wing, and the AVS would be fitted with a conventional tricycle undercarriage allowing normal take-offs and landings.

Boeing is understood to have dropped out of the project by around 1967, although the design continued to evolve into the definitive A400 version that had the look of a Panavia Tornado predecessor. In 1968, the AVS was rejected by the Luftwaffe which had re-evaluated its immediate needs. A decision had been taken to buy a substantial number of F-4E Phantoms and begin development of a new variable-geometry multi-role combat aircraft with the UK and Italy. AVS was at an end, although the remaining partner Fairchild

ABOVE Front view of the EWR VJ 101C X-2, displayed at the Deutsches Museum at Schleissheim near Munich. *Deutsches Museum*

RIGHT This variant of the VJ 101C, referred to as the X-4, was proposed in late 1965 and it mainly differed from earlier prototypes in changes to the propulsion system. X-4 would have been powered by two swivelling wingtip-mounted Rolls-Royce/MAN Turbomotoren RB.153 engines. In addition, the two forward turbojets used in the X-1 and X-2 would be replaced by Rolls-Royce RB.162-31 lift engines. The X-4 would be designed from the outset to carry external stores. *Bill Rose*

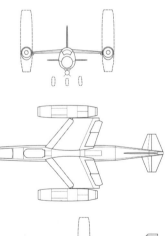

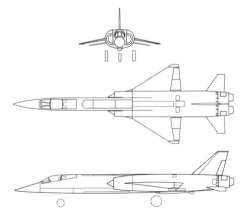

ABOVE The high-performance EWR VJ 101D, which was expected to be the VJ 101C's true successor. It would have entered service with the Luftwaffe during the 1970s as its operational VTOL strike fighter. *Bill Rose*

Republic continued to use research data from the project, eventually designing a smaller-sized strike fighter based on the original concept which would be powered by a single P&W F100 engine with downward-vectored thrust for VTOL and two additional swing-out engines carried in the forward fuselage. This small single-seat fighter known as the FR-150 was primarily intended for naval use, but failed to generate official support.

Heinkel left the VTOL fighter project in 1964 and a new company was formed on 6 June 1968, known as Messerschmitt-Bölkow GmbH. Heading the board of this new larger, stronger organisation were Willy Messerschmitt and Ludwig Bölkow and one year later Messerschmitt-Bölkow merged with the Hamburger Flugzeugbau GmbH (HFB), which had originated as Blohm & Voss. The unification of West Germany's aviation industry was now proceeding exactly as anticipated in higher circles.

West Germany's Nuclear Strike Fighter

By the late 1950s, senior Luftwaffe officials were becoming preoccupied with the need for future VTOL combat aircraft, anticipating the wholesale destruction of their airbases in a major East-West clash. Other NATO members reached similar conclusions, with the ability to build an effective flat-rising VTOL fighter becoming a realistic possibility during the early 1960s. Several countries were already working on designs for VTOL interceptors and strike fighters, with EWR-Süd in West Germany starting work on a supersonic interceptor to eventually replace the F-104G. However, the Luftwaffe and the *Aeronautica Militare Italiana* (Italian Air Force) were considering a more advanced VTOL replacement for their subsonic Fiat G.91 strike fighters, which were about to enter service. These would need to be capable of delivering tactical nuclear weapons provided by the Americans in a Third World War scenario. This specific requirement was primarily responsible for the overall design of the aircraft, although the nuclear strike role was not disclosed to the public.

NATO was largely in agreement that most of the key airfields would be lost at the start of a major conflict with Eastern Bloc forces and the ability to operate from improvised sites seemed the obvious way forward. In 1961, NATO's NBMR-3 was issued. This led to a project known as *Vertikalstartendes Aufklärungs und Kampfflugzeug* (V/STOL Reconnaissance and Strike Aircraft) 191 (VAK 191).

Several proposals were carefully reviewed, although NATO failed to reach an agreement on how to proceed. Nevertheless, the West German and Italian proposals won considerable support in many quarters. Focke-Wulf Flugzeugbau GmbH had started to develop its Fw 1262 proposal for VAK 191 in September 1961 before the NATO report was published. The aircraft (VAK 191B) was similar in appearance to the Hawker P.1127, but Focke-Wulf's designers concluded that the Pegasus engine was unnecessarily large for normal flight and better performance would be attained using a smaller unit, supplemented by two separate lift engines.

The British withdrew from the NATO contest in order to develop the Hawker P.1127 independently, although UK contractors expressed interest in participating in development of the West German VAK 191B. Italian manufacturer Fiat continued to develop its G.95/4 (the VAK 191D), but this would soon be

ABOVE Close-up of RB.193 engine exhaust detail. *Deutsches Museum*

LEFT Crucial to the development of the VAK 191B was the advanced propulsion system produced by Rolls-Royce in association with MAN Turbomotoren. This photograph shows the aircraft's main engine, which was an RB.193-12 lift/cruise, high-bypass turbofan, initially designed by Bristol Siddeley, who received a Federal German Ministry of Defence contract for full development in December 1965. During the following year, Bristol Siddeley became a division of Rolls-Royce. Part of the arrangement stipulated that West German manufacturer MAN Turbomotoren would be the engine's principal contractor. Utilising various features developed for the Spey engine, the new vectored-thrust RB.193-12 has often been described as a scaled-down Pegasus, having the same pairs of hot and cold swivelling thrust nozzles, used for lift and normal flight. The RB.193-12 weighed 1,742lb (790kg) and provided 10,150lb (45.14kN) of thrust. The first successful test run was completed in December 1967, which included rotation of the thrust vectoring nozzles. By late 1969 the engine had completed a 25-hour flight clearance requirement. Rolls-Royce.

In July 1965, West Germany and Italy signed a memorandum of agreement to jointly build at least one test rig, followed by three single-seat prototypes, three two-seat prototypes and a static test example. The cost would be split 60/40, with West Germany the dominant partner. This was followed by an official contract to Rolls-Royce and Motoren-und-Turbinen Union (MTU) for development of the RB.193 twin-shaft vectored-thrust turbofan engine. The first prototype engine would run two years later and complete its 25-hour flight clearance test during December 1969, with the delivery of nine engines to VFW in September 1970. In addition, eighteen RB.162-81 turbojet lift engines were delivered to VFW. Fiat was planning to build three two-seat prototypes, but this was cancelled, with the company switching to development and manufacture of the forward section, wings and tail section. Construction of the first VAK 191B began at Bremen and, in visual terms, the aircraft looked very similar to the British Kestrel. Nevertheless there were many engineering differences and the VAK 191B was far from being a clone.

The compact RB.193 would be installed at the aircraft's centre of gravity and, unlike the Harrier, raised into place from underneath. Both RB.162-81 turbojets would be mounted with a slight rearward inclination of 12.5°, providing just enough performance for an emergency landing in the event of a main engine failure. Low-speed flight control would be provided by air bleed from the engines and channelled to the front and rear of the fuselage and wingtips. Control surfaces took over during normal flight, with a number of new technologies being introduced, such as fly-by-wire with multiple redundancy. An empty bay was located below the main engine and this was intended for a weapons or reconnaissance pack, although most stores would be carried beneath the wings. The airframe and wings were mainly fabricated from aluminium alloy, the undercarriage was similar in layout to the Hawker

abandoned, with the company becoming a participant in the VAK 191B project. Rolls-Royce now became the main engine developer for VAK 191B, providing the RB.193-12 vectored thrust lift/cruise turbofan, in association with MAN Turbo (the future MTU).

A new northern consortium was formed to develop the VAK 191B, drawing on the expertise of Focke-Wulf, Weserflug and Heinkel engineers, known as *Vereinigte Flugtechnische Werke* (VFW). This government-promoted arrangement would eventually lead to a series of company mergers and takeovers. Design work on the VAK 191B continued, with a full-sized mock-up being completed at VFW Bremen. It should also be noted that, from March to November 1965, Luftwaffe pilots participated in a full evaluation of the British Kestrel FGA.1 (an improved P.1127) at RAF West Raynham in Norfolk. Useful as this may have been in terms of gaining hands-on experience, it seems that the Luftwaffe was already committed to the development of a West German VTOL combat aircraft.

RIGHT Drawing showing two of the VAK 191B prototypes, displaying minor differences. Top, D-9563 lower, D-9564. *Bill Rose*

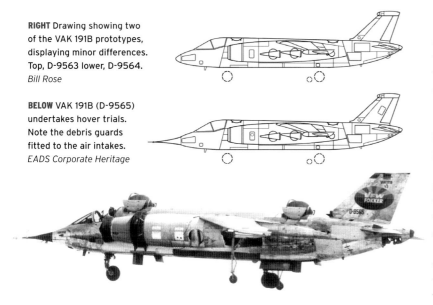

BELOW VAK 191B (D-9565) undertakes hover trials. Note the debris guards fitted to the air intakes. *EADS Corporate Heritage*

During the development programme approximately 8,900 hours of wind tunnel testing were undertaken, with emphasis on VTOL transition to level flight, transonic speeds and anticipated problems with engine exhaust recirculation. The work was undertaken at many different facilities located at Amsterdam, Bedford, Bremen, Brunswick, Cologne, Emden and Fiat in Italy. The cost of the project was substantial for that period, with VFW estimating a figure approaching DM500 million to complete the three airworthy prototypes. Pilots prepared to fly the aircraft, training with the SG-1262 Schwebegestell test rig, and aircraft would later be tested using the telescopic pylon used during the VJ 101C project.

In April 1970, the first VAK 191B prototype (D-9563) was completed at Bremen and rolled out, making a brief first flight on 10 September 1970, flown by former VJ 101C test pilot Ludwig Obermeier, who now headed the VAK 191B flight team. All engine inlets were covered with screening to prevent the ingestion of debris during low-level trials and this would continue for much of the programme. Restrictions on testing at Bremen eventually led to the first aircraft being transported to the Luftwaffe's test facility at Manching in Bavaria. This operation was undertaken using a Sikorsky S-64 helicopter, with the VAK 191B slung underneath. Although a little unorthodox, this was considered the easiest way to move the aircraft as it avoided full disassembly for road transport.

The other two VAK 191B prototypes (D-9564 and D-9565) built at Bremen were also moved to Manching in the same manner, using the Sikorsky S-64 helicopter. VAK 191B (D-9563) made the first transition from vertical to horizontal flight on 26 October 1972, reaching a speed of 250mph (400km/h). All three prototypes were now available for testing and the US Navy was taking a considerable interest in the project. Chief of Naval Operations Elmo Zumwalt was promoting the idea of smaller, cheaper carriers, leading to the Sea Control Ship (SCS) project, which would involve the use of VTOL strike fighters. This made the VAK 191B a potential candidate for further development and various improved versions were designed, with some wind tunnel testing of models. The VAK 191B Mk 2 would have been fitted with a new wing providing a 50% increase in area, allowing conventional runway operations and improved manoeuvrability. The main engine's performance would be increased by 30% and the lift engines' thrust uprated by 5%. In turn, maximum speed, payload capacity and range would have improved. New avionics were anticipated, along with the option of various internal weapons, reconnaissance and electronic warfare packs. In addition, there would be provision for underwing stores.

A further development was the VAK 191B Mk 3, using Rolls-Royce/Allison J99-type lift engines, each providing

Kestrel and the forward pressurised cockpit was equipped with a Martin-Baker Mk 9 ejector seat.

The VAK 191B was originally designed for a specific mission. In an all-out war the aircraft would operate from a dispersed or improvised site and deliver a single free-fall nuclear weapon. However, changing NATO strategy moved away from this to a more flexible response, requiring an increased capability. The aircraft had been initially expected to fly at low level to avoid detection by enemy radar. For this reason, the VAK 191B was built with small, highly loaded wings to counteract low-level turbulence. The wing design was acceptable for VTOL operations but rather unsatisfactory for horizontal take-offs and landings. VAK 191B was also originally intended to be capable of brief supersonic performance, but the relatively small engine provided insufficient power to allow this. In comparison, the shorter Harrier had a more powerful engine and somewhat larger wing making it more versatile and able to function in much the same way as a conventional jet fighter.

BELOW LEFT The relatively refined VAK 191B Mk 3, offering improved performance. *Bill Rose*

RIGHT VAK 191B Mk 4, using a larger swept wing to improve the aircraft's performance and capability. This version was closely studied and considered by the US Navy. *Bill Rose*

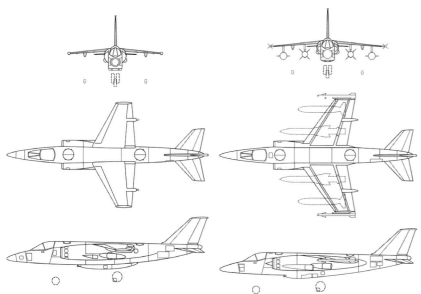

an anticipated 7,000-8,000lb (31-35kN) of thrust. This was followed by the VAK 191B Mk 4 design, equipped with the RB.193-30/P main engine producing an anticipated 18,300lb (81kN) of thrust, plus two XJ-99 lift engines, each providing 14,400lb (64kN) of thrust. The wing area would be double that of the original design and the wingspan would be 26.5ft (8m), with a length of 50ft (15.2m) and a height of 14ft (4.26m). In addition to VTOL, normal horizontal landings and take-offs would be possible and the aircraft would be capable of undertaking a variety of different roles.

During the early 1970s, the Mk 4 appears to have generated considerable interest with the US Navy as a possible Sea Control attack fighter and at least one proposal was submitted for consideration. The only available artwork shows a USN modified version of the Mk 4 carrying two underwing AS.34 Kormoran anti-shipping missiles and two drop tanks. Two further single-seat versions of the VAK 191B were the Mach 1.5 Mk 5, equipped with an advanced version of the Pegasus engine, and the Mk 6, with Mach 1.8 performance. Both of these designs featured slightly stretched fuselages, larger wings and were designed to have multi-role capabilities.

Trials of the VAK 191B aircraft continued at Manching until 1975, with Professor Rolf Riccius as project director, and all three prototypes made 91 flights lasting for a total of approximately 120 hours. Chief Test Pilot Ludwig Obermeier or his colleague Horst Philipp made the majority of flights. A number of problems arose during these trials, but the only major incident was the loss of a lift engine during an otherwise routine flight. This led to the VAK 191B making its only conventional horizontal landing, which the aircraft was not designed for. The small wings meant that a very high landing speed of 212mph (340km/h) was required and this exceeded the maximum tyre rating of 185mph (300km/h). Fortunately, this rather risky touchdown took place without any serious consequences. Nevertheless, the VAK 191B remained tied to its original design specification and lacked the capabilities and flexibility of the British VTOL strike fighter.

Having started out as a VTOL aircraft that would deliver a single nuclear bomb to the intended target at low level, its future was probably sealed from the outset. Furthermore, it would soon be possible to undertake exactly the same mission more easily and effectively using a nuclear-tipped Tomahawk cruise missile launched from an improvised site. Generally speaking, the VAK 191B proved useful for the development of various technologies that would find their way into future military aircraft such as the Panavia Tornado and this project could undoubtedly be credited with helping to reform the German aerospace industry into something more dynamic.

All three aircraft have survived, with the first prototype on display at the Deutsches Museum at Schleissheim near Munich. The second VAK 191B belongs to the *Wehrtechnische Studiensammlung* (Military technical collection) at Koblenz and the third aircraft is stored at EADS, Bremen.

Italy's VTOL Strike Fighter

The Fiat G.95 was a direct competitor to the VAK 191B, receiving the NATO reference VAK 191D. In retrospect, it was possibly a slightly better design but failed to become the outright winner of the NBMR-3 contest and Fiat was finally encouraged to abandon the proposal and become a development partner in the VAK 191B project. The G.95 began as a study to find a VTOL successor to the Fiat G.91 strike fighter, which was about to enter service with the *Aeronautica Militare Italiana* and the Luftwaffe. The G.95 project was undertaken by a team working at Turin under the direction of Professor Giuseppe Gabrielli (1903-1987), a highly respected designer responsible for many classic aircraft, including

the Fiat G.91. The preliminary report to Fiat's board was well received and in addition to company funding, the project also received substantial support from the Italian government. The initial G.95 design was based directly on the G.91, using the same rear section of fuselage and a single engine for horizontal flight. Two small additional turbojets were positioned in the forward lower fuselage to provide extra lift for enhanced STOL performance but not VTOL.

This design rapidly gave way to a more advanced VTOL version with the reference G.95/3, using a different propulsion layout of twin cruise engines with a thrust deflection system for VTOL, supplemented by four lift engines. The fuselage was redesigned completely, the wingspan was reduced and the tailplane was moved to the top of the tail fin. There is some confusion about the history of follow-on versions, because the G.95/3 was succeeded by the very sophisticated supersonic G.95/6, which was submitted for NMBR-3. This VTOL proposal was to be powered in level flight by two afterburning Rolls-Royce-MAN Turbomotoren RB.153-61 turbofan engines and to use six Rolls-Royce RB.162-31 lift engines for VTOL. Weapons, including a single nuclear free-fall bomb carried inside a central bay. It is also possible that this section was considered to accommodate extra fuel, with stores carried underwing or semi-externally.

Nothing appears to be currently known about the GR.95/2 or GR.95/5, which do not seem to have progressed beyond the initial concept phase. Nevertheless, the aircraft design receiving the most attention at Turin was the compact Fiat G.95/4, which was closer to the VAK 191B in terms of performance. Designed to undertake a nuclear strike mission from improvised sites using full VTOL, the G.95/4 would have a maximum range of 230 miles (370km), flying the first part of the mission at an altitude of 490ft (150m) at Mach 0.6. There would be a five-minute allowance for high-speed loiter in the target area and, after weapon release, the aircraft would return to its base at Mach 0.92. A brief maximum speed of Mach 1.2 –1.4 was considered possible. Fiat initially planned to use two General Electric J85-GE-15 turbojets for normal flight and four Rolls-Royce RB.162-31 lift engines fitted with swivelling nozzles. But, as the project advanced, it was agreed with the West German government that, should the G.95/4 be selected for NATO use, the main engines would be replaced with Rolls-Royce/MAN Turbomotoren-developed RB.153-61 turbofans, each producing 7,000lb (31.13kN) of thrust. Four Rolls-Royce RB.162-31 engines would provide the lift during VTOL. Two sets of louvred doors covered the upper lift engine inlets and these would fully open during VTOL. There would also be ventral shutters to cover the engine exhausts during horizontal flight. A compressor air bleed reaction control system would be functional during low-speed operations, with nozzles at the nose and wingtips.

Anticipated maximum VTO weight was 16,000lb (7,257kg) with this rising to 17,600lb (7,983kg) for the proposed G.95/4A reconnaissance variant. This variant was requested by the *Aeronautica Militare Italiana* to replace the existing G.91R and it was to be fitted with a different forward section that carried two cameras. Although originally optimised for high-speed, low-level flight, Gabrielli designed the GR.95/4 (and apparently the GR.95/6)

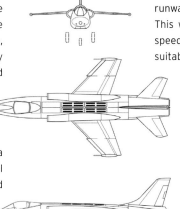

ABOVE Fiat's G.95.4 VTOL strike fighter, originally intended to become a replacement for the Fiat G.91. *Bill Rose*

BELOW The high-performance Fiat G.95.6 VTOL strike fighter. *Bill Rose*

to be capable of making an emergency horizontal runway landing in the event of a lift engine failure. This would need to be undertaken at relatively high speed and there was considerable attention given to a suitable undercarriage design and the type of tyres.

A model of the G.95/4 was displayed at the Le Bourget Air Show in 1963 and, with wind tunnel testing of models under way, Fiat built a tethered test rig at Turin to duplicate the strike fighter's handling properties. Essentially, this was little more than a manned framework carrying two Rolls-Royce RB.108 lift engines. The cockpit was located in the forward section of the framework, which had similar overall dimensions to the G.95/4. Air bleed from the engine's compressor stages was ducted to nozzles at either end of the rig and the wingtip positions. Despite being locked to a central column, the rig could turn horizontally through 360° and was designed to allow adequate movement through the two other axes. Testing provided useful data for the G.95/4 and later the VAK 191B projects.

Although the West German VTOL strike fighter had been selected, work on the G.95/4 continued, albeit at a considerably reduced level. Fiat now agreed to become the junior partner in development of the VAK-191B and there were rather unrealistic estimates that 1,000 of these aircraft would be built. Fiat would be responsible for development and manufacture of the wings, tail and forward section at Turin, along with three complete two-seat prototypes. The VAK 191B programme began well, but NATO thinking altered and there was a shift towards the use of a VTOL strike fighter equipped with conventional weapons. The aircraft had been designed to operate from an improvised site and undertake a single mission at low altitude, with no guarantee of returning to base. Now all that had changed and NATO required flexibility and repeated missions, calling for a totally different warplane. It was becoming clear that the VAK 191B was unsuitable and Fiat dropped plans to build the two-seat aircraft.

The West German VTOL design would be used as a purely experimental aircraft to develop technologies for future projects. In February 1967, Fiat largely pulled out of the programme, diverting funds to the development of an advanced twin-engined version of the Fiat G.91, known as the G.91Y. The first production version of this design would enter service with the *Aeronautica Militare Italiana* in 1970. It is hard to say exactly when work on the Fiat G.95/4 ended, as there are reports indicating that low-level studies were still taking place in 1968. Nevertheless, by this time, the focus of attention had shifted to the NATO Multi-Role Combat Aircraft (MRCA) project, that would eventually lead to the Panavia Tornado.

French VTOL Flat Risers

French interest in VTOL combat aircraft pre-dated NBMR-3 by many years, although the C.450 Coléoptère project failed to generate official support and the SNECMA VTOL programme ended when its C.450 prototype crashed. But the VTOL strike fighter concept was far from dead and in September 1960 the government encouraged Dassault and Sud Aviation to begin a joint project to develop a supersonic flat riser, based on the Mirage III fighter. This quickly led to a proposal using a modified wing from a Mirage III prototype and a fuselage designed by Sud Aviation. Official approval was granted on 2 February 1961 and the aircraft was given the name Balzac V. This was not taken from the famous French playwright and novelist Honoré de Balzac, but the telephone number (BALZAC 001) of a well-known Paris movie agency (Publicité Jean Mineur), as the prototype had been assigned the reference 001. The V stood for VTOL. If tests involving the Balzac V progressed well, it was planned to build one or two prototypes of a larger VTOL design known as the Mirage IIIV (3V).

The Balzac would be equipped with eight lift engines vertically positioned in the fuselage and a single engine for horizontal flight. The more advanced Mirage IIIV would be fitted with eight Rolls-Royce RB.162-1 lift engines, but these would not be available until 1963, so a decision was taken to use eight Rolls-Royce RB.108-1A lift turbojets, each providing 2,160lb (9.6kN) of thrust. Four dorsal intakes supplied air to these engines, with

covers that closed over the inlets and exhausts during horizontal flight to reduce drag. Furthermore, in the event of a single engine failure, the diagonally opposite turbojet would be throttled back to ensure some degree of stability. The lift engines were located in pairs alongside the main engine's duct and around the aircraft's centre of gravity.

A later modification to the lift system would see the use of a door below each engine, which was designed to act as an exhaust deflector to aid extremely short horizontal take-offs. Approximately 11% of the lift engine's thrust was bled off to supply the Balzac's low-speed reaction control system, with air being ducted to the nose, tail and wingtips. The Mirage would normally be equipped with a SNECMA Atar turbojet, but, in view of the space occupied by the lift engines, it was decided to install a single, non-afterburning Bristol Siddeley Orpheus BOr 3 Cruise turbojet, which provided 4,850lb (21.57kN) of thrust. The complex internal arrangement of engines also meant that there was no possibility of applying the area rule to the fuselage so, with the engine's limited thrust-to-weight ratio, it would be restricted to subsonic speeds. On the other hand, this was hardly an important consideration for an experimental VTOL aircraft.

Furthermore, there were limitations on endurance, with the six fuel tanks holding a total of 362 (UK) gallons (1,650 litres), which allowed no more than 12 minutes of flight with all nine engines in operation. The

BELOW The experimental Dassault Balzac V-001 at the start of the test programme. *Dassault Aviation*

RIGHT The Dassault Balzac V hovering above the runway in an early untethered test flight. *Dassault Aviation*

LEFT The Dassault Balzac V seen on a snow-covered runway during STOL trials. Note the deflector flaps fitted to the lift engine exhaust ports. *Dassault Aviation*

RIGHT The Balzac V, with undercarriage fully retracted and lift engines still operational, makes the transition to level flight. *Dassault Aviation*

ABOVE The Balzac V after crashing at the *Centre d'Essais en Vol*, Melun-Villaroche, on 10 January 1964. Test pilot Jacques Pinier was killed in the accident, although the aircraft was repaired and continued flying. *Armée de l'Air*

BELOW USAF test pilot and VTOL expert Major Phil Neale, who was tragically killed in the second Balzac V accident. The aircraft was totally destroyed on this occasion. *USAF*

airframe was mainly constructed from aluminium alloy and utilised elevons and a rudder for normal flight. The forward-positioned pressurised cockpit provided the pilot with good visibility and the aircraft was fitted with a fully retractable tricycle undercarriage. As an experimental aircraft, the Balzac carried no weapons.

On 12 October 1962, test pilot René Bigand made the first of two tethered hover flights at Melun-Villaroche. This was followed, on 18 October 1962, by the aircraft's first untethered hovering flight and, eventually, the first conventional flight on 1 March 1963. A couple of weeks later the Balzac made a transition from vertical lift-off to horizontal flight and a full cycle, including vertical landing, took place on 29 March 1963. Aside from limited endurance, the project was progressing well and Balzac V was demonstrated to the public at the Paris Air Show in June 1963, performing flawlessly. However, all this changed on the 125th test flight at the *Centre d'Essais en Vol*, Melun-Villaroche, on 10 January 1964. Test pilot Jacques Pinier was hovering in the aircraft at an altitude of about 329ft (100m) when there was a sudden loss of control and Balzac V rolled over. The port wing struck the ground and the aircraft overturned. There was a brief fire, brought under control by an emergency response team, but the pilot was killed in the accident.

Apparently, he said nothing during the rapid descent and made no attempt to eject. A subsequent inquiry decided that the pilot had turned the aircraft into a crosswind to reduce the effect of drift. This had led to loss of control when the three-axis auto-stabilisation system's limits were exceeded. Although the Balzac V appeared to be a write-off, the examining engineers found that most of the airframe was intact and all the engines were fully functional. As a result of this, it was decided to restore the aircraft and resume test flights. Whether or not there was any political pressure to continue with the project is unknown.

On 2 February 1965, the Balzac V resumed test flying. The USAF was now taking a serious interest in the Mirage VTOL project and had sent a four-man evaluation team to appraise the programme. Things proceeded well, until 8 September 1965, when the Balzac V crashed for a second time with tragic consequences for the pilot. Hovering at low altitude, there was a sudden loss of engine power and USAF test pilot Major Phil Neale (1930–1965) made an unsuccessful low-level ejection. Seconds later, the aircraft smashed into the ground and was destroyed. This might have ended the project, but the Balzac V had set the stage for the larger more powerful Mirage IIIV, which was closer to a production aircraft and already undergoing trials. The Mirage IIIV was always going to be a costly and challenging aircraft to develop and Dassault had started looking for co-operation and financial assistance from overseas contractors in early 1961. This initially led to a meeting between company officials from Dassault and the British Aircraft Corporation (BAC), which took place on 27 October 1961. It resulted in the RAF and Royal Navy expressing considerable interest in the proposed French VTOL strike fighter. Unfortunately for the French, there was already a British VTOL combat aircraft in development and the UK government favoured this design over the Mirage.

Dassault then approached Boeing with the offer of a technology transfer deal and both companies signed an agreement on 23 December 1961. Boeing's main interest was VTOL stabilisation systems, but it agreed to assist Dassault with a submission for NBMR-3. The US contractor was also obliged to involve the Pentagon in this arrangement, which generated considerable interest in upper USAF circles. Eventually, the USAF began to seriously consider buying three Boeing-assembled two-seat Mirage IIIV aircraft for flight-testing. And after prolonged debate the deal almost came together in May 1964, but was put on indefinite hold at the last minute and ultimately never happened.

There was also an attempt to involve the West Germans with development of the Mirage IIIV and a provisional agreement was reached for them to take three prototypes in 1963. This came down to two aircraft, but the proposal was finally abandoned during the following year. Design work for the Mirage IIIV started on 29 August 1961, with Dassault and Sud Aviation receiving official contracts to build two prototypes. The new aircraft would be much larger and heavier than the Balzac V, with numerous design changes such as a more robust undercarriage. The Mirage III airframe was adapted to house eight Rolls-Royce RB.162-31 lift turbojets, each providing 4,409lb (19.61kN) of thrust. In an attempt to reduce weight as far as possible, these engines were fitted with fibreglass casings and used plastics in certain areas. For horizontal propulsion, the Mirage IIIV was to be fitted with a single afterburning SNECMA TF 104B turbofan (a modified Pratt & Whitney JTF10), producing a maximum thrust of 13,668lb (60.8kN).

But the newly designed SNECMA TF 104B proved troublesome and continued to undergo evaluation in a specially modified Mirage IIIC, renamed the Mirage IIIT. Subsequently, a decision would be taken after a

few test flights in the Mirage IIIV to replace the engine with a more powerful TF 106. This was another relatively new P&W design, which also suffered with problems. It virtually goes without saying that an air-bleed reaction control system was used for low-speed flight. In normal flight, the aircraft used similar control surfaces to those employed on the conventional Mirages. Armament was also considered for a possible production aircraft and this would comprise two 30mm DEFA cannon, each with 125 rounds. In addition, there would be a centrally located weapons bay, with a payload limit of 1,200lb (544kg). This would allow the carriage of two air-to-air missiles, one tactical nuclear weapon or a reconnaissance pack.

The first free-hovering test flight of Mirage IIIV-01 was undertaken by René Bigand on 12 February 1965 at Melun-Villaroche. Various issues arose that included problems with the TF 104B turbofan and a realisation that the lift engines were not producing sufficient thrust. Further test flights were undertaken, with the TF 104B finally being replaced by the supposedly superior TF 106 and the aircraft was ready for its 15th test flight in December 1965. Unfortunately, there was dwindling official support for the project. The second Balzac V crash had generated widespread negative feelings and the idea of developing an operational VTOL strike fighter seemed increasingly unrealistic. There were serious concerns about payload, range and performance, the main engine continued to be troublesome, the lift engines were considered underpowered and frequent problems arose with exhaust re-ingestion and debris being sucked into the engines during VTOL, causing damage and stalls.

Clearly the project was in serious difficulty and things became worse on 24 March 1966, when test pilot Jean-Marie Saget made the first complete transition flight and experienced fairly serious instability. As an immediate consequence, the project was temporarily halted, although Mirage IIIV-01 would soon make a runway take-off without the lift engines and reach a level speed of Mach 1.35. By spring 1966, Mirage IIIV-02 had been completed and this aircraft was equipped with a new afterburning SNECMA TF 306C turbofan providing a further increase in performance. There were various other modifications and minor improvements, such as newly designed lift

engine intakes. The second Mirage IIIV took to the air on 22 June 1966, flown by Jean-Marie Saget, and on 12 September 1966 the aircraft attained Mach 2.03 in level flight. This remains a record for any VTOL aircraft. Both prototypes continued to fly at Istres and Melun-Villaroche until 28 November 1966, when senior test pilot Bernard Ziegler (1933–) took to the air at Istres in the second Mirage. He found the aircraft impossible to control and ejected, with the Mirage smashing into the ground and catching fire. It was totally destroyed and as a direct consequence the French government decided it was time to close the project. In fact, this was almost the opportunity they had been waiting for, as it was clear that this very expensive programme would be going nowhere.

The Balzac V completed 179 flights, the Mirage IIIV-01 made 40 flights and the Mirage IIIV-02 undertook 24 flights. This VTOL project was simply a step in the wrong direction. The use of eight lift engines created a serious weight penalty and introduced significant maintenance and reliability issues. Fuel consumption was prohibitive, placing serious restrictions on hover time, possible combat range and payload. Furthermore, there seemed little scope to improve this situation in future versions. Many lessons were learned from the Mirage VTOL programme and various technical spin-offs found their way into future designs, but in overall terms this was a dead-end project that killed two pilots and cost a small fortune. Mirage IIIV-01 was eventually passed to the Musée de l'Air et de l'Espace at Le Bourget, where it is currently on display.

LEFT The first Mirage IIIV prototype hovers above the airfield with its lift engine air-intake doors raised. *Dassault Aviation*

RIGHT The first Mirage IIIV prototype VTOL strike fighter stands on the runway while preparations are made for a test flight. *Dassault Aviation*

BELOW The second Mirage IIIV hovers above the runway. There were various minor differences between this aircraft and the first prototype. Noticeable in this photograph are the changes to the air-inlet doors for the lift engines. *Dassault Aviation*

Double Deltas

Designed as a competitor for the anticipated VTOL Mirage project, Sud Aviation's X-600 was submitted for official approval in late 1959. The concept was broadly similar to the Mirage III, but utilised a double-delta wing similar in design to that of the Saab J 35 Draken. The X-600 was roughly midway in size and weight between the Balzac V and the Mirage IIIV and the intention was to power it in horizontal flight with an engine in the class of a Rolls-Royce/MAN RB.153-61 turbofan producing 6,850lb of thrust (30.5kN) and 11,750lb (52.3kN) with the afterburner. This was expected to provide a maximum speed of Mach 2 at altitude. There would be six centrally located engines for VTOL operations and the preferred choice was RB.162-31 turbojets, each producing 4,409lb (19.61kN) of thrust. Sud Aviation suggested a development period of seven years for this aircraft, which seems rather lengthy for the era. Perhaps this delay contributed to the Mirage VTOL programme being given the green light?

Two other British designs appear to be either connected with, or inspired by, the Saab Draken. In 1961, Geoffrey Light Wilde (1917-2007), who headed the Advanced Projects Design Office at Rolls-Royce in Derby, disclosed details of a strike fighter proposal he was working on. Wilde had been interested in VTOL aircraft for some time and his double-delta proposal was similar in many ways to the X-600 and much like a VTOL Draken in appearance. The fighter utilised four central lift engines and this configuration was apparently based on research provided by the experimental Short SC.1, which is discussed later in this chapter.

The Rolls-Royce VTOL strike fighter would be capable of high subsonic speed at sea level and supersonic speed at altitude. Wilde also anticipated an ability to carry a military payload that equalled approximately 10% of the aircraft's gross weight. The single afterburning cruise engine would be similar in specification to that chosen for the X-600, while the four unspecified lift engines were each expected to provide about 6,000lb (26.6kN) of thrust. The other British design for a VTOL double delta was produced by Hawker at Kingston-upon-Thames in 1957. This differed considerably from the other two proposals and was probably a little larger. Assigned the company reference P.1126, it was to be powered by two Bristol Siddeley Orpheus BOr 3 cruise turbojets, providing 4,850lb (21.57kN) of dry thrust. In addition, there would be two separate units containing a total of twelve Rolls-Royce RB.108-1A turbojets, each producing 2,160lb (9.6kN) of thrust. During VTOL and transition, upper doors would open and the turbojets would be turned downwards into an upright position, providing lift. It appears that the P.1126 was never intended to have supersonic performance.

BELOW Three VTOL strike fighter proposals that seem to have been strongly influenced or inspired by the Saab J 35 Draken:

LEFT: The Sud Aviation X-600 using six vertically mounted lift jets.

CENTRE: A proposal from Rolls-Royce, which would use four lift engines.

RIGHT: The Hawker P.1126, equipped with 12 extra engines mounted on two panels that would swing downwards into a vertical position to facilitate VTOL. All three drawings are closely based on available illustrations and information, but may not be exactly to scale. *All: Bill Rose*

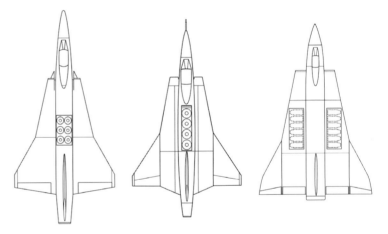

English Electric (Later BAC) VTOL Strike Fighter

In 1960, English Electric designers Frank Willcox and Gerald Walley began work on a VTOL combat aircraft that appears to have been intended to directly rival work taking place in France and also as a proposal for NATO's NBMR-3. This single-seat aircraft would have been similar in size to the Mirage 111V, although its centrally positioned wing was not a true delta, with clipped wingtips. A single, centrally positioned afterburning turbojet would provide propulsion for normal flight, plus eight separate lift engines for VTOL, probably envisaged as Rolls-Royce RB.162-31 turbojets, each producing 4,409lb (19.61kN) of thrust. These would be vertical during VTOL and swivel to a dormant position, in-line with the fuselage during horizontal flight. Low-speed handling, up to the point of transition, would involve the use of an air-bleed reaction control system, and large elevons and a tail rudder would be used during normal flight. In addition to VTOL operations from improvised sites, this aircraft would be fitted with a conventional tricycle undercarriage for horizontal runway take-offs and landings. The aircraft would be capable of high subsonic speed at low level and supersonic speeds at altitude. Weapons would be carried in a ventral bay, undoubtedly with space for a tactical nuclear weapon, air-to-air missiles or a reconnaissance camera pack. It also seems likely that additional stores might have been carried beneath the wings if required.

Several versions of this design were produced that included a high-performance STOL variant, using fewer engines and blown flaps. Some details of English Electric's VTOL strike fighter design can be found in UK

Patent 993731, applied for in January 1962 by the British Aircraft Corporation, which had then officially replaced the company. It is unclear if development progressed much further than the drawing board but the project failed to generate any lasting interest and was soon forgotten.

LEFT An English Electric/BAC design produced in 1962 for a strike fighter with VTOL capability in roughly the same class as the Mirage IIIV. *British Aerospace*

RIGHT One of several designs produced by English Electric/BAC in the early 1960s for VTOL/STOL strike fighters, this proposal used four forward-positioned lift engines to allow very short take-offs, although would not have been capable of VTOL. *British Aerospace*

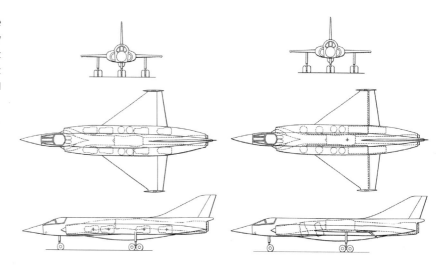

Rolls-Royce and Short Brothers

At the start of the 1950s, Rolls-Royce began work on a VTOL test platform known as the Thrust Measuring Rig (TMR), which was conceived by the jet engine pioneer Dr Alan Arnold Griffith (1893-1963). The TMR's purpose was to explore VTOL and hover. Two Rolls-Royce Nene turbojets would power this manned machine, with combined exhausts ducted downwards at the platform's centre. Stabilising the TMR was a reaction control system, generally referred to as puffers, using air bleed from the compressor stages of the engines. Approval to proceed with the project was granted and the first (of two) TMRs was completed in 1953, with the appearance of this metal framework on legs carrying two engines soon leading to it being called the Flying Bedstead (Serial No: XJ314). The first tethered flight took place on 3 July 1953 at Hucknall Aerodrome, Nottinghamshire, and the TMR undertook its first manned free flight on 3 August 1954, flown by the company's chief test pilot Ronald Thomas Shepherd OBE (1896-1955). Controlling the TMR was always difficult, partly due to the throttle lag of the Nene engines, which provided a total thrust of about 8,100lb (36kN) of which approximately 8% was diverted to the puffers. With a loaded weight of 7,500lb (3,401kg) that included 1,385lb (628kg) of fuel, this was enough to keep the TMR airborne for a maximum of about 11 minutes.

In July 1956, XJ314 was transported to the RAE at Bedford for further testing, where it crashed on 16 September 1957, killing the pilot. Soon after this, the second TMR (XK416) made its first flight at Hucknall Aerodrome, only to crash a few days later. Subsequently, some of the parts from this rig were used to rebuild the XJ314, although it soon became a museum exhibit. In the meantime, Griffith had been responsible for development of the very compact Rolls-Royce RB.108 turbojet and in September 1953 the MoS issued a

request (ER.143T) to various contractors for an experimental VTOL aircraft powered by these lift engines (that had yet to be bench tested). Two prototypes were required for use by the RAE, primarily for the development of new VTOL control systems. Short Brothers at Belfast was one of the companies that responded. Its proposal was judged the best and a contract was issued on 15 October 1954. Much of the initial development was undertaken by the company's chief designer David Keith-Lucas (1911-1997). The VTOL design was given the company reference PD.11, but then redesignated as SC.1, with the official serials XG900 and XG905 being issued for both prototypes.

The SC.1 was a compact tailless delta, fitted with four centrally located RB.108 lift engines positioned vertically and able to swivel. A fifth horizontal RB.108 turbojet would be used for normal flight and all engines were connected to an air-bleed system providing reaction control at the nose, tail and wingtips. In horizontal flight the lift engines would

LEFT The Rolls-Royce Thrust Measuring Rig (TMR), better known to most people as the Flying Bedstead. It was first tested on 3 July 1953 at Hucknall Aerodrome, Nottinghamshire, by the company's chief test pilot Ronald Thomas Shepherd OBE. Rolls-Royce

BELOW Cutaway drawing showing the interior detail of the Short SC.1 experimental VTOL aircraft. *Short Brothers*

TOP LEFT The Short SC.1 during hover trials. *Short Brothers*

TOP RIGHT The Short SC.1 demonstrates its VTOL capability. *Short Brothers*

RIGHT Hanging almost motionless above the runway, the Short SC.1 during VTOL trials. *Short Brothers*

be shut down, with compressor air from the horizontal engine being used to restart the four vertical turbojets.

Because the SC.1 was intended for relatively low-speed testing, the tricycle undercarriage was fixed in position to reduce weight and mechanical complexity.

The overall length was 30ft (9.14m), with a wingspan of 23.5ft (7.16m) and a wing area of 211.5ft^2 (19.64m^2), so the SC.1 was a very compact machine with what might be described as an integral forward cockpit, providing an excellent view for the pilot. Most of the aircraft was built from aluminium alloy, apart from some sections of the engine bays made from titanium. Maximum VTO take-off weight was 7,800lb (3,538kg), with the four lift engines providing 8,520lb (37.9kN) of thrust. In level flight, the maximum speed was relatively pedestrian, but the SC.1 was a VTOL test-bed and high performance was never a consideration. The first SC.1 (XG900) was completed in November 1956, although it lacked the lift engines and was fitted with only a single horizontal RB.108. Taxiing trials began at Belfast in December 1956. The aircraft was then transported (partly by sea) to Boscombe Down, where the first conventional flight was made on 2 April 1957 by company test pilot Tom Brooke-Smith. Apparently, the SC.1 proved more difficult to handle than expected.

The second SC.1 (XG905) was ready for testing in May 1958, by which time the project had become public

knowledge. Four Roll-Royce RB.108 lift engines were installed in the aircraft and hovering tests were under way at Belfast. With the aircraft tethered to a substantial gantry, the first piloted jet lift was completed on 26 May 1958. These tests continued without any major problems and the first untethered hover took place on 25 October 1958. By the following year XG905 had undergone a number of engineering modifications and was moved to RAE Bedford. The main concern for the VTOL lift system was ingestion of hot exhaust gas and debris, although the high rate of fuel consumption (when running all five engines) and the pilot's workload were also serious issues.

After initial trials at Boscombe Down were completed, XG900 was returned to Belfast, where installation of the lift engines and a number of minor modifications took place. By the start of summer 1960 it was ready to resume testing, with upgraded undercarriage shock absorbers and new automatic engine covers. XG905 had completed its first successful transition on 6 April 1960 and was demonstrated at the Farnborough Air Show by Tom Brooke-Smith. The following year the SC.1 was flown across the Channel to appear at the Paris Air Show. The first prototype was now moved to RAE Bedford, while the second SC.1 returned to the workshops at Belfast, where it received a new auto-stabilisation system. Former RAE test pilot J. R. Green joined Shorts in August 1963 and one of his initial tasks was to evaluate the auto-stabilisation system fitted to XG905. On 2 October 1963, he lost control of the aircraft above the Belfast airfield and XG905 plunged to the ground from a height of about 30ft (9.1m). Green was killed in the crash, although the SC.1 was found to be repairable and a decision was taken to keep the aircraft in service. Various improvements were made to the control systems, with flights resuming in 1966. These trials continued until 1971, when the project officially ended. XG900 would eventually become part of the London Science Museum's aircraft collection and XG905 was presented to the Ulster Folk & Transport Museum in Northern Ireland.

Advanced Belfast Designs

Before trials of the first SC.1 began, designers working at Short Brothers were already considering the possibility of utilising the VTOL engine technology for future civil and military aircraft, in particular an advanced combat aircraft that might enter service in the late 1960s. This aircraft would be powered by at least four lift engines and one or two turbojets for horizontal flight. The overall propulsion system was similar in concept to that of the SC.1. Possible applications included a multi-role fighter, or an interdictor, equipped with small wings to improve high-speed handling at low altitude. The suitability of a flat riser for operations from a smaller warship or merchant ship was also obvious from the outset.

The initial proposal was a relatively lightweight single-seat strike fighter, clearly derived from the SC.1. Four centrally positioned engines provided lift and two horizontal turbojets (probably non-afterburning) in the rear fuselage propelled the aircraft in normal flight. These were fed by inlets on the forward inner wing section. Short stubby wings were moved well back, with a single tail fin. In common with the VAK 191B, this formula would probably have led to an inability to take-off safely and land horizontally. The accepted system of compressor-bleed air would have been used for low-speed control, with elevons and a rudder for normal flight. The forward-positioned cockpit would afford good visibility and a tricycle undercarriage was intended. There is no way of knowing what kind of armament this aircraft was expected to carry and the options would be very limited. However, as the SC.1 project progressed, there was increased concern about range, payload and performance, leading to a significant re-evaluation of propulsion systems intended for future concepts. The designers and engineers now reappraised their strike fighter concept, producing a revised concept fitted with swivelling engines in underwing nacelles for VTOL and horizontal flight. In addition, this aircraft would be fitted with two vertically positioned turbojets just behind the cockpit to balance the lift system and two turbojets in the rear fuselage for horizontal flight. These would be fed from a dorsal air intake just ahead of the tail fin and equipped with a downward vectoring exhaust system for use during VTOL operations.

A further Shorts design for a lightweight VTOL strike fighter moved even further from the original concept. This was a sleek-looking canard, with a forward-positioned cockpit, a sharply swept wing with swivelling engine nacelles at the tips and a single swept tail fin. Two engines would be positioned vertically behind the cockpit and an additional turbojet in the rear fuselage was omitted. A conventional tricycle undercarriage was fitted, allowing normal runway take-

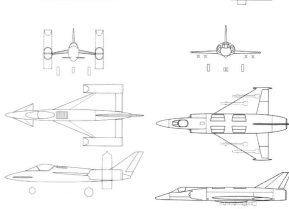

LEFT This early design for a VTOL strike fighter was directly based on the Short SC.1, using four centrally located lift engines. *Bill Rose*

RIGHT A second proposal for a lightweight VTOL strike fighter produced by designers working at Shorts. This design features engines in underwing nacelles that swivel into an upright position for VTOL operations. *Bill Rose*

LEFT A third Short VTOL strike fighter design with a completely revised canard configuration and further alterations to the propulsion layout. *Bill Rose*

RIGHT The Short PD.56 strike fighter configured as an interceptor, with four underwing AIM-9 Sidewinder missiles. *Bill Rose*

offs and landings, and this aircraft was probably expected to have supersonic performance when fitted with suitable engines. It was not possible to determine the exact company references for these studies at the time of writing, although none progressed much further than initial evaluation.

By the early 1960s, external developments led the designers to turn their attention towards a rival for the French VTOL Mirage. The company's new chief project designer Frank H. Robertson was largely responsible for this study, which received the company designation PD.56. This was in the same general class as the Dassault Mirage IIIV and it would utilise eight RB.162 engines for lift and an afterburning Rolls-Royce RB.168 engine for normal flight. It was expected to achieve high subsonic speed at low level and supersonic speed at medium altitudes. The strike-fighter would be capable of high altitude interception, provisionally armed with four underwing Sidewinder AAMs, or alternatively, the delivery of a single tactical nuclear weapon and there would be the further option of reconnaissance missions. A fully retractable tricycle undercarriage was fitted, allowing conventional take-offs and landings. A two-seat version may have been considered and some wind tunnel testing of models is thought to have been undertaken. PD.56 was submitted to NATO as a contender for NBMR-3, but generated less interest than the Mirage and progressed no further.

Lockheed Projects

Lockheed produced hundreds of different designs for VTOL fighter aircraft from the late 1940s onwards. With substantial budgets and research facilities available, there was rapid progress from turboprop-powered tailsitters to concepts for supersonic VATOL strike fighters. However, by the mid-1950s official interest in tailsitters was rapidly declining as the many disadvantages became increasingly apparent. Lockheed had already explored the idea of converting its most advanced supersonic fighter to a VATOL design (CL-295) and began to investigate the possibility of using the same approach to develop an effective flat-rising fighter. Kelly Johnson, who headed Lockheed's Skunk Works, was primarily responsible for designing the F-104 fighter and he would continue to promote the adaptation and development of this aircraft for new roles throughout its life. A VTOL fighter based on the F-104 had a number of commercial advantages, such as a shorter development period, the use of many proven systems and a reduction of manufacturing costs.

The first identifiable study for a single-seat horizontal VTOL multi-role version of the F-104G was given the company reference CL-521-1. The exact date for this design series is unclear, but somewhere in the region of 1958-1960 seems reasonable and it was directly aimed at the European market. The basic F-104G airframe would remain largely unchanged, with an afterburning General Electric J79-GE-11A turbojet providing propulsion for normal flight.

The visible difference between the CL-521-1 and F-104G would be the large wingtip pods, each housing four vertically positioned lift engines. Some sources indicate that Rolls-Royce RB.108 turbojets were initially considered, which might have been modified and built under licence by Continental. Fuel would also be carried in the pod, which was fairly substantial in size, with a

suggested length of 26.75ft (8.15m). It would be possible to transfer this fuel to the fuselage for main engine use and vice versa and the engine pods would be easily removable, returning the aircraft to its earlier non-VTOL form and allowing the carriage of wingtip fuel tanks or missiles. Lockheed suggested that this particular design would be cost-effective to develop, with the advantage of easy access for inspection, maintenance and repair.

CL-521-1 would be able to operate from conventional runways when VTOL was judged unnecessary or to increase range/payload, although carriage of the engine pods would create a significant drop in performance, lowering the maximum speed to about Mach 1.4 at best, with a combat radius of 287 miles (460km). It remains unknown if there were any further designs for a VTOL Starfighter in this particular series, but there were similar proposals that appeared rather confusingly in separate design programmes.

Another attempt to adapt the F-104G for VTOL operations is listed as CL-704 and it seems that many of Lockheed's designations were assigned in a fairly random manner. Available detail suggests this particular concept was intended for NATO reconnaissance missions from improvised sites in Europe, with a secondary strike capability. It seems that there were another 34 numbers assigned to the CL-704 studies, but the documentation no longer exists at Lockheed-Martin. In all probability, each reference showed little more than engineering variations to the original design. The propulsion system appears to be identical to the CL-521-1, with a General Electric J79-GE-11A turbojet used for level flight and eight lift jets in the wingtip pods. Range, maximum speed and weight all seem similar, although, like the RF-104G, three KS-67A cameras would have replaced the internal cannon located in the forward fuselage.

BELOW LEFT One of many proposals to adapt the Lockheed F-104 Starfighter into a VTOL strike fighter, primarily for European operations. This proposal, with the company reference CL-802-12, would use no fewer than 12 lift engines. *Pete Clukey Lockheed Martin/Restoration by Bill Rose*

CENTRE The Lockheed CL-802-7 was a heavy VTOL fighter design with a fairly conventional appearance, equipped with an internal weapons bay and four underwing hardpoints for stores. *Lockheed Martin*

RIGHT This Lockheed VTOL canard design was given the company reference CL-802-14-3 and would have been equipped with ten lift engines and two larger afterburning cruise turbojets in tail-mounted nacelles. Weapons would be carried internally or underwing. *Pete Clukey Lockheed Martin*

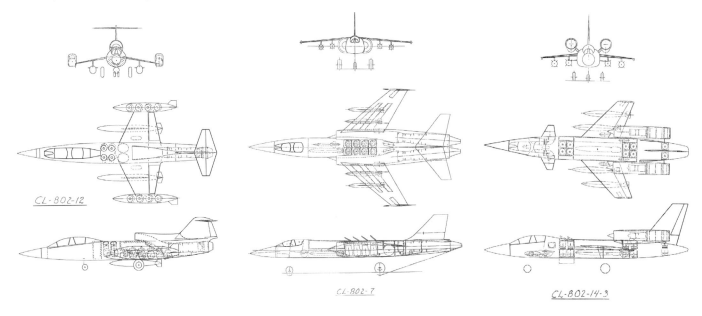

CL-802-12

CL-802-7

CL-802-14-3

Yet another proposed VTOL development of the Starfighter was the CL-802-12, which would be configured for a variety of roles, including close-support, light observation and high-priority cargo transport. The two-seat CL-802-12 starts to differ considerably from the F-104, with changes to the propulsion system. Although this aircraft retains the same overall length as the F-104G/TF104G, the General Electric J79-GE-11A is now moved further rearward, minus the afterburner. A total of 12 Continental Model 365 lift engines, each rated at 4,000lb (17.79kN) thrust, would be used, with four in each wingtip pod and a further pack of four positioned directly behind the second crew member. This revision meant that the air inlets on each side of the fuselage were removed and replaced by a single large dorsal intake, with its opening close to the middle of the aircraft. In keeping with all the other VTOL Starfighters, this proposal would retain a fully retractable undercarriage, allowing normal runway operations. Many other designs were considered for the CL-802 series, but most differed considerably from this one and were to all intents and purposes unconnected.

The CL-802-12 would have been unable to match the performance of any previously described VTOL Starfighters and its maximum speed would have been Mach 1 or less. It is also probable that all these VTOL designs using wingtip pods would have required some strengthening. There is no indication in remaining documents if any of these proposals were built as models and no evidence to show if experimental engine pods were ever tested on an aircraft.

Two further concepts from the extensive CL-802 series of studies would deviate considerably from the earlier Starfighter-based designs. CL-802-7 proposed a slightly larger combat aircraft with a relatively conventional appearance, powered by two advanced, unspecified afterburning turbofans and eight centrally located lift engines. This aircraft would be equipped with a fully retractable tricycle undercarriage. It carried a crew of two and there would be an internal weapons bay and provision for underwing stores. Maximum speed in level flight would be in excess of Mach 2. A canard version of this design with the Lockheed reference CL-802-14-3-2 utilised a somewhat different engine layout, with the two main engines housed in nacelles attached to the rear fuselage. Ten Continental lift engines were envisaged, with four located just behind the cockpit area, another four in the fuselage section just behind the main wing's trailing edge and a further two towards the tail of the aircraft. This design would be flown by a crew of two, with a maximum speed of Mach 2 available in level flight. The aircraft would be equipped with a tricycle undercarriage and capable of conventional runway take-offs and landings. CL-802-14-3-2 was expected to be equipped with a rotary cannon,

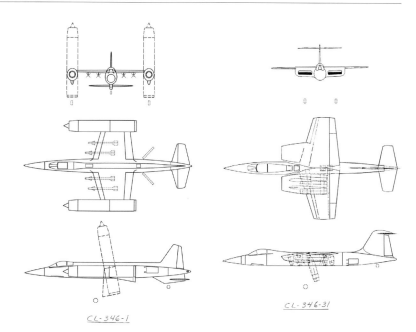

CL-346-1

CL-346-31

with other weapons carried internally or beneath the wings. Many interrelated Lockheed VTOL combat aircraft designs were produced during the late 1950s and early 1960s. One concept for a nuclear strike and air defence aircraft has the company reference CL-346-1. Its fuselage has some similarities to a Starfighter, but without an engine. In this study, afterburning J79 engines were contained in wingtip nacelles.

These would swivel downwards for VTOL operations and this was made possible by raising the front of the aircraft with two forward-positioned long struts with wheels, while the rear of the fuselage rested on a tailwheel. This design has the look of an aircraft intended to undertake STOL rather than VTOL and it is unclear how the designers hoped to stabilise the aircraft efficiently at low speeds. Nevertheless, the CL-346-1 was expected to be capable of reaching Mach 2 and a maximum altitude of 60,000ft (18,288m). For interception, the aircraft could carry four Sidewinder missiles beneath the wings and, for a tactical nuclear strike, a single bomb beneath the fuselage. This design was later revised with a different propulsion system housed within the inner wing section, with swivelling units and four additional lift engines in the fuselage. A Starfighter tailplane arrangement was fitted along with the long front undercarriage struts and tailwheel to provide adequate exhaust clearance during take-off. This concept received the company reference CL-346-31, but little is known about the other designs in this series.

Lockheed also investigated the possibility of a VTOL heavy fighter/light bomber under project number CL-407. Many designs were reviewed for this series, but CL-407-37/40 was a canard delta with powerful afterburning engines in the rear fuselage capable of swivelling for VTOL. These would have been balanced by three lift jets located immediately behind the

LEFT This Lockheed design for a supersonic VTOL fighter was given the company reference CL-346-1. The unusual undercarriage was necessary to allow sufficient exhaust clearance for the swivelling engines. *Bill Rose*

RIGHT Similar to other designs in the same series, the Lockheed CL-346-31 would be fitted with a different wing and revised engine layout. *Pete Clukey Lockheed Martin*

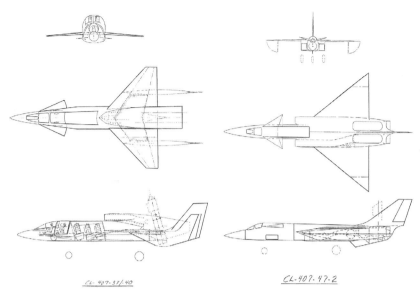

CL-407-37/.40

CL-407-47-2

LEFT This Lockheed two-seat, canard strike fighter has the reference CL-407-37/40. The main engines would tilt backwards during VTOL, balanced by three lift engines behind the cockpit area. *Pete Clukey Lockheed Martin*

RIGHT The Lockheed CL-407-47-2 was designed as a VTOL strike fighter with a canard configuration and delta wing. Like other concepts in the CL-407 series, the main engines would swivel backwards during VTOL. *Pete Clukey Lockheed Martin*

cockpit. The anticipated performance for some designs in this series was as high as Mach 3 in level flight, with a ceiling of 70,000ft (21,336m).

Lockheed's CL-706 began as a one-man shipboard multi-role combat aircraft that evolved into an all-weather VTOL close-support aircraft with USAF and US Marine Corps applications. Few documents relating to this large study undertaken between January 1962 and May 1963 have survived. However, there are some details of Model CL-706-13, which was a proposal for a heavily armed VTOL combat aircraft. It would have been equipped with 10 vertically positioned Continental lift engines. Four would be located in a forward fuselage section and three in each wingtip nacelle. In addition, the aircraft would be propelled in level flight by two afterburning turbofans, providing a high subsonic performance. The aircraft would be equipped with a

rotary cannon and capable of carrying free-fall bombs, rockets and air-to-surface missiles. CL-706 would be 50ft (15.24m) in length, with a wingspan of 27.5ft (8.38m) and a wing area of 250ft^2 (23.2m^2). Gross weight was expected to be in the region of 32,000lb (14,500kg).

Lockheed followed these studies with the construction of an experimental VTOL test rig that was jointly funded by Lockheed and the USAF and assigned the company reference CL-757. This vehicle was little more than an open framework with a cockpit area providing accommodation for a pilot and observer in a side-by-side arrangement. The CL-757 was 23ft (7m) in length and 32ft (9.75m) wide, with a gross weight of 7,920lb (3,592kg). Propulsion was provided by six upright J85 turbojets on each side of the craft and these engines were supplied and fitted by USAF technicians. Testing took place at Edwards AFB and exact dates were unavailable at the time of writing but are understood to have been mid-1963. In total, only 19 test flights were undertaken and initially these were tethered. The USAF test pilot undertaking some of these flights was VTOL expert Major Phil Neale, who was later assigned to the Dassault Balzac V programme in France. Apparently, there were problems with flight control, noise, vibration and exhaust re-ingestion leading to stalls. The value of this brief test programme remains unclear.

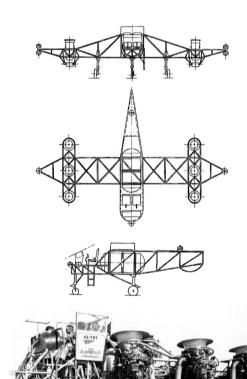

RIGHT Initial design for the multi-engined Lockheed CL-757 test rig, built and tested by Lockheed/USAF during the early 1960s. *Pete Clukey Lockheed Martin*

LEFT Primarily intended for close support, the Lockheed CL-706-13 was a subsonic VTOL concept dating from the early 1960s. *Pete Clukey Lockheed Martin*

RIGHT The Lockheed CL-757 test rig during hover trials. *USAF*

Chapter Four: Aircraft Details

Bell D-109-1
Crew: 1
Wingspan: 31.8ft (9.7m)
Wing Area: N/A
Length: 47.1ft (14.4m)
Empty Weight: N/A
Gross Weight: 19,640lb (8,912kg)
Rate of Climb (at sea level): 19,150ft/min (5,836m/min)
Ceiling: 54,400ft (16,581m)
Maximum Speed: 650mph+ at 30,000ft (1,046km/h+ at 9,144m)
Powerplant: 2 x Allison J33-A-16 turbojets, each rated at approximately 4,000lb (17.8kN) static thrust, plus 2 x solid fuel rocket boosters, rated at 6,500lb 28.9kN thrust
Armament: 4 x (unspecified calibre) cannons and underwing provision for 4,000lb (1,814kg) payload

Bell D-139
Crew: 1
Wingspan: 33.4ft (10.2m)
Wing Area: N/A
Length: 59.7ft (18.2m)
Empty Weight: N/A
Gross Weight: 20,960ft (9,507kg)
Rate of Climb (at sea level): N/A
Ceiling: N/A
Maximum Speed: 682mph (1,096km/h) at 35,000ft (10,668m)
Range: N/A
Powerplant: 1 x P&W J75 turbojet with an estimated minimum dry thrust of 17,000lb (75.6kN) and 24,000lb (106kN) with afterburner
Armament: 1 x 20mm Gatling gun

Bell D-188 (Revised D-139)
Crew: 1
Wingspan: 33ft (10m)
Wing Area: N/A
Length: 61ft (18.6m)
Empty Weight: 22,011lb (9,984kg). Production Ver: 23,021lb (10,442kg)
Gross Weight: 32,414lb (14,702kg). Production Ver: 34,164lb (15,496kg)
Maximum Speed: Mach 2.02 at altitudes above 25,000ft. Production Ver: Mach 2.2
Ceiling: 57,000ft (17,373m). Production Ver: 60,000ft (18,288m).
Range: N/A
Powerplant (Production Ver): 2 x J79-GE-X207 afterburning turbojets and nine modified J85-GE-1 turbojets for lift
Armament: 1 x 20mm Gatling gun; air-to-surface rockets, Sidewinder AAMs

Bell D-188A Configuration 2 (Provisional Military Designations: XF3L and XF-109)
Crew: 1
Wingspan: 23.66ft (7.2m)
Wing Area: 194ft² (18.02m²)
Length: 54.9ft (16.7m)
Height: 12.25ft (3.73m)
Empty Weight: 12,805lb (5,808kg)
Gross Weight: 22,670lb (10,282kg)
Maximum Speed: Mach 2.3
Combat Radius (VTOL, max weapons load): 270 miles (500km) rolling take-off greater; in-flight refuelling available
Ceiling: 60,000ft (18,000m)
Powerplant: 8 x General Electric J85-GE-5 turbojets (six afterburning); maximum static thrust per engine 2,600lb (11.56kN), with afterburning engines providing 3,850lb (17.1kN)
Armament: Guns: 2 or 4 x 20mm (0.79in) cannon. Rockets: 108 x 2.75in (70mm) rockets. Bombs: 4,000lb (1,800kg). Missiles: 4 x AIM-9 Sidewinder AAMs or 2 x Bullpup AGMs

Avro-Canada 1956 VTOL Visual Fighter
Crew: 1
Wingspan: 25.25ft (7.6m)
Wing Area: Forward 70ft² (6.5m²). Aft 145ft² (13.4m²)
Length: 50ft (15.24m)
Height: 9.75ft (2.97m)
Empty Weight: 11,250lb (5,102kg)
Gross Weight: 16,250lb (7,370kg)
Maximum Speed: Mach 1.75
Rate of Climb: 55,600ft/min (16,946m/min) at sea level
Ceiling: 62,000ft (18,897m)
Combat Radius: 115 miles (185km)
Powerplant: 4 x Bristol (Orenda manufactured) Orpheus II turbojets, each producing 5,760lb (25.6kN) static thrust
Armament: Weapons bay carrying 2-inch (50mm) rockets, or four Sidewinder AAMs

Sud Est X-115
Crew: 1
Wingspan: 22ft (6.7m)
Sweep (leading edge): 0°
Wing Area: 129ft² (12m²)
Length: 37.4ft (11.4m)
Height: 8.9ft (2.7m)
STO Weight: 8,500lb (3,860kg)
VTO Weight: 6,140lb (2,785kg)
Maximum Speed: Mach 1.6
Ceiling: 50,000ft (15,240m)
Range: N/A
Powerplant: 2 x afterburning SNECMA R.105 turbojets, with a maximum thrust of 4,000-5,000lb (17.8-22.2kN); engines would

rotate downwards by 45° during take-off and landing
Armament: Cannons, possibly two air-to-air missiles

Heinkel He 231 Flat Riser (Ver 1)
Crew: 1
Wingspan: 20.33ft (6.2m)
Wing Area: N/A
Sweep (leading edge): Main Wing: 45°; Canard: 60°
Length: 33.8ft (10.3m)
Empty Weight: 10,140lb (4,600kg)
Maximum Take-off Weight: 16,534lb (7,500kg)
Maximum Speed: Mach 2+
Ceiling: 60,000ft+ (18,288m+)
Range: N/A
Powerplant: 4 x afterburning General Electric J85-GE-5 turbojets, each producing 2,600lb (11.56kN) thrust per engine and 3,850lb (17.1kN) with afterburner
Armament: 1 x 25mm Oerlikon cannon and 2 x air-to-air missiles

Messerschmitt P 1227/VJ 101B
Crew: 1
Wingspan: 18.33ft (5.590m)
Sweep (leading edge): 60°
Wing Area: N/A
Length: 53.6ft (16.35m)
Height: 13.3ft (4.03m)
Empty Weight: N/A
Gross Weight (VTO): 15,432lb (7,000kg)
Maximum Speed: Mach 2.2
Ceiling: 65,000ft (19,812m)
Powerplant: Version 1: 4 x Rolls-Royce/MAN Turbomotoren RB.145 turbojets, producing 2,787lb (12.4kN), with afterburning, 3,650lb (16.24kN) for horizontal flight and lift using thrust diverters, plus 1 lift engine thought to be a proposed version of the RB.106. Version 2: an additional forward lift engine
Armament (proposed): 4 x AIM-9 Sidewinder AAMs

Messerschmitt XVJ 101B-002 Compact Version
Crew: 1
Wingspan: 19.1ft (5.84m)
Sweep (leading edge): 57°
Wing Area: N/A
Length: 38.5ft (11.75m)
Height: 12ft (3.75m)
Empty Weight: N/A
Gross Weight: N/A
Maximum Speed: Mach 2
Ceiling: 60,000ft (18,288m)
Range: N/A
Powerplant: 2 x Rolls-Royce/MAN Turbomotoren RB.145 turbojets, each

producing 2,787lb (12.4kN) static thrust and 3,650lb (16.24kN) with afterburner, plus 1 x lift engine
Armament (proposed): N/A

EWR VJ 101C (X-2)
Crew: 1
Wingspan: 20.2ft (6.16m)
Wing Area: 200ft^2 (18.6m^2)
Sweep (leading edge): 40°
Length: 51.5ft (15.7m)
Height: 13.5ft (4.1m)
Empty Weight: 9,127lb (4,140kg)
Maximum VTOL Take-off Weight: 13,2501b (6,010kg)
Maximum Speed: Mach 1.14
Ceiling (during testing): 33,000ft (10,000m)
Range: N/A
Powerplant: 6 x Rolls-Royce/MAN Turbomotoren RB.145 turbojets, each producing 2,787lb (12.4kN) static thrust and 3,650lb (16.24kN) with afterburner
Armament: None

EWR VJ 101D 'Dora'
Crew: 1 or 2
Length (Without Pitot): 72ft (21.9m) estimated
Wingspan: 33ft (10m) estimated
Wing Area: N/A
Wing Sweep (leading edge): 44° estimated
Empty Weight: N/A
Gross Weight: 35,000lb (15,875kg)
Maximum Speed: Mach 2+
Ceiling: 65,000ft (19,812m)
Range: 287 miles (462km)
Powerplant: 2 x Rolls-Royce/MAN Turbomotoren RB.153-61 turbofan lift/cruise engines, each producing 6,850lb (30.5kN) static thrust and 11,750lb (52.3kN) with afterburner; 5 x Rolls-Royce RB.162-31 lift engines, each producing 4,409lb (19.61kN) of thrust
Armament: 4 x air-to-air missiles, or 1 x free-fall tactical nuclear weapon.

EWR-Boeing-Fairchild AVS
Crew: 1 or 2
Wingspan: Fully Extended: N/A. Retracted: 33ft (10m)
Wing Area: N/A
Sweep (leading edge): Fully Retracted 72°
Length: 72ft (21.9m) estimated
Empty Weight: N/A
Gross Weight: 35,000lb (15,875kg)
Maximum Speed: Mach 2
Ceiling: 65,000ft (19,812m)
Range (Depending on Mission): VTOL 275 miles (442km)
Ferry Range: 2,500 miles (4,630km)
Powerplant: West German Version: 2 x Rolls-Royce/MAN Turbomotoren RB.153-61 turbofans, each producing 6,850lb (30.5kN)

thrust dry and 11,750lb (52.3kN) with afterburner. US Version: unspecified GE or P&W turbofans; 4 x Rolls-Royce/Allison XJ-99 lift engine, each providing 8,767lb (39kN) thrust
Armament: Unspecified; maximum weapons load: 16,000lb (7,257kg)

VFW VAK 191B
Crew: 1
Wingspan: 20.2ft (6.16m)
Wing Area: 134.5ft^2 (12.5m^2)
Length: 53.8ft (16.40m)
Length (without probe): 48.29ft (14.72m)
Height: 14.1ft (4.30m)
Empty Weight: 12,257lb (5,560kg)
Maximum Take-off Weight: 19,841lb (9,000kg)
Maximum Speed: 685mph (1,102km/h)
Combat Radius (production version): 246 miles (400km)
Ceiling: 49,200ft (15,000m)
Powerplant: 1 x Rolls-Royce/MAN Turbomotoren RB.193-12 lift/cruise turbofan, 10,150lb (45.14kN); 2 x Rolls-Royce RB.162-81 F 08 lift turbojet, each rated at 5,587lb (24.85kN) of thrust
Armament: None for prototype aircraft

VFW VAK 191 Mk 4
Crew: 1
Wingspan: 26.5ft (8m)
Wing Area: 279.7ft^2 (26m^2)
Length: 50ft (15.2m)
Height: 14ft (4.26m)
Empty Weight: 18,540lb (8,410kg)
Maximum VTO Weight: 29,982lb (13,600kg)
Maximum Speed: Mach 1.2 estimated
Ceiling: 50,000ft+ (15,240m+)
Unrefuelled Combat Radius (Depending on Mission): VTOL: 275 miles (442km) approx
Powerplant: 1 x Rolls-Royce/MAN Turbomotoren RB.193-30/P lift/cruise turbofan, producing 18,300lb (81.4kN) maximum thrust; 2 x Royce/Allison XJ-99 lift engine, each providing 8,767lb (39kN) thrust
Armament: 1 or 2 x 25mm cannon, AIM-9 Sidewinder AAMs, Kormoran anti-shipping missiles, Bullpup or Harm air-to-surface missiles, ground-attack rockets, free-fall bombs, tactical nuclear weapons (US Ver)

Fiat G.95/4
Crew: 1
Wingspan: 21.7ft (6.62m)
Wing Area: 151ft^2 (14m^2)
Length: 46ft (14m)
Height: 15.1ft (4.6m)
Empty Weight: 8,378lb (3,800kg)
VTO Weight: 16,000lb (7,257kg)
Maximum Speed: 750mph (1,200km/h)
Cruise Speed: 572mph (920km/h)
Maximum Speed (at altitude): Mach 1.2-1.4

Maximum Speed (sea level): Mach 0.92
Operational Ceiling: 33,000ft (10,000m)
Maximum Ceiling: 50,000ft (15,240m) estimated
Range: 280 Miles (450km)
Powerplant: Main Engines: 2 x Rolls-Royce/ MAN Turbomotoren RB.153 engines, each producing 7,000lb (31.13kN) of thrust; 4 x Rolls-Royce RB.162-31 engines, each producing 4,409lb (19.61kN) of thrust
Armament: 2 x 30mm DEFA cannons, Sidewinder AAMs, air-to-surface rockets, free-fall bombs

Fiat G.95/6
Crew: 1
Wingspan: 26.25ft (8m) estimated
Sweep (leading edge): 44.5°
Length: 59ft (18m) estimated
Empty Weight: N/A
VTO Weight: N/A
Maximum Speed: Mach 2
Ceiling: N/A
Powerplant: 2 x Rolls-Royce/MAN Turbomotoren RB.153 engines, each producing 7,000lb (31.13kN) of static thrust and 11,750lb (52.3kN) with afterburner; 6 x Rolls-Royce RB.162-31 lift engines, each producing 4,409lb (19.61kN) of thrust
Armament: 2 x 30mm DEFA cannons, AAMs, air-to-surface rockets, free-fall bombs

Dassault Balzac V
Crew: 1
Wingspan: 24ft (7.3m)
Wing Area: 292.78ft^2 (27.2m^2)
Sweep (leading edge): 60°
Wing Loading: 52.7lb/ft^2 (257.3kg/m^2)
Length: 42.98ft (13.1m)
Height: 15ft (4.57m)
Empty Weight: 13,500lb (6,123.5kg)
Gross Weight: 15,432lb (7,000kg)
Maximum Speed (sea level): 686mph (1,104km/h); Mach 0.92
Endurance: 12-15 minutes
Ceiling: N/A
Range: N/A
Powerplant: 1 x Bristol Siddeley Orpheus BOr 3 Cruise turbojet, providing 4,850lb (21.57kN) thrust. 8 x Rolls-Royce RB.108-1A lift turbojets, each producing 2,160lb (9.6kN) thrust;
Armament: None

Dassault Mirage IIIV
Crew: 1 (2-seat version considered)
Wingspan: 29ft (8.83m)
Wing Area: N/A
Length: 53.5ft (16.30m)
Height: 18.25ft (5.56m)
Empty Weight: 14,880lb (6,750kg)
Gross Weight: 29,630lb (13,440kg)
Maximum Speed: Mach 2.03

Ceiling: N/A
Range (Production Aircraft): Originally expected to be 290 miles (537km)
Powerplant: V-01: 1 x Afterburning SNECMA TF104B turbofan, providing a maximum thrust of 13,668lb (60.8kN); this was replaced with an afterburning SNECMA TF106 turbofan, producing 16,534lb (73.5kN) of thrust. V-02: 1 x SNECMA TF306C turbofan engine providing 11,700lb (52kN) of static thrust and 20,500lb (91kN) of thrust with afterburner; in addition, each prototype carried 8 x Rolls-Royce RB.162-31 lift turbojets, each providing 4,409lb (19.61kN)
Armament (Production Aircraft): 2 x 30mm DEFA cannon with 125 rounds each, plus 1,200lb (544 kg) of ordnance carried in internal weapons bay

Sud Aviation SA X-600
Crew: 1
Wingspan: 23.6ft (7.2m)
Wing Area: N/A
Length: 47.9ft (14.6m)
Empty Weight: 10,086lb (4,575kg)
Maximum VTO Weight: 19,555lb (8,870kg)
Maximum Speed: Mach 2
Ceiling: N/A
Range: N/A
Powerplant: 1 x Rolls-Royce/MAN RB.153-61 turbofan producing 6,850lb of thrust (30.5kN) and 11,750lb (52.3kN) with afterburner; lift: 6 x RB.162-31 turbojets, each producing 4,409lb (19.61kN) of thrust
Armament: None for prototype

Short SC.1
Crew: 1
Wingspan, 23.5ft (7.16m)
Wing Area: 211.5ft² (19.64m²)
Sweep (leading edge): 54°
Airfoil: NACA 0010
Length (including nose probe): 30ft (9.14m)
Height: 10.66ft (3.24m)
Fuel Capacity: 220 (UK) gallons (1,000 litres)
Empty Weight: 6,260lb (2,839kg)
Maximum Take-off Weight: VTO 7,800lb (3,538kg); Conventional 8,050lb (3,651kg)

Maximum Level Speed: 246mph (396km/h)
Cruise Speed: 100mph (160km/h)
Ceiling: 8,000ft (2,438m)
Range: 150 miles (241km)
Powerplant (VTOL): 5 x Rolls-Royce RB.108 turbojets, each providing 2,130lb (9.47kN) of thrust; one used for horizontal flight, four used for VTOL
Armament: None

Lockheed CL-521
Crew: 1
Wingspan: 21.75ft (6.62 m). Span (with engine pods): 27.95ft (8.5m)
Wing Area: 196.1ft² (18.22m²)
Length (without probe): 54.75ft (16.68m)
Height: 13.5ft (4.11m)
Gross VTO Take-off Weight: 34,500lb (15,648kg)
Landing Weight: 23,500lb (10,659kg)
Maximum Speed: Mach 1.4 approx
Ceiling: 50,000ft (15,240m)
Combat Radius VTOL: 287 miles (460km)
Combat Radius STOL: 420 miles (670km)
Powerplant: 1 x General Electric J79-GE-11A afterburning turbojet, producing 10,000lb (48kN) of dry thrust and 15,600lb (69kN) with afterburner; 8 x RB.108 or Continental Model 365 lift engines each rated at 4,000lb (17.79kN) static thrust
Armament: 1 x 20mm (0.78in) T171 Vulcan 6-barrelled Gatling cannon, 725 rounds Seven hardpoints with a total capacity of 4,000lb (1,814 kg); typically, AIM-9 Sidewinder AAMs, ground-attack rockets, free-fall bombs and a nuclear weapon capability

Lockheed CL-346-1
Crew: 1
Wingspan: 28.66ft (8.73m)
Wing Area: 330ft² (30.65m²)
Length: 54.6ft (16.6m)
Height: 14.66ft (4.4m)
Gross Weight: 30,500lb (13,834kg)
Empty Weight: 20,500lb (9,294kg)
Maximum Speed: Mach 2
Ceiling: 60,000ft (18,288m)

Powerplant: 2 x General Electric J79-GE-11A afterburning turbojets in swivelling nacelles, each providing 10,000lb (44.4kN) of dry thrust and 15,600lb (69kN) with afterburner
Armament: 1 x 20mm rotary cannon, 4 x AIM-9 Sidewinder AAMs, various underwing stores including free-fall conventional and nuclear bombs

Lockheed CL-706-13
Crew: 1
Wingspan: 27.5ft (8.3m)
Wing Area: 250ft² (23.22m²)
Length: 50ft (15.24m)
Height: 16ft (4.87m)
Empty Weight: N/A
Take-off Weight: 32,000lb (14,514kg)
Maximum Speed: High subsonic
Ceiling: 50,000ft (15,240m)
Range: N/A
Powerplant: 2 x afterburning General Electric GE X-84 turbofan engines, each producing an estimated maximum thrust of 20,100lb (89.4kN); 10 x Continental Model 365 lift engines each rated at 4,000lb (17.79kN) static thrust
Armament: 1 x 30mm cannon; hardpoints for a range of different weapons

Lockheed CL-802-14-3 2
Crew: 2
Wingspan: 27.4ft (8.35)
Wing Area: N/A
Sweep (leading edge): 45°
Length: 61ft (18.59m)
Height: 20ft (6m)
Maximum Speed: Mach 2
Ceiling: 60,000ft (18,288m)
Range: N/A
Powerplant: 2 x General Electric J79-GE-11A afterburning turbojets, each providing 10,000lb (44.4kN) of dry thrust and 15,600lb (69kN) with afterburner; 10 x Continental Model 365 lift engines each rated at 4,000lb (17.79kN) static thrust
Armament: Air-to-air missiles, air-to-surface missiles; provision to carry a tactical nuclear weapon internally

Chapter 5 Fans, Augmentation and the Sea Control Ships project

During the late 1950s, engineers looked at various ways to improve short take-off performance by using methods of fan in wing lift. The Chance Vought Corporation was one of the first companies to study these ideas in detail and it soon led to a very promising VTOL system for civil and military aircraft. Another lift system with considerable potential for a VTOL fighter was devised and patented in the 1960s by De Havilland Aircraft of Canada at Downsview, Ontario. This used relatively simple thrust augmentation ejector slots on each lower side of the fuselage. Yet another method of lift was devised by Rockwell, which directed the exhaust flow from an aircraft's main engine into a wing-mounted flap system. This won considerable favour with the US Navy in the 1970s, which was looking for an advanced supersonic VTOL fighter for its Sea Control Ships project. Each system seemed to promise development into an efficient VTOL system and these multi-million dollar projects are described in this chapter.

ABOVE Company artwork showing the first XFV-12A prototype making a landing on a carrier. *Rockwell International*

Vought's Adam Project

The origins of this programme can be traced to an engineer called Byron R. Winborn (1910-1997), who served as a Technical Intelligence Officer with the USAAF during World War 2. In the postwar years he worked as a gas turbine development engineer for the General Electric Company, before joining Chance Vought Aircraft at Dallas. In 1958, Winborn produced his first proposals for a new propulsion system called Air Deflection and Modulation (ADAM). Winborn hoped to fully develop a ducted fan system for light transport aircraft that would provide significantly enhanced STOL performance using wing-mounted propulsive pods channelling the fan flow downwards to increase lift. The initial layout envisaged four high-bypass ratio fans in ducts below the inner wing section, with an equal number of gas generators (small turbojets) above each unit, providing power to drive the fans via hot gas ducting. A system of flaps would be used to channel the airflow downwards at slow speeds and rearwards, providing thrust for level flight in combination with exhaust from the engines.

As the project progressed it was realised that there was considerable potential to refine the concept and apply it to a combat aircraft, perhaps providing a VTOL and hover capability. In this type of aircraft the four-fan system would be fully integrated into the wing and the gas generators would be housed within nacelles on each side of the fuselage. The propulsion system also led to an unusual overall configuration, with booms outboard of the thick wing sections, housing landing gear and carrying horizontal fins, later set at a dihedral angle. Upright tail fins were also tested on models and it was finally determined that a single tail fin with rudder should be placed at the rear of the fuselage. The large flaps behind the wing, used for flow deflection, would become elevons in normal flight. With the support of NASA Langley and NASA Ames, it was decided to build a one-quarter-scale model of a lightweight aircraft and Vought received funding from the USAF and US Army to study military applications for the ADAM system. The USAF was primarily interested in a strike fighter or close-support aircraft

able to operate from an improvised site, and the US Army was seeking a tactical light transport with excellent STOL or ideally full VTOL.

Once NASA began wind tunnel testing, a number of issues became apparent, with the most significant being a centre of gravity location, which meant that the aircraft needed to be redesigned with more weight at the tail end. There were also pitch problems and this was addressed with a decision to install a lift fan at the front of the aircraft. The original ADAM I design, which dated from 1959, had now rapidly evolved into ADAM II. Many modifications and engineering changes were

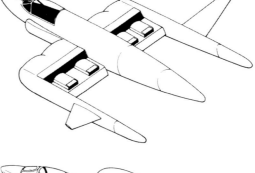

TOP LEFT Basic configuration of the ADAM I design from April 1962. *Ling-Temco-Vought*

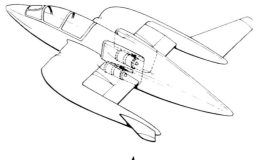

CENTRE LEFT This drawing shows the revised positioning for the gas generators and the air inlets for the later ADAM I designs. *Ling-Temco-Vought*

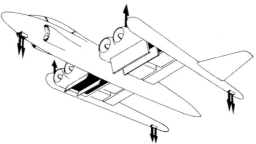

BELOW LEFT The proposed hover pitch control system for the initial ADAM I design. *Ling-Temco-Vought*

BELOW LEFT The two-seat Vought ADAM I basic configuration proposed in November 1962. Note the twin tail fins. *Ling-Temco-Vought/Bill Rose*

BELOW CENTRE A photo-montage, showing the basic ADAM I in flight. *Tony Buttler/Bill Rose*

BELOW RIGHT Single-seat, twin-tail fin ADAM 1 concept. *Ling-Temco-Vought*

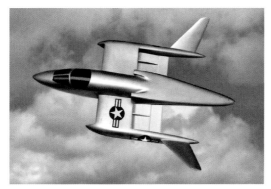
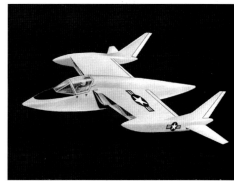

ABOVE The significantly revised ADAM II configuration, produced in December 1967. *Ling-Temco-Vought*

made, with the number of gas generators being reduced to two and these were moved into the fuselage. Vought was confident that in the event of one engine failing, the revised system would allow the aircraft to remain flyable. The forward pitch control lift fan was initially designed to be driven by the gas generators using a lengthy connecting shaft, although this was soon replaced by gas ducting, which was regarded as more satisfactory. It was also obvious that the forward lift fan would make it very difficult to install a radar system and this

problem would be reviewed throughout the ADAM II programme, with various attempts being made to rectify matters.

Another area of some concern was the retractable undercarriage, which proved troublesome. Initially, ADAM II used a tricycle layout, but there were centre of gravity problems, which required repositioning and then it was realised that the nosewheel would interfere with the forward lift fan. Further changes were made throughout the development of ADAM II, with the final adoption of a B-47-style tandem layout, with stabilising

ABOVE An ADAM II model with twin tail fins is supported upside down in the LTV low-speed wind tunnel. *Ling-Temco-Vought*

ABOVE Rear view of the scale-sized ADAM II model in the 16ft Transonic Tunnel at NASA Langley. These tests, with the reference 228, were undertaken in 1967. *NASA*

TOP ROW LEFT Artwork showing a USAF ADAM II aircraft operating in the close-support role. It was anticipated that ADAM II aircraft would start to enter service in the late 1970s. *Ling-Temco-Vought*

TOP ROW CENTRE This original piece of company artwork dating from February 1967 shows a single-seat Vought ADAM II aircraft in clean condition. By this stage in the project there had been numerous modifications to the propulsion system and aerodynamics. *Ling-Temco-Vought*

TOP ROW RIGHT A scale-sized model of an LTV ADAM II basic configuration aircraft equipped with hardpoints carrying bombs. The nose intake for the forward fan and wing fans are clearly visible in this photograph dating from about 1967. *Ling-Temco-Vought*

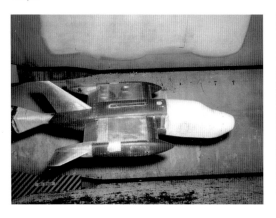

ABOVE A 1/6-size ADAM II scale model is tested in the 16ft Transonic Tunnel by NASA Langley Research Center during 1967. *NASA*

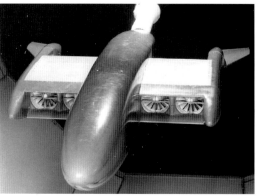

ABOVE Forward view of a detailed ADAM II scale model, undergoing wind tunnel trials at NASA Langley in the late 1960s. *NASA*

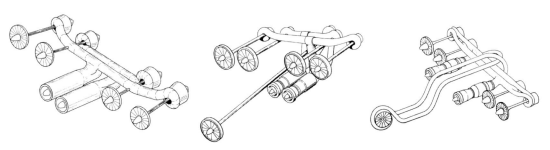

TOP LEFT This drawing shows one of the early ADAM ducting systems. *Ling-Temco-Vought*

TOP CENTRE This later ADAM hot gas ducting system is coupled to a forward shaft-driven fan. *Ling-Temco-Vought*

TOP RIGHT Eventually the forward fan in the ADAM propulsion system would be directly incorporated into the hot gas ducting system. *Ling-Temco-Vought*

outrigger wheels carried in the booms. ADAM II had by this stage been developed into several different proposals for strike fighters, close-support and reconnaissance aircraft, all having a full VTOL and hover capability. A single-seat ADAM II fighter known as V-482 was expected to have a gross weight of 17,400lb (7,892.5kg) and a combat radius of at least 290 miles (466km) using VTOL, and somewhat further with STOL. Performance, although not specifically noted, was high subsonic. A slightly larger two-seat variant, assigned the company reference V-485, was intended primarily for use as a strike fighter. It would have more powerful engines, an anticipated gross weight of approximately 30,000lb (13,608kg) and might be capable of near-supersonic speed. Weapons carried by these aircraft included a single rotary cannon, AIM-9 Sidewinder missiles, air-to-surface rockets and free-fall bombs.

ADAM II was followed by a series of designs known as ADAM III, which were more sophisticated. Sleeker in appearance, with anticipated supersonic performance, these concepts carried the gas generators in the wing roots next to the fans, with the forward lift fan being eventually repositioned behind the cockpit area, allowing the installation of radar equipment in the nose. After Vought re-formed into Ling-Temco-Vought (LTV), the new management team was convinced that ADAM was a project of significant importance to the company that required ongoing support and promotion. The USAF and US Army continued to provide financial assistance and LTV executives believed that a campaign of aggressive lobbying would win over the US Navy, leading to the construction of a proof-of-concept prototype.

However, things began to go seriously wrong in 1965 when the USAF and US Army decided to end their

involvement with the ADAM project. At that time the Harrier VTOL fighter was undergoing trials and it is likely that this had a bearing on the matter. Despite this rejection, LTV continued to persevere with the project and design work on ADAM III carried on until the end of 1968, when the company accepted that the US Navy or Marine Corps could not be encouraged to fund further development. ADAM seems to have been a promising propulsion system, but it remains unknown if it would have worked successfully in a full-sized prototype.

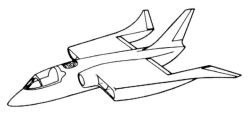

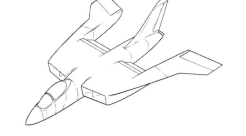

LEFT TOP An early ADAM III concept from May 1968, with the forward fan located ahead of the cockpit. Streamlining would improve performance in level flight. *Ling-Temco-Vought*

LEFT CENTRE This revised ADAM III concept has the forward fan relocated to behind the cockpit area, allowing for the fairly easy installation of a radar unit. The design dates from June 1968. *Ling-Temco-Vought*

LEFT BOTTOM This ADAM III proposal was given the reference 3-28-11.70. Fitted with twin booms and a single tail fin, it may have been intended to provide marginal supersonic performance. It is unclear if a forward fan was fitted. No details are available for this specific model. *Ling-Temco-Vought*

De Havilland Canada VTOL Fighter Project

During the 1950s, aerodynamicist Don Whittley worked for John Frost's Special Projects Group (SPG) at Avro-Canada, Malton, Ontario. He was heavily involved in the development of a highly classified USAF disc-shaped VTOL interceptor and the Avrocar (see the author's previous book *Flying Saucer Technology*).

Unfortunately, the Avrocar failed to perform as anticipated and soon after this Avro-Canada folded when its outstanding CF-105 Arrow supersonic fighter was

cancelled for what appears to have been purely political reasons. In 1962, Whittley and his colleague Doug Garland (who also worked for the SPG as an aerodynamicist) were recruited by De Havilland Canada (DHC). Both worked on the Buffalo transport aircraft and during this period Whittley produced some interesting proposals for VTOL aircraft. By 1966, a small team headed by Whittley had developed a comprehensive design for an entirely new type of lift system. Intended

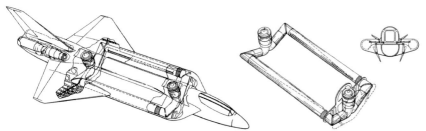

for use with a strike fighter having superior performance to the British Harrier, this concept received full backing from DHC's senior management, who secured interest from the Canadian Department of National Defence and the Pentagon, who arranged for NASA Ames to provide technical assistance.

The system would utilise two small turbojet engines channelling their exhaust into two conduits called augmentors along the lower side of the fuselage, which released gas through a series of nozzles. Air would also be drawn down through openings by the gas leaving the augmentors. Flaps provided control of the downward flow and the system was supplemented by a reaction control system to stabilise and control the aircraft at low speed, with nozzles located fore, aft and at the wingtips. Following small-scale laboratory experiments involving desktop-sized models lifted by compressed air, several patents were filed and the project moved to the next phase. This involved the construction of a scale-sized proof-of-concept, jet-powered unmanned demonstrator. Never intended for free flight, this engineering model formed part of a variable-height test rig. A compact Orenda-built, General Electric J85 turbojet provided the power for the lift system and, following a series of successful trials at Downsview, the model was shipped to NASA Ames for testing in its 40ft x 80ft (12m x 24m) wind tunnel.

Soon after this, DHC built a larger model powered by a General Electric J97 turbojet engine, which was tested in a rig at Downsview and eventually shipped to NASA Ames for wind tunnel testing. Whittley had already outlined various proposals for a strike fighter, with several unpowered scale models being completed and wind tunnel tested. The initial concept was for an aircraft with an approximate overall length of about 60ft (18.2m). The wing was positioned towards the rear of the fuselage and there was a single tail fin. This design would allow for one or two crew members in a forward-positioned cockpit. Lift would be provided by two compact gas generators feeding two augmentor conduits via manifolds. A rectangular section would be formed around the aircraft's centre of gravity and a weapons bay would be located within this area. Flaps would control the downward flow of exhaust gas and the additional air drawn from above the fuselage. This mixing of cold air with hot exhaust gas leaving the

ABOVE LEFT This drawing shows a De Havilland Canada VTOL fighter proposal that first appeared in a US Patent filed in 1969. It seems to be very close in general specification and appearance to a later VTOL fighter given the company reference P-71-30, which was submitted to the US Navy for its early 1970s Sea Control Ships project. *DHC*

ABOVE RIGHT Detail of the original DHC lift system powered by two gas generators, which was intended for use with its VTOL fighter aircraft. The upper right cross-section drawing shows the flap system. *DHC*

BELOW A small DHC proof-of-concept VTOL demonstrator, powered by a J97 engine. *DHC*

augmentors would reduce velocity and temperature, lessening runway/surface erosion and lowering noise. Trials had already indicated that the system would be significantly quieter than other VTOL lift methods such as the Harrier's Pegasus engine. It was also claimed that, in the event of one engine failing, the system would have sufficient power to keep the aircraft airborne.

In level flight the aircraft would be powered by two afterburning turbojets mounted in the fuselage, providing supersonic performance. An undercarriage would also permit horizontal take-offs and landings without the use of the augmentation system, although the main purpose of this design was to provide a fighter aircraft capability for helicopter-carrying carriers and suitable warships. The project continued into the early 1970s, with DHC submitting a proposal with the company reference P-71-30 to the US Navy for a small carrier project (see the next section). DHC's design, which had a very similar appearance to an aircraft shown in US Patent 3,602460, filed in June 1969, was up against some excellent competition and finally met with rejection.

DHC then produced a more advanced VTOL fighter concept with a canard layout and twin tail fins. There were no takers, although company-sponsored research continued. Then General Dynamics took an interest in DHC's lift system and the idea of utilising it for an advanced version of the F-16 had become a serious possibility. This proposal is discussed in a later section of this chapter.

BELOW RIGHT One of De Havilland Canada's designs for an advanced VTOL canard fighter aircraft using its external augmentor lift system. *DHC*

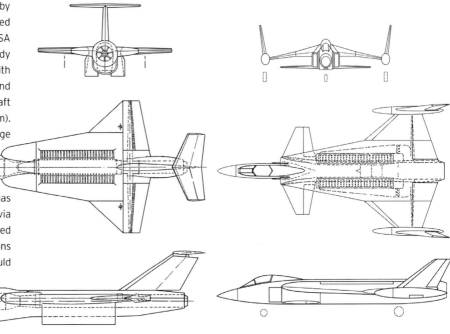

Rockwell XFV-12A

In 1970, President Richard M. Nixon nominated Elmo Russell Zumwalt (1920–2000) to become the next Chief of Naval Operations. After assuming the post and becoming a full Admiral in July 1970, Zumwalt set about a major plan to upgrade or replace many of the Navy's ageing vessels, with cost savings as a priority. His plan, known as High-Low, aimed to introduce several new state-of-the-art nuclear-powered vessels, while replacing older craft with cheaper modern alternatives, such as the flexible Sea Control Ships (SCS) that could be obtained in larger numbers.

These were very compact aircraft carriers that would carry helicopters mainly intended for anti-submarine warfare and a small number of VTOL strike fighters. The primary function of these light carriers would be convoy defence, but they could be effectively used in various other roles. Zumwalt hoped to have at least eight SCS in service by the 1980s and each vessel would have a length of 620ft (189m), a beam of 80ft (24.3m) and a full displacement of about 13,736 tons (12,461 metric tonnes). Gas turbine propulsion would be used and a SCS would have a complement of 76 officers and 624 enlisted men. Initially, it was planned to carry about sixteen helicopters and three Harrier VTOL fighters, so a practical assessment was undertaken in mid-1971, using the USS *Guam* (LPH-9), an 'Iwo Jima' class amphibious assault ship. Trials began at the start of 1972, with eventual deployment taking place in the Atlantic and the USS *Guam* acting as an SCS, carrying a number of Marine Corps AV-8A Harriers and Sea King ASW helicopters. After these operations had been completed the USS *Guam* resumed its role as an amphibious assault ship on 1 July 1974. While the trials went reasonably well, it had already been decided that the US Navy required a new supersonic VTOL fighter for the SCS and each carrier would be expected to operate at least six of these aircraft.

The main requirement for this aircraft would be the interception of long-range Soviet aircraft such as the Tu-95 Bear, with secondary roles that might include anti-shipping and reconnaissance operations. This resulted in requests for new designs being issued to all major aerospace contractors in late 1972. There were about a dozen initial submissions and the Navy's final choice was the North American/Rockwell XFV-12A.

For more information on other Sea Control fighter proposals see the next section.

The XFV-12A used a system of thrust augmentation that redirected the single main engine's exhaust output through ducts and into an arrangement of wing-mounted outlets to provide a VTOL and hover capability. In normal flight the aircraft would have a similar performance to the F-4 Phantom, with a maximum speed in excess of Mach 2 and AIM-7 Sparrow missiles

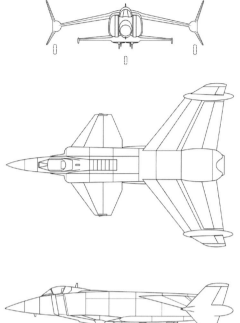

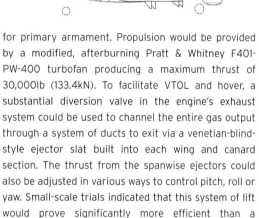

for primary armament. Propulsion would be provided by a modified, afterburning Pratt & Whitney F401-PW-400 turbofan producing a maximum thrust of 30,000lb (133.4kN). To facilitate VTOL and hover, a substantial diversion valve in the engine's exhaust system could be used to channel the entire gas output through a system of ducts to exit via a venetian-blind-style ejector slat built into each wing and canard section. The thrust from the spanwise ejectors could also be adjusted in various ways to control pitch, roll or yaw. Small-scale trials indicated that this system of lift would prove significantly more efficient than a directional thrust Pegasus engine.

ABOVE Admiral Elmo Zumwalt who became Chief of US Naval Operations in 1970 and was responsible for the Sea Control Ships project. *US Navy*

LEFT General appearance of the Rockwell XFV-12A supersonic VTOL fighter. *Bill Rose*

BELOW This shows details of the forward lift system in the canard wing. *Rockwell International*

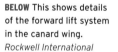

An additional air inlet for the engine was positioned behind the cockpit for use during VTOL, presumably to avoid problems with exhaust re-ingestion. Transition to horizontal flight was expected to function without difficulty and in level flight the XFV-12A would be capable of speeds well in excess of Mach 2 at altitude. However, there were some obvious disadvantages to this system and the variable-position ejectors restricted the carriage of stores underwing. This meant that any missiles or free-fall bombs would have to be partly recessed under the fuselage. It was a very unsatisfactory situation as there was no space for drop tanks or a reconnaissance pod. While the original Navy requirement for weapons carriage was not very demanding, it remains hard to understand how this shortcoming failed to be identified by the Navy at an early stage in the XFV-12A's development. Nevertheless, assembly of the first of two prototypes was approved, with work beginning at Rockwell International's facility at Columbus, Ohio, in 1973. To keep costs as low as possible, the XFV-12As were built from as many off-the-shelf components as possible. This is a common practice with prototypes. The nose section, much of the cockpit, the canopy and landing gear were all parts used for the A-4 Skyhawk, while sections of the wings, fuel tanks and air

inlets were adapted from F-4 Phantom components. In total, these parts accounted for about 35% of each prototype. The overall dimensions of the XFV-12A were 43.8ft (13.35m) in length and a wingspan of 28.5ft (8.7m). Empty, the aircraft weighed 13,800lb (6,259kg) and Rockwell remained confident that a fully laden aircraft would easily exceed twice the speed of sound in level flight. With work on assembly of the predominantly aluminium alloy airframes under way, engine trials began in 1974, followed by free-flight model tests in NASA Langley's Full Scale Wind Tunnel. Although the model flew well as a conventional design, the findings for VTOL proved very unsatisfactory, with NASA concluding that the anticipated thrust augmentation system would produce insufficient power to satisfy lift requirements.

However, the Navy persevered with the project and the first XFV-12A was rolled out in 1977. Ground tests began at Columbus, Ohio, in July 1977 and the external finish was altered, probably for perceived PR reasons, prior to an official unveiling on 26 August 1977. Full completion of the second prototype was now put on hold as a cost-saving measure, while the first prototype was shipped to NASA Langley in early 1978 to undergo tethered trials conducted by a team of NASA, US Navy and Rockwell engineers.

LEFT The XFV-12A was repainted in these new colours and eventually the Navy insignia appears to have been removed, perhaps signifying an official desire to portray the aircraft as an experimental design, primarily intended for research purposes. *Rockwell International*

BELOW The Rockwell XFV-12A is prepared for testing under a gantry at the NASA Langley Research Center. *NASA*

These trials lasted for six months and, as NASA had predicted, the XFV-12A's propulsion system was incapable of providing adequate vertical thrust. Scaling up the design from a laboratory experiment had failed to work as intended, with only enough power available to support about 75% of the aircraft's weight. It seemed that the ducting system was acting as a huge drain on performance. Rockwell engineers were already proposing a revised version of the aircraft powered by two side-by-side cruise engines; in addition there would be various modifications to allow the carriage of various stores below the fuselage and launch rails at the wingtips for Sidewinder AAMs. This future option aside, the attempts to rectify the lift problem had generated a massive cost overrun and in 1981 the Navy finally decided to abandon the XFV-12A programme. The first prototype remained at Langley for some years and was finally scrapped. It is unclear what happened to the second aircraft, but this was almost certainly broken up for scrap. Although the XFV-12A turned out to be a disastrous waste of money, the US Navy would continue to investigate the viability of VTOL fighters for many years to come. Had it selected one of the alternative candidates for the SCS project, things might have been very different.

Some Alternatives for the SCS Project

ABOVE Two General Dynamics/Convair Model 200A VTOL fighters intercept enemy aircraft. *US Navy*

Informal discussions about a supersonic shipborne VTOL fighter for the SCS project had been taking place with major aerospace contractors since the start of 1971 and eventually official requests were issued for designs, with (according to some sources) around 12-15 responses, including overseas entries such as the DHC strike fighter and an advanced version of the VAK 191B (initially the Mk 3). However, the number of submissions was quickly reduced by half, to include the General Dynamics/Convair Model 200, the Vought V-517, the Grumman Type 607, the Fairchild FR-150, the Boeing 908-535 Nutcracker, a McDonnell Douglas-developed supersonic version of the Harrier (Lockheed produced something very similar, which is discussed in the final chapter) and the North American/Rockwell XFV-12A. As described in the previous section, the XFV-12A was the winner of this competition, but the other designs, which in some cases appear to have been superior, are worthy of some discussion. In second place to the Rockwell XFV-12A was the General Dynamics/Convair Model 200A VTOL strike fighter with the ability to make horizontal carrier or airfield landings. This was a canard design, bearing a strong resemblance to the current Saab JAS 39 Gripen fighter. It had a similar wingspan, length, weight and roughly equal performance in normal flight.

The Model 200A would have been powered by an afterburning engine derived from the Pratt & Whitney JTF22A-30A, producing a maximum thrust of 26,800lb (119.1kN). An essential feature of this aircraft's VTOL lift system was the three-bearing downward-vectoring exhaust nozzle. This technology appears to have been directly related to propulsion methods pioneered in West Germany during the EWR-Süd VJ 101D and EWR-Süd-Fairchild Hiller Republic AVS programme. The P&W thrust direction system for the main engine would function in association with two vertically positioned engines located behind the cockpit area, providing additional lift and balancing the aircraft. These were initially of unspecified manufacture with individual thrust requirements of at least 10,500lb (46.7kN). Some documentation indicates that the eventual preference was for the Allison J99 engine (when available) and both would be shut down during horizontal flight, with doors covering the air inlets and exhaust areas. In addition, a reaction control system would bleed air from the compressor stages of these engines, ducting it to the nose and wingtips during VTOL operations.

The designers of the Model 200A insisted that it

ABOVE A General Dynamics/Convair Model 200A VTOL fighter lifts off from a small US Navy carrier. *US Navy*

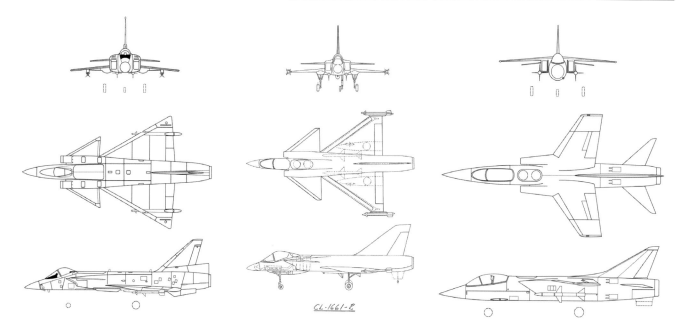

CL-1661-2

LEFT The General Dynamics/Convair Model 200A VTOL strike fighter, having a similar appearance to the later Saab JAS 39 Gripen fighter. *Bill Rose*

CENTRE Lockheed's CL-1661-2 design for a VTOL supersonic strike fighter, which appears to be a direct competitor to the Convair Model 200A. *Pete Clukey Lockheed Martin*

RIGHT One of the proposed production versions of the Ling-Temco-Vought V-517 VTOL strike fighter, which utilised a slightly revised propulsion system. *Bill Rose*

would be possible to make an emergency return home on just two lift engines and a short conventional landing with one failed lift engine. This aircraft would have utilised a multiple redundancy fly-by-wire control system and computerised VTOL management package. Some systems would probably have been common to the F-18A, such as radar, self-protection jamming equipment and chaff/flare dispensers. The aircraft would be supported on a fully retractable tricycle undercarriage and the forward pressurised cockpit would provide excellent visibility for the pilot. Several closely related variants were proposed, such as a conventional take-off fighter and a two-seater, having the advantage of commonality of components. Armament for all versions would include an internal 20mm M61A1 Vulcan cannon, two AIM-7 Sparrow AAMs in semi-recessed locations beneath the fuselage and the option of two AIM-9 Sidewinder AAMs either below the wings or mounted on the wingtips. Other possibilities included anti-shipping weapons and free-fall bombs. Although the Model 200A was considered technically complex, it might have been more successful than the XFV-12A and would have probably flown. Whether the aircraft could have met all the US Navy's requirements for an affordable price is an entirely different matter.

Another strike fighter design with a very similar appearance to the Model 200A was the Lockheed CL-1661-2. It had almost identical overall dimensions, weight, armament and powerplant and virtually the same lift arrangement. It has not been possible to obtain any more than the basic specifications for this concept, but it looks as if Lockheed studied the Model 200A and concluded it could produce an aircraft that met exactly the same requirement. Alternatively, the US Navy may have issued the company with very specific requirements. While the CL-1661-2 does not appear on any available SCS

documentation, it is too similar to the Model 200A to have been anything other than an unacknowledged submission for this competition.

The entry from Ling-Temco-Vought (LTV) had a broadly similar specification to the Model 200A, but a more conventional appearance. Initially given the company reference V-517, there were at least four variants of this design listed as V-517A to V-517D. The first two designations were assigned to prototypes, with V-517A being equipped with a P&W JTF10A-42A main engine and V-517B being fitted with a P&W JTF22A-30A. V-517C and D are thought to have been proposed production versions that would use a slightly more powerful P&W JTF22A-30B engine. The prototypes would also be fitted with three upright Rolls-Royce RB.162-81 F 08 lift turbojets, each rated at 5,587lb (24.85kN) thrust, while the production aircraft would utilise two of the more powerful Allison J99 lift jets. Estimated weights for the production aircraft were 18,152lb (8,234kg) empty and a maximum of 27,480lb (12,465kg) for VTO. This would have provided a very similar performance to the Convair or Lockheed designs. Other changes that would only become evident on a production model included folding wings and armaments. However, soon after submitting the V-517 to the US Navy, there was a decision taken by designers at LTV to modify the lift system, leading to the V-520. Forward lift would now be provided by two Allison J99 turbojets that swung out of the fuselage ahead of and below the main engine air intakes.

The Grumman Model 607 was yet another proposal, intended to meet US Navy requirements for a SCS VTOL supersonic fighter. Built around the P&W JTF22A-30B turbofan, the Model 607 was fitted with a conventional rear exhaust and two swivelling nozzles on the rear of the fuselage for use during VTOL. In addition, there would be two almost vertically positioned Grumman

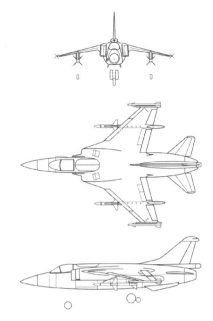

GLE-607A lift jets in tandem behind the cockpit, each rated at 11,535lb (51kN) thrust. During low-speed operations, the aircraft would utilise a reaction control system, with conventional control surfaces being used during normal flight. The forward-positioned pressurised cockpit would provide good visibility for the pilot and the aircraft would be supported at rest by a fully retractable bicycle undercarriage with outriggers and small wheels carried in wing nacelles. Grumman indicated that it would be relatively easy to build a land-based version intended for conventional take-off and landing that would have superior performance due to lower weight. There was a minor upgrade to the design in July 1972, with a number of aerodynamic improvements and relatively minor changes taking place, including the provision to fold the wings for hangar deck storage. This resulted in the proposal being redesignated as the Model 607A. It had been originally suggested that the specified 20mm M61A1 cannon might be carried in a separate underwing pod, but it was moved to the port wing root during this design upgrade. Other weapons carried by the Model 607 would be the normal complement of Sidewinder/Sparrow air-to-air missiles or, alternatively, Harpoon air-to-surface missiles. Drop tanks to extend the aircraft's range were another option.

The aircraft proposed for Sea Control operations by Fairchild Republic received the company reference FR-150 and not surprisingly utilised the Pratt & Whitney F100 (JTF22A-30A) turbofan with the three-bearing thrust deflection nozzle. This design would utilise two Allison J99 lift engines carried inside the forward fuselage section that would swing out when required for VTOL. In most respects, this was a scaled down version of the AVS VTOL strike fighter, which was under joint development with EWR-Süd (see the previous chapter). As might be expected, weight, armament and anticipated performance all complied with US Navy requests.

Boeing's entry for a SCS fighter was totally different from the previously described proposals, being a VATOL design that used a cable and hook system, developed by Ryan. Assigned the company reference 908-535, this was a sleek, impressive-looking canard design, with the promise of very high performance in normal flight. It was initially intended to function in a somewhat similar manner to the postwar Fairey flying wing fighter, with the aircraft being hung over the side of the ship for launch. Another feature would be a forward swivelling cockpit, designed to remain horizontal during take-off and landing. This was responsible for the name Nutcracker being applied to the proposal. Initially, there were no plans to fit a conventional undercarriage to the 908-535, but it was soon decided that fully retractable landing gear was desirable and necessary. The exact reason for this change in thinking is unclear. This aircraft would have the highest performance of any SCS design, with a maximum speed of Mach 2.8 at 70,000ft (21,336m), provided by two powerful GE turbofans, still in development. It appears that vanes in the exhaust flow and a reaction control system would control the aircraft at low speeds while it was in a vertical position. This design complied with most of the US Navy's requirements regarding weight, dimensions and armament, but major modifications to the carrier would be necessary. The only advantage offered by the Boeing Nutcracker appears to have been the very high, seemingly unnecessary, performance. The take-off and landing of a tailsitting design had already been established as very demanding in difficult maritime conditions, although there might have been scope for improvement with a sufficiently advanced computerised control system. The aircraft would be mechanically complex, very expensive to develop and the ship carrying this aircraft would need to be extensively adapted. With this in mind, it is surprising that the Boeing fighter reached the second stage of this contest.

At about the same time, a very unusual variant of the F-16 fighter was conceived which would take off and land vertically from a special ramp intended for marine

ABOVE The high-performance Boeing 908-535 Nutcracker, designed for VATOL operations and featuring an unusual tilting cockpit. This design would have required special launch ramps. *Boeing*

LEFT Grumman's Model 607 supersonic VTOL fighter, designed in the early 1970s to meet the US Navy's SCS project. *Bill Rose*

applications. The aircraft's nose section was designed to swivel forward to maintain a horizontal attitude, although rather unexpectedly the aircraft would be fitted with a normal retractable undercarriage, allowing horizontal take-offs and landings. NASA Langley undertook various wind tunnel tests with a scale model of the upright VTOL F-16 and similarly functioning models of the F-17 and F-18, although this idea never progressed beyond an initial research study.

Undoubtedly, the two best options for a Sea Control fighter would have been the General Dynamics/Convair Model 200 or, alternatively, a next-generation supersonic Harrier, developed by McDonnell Douglas. As things turned out, the Rockwell XFV-12A proved to be totally useless and the Convair Model 200A progressed no further. Was a supersonic VTOL fighter really necessary for the US Navy's needs at that time? In the early 1980s, the Royal Navy played a key role in winning the Falklands War, using small aircraft carriers operating subsonic Sea Harriers. They repeatedly engaged supersonic Dagger A (an IAI Mirage clone) and Mirage fighters, shooting down 10, with no losses due to enemy aircraft. Admiral Zumwalt's High-Low plan resulted in the Pegasus class of missile patrol boats and the Oliver Hazard Perry (FFG-7) class of guided missile frigates, but most of the other ideas like SCS would fall by the wayside. Zumwalt retired from the Navy on 1 July 1974.

US Navy Interest Continues

Despite the SCS project failing to find favour with the US Navy, interest in VTOL strike fighters was maintained within the Pentagon by Britain's use of Harriers in very difficult conditions during the South Atlantic conflict of 1982. Deliveries of the new McDonnell Douglas F/A-18 Hornet were under way and the first US Marine Corps unit equipped with these aircraft became operational in January 1983. However, planners were trying to look 20 years ahead and determine what kind of shipborne strike fighter might be available to replace the F/A-18. A largely classified programme was already under way to develop a cutting-edge stealth attack aircraft (the A-12A Avenger II) and despite wasting a great deal of money on the unsuccessful XFV-12A, a supersonic VTOL fighter remained high on the US Navy's shopping list. From June 1981 onwards, McDonnell Douglas, General Dynamics, Vought and Rockwell all undertook a largely unpublicised series of studies into the development of a single-engined supersonic VTOL strike fighter. The project was run by the Navy in association with NASA Ames who were responsible for wind tunnel evaluation of the most successful designs in model form.

Some aspects of this new VTOL fighter requirement had shifted from convoy defence to sea-based strike operations, but the usefulness of being able to operate from a small carrier that lacked any launch or arrestor equipment endured. This meant total reliance on VTOL, although the aircraft would also be expected to make conventional take-offs and horizontal landings from larger carriers and runways when needed. Maximum speed was set at a minimum of Mach 1.6, with a VTO weight of about 20,000lb (9,071kg), extending to a STO strike mission weight of 40,000lb (18,134kg). Agility, range and capability were all considerations, with no plans to involve the USAF in any kind of joint development programme. McDonnell Douglas proposed an advanced canard VTOL fighter with a clear Harrier

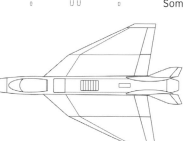

ABOVE General appearance of the Rockwell Baseline VTOL fighter proposal. A second version, simply referred to as The Alternative, was essentially the same concept with a revised wing profile, allowing different positions for the augmentors. *Bill Rose*

RIGHT This illustration shows some of the proposed modifications that might be made to the Rockwell Baseline VTOL fighter if it progressed to the hardware stage. These included a fuselage extension, canards, and wingtip fins. *Rockwell International*

ancestry and details of this Mach 2 proposal can be found in the next chapter, which includes a section on specialised Harrier-related projects.

Somewhat surprisingly, the idea of using a thrust augmentation system, already attempted with the Lockheed XV-4A Hummingbird and the Rockwell XFV-12A, was able to generate renewed interest, despite both projects proving unsuccessful. Engineers at Rockwell remained convinced that thrust augmentation could be made to work and produced a series of revised designs that attempted to address most of the shortcomings of the supersonic VTOL fighter they devised for the SCS project. At around the same time De Havilland Canada, in association with General Dynamics, was also investigating the idea of combining an advanced version of a proven combat aircraft with its augmentation lift system that was originally developed for the SCS fighter. The ongoing Rockwell programme considered a twin-engined replacement for the XFV-12A, followed by stretched version with a narrower wingspan and forward strakes, which received the company designation 026E. This proposal then gave way to two broadly similar single engine designs that differed considerably from the previous canards and were both virtually deltas, with twin tail fins.

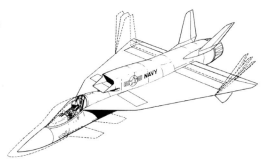

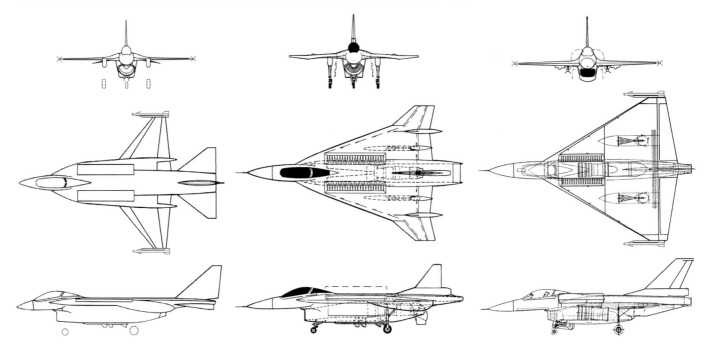

The first proposal, known as the Baseline Model, can be found in some documentation with the company reference 141-023Q. The other concept was simply known as the Alternative Model and received the reference 84884-002F. The principal difference between the two designs was the wing profile, with the Baseline configured for lateral augmentors and the Alternative adapted to allow longitudinal augmentors. The Baseline and Alternative designs were studied in some detail by Rockwell from June 1981 to February 1982, under Contract NAS2-11002, sponsored by the US Navy and NASA Ames Research Center.

The Navy was looking for increased mission flexibility, with two distinct requirements. The first was a VTOL supersonic interception with a combat radius of 172 miles (276km) and the second was a VTOL/STOVL strike or air defence mission with an operational range of 345 miles (555km). Various ways of making the extended range possible were examined, such as a conventional take-off, the use of a ski-ramp and different armament or fuel loads. The principal weapons considered were AIAAM, AMRAAM, AGM-84A Harpoon and AGM-88 HARM, although the carriage of AGM-65 Maverick AGMs and free-fall bombs must have been reviewed. It is not known if there were plans to carry a cannon internally or in a nacelle.

Power would be provided by an advanced afterburning Pratt & Whitney JT69 twin-spool turbofan that was still in the early stages of development. This had an anticipated dry thrust of 20,600lb (91.6kN) and a maximum of 33,800lb (150kN) with afterburner. Availability of the engine was expected to be in 1987 at the earliest. During lift, the exhaust would be diverted into a system of wing-mounted augmentor flaps, with different locations for each variant. This was the only major difference between the two designs. After lift-off,

thrust would be progressively diverted to the aircraft's rear nozzle, followed by full retraction of the flaps. In addition, a reaction control system would operate during VTOL and hover, with control by elevons and rudders in normal flight. The US Navy set the maximum required speed at a conservative Mach 1.6, although Rockwell determined that Mach 1.9 was possible without too much difficulty. The ceiling was also set at 50,000ft (15,240m), although Rockwell indicated that it could easily surpass that figure if required. In the event that either the Baseline or Alternative designs were selected for prototyping, then 56% of the airframe and wing was to be fabricated from aluminium alloy, with 36% use of titanium alloy in load-bearing or hot sections and the remainder made from steel or composites. Fuel would be carried in tanks within the fuselage and wing. The estimated maximum fuel weight was between 5,400lb (2,449kg) and 5,700lb (2,585kg) for the two variants. Horizontal flight control would be handled by a multiple redundancy fly-by-wire system and it is probable that sophisticated control of all VTOL operations was envisaged. The cockpit would have afforded excellent visibility for the pilot and it appears that a side-by-side two-seat aircraft was considered. The main engine inlet was above and behind the cockpit, placed here to minimise exhaust re-ingestion problems, but possibly intended to improve the stealth characteristics of this aircraft. Although Contract NAS2-11002 appears to have progressed no further, Rockwell outlined a number of ideas for further variants of its VTOL strike fighter. They included various changes to the wing design, vertical fins with control surfaces mounted on the wing, larger elevons and a new type of all-movable canard. Other options were a stretched forward fuselage section and different cockpit canopy that would improve engine inlet flow

LEFT This was General Dynamics' second attempt to produce a hybrid based on the earlier DHC P-71-30 VTOL fighter design and the F-16. It received the designation E-2. *General Dynamics Corp*

CENTRE The General Dynamics E-3 study was a combination of the crank-winged F-16XL and the DHC augmentor lift system, with a Rolls-Royce engine providing propulsion. *General Dynamics Corp*

RIGHT The E-7 was the production design that emerged from the General Dynamics E series of VTOL fighter designs. The crank wing had given way to a delta, with wingtip missiles and provision for underwing stores. It remains hard to say how close this concept came to being built as a fully functional prototype, but there was considerable Pentagon interest. *General Dynamics Corp*

LEFT A small-scale model of the General Dynamics E-7, showing the upper augmentor inlets open. This was wind tunnel tested at NASA Ames during the 1970s, encouraging the construction of a full-sized test model. *NASA*

BELOW A full-sized test model of the General Dynamics E-7 was built and underwent wind tunnel testing at NASA, with the programme lasting into the 1980s. *NASA*

and pilot visibility.

An alternative VTOL fighter under consideration by the US Navy was proposed by General Dynamics and based on work carried out by De Havilland Canada that began in the 1960s. It used a thrust augmentation system that had been proposed for an SCS fighter in the 1970s, but met with early elimination. Some time after this, General Dynamics saw considerable potential in DHC's lift technology and planned to integrate it with an advanced version of its F-16 fighter. This was now being referred to as the Ejector Lift (EL) system, which differed in many ways from Rockwell's contemporary design, using a turbofan with afterburner and vectorable exhaust at the lower centre of the fuselage. Fan air would be channelled to cordwise ejectors on each forward wing root section to provide VTOL lift and this would be directed rearward to a tail outlet during level flight. There would also be a reaction control system for low-speed pitch, yaw and roll adjustment. Normal control surfaces would be used in horizontal flight.

All this was packaged into a highly modified F-16 fighter, which steadily evolved into an aircraft resembling the big-wing prototype F-16XL. The Navy initially felt that a VTOL combat aircraft in the 30,000lb (13,607kg) class would be too small for effective fleet air defence and incapable of meeting range or payload requirements for deep strike missions. While General Dynamics believed it would be possible to produce a VTOL fighter capable of meeting basic requirements, it also realised that it would be possible to meet most of the Navy's needs if a 400ft (122m) deck run was used in preference to VTO. Landing would still be vertical, allowing the safe return of any expensive unused weapons. There was some resistance to this idea, although the Navy agreed to further development before dismissing the proposal. The first design in the General Dynamics E Series (E-1) was based on an aircraft that amalgamated features from the DHC P-71-30 and a standard F-16. It was proposed that an afterburning Rolls-Royce IIF-35 turbofan (still in development) would be used and this might be replaced by a proposed Rolls-Royce J-engine in the first pre-production models. However, design changes soon resulted in the E-2, with further augmentor and engine modifications. Although the aircraft's low-speed performance would meet most requirements, there

were problems caused by the positioning of the augmentor ejectors and boxes in strake sections, which meant the wing was too far back and the E-2 would be incapable of reaching supersonic speeds.

It was then decided to re-equip the design with an F-16XL cranked-arrow wing, with initial calculations indicating that the change would rectify the problem, although a propulsion upgrade to the Rolls-Royce J-engine was considered desirable. This version became the E-3. Further exhaust system modifications led to the E-4, although this design was regarded as a step backwards and abandoned, with the design team reverting to the E-3. With uncertainty about funding for full development of the Rolls-Royce IIF-35 engine and concerns about the J-engine, it was decided to look for an alternative and the General Electric F101DFE (which evolved into the very successful F110) was selected as the most promising replacement. This led to the E-5, E-6 and E-7, with the wing becoming a near-delta, and the propulsion system received the more general designation E-X. With the ejector lift units buried within the wing roots and covered by doors and folding flaps, there would be considerable scope to carry underwing stores and it was also planned to fit wingtip AAMs to production versions.

Despite becoming a very complex piece of machinery with some limitations, there was sufficient enduring US Navy interest to encourage the testing of scale and full-sized models of the E-7 at NASA Ames, using the 40ft x 80ft (12m x 24m) wind tunnel. This began at some point in 1982 and appears to have continued for several years. These trials led to various suggestions for propulsion and aerodynamic modifications, including the possibility of adding canards, although this would have required a lengthening and substantial rebuild of the forward fuselage section, which was probably not a realistic option. Although it was finally determined that the E-7 could meet the US Navy's requirements if a short take-off run and a 6° ski-jump were used, there was a lack of official support for further development and the project was cancelled.

From the time of the SCS fighter requirement, Vought worked on many different VTOL fighter concepts, leading to the SF Series of fighters designed for VATOL using a complex ramp built into the carrier. SF aircraft would also be capable of making conventional horizontal take-offs and landings. The Vought SF Series probably represents the last time any government department or contractor took a serious interest in VATOL fighter development. Designs are believed to have started with the SF-100 and concluded with the SF-121 (or possibly slightly higher). In some cases the differences between variants is relatively minor, involving changes to wing area or fins.

The series was generally referred to as Superfly and

it is unclear if this developed from the 'SF' designation or was responsible for it. The first design that appears in reference material was the SF-106, a compact twin-engined fighter with similar dimensions and weight to an SCS proposal like the Convair Model 200A. Designed with an area rule fuselage, the SF-106 was somewhat minimalistic, with the intention of being low weight, affordable, easy to maintain and effective in combat. Twin-engined aircraft have generally been preferred by the US Navy and SF-106 was expected to be capable of vertical landing with one engine disabled. Models of the SF-106 are known to have been tested in Vought's 4ft x 4ft (1.2m x 1.2m) wind tunnel at speeds of Mach 2.4 and up to a 35° angle of attack. However, as this concept evolved, the twin tail fins were replaced with a large single fin with rudder and canards added. Extensive use of composite materials was proposed, with projected structural weight savings of about 20%. Flight control would be achieved using a digital fly-by-wire system and it was anticipated that fully automated control of take-off and transition would be possible. Engines are not discussed in any detail within available documents and appear to have been a secondary consideration. However, it seems likely that a turbofan such as the General Electric F110 would have been pencilled in as a possible future option.

Low-speed control of the aircraft would be achieved using vectored thrust and a reaction control system using air bleed from the engine compressors. The Superfly would be capable of making a vertical or horizontal deck landing, using a fully retractable tricycle undercarriage, which would also aid deck handling. In addition, the aircraft could operate as a conventional strike fighter from any carrier or land runway, with the ability to carry a substantial payload. The forward-positioned pressurised cockpit would provide good visibility for the pilot and it was planned to fit a forward- tilting ejector seat to assist the pilot during VTOL operations. Depending on the engines, a maximum speed of Mach 2.4 was theoretically possible, although speed, range and payload capability were all dependent on the form of take-off employed and the mission requirement. For example, a VTO lift-off and supersonic intercept at Mach 1.6, carrying four air to air missiles, would be limited to a combat radius of 172 miles (278km). Other missions including strike/interdiction might be double this range, further extended with drop tanks or in-flight refuelling. Although VATOL was now largely out of favour, the Superfly represented the most advanced concept produced for this type of combat aircraft. It would have used many advanced technologies and promised good performance. However, there were no naval vessels equipped with the necessary platforms for take-off and landing and little enthusiasm for spending the kind of money necessary to build new ships or undertake major

rebuilds of existing aircraft carriers. One of the final Superfly designs represented a significant change to the series, with the aircraft being re-engineered as a flat riser. Similar in appearance to the later Superfly designs, this aircraft would carry one or more upright-mounted lift engines directly behind the cockpit area. In addition, the two axisymmetric gimballed nozzles would be replaced by 90° vectoring nozzles.

Vought completed the Superfly study for NASA under contract NAS2-9772 in 1978. The findings were then presented to the Ames Research Center and Vought turned its attention to a more advanced VTOL flat riser powered by a Tandem Fan (TF) system. The new study, commissioned by the US Navy and NASA Ames, made full use of research undertaken during the Superfly study and a seperate development known as V-536. This was a Vought VTOL fighter study based on the use of two TF engines, cross-coupled to maintain thrust symmetry and allow vertical landings with only one engine operational. It is unclear how many different designs were produced during the new Vought TF study, but the definitive version to emerge from this project was the TF120.

This compact, sleek-looking aircraft had a forward fuselage section resembling an F-4 Phantom with air inlets on each side of the cockpit. The body was essentially a blended wing design with twin tail fins, canards and small control fins on the lower air inlets. The aircraft would be equipped with a fully retractable tricycle undercarriage and capable of operating from carriers and land bases. An advanced control system would manage all aspects of flight from VTOL to cruise, with the ability to compensate for component failure and combat damage. TF120 would have a maximum speed of Mach 2.4 and a ceiling of 66,550ft (20,284m). Using a short take-off run, the maximum strike range was calculated at 597 miles (960km), using drop tanks and carrying laser-guided bombs. In-flight refuelling would obviously sidestep this issue.

The propulsion system would comprise of a

ABOVE One of the many different all-metal wind tunnel models used in the development of the Vought SF series of VATOL fighter proposals. Models in this series were tested in Vought's 4ft x 4ft (1.2m x 1.2m) wind tunnel at speeds up to Mach 2.4 and up to a 35° angle of attack. *Vought Corporation*

BELOW Vought's SF-106 Superfly VATOL fighter. *Vought Corporation*

LEFT Comparison between the Vought SF-106 (top) and SF-120. *John Luc Seligman*

RIGHT One of the final concepts in the Superfly series. Vought reconfigured the design to become a 'flat riser' with an additional forward lift engine and changes to the main exhaust system. *Bill Rose*

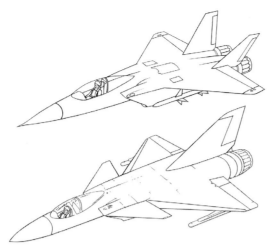

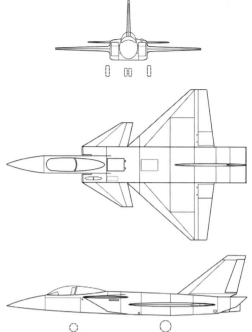

powerful core engine driving two separate fan stages coupled by a single shaft. Between these sections would be a fairly complex transition stage that functioned only at low speed. It contained a flow diverter, which blocked off the first section (making it effectively a separate forward engine) and channelled air via an afterburner into a ventral exhaust nozzle. At the same time, the rear fan stage would draw air through a shuttered dorsal inlet (also part of the transition stage) into the engine, with exhaust leaving the rear of the aircraft via a vectoring nozzle (now pointing downwards). Control of pitch would be possible by differential variation of thrust, with a reaction control system handling roll and yaw. During cruise, the diverter would be fully open, the upper inlet and lower exhaust nozzle closed and the rear vectoring nozzle raised to a horizontal position, with the overall system functioning as a low-bypass turbofan. In the early 1980s there was great optimism that this system could be made to work. Vought suggested that a fighter based on the TF120 could be operational by the mid-1990s, but insurmountable technical problems seem to have arisen and the project was finally abandoned.

Northrop also participated in VTOL fighter studies sponsored by NASA Ames Research Center and the US Navy during the early 1980s. The company produced designs for a stealthy VATOL and an advanced flat riser, which were both considered for service entry in the mid-1990s. Northrop's VATOL concept reviewed by NASA was given the company designation N338-12 and

RIGHT Vought's successor to the Superfly series was this advanced, high-performance VTOL strike fighter with the designation TF120. *Vought Corporation*

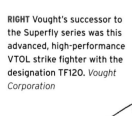

it might be described as looking rather like a slightly smaller, tailless F/A-18, with stealthier dorsal air intakes. Perhaps this appearance is not too surprising when you appreciate that Northrop was originally responsible for the F/A-18, which was then taken over by McDonnell Douglas. Like the F/A-18, the N338-12 would be twin-engined and fitted with leading-edge extensions (LEX) to improve lift, allowing good control at high angles of attack and making the aircraft very manoeuvrable.

As a VATOL design, this fighter would be launched from an upright ramp using an attachment hook system. It was also expected to make computer-assisted vertical landings on the ramp. In addition, the N338-12 would be fitted with conventional fully retractable tricycle landing gear, allowing horizontal take-offs and landings. The underside of the aircraft was relatively clean, so there was plenty of space for underwing stores. Engines suggested for this aircraft are unspecified non-afterburning Pratt & Whitney turbojets, and low-speed control would be achieved with gimballed axisymmetric nozzles able to deflect ±30° in pitch and ±15° in yaw. Additional air-inlet doors would open at low speeds and the aircraft's overall stability would be maintained by a reaction control system, with air bleed from the engine compressors. Normal flight control would be undertaken with substantial elevons and an all-moving tail unit. In common with most other VATOL fighter designs, the pilot's ejector seat would swivel to provide an improved view during take-off and vertical landing.

The suggested VTOL gross weight for this aircraft was 30,000lb (13,608kg) and although somewhat less than the F/A-18, it would be able to match the un-refuelled combat radius of the conventional strike fighter. Maximum speed is not specified in any of the official documentation currently available, but it

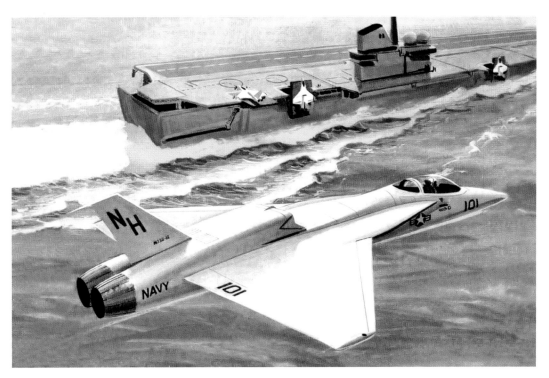

LEFT Company artwork showing the Northrop N338-12 VATOL fighter in flight. This proposal drew on design experience gained during development of the F/A-18 fighter and the similarities are fairly apparent. *Northrop Grumman*

seems fair to assume that, although the engines were non-afterburning, the N338-12 was expected to be capable of marginal supersonic performance. Like all the other VATOL studies conducted during this period, the design went no further than the wind tunnel testing of models. Running in parallel with this design was another Northrop study to develop a flat-rising supersonic combat aircraft. Details of the entire study are not available, but the design finally reaching NASA Ames for full evaluation was given the company designation N382-20.

This was a single-engined VTOL fighter, fairly closely based on the earlier Northrop N336 twin-engined concept. N382-20 was a canard with tail fins mounted on two short booms extending from the trailing edge of the near-delta wing. It would be supported on the ground by a conventional tricycle undercarriage, allowing conventional take-offs and landings. Propulsion took the form of a single General Electric variable-cycle afterburning turbofan engine providing VTOL and cruise, using a forward-positioned remote augmented lift system (RALS) and augmented deflector exhaust nozzle (ADEN) at the rear. The intended engine remains unclear, although it is quoted in one Northrop document as having an expected dry thrust of 42,345lb (188kN) and being capable of supercruise without the need for afterburning. The forward RALS exhaust unit was located just behind the cockpit section. During VTOL operations it would be possible to control pitch with thrust modulation between the forward and aft nozzles. Yaw was controlled by the lateral direction of the forward nozzle, with roll handled by the aircraft's reaction control system. In conventional flight, elevons,

canards and rudders on each tail fin would provide full control. One document dealing with the N382-20 suggests that all-moving tail fins were initially considered. Thrust vectoring, using the ADEN nozzle, was also available to improve high-speed manoeuvring.

The N382-20 would be capable of making conventional take-offs and landings, with a distance of 600ft (183m) being quoted for a normal load, when using vectored thrust. Significant gains in payload and range would be possible using rolling take-offs and in-flight refuelling was available. The airframe would be built from aluminium and titanium alloy, with graphite epoxy in large-scale use for the wing, canards, tail fins and many fuselage sections. Armament comprised a single 20mm cannon with 500 rounds and a ventral bay carrying two AMRAAMs and two ASRAAMs. Additional stores could be carried underwing. After completion of this study for NASA Ames, there was further interest shown by the USAF, with an evaluation being undertaken by the Flight Dynamics Directorate, Wright Laboratory at Wright-Patterson AFB, Ohio. This lasted until late 1991. Like all the other American VTOL fighter concepts of this period, the Northrop design progressed no further than wind tunnel tests of models.

BELOW Northrop's advanced single engine N382-20 VTOL strike fighter. *Bill Rose*

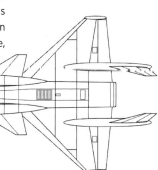

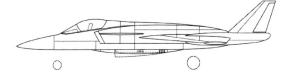

Chapter Five: Aircraft Details

Vought Adam II V-482
Crew: 1
WingSpan: 40ft (12m)
Length: 50ft (15.2m) approx
Height: N/A
Gross Weight: 17,400lb (7,892.5kg)
Maximum Speed: High subsonic
Ceiling: N/A
Range (VTOL): 290 miles (466km) approx
Powerplant: 2 x unspecified General Electric gas generators
Armament: 1 x 20mm cannon, 2 or 4 x AIM-9 Sidewinder AAMs

Vought Adam II V-485
Crew: 2
WingSpan: 40ft (12m)
Length: 59.5ft (18m)
Height: 15ft (4.5m)
Gross Weight: 30,000lb (13,608kg) approx
Maximum Speed: Mach 0.95 approx
Ceiling: N/A
Range: N/A
Powerplant: 2 x unspecified General Electric gas generators
Armament: 1 30mm cannon, Sidewinder AAMs, free-fall bombs, rockets

De Havilland Canada P-71-30
Crew: 1 or 2
Span: 30ft (9.14m)
Wing Area: N/A
Length: 60ft (18.28m)
Height: 18ft (5.48m) approx
Maximum Speed: Mach 2 at altitude
Range: N/A
Powerplant: 2 x afterburning turbojets; 2 x gas generators
Armaments: Sidewinders AAMs, rockets, free fall bombs

Rockwell XFV-12A
Crew: 1
WingSpan: 28.5ft (8.7m)
Wing Area: 293ft^2 (27.2m^2)
Length (excluding probe): 43.8ft (13.35m)
Height: 10.3ft (3.15m)
Empty Weight: 13,800lb (6,259kg)
Maximum VTO Weight: 19,500lb (8,845kg)
Maximum STO Weight: 24,250lb (11,000kg)
Maximum Speed: Mach 2.4 (2560km/h; 1380kt)
Ceiling: 50,000ft+ (15,240m+)
Range: N/A
Minimum Take-off Run: 300ft (91m) at max weight
Thrust/Weight: 1.5
Powerplant: 1 x Pratt & Whitney F401-PW-400 augmented turbofan, producing an estimated maximum thrust of 30,000lb (133.4kN)

Armament: One internal 20mm M61A1 Vulcan cannon 639 rounds; 2 x AIM-7 Sparrow (carried under fuselage) and 2 x AIM-9L Sidewinder AAMs or 4 x AIM-7, or Zuni 127mm rockets

Convair Model 200A
Crew: 1
Span: 27.8ft 10in (8.47m)
Wing Area: N/A
Length: 51.12ft (15.58m)
Height: 18ft (5.49m)
Maximum Take-off Weight VTO: 25,000lb (11,339kg) approx
Maximum Take-off Weight CTO: 30,000lb (13,607kg)
Maximum Speed: Mach 2
Ceiling: 55,000ft (16,764m)
Range: N/A
Powerplant: 1 x Pratt & Whitney F100 (JTF22A-30A) turbofan, rated at 14,000lb (62.2kN) dry and 26,800lb (119.1kN) with afterburning; 2 x Allison J99 lift jets, each rated at 11,200lb (49.8kN) thrust
Armament: 1 x internal 20mm M61A1 Vulcan cannon with 600 rounds; 2 x AIM-9L Sidewinder AAMs, 2 x AIM-7 Sparrow (carried under fuselage), AGM-84 Harpoon missiles or Zuni 127mm rockets

Lockheed CL-1661-2
Crew: 1
WingSpan: 28.2ft (8.6m)
Wing Area: 400ft^2 (37.16m^2); Canard Wing: 83ft^2 (7.7m^2)
Sweep (leading edge): 56°; Canard Wing: 53°
Length: 51.33ft (15.6m)
Height: 19.4ft (5.9m)
Empty Weight: N/A
Maximum VTO Weight: 28,000lb (12,700kg)
Maximum Speed: Mach 2
Ceiling: 55,000ft (16,764m)
Range: N/A
Powerplant: 1 x Pratt & Whitney F100 (JTF22A-30A) turbofan, rated at 14,000lb (62.2kN) dry and 26,800lb (119.1kN) with afterburning; 2 x Allison J99 lift jets, each rated at 11,200lb (49.8kN) thrust
Armament: 1 x 20mm M61A1 Vulcan cannon in ventral pack; 2 x AIM-9L Sidewinder AAMs, 2 x AIM-7 Sparrow (carried under fuselage), or other unspecified stores

LTV V-517/520
Crew: 1
WingSpan: 28.72ft (8.75m)
Wing Area: 275ft^2 (25.5m^2)
Sweep (leading edge): 35°
Length: 53ft (16.15m)
Height: 16.5ft (5m)
Empty Weight: 18,152lb (8,234kg)

Maximum VTO Weight: 27,480lb (12,465kg)
Maximum Speed: Mach 2
Ceiling: 55,000ft (16,764m)
Range: N/A
Powerplant (main engine): V-517A: 1 x P&W JTF10A-42A. V 517B: 1 x P&W JTF22A-30A. V-517C/D, V-520: 1 x Pratt & Whitney F401 (JTF22-30B) turbofan, rated at 15,650lb (69.6kN) dry and 27,500lb (122.3kN) thrust with afterburner
Lift Engines: V-517A/B: 3 x Rolls-Royce RB.162-81 F 08 lift turbojets, each rated at 5,587lb (24.85kN) of thrust. V-517C/D, V-520: 2 x Allison J99 Lift engines; different location for V-520
Armament (production aircraft): 1 x 20mm M61A1 Vulcan cannon with 600 rounds; 2 x AIM-7E/F Sparrow AAMs (carried under fuselage), 2 x AIM-9L Sidewinder AAMs (or a total of 4 AIM-7 AAMs), Zuni 127mm rockets, free-fall bombs

Grumman Model 607
Crew: 1
Span: 31.5ft (9.6m)
Wing Area: 365ft^2 (33.9m^2)
Length: 52ft (15.8m)
Height: 16ft (4.88m)
Empty Weight: 19,204lb (8,711kg)
VTO Weight: 30,000lb (13,950kg)
Maximum Speed: Mach 1.2 at sea level; Mach 2.0 at altitude
Ceiling: 50,000ft+ (15,240m+)
Combat endurance: 1.72 hours at 345 miles (555km) (conventional take-off)
Poweplant: 1 x Pratt & Whitney F401 (JTF22A-30B) lift/cruise turbofan producing 15,650lb (69.6kN) dry thrust and 27,500lb (122kN) thrust with afterburner; 2 x Grumman GLE-607A lift jets, each providing 11,535lb (51kN) thrust
Armament: 1 x 20mm M61A1 Vulcan cannon, 2 x AIM-9L Sidewinder AAMs, 2 x AIM-7E/F Sparrow AAMs, AGM-84 Harpoon missiles or Zuni 127mm rockets

Fairchild Republic FR-150
Crew: 1
Span: 26ft (7.92m)
Wing Area: N/A
Length: 53ft (16.15m)
Height: N/A
Empty Weight: N/A
Maximum VTO Take-off Weight: 25,000lb (11,339kg)
Maximum CTO Take-off Weight: 33,560lb (15,222kg)
Maximum Speed: Mach 1.2 at sea level; Mach 2.0 at 40,000ft (12,192m)
Ceiling: 50,000ft+ (15,240m+)
Range: 345 miles (555km)

Powerplant: 1 x Pratt & Whitney F100 (JTF22A-30A) turbofan, rated at 14,000lb (62.2kN) dry and 26,800lb (119.1kN) with afterburning; 2 x Allison J99 lift jets, each rated at 11,200lb (49.8kN) thrust

Armament: 1 x 20mm M61A1 Vulcan cannon, 2 x AIM-9L Sidewinder AAMs, 2 x AIM-7E/F Sparrow AAMs, 2 x AGM-84 Harpoon AGM or Zuni 127mm rockets

Boeing 908-535/D-180
Crew: 1
Span: 25.5ft (7.77m)
Sweep: From 80° to 55°
Wing Area: 435ft² (40.4m²)
Length: 49.5ft (15m)
Height: N/A
Empty Weight: N/A
Gross Weight: 24,150lb (10,954kg)
Maximum Speed: Mach 2.8 at 70,000ft (21,336m)
Ceiling: 75,000 (22,860m)
Powerplant: 2 x General Electric YJ101 turbofans, each rated at 15,000lb (66.7kN) dry and 27,000lb (120kN) thrust with afterburner
Armament: 1 x 20mm M61A1 Vulcan cannon, 2 x AIM-9L Sidewinder AAMs, 2 x AIM-7E/F Sparrow AAMs or 2 x AGM-84 Harpoon AGM

Rockwell Baseline and Alternative VTOL
Crew: 1 (Possibly 2)
WingSpan: 31.5ft (9.6m)
Wing Area: Baseline 422.9ft² (39.28m²). Alternative 548ft² (51m²)
Sweep (leading edge): Baseline 48° & 64°. Alternative 60°
Height: 14.3ft (4.35m)
Length: 52.25ft (15.92m)
VTO Weight: 25,000lb (11,339kg)
STO Weight: 29,400lb (13,335kg)
Maximum Speed (Baseline): Mach 1.9 at altitude
Ceiling: 50,000ft+ (15,240m+)
VTOL Combat Radius (Supersonic Intercept): 172 miles (276km)
VTOL Combat Radius (Strike/Air Defence): 345 miles (555km)
STOL Strike Range: 460 miles (740km)
Powerplant: 1 x afterburning Pratt & Whitney JT69 turbofan, with an expected dry thrust of 20,600lb (91.6kN) and a maximum of 33,800lb (150kN)
Armament: Up to 4 x AIAAM, AMRAAM, AIM-7 Sparrow or AIM-9L Sidewinder AAMs; AGM-84A Harpoon AGM, AGM-88 HARM AGM, AGM-65 Maverick AGM, or free-fall bombs; 2 x 166-gallon (754-litre) drop tanks, target designation pod, ECM or reconnaissance equipment

General Dynamics E-7
Crew: 1
WingSpan: 32.4ft (9.87m)

Wing Area: 630.6 ft² (58.58m²)
Sweep (leading edge): 60°
Height: 17ft (5.18m)
Length: 49.4ft (15m)
Maximum VTO Take-off Weight: 21,800lb (9,888kg) approx
Gross Weight STOL (6° ski-jump): 35,500-37,500lb (16,100-17,000kg)
Maximum Speed: Mach 1.7
Ceiling: 50,000ft (15,240m) approx
Range: 172-345 miles (276-555km) depending on mission; range extension using drop tanks and/or in-flight refuelling possible
Powerplant: 1 x modified General Electric F101DFE turbofan (development model for the F110) with an expected dry thrust of 17,000lb (75.6kN) and 29,000lb (129kN) with afterburner
Armaments: 2 x AIM-9s and 2 x AMRAAMs; laser-guided bombs, possibly other stores

Vought SF-121 Superfly
Crew: 1
WingSpan: 28.53ft (8.70m)
Wing Area: 354ft² (32.89m²); Canard Area: 52.6ft² (4.88m²)
Sweep (leading edge): 50°; Canard Wing: 60°
Length: 45.25ft (13.79m)
Height: 14.17ft (4.32m)
Empty Weight: N/A
VTOL Take-off Weight: 23,375lb (10,603kg)
Maximum CTOL Take-off Weight: 33,375lb (15,138kg), within 400ft (122m)
Maximum Speed: Mach 2.4
Acceleration from Mach 0.8 to Mach 1.6 at 36,000ft (10,975m): 44.6 sec
Ceiling: 60,650ft (18,486m)
Range: Supersonic intercept at Mach 1.6; 172 miles (278km); Surface Strike: 345 miles (555km)' range greater with drop tanks or in-flight refuelling
Powerplant: 2 x unspecified advanced technology mixed flow afterburning turbofans, each with an expected dry thrust of 16,375lb (72.8kN)
Armament: 1 x M61A1 20mm six-barrel cannon with 603-round capacity drum. It was hoped to replace this with a 25mm three-barrel cannon using caseless ammunition, but the technology proved unreliable. Up to 4 x AIAAM, AMRAAM, AIM-7 Sparrow or AIM-9L Sidewinder AAMs; AGM-84A Harpoon AGM, AGM-88 HARM AGM, AGM-65 Maverick AGM, or free-fall/laser-guided bombs; 2 x 250-gallon (946-litre) drop tanks, target designation, or reconnaissance equipment

Vought TF120
Length: 46ft (14.02m)
WingSpan: 28ft (8.53m)
Wing Area: 350ft² (32.5m²); Canard Area: 20.8ft² (1.93m²)
Sweep (leading edge): 50°

Height: 11.67ft (3.55m)
Empty Weight: 14,253lb (6,465kg)
Gross Weight: 24,940lb (11,312kg)
Maximum Speed: Mach 1.2 at sea level, Mach 2.4 at altitude, and a supercruise capability Acceleration from Mach 0.8 to Mach 1.6 at 36,089ft (10,999m) in less than 60 seconds
Ceiling 66,550ft (20,284m)
Range: VTO Supersonic Intercept: 230 miles (370km). VTO Subsonic Fighter Escort: 622 miles (1,000km). Short take-off: Combat Air Patrol, with four air-to-air missiles and two 308-gallon (1,400-litre) drop tanks: 964 miles (1,550km). Short take-off Interdiction/Strike: 4 x laser-guided bombs, 2 x AAMs and drop tanks: 597 miles (960km)
Powerplant: 1 x afterburning mixed flow, augmented turbofan, driving a remote front fan through an extension shaft; suggested ratings for this proposed engine were: 25,000lb dry (111kN), 34,000lb (151kN) with afterburner, possibly rising to 42,960lb (191kN) with development
Armament: 1 x 20mm M61A1 Vulcan cannon with 400 rounds, 4 x AMRAAMs, laser-guided bombs, probably air-to-surface missiles

Northrop N338-12
WingSpan: 32.6ft (9.9m)
Sweep (leading edge): 50°
Wing Area: 500ft² (46.45m²)
Height: 13.3ft (4m)
Length: 15.8m (51.7ft)
VTO Gross Weight: 30,000lb (13,607.7kg)
Maximum Speed: Supersonic
Ceiling: 50,000ft (15,249m) estimated
Range: 575 miles (925km) (escort fighter mission)
Powerplant: Unspecified Pratt & Whitney variable-geometry turbojets
Armament: 1 x 20mm cannon, AMRAAM, ASRAAM or Sidewinder AAMs, Harpoon AGM, HARM AGM or free-fall bombs

Northrop N382-20
WingSpan: 32.4ft (9.87m)
Wing Area: 495.3ft² (49.5m²); Canard Area: 45.5ft² (4.22m²)
Sweep (leading edge): Wing 50°; Canard 60°
Height: 14.25ft (4.34m)
Length: 40.7ft (14.84m)
VTO Gross Take-off Weight: 30,000lb (13,607.7kg)
STO Gross Weight: 35,000lb (15,857kg)
Maximum Speed: Mach 1.8 estimated
Ceiling: 50,000ft (15,249m)
Range: 575 miles (925km) (escort fighter mission)
Powerplant: Unspecified GE afterburning turbofan rated at 42,345lb (188kN) dry
Armament: 20mm cannon with 500 rounds; 2 x AMRAAM and 2 x ASRAAM internal AAMs; underwing stores

Chapter 6 Harriers and Advanced VTOL Designs

This final chapter initially covers the Harrier and its known clones, or models using similar engine technology, including various supersonic proposals. One particularly interesting design was the very advanced Republic Fokker D-24 multi-role VTOL combat aircraft, which was probably too far ahead of its time.I have briefly described the troubled, very costly Lockheed Martin F-35B, which might be seen as a present-day descendant of the SCS fighter programme, and concluded with VTOL fighter developments in the Soviet Union.

ABOVE A line-up of Tripartite Kestrels at RAF West Raynham in Norfolk during early 1965. *BAe*

The Harrier

The British Harrier is the best-known VTOL strike fighter and the only design to see operational service. Many authors have written in considerable detail about the Harrier and its engine, so I have restricted this section to a basic outline, spending most of my time examining the more unusual developments and proposed variants of this exceptional aircraft. It also needs to be mentioned that although the Harrier has often been referred to as a 'Jump Jet' or a vertical take-off fighter, it appears that no version has ever operated this way in a combat situation. This is certainly the case with RAF and Royal Navy aircraft and it was one of the first things I discussed with the UK Ministry of Defence when starting work on this book. As far as I have been able to ascertain, no overseas operator of the Harrier has ever used full VTOL in any combat situation.

Normally, an operational Harrier would make a short take-off run to become airborne, allowing the carriage of an adequate payload. A vertical landing might be undertaken on return to an aircraft carrier. I have personally watched several different Harriers demonstrate vertical take-offs, but this method severely limits payload and/or range. Newspaper reports of Harrier 'Jump Jets' using their VTOL capability during the Falklands War are all incorrect and a 780ft (238m) metal strip was employed as a makeshift runway at the Forward Operating Base. However, as one near exception to this rule, two Harriers were prepared to undertake short-range VTOL air defence operations from the deck of the merchant ship Atlantic Conveyor during the Falklands Campaign. Several VTOL transfers were also made between this ship and the RN aircraft carrier HMS *Hermes*.

The origins of the Harrier can be traced back to a well-respected French aeronautical engineer called Michel Henri Marie Joseph Wibault (1897-1963), who became interested in VTOL and disc-shaped aircraft during the immediate postwar years. By 1950, he was designing a high-speed circular-shaped strike aircraft that would be capable of operating from improvised sites. (See the author's previous book *Flying Saucer Technology* by Midland Publications.) As Wibault's aircraft steadily evolved, becoming progressively more conventional in appearance, he began to look for a new propulsive system. This would lead to a concept involving four separate blower units powered by a Bristol BE.25 Orion turboshaft engine producing 8,000hp (5,970kW). Each blower would be positioned around the aircraft's centre of gravity and capable of being rotated to provide downward or horizontal thrust. With several designs completed, Wibault approached the French government, but his ideas were swiftly rejected. He then visited the NATO Mutual Weapons Development Programme (MWDP) office in Paris where his research was recognised as having considerable potential and immediately forwarded to the US for examination by the MWDP's senior aerodynamic consultant, Dr Theodore von Kármán (1881-1963).

Wibault's work clearly made quite an impression on von Kármán, who then passed the details to Sir Stanley Hooker (1907-1984) at Bristol Aero Engines in England. In turn, Hooker arranged to meet Wibault and immediately decided that his propulsion design had considerable potential. As a result, Hooker assigned Gordon Lewis (1924-2010), Pierre Young and Neville Quinn to examine Wibault's ideas in detail. The engineers quickly realised that the concept could be significantly improved by a rearrangement of the propulsive system, which would duct some of the engine's airflow through two swivelling forward outlets, while retaining a fairly uncomplicated exhaust at the rear. It resulted in the construction of an experimental Orion-based engine called the BE.48. This was soon replaced by the BE.52 and the BE.53, based on the Orpheus turbojet fitted with a larger compressor fan.

Wibault was now on Bristol's payroll as a technical consultant and is said to have been delighted with the way this project was going. At the start of 1957, Bristol Siddeley Engines Ltd applied for a UK patent on behalf of Wibault and Lewis for the new engine, although there was no suitable aircraft in development to make use of it. However, Hawker Aircraft's chief designer Sir Sydney Camm (1893-1966) was already following the development of this new engine and assigned Ralph Hooper (1926-), who was assisted by (Prof) John Fozard (1928-1996), to design a suitable airframe. The first rather crude, straight-wing, two-seat proposal received the company reference P.1127. It was barely recognisable as being related to later designs, but started to evolve almost immediately, with a decision being taken to channel the BE.53 engine's main exhaust through two rear vectoring nozzles as opposed to a single outlet. At the same time Bristol

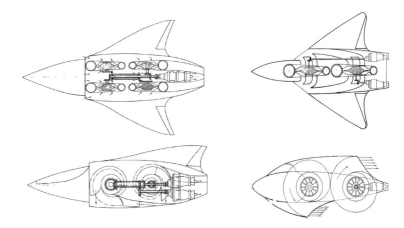

LEFT An original Wibault design for a VTOL fighter, using a turbojet engine driving four blower units. This concept is a very early ancestor of the British V/STOL Harrier. *US Patent Office/Bill Rose*

RIGHT Schematic for a VTOL fighter propulsion system produced by Henri Wibault in the early 1950s. *US Patent Office/Bill Rose*

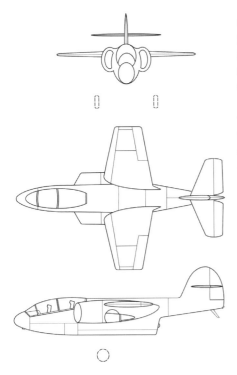

ABOVE This drawing is directly based on the first Hawker P.1127 concept that would progressively evolve into the Harrier. At this point, the two-seat design had little in common with the later designs. Bill Rose

continued to refine the BE.53, raising the thrust to about 10,000lb (44.5kN), which ensured the success of this lightweight VTOL strike fighter.

Unfortunately, the late 1950s were a bad time for UK aircraft manufacturers, with the government slashing defence spending and suggesting there was little future need for manned combat aircraft, as missiles would be taking over. Nevertheless, Colonel Bill Chapman of the MWDP remained supportive of Wibault's concept and a deal was struck with Bristol to provide further financial support for engine development. At the same time, Camm managed to convince Hawker's board to fund the construction of a prototype and it agreed to this in August 1958. Further improvements were made to the engine which had been called the Pegasus and, in addition to various engineering refinements, the maximum thrust was now theoretically in the region of 13,500lb (60kN).

The design began to find favour with senior RAF officials, who were willing to disagree with the government's stance on development of new military aircraft. Subsequently, the MoS reviewed the possibility of purchasing two P.1127 prototypes for official evaluation. NASA now lent some support to the project with wind tunnel testing, but there were ongoing problems with the Pegasus engine, which began bench tests in August 1959 and continued to underachieve.

The first P.1127 was largely completed by July 1960 and assigned the official serial reference XP831, although the first engine was not delivered until the end of August 1960. Test pilot Bill Bedford made the first tethered flight on 21 October 1960 at Dunsfold Aerodrome and the aircraft handled very badly, leading to further modifications, although the overriding problem was insufficient engine power. The first untethered hover took place on 19 November 1960 and

XP831 was then transferred to the RAE, followed by the second prototype XP836, which made its first rolling take-off on 7 July 1961. Flight-testing continued to be undertaken by Bill Bedford and his deputy Hugh Merewether, who were able to perform vertical and short take-offs followed by vertical landings.

The P.1127 was fairly conventional in appearance and now recognisable as an early type of Harrier, with large air inlets on each side of the fuselage just aft of the cockpit and four swivelling (hot and cold) exhaust nozzles on each side of the fuselage below the wing. On the ground, P.1127 was supported by a single retractable nosewheel and a second tandem retractable strut with two wheels about midway along the fuselage. Outriggers at each wingtip guaranteed stability and would be a feature of all future Harrier designs. The aircraft was also relatively compact, with an overall length of 41.16ft (12.54m) and a short wingspan of 24.33ft (7.41m). Empty, the P.1127 weighed about 10,200lb (4,626kg), making vertical take-off in ideal conditions difficult with the limited engine power, although development of the Pegasus was still at an early stage, with ongoing improvements taking place. Low-speed control was assisted by the puffer system, using compressor -bleed air, which initially proved rather unsatisfactory and required a significant redesign.

Four more Hawker P.1127 prototypes were ordered (XP972, XP976, XP980, XP984) and a range of improvements were made to the aerodynamics and engines, with the last of this series (XP984) being fitted with a new wing and eventually the more powerful Bristol Siddeley Pegasus 5, rated at 15,000lb (66.7kN). This aircraft would become the first version of a second series of aircraft called the Kestrel. Many 'firsts' were achieved by the P.1127, with XP836 attaining Mach 1.2 in a shallow dive during December 1961, and Bill Bedford conducted take-off and landing trials with XP831 on the carrier HMS *Ark Royal* (R09) during February 1963. Accidents and mishaps with the P.1127 were frequent, with the first three prototypes crashing. The original aircraft (XP831) made a hard emergency landing at the 1963 Paris Air Show, although it was fully repaired and became a museum exhibit. None of the pilots involved in any of these incidents were seriously injured.

LEFT The Hawker P.1127 (XP972) demonstrated at Farnborough on 8 September 1962. *TSRL*

RIGHT Side view of the first P.1127 prototype. *BAe*

The Kestrel

Even before the first prototype flew, government indecision placed the P.1127 in difficulty. NATO had issued requirements for a supersonic VTOL strike fighter and the French were developing a VTOL version of the Mirage, powered by Rolls-Royce engines. This appeared to be the front-runner, with the Americans taking an immediate interest in the project and considering buying an advanced version.

Fortunately for the British, the MWDP encouraged a joint development programme with the West Germans, which led to an agreement in early 1961. This saved the P.1127 project and it seems that West Germany was happy to fund this project, while proceeding with the development of another somewhat similar VTOL combat aircraft (the VAK 191B). As a consequence, the Pentagon agreed to additional funding for the construction of new British aircraft for use by a specialist unit based in Norfolk, England, known as the Tripartite Evaluation Squadron (TES). An agreement was formally signed on 16 January 1963 and nine improved P.1127s were placed on order. These aircraft would be renamed the following year as the Kestrel, Fighter-Ground Attack Version 1 (FGA.1).

Similar in appearance to the final P.1127 prototype and equipped with the more powerful Pegasus 5 turbofan, the first Kestrel flew on 7 March 1964. Aside from numerous engineering improvements, the new aircraft was now equipped with underwing pylons allowing the carriage of drop tanks and practice bombs. The TES was based at RAF West Raynham in Norfolk and commenced operations during March 1965. Pilots making up the squadron were from the RAF, Luftwaffe, USAF, US Navy and US Army, but surprisingly, not the US Marine Corps, who would eventually become the only US operators.

Trials generally went well, with tests also taking place in intentionally difficult conditions at nearby RAF Bircham Newton. In total, 938 flights were made and one Kestrel was destroyed in a take-off accident, although the US pilot escaped without injury. The TES came to an end in November 1965 and the following year, two Kestrels were retained by the British, while six others were taken to the US for further evaluation and redesignated XV-6A.

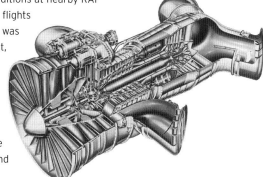

BELOW Artwork showing the interior detail of a Rolls-Royce Pegasus turbofan engine. *Rolls-Royce*

The Harrier

Various advanced designs based on the Kestrel were now under way and I intend to return to supersonic proposals in a later section. Aside from this, there was considerable official UK interest in further development of the Kestrel into a subsonic strike-reconnaissance aircraft for the RAF. This would lead to the Harrier Ground Attack-Reconnaissance 1 (GR.1), with a contract being issued for six pre-production aircraft on 17 February 1965. Although resembling the Kestrel, the GR.1 was actually a substantial design revision undertaken by a team now headed by John Fozard. With the design-to-construction time being more rapid than today, the first GR.1 flew on 31 August 1966. Following this initial batch of aircraft, the first production GR.1 flew on 28 December 1967 and entered RAF service the following year, followed by a two-seat conversion trainer called the Harrier T.2. Both aircraft were broadly similar in most other respects, being fitted with the more reliable and higher-powered Pegasus 6 Mark 101 turbofan, providing a maximum thrust of 19,000lb (84.5kN), with the addition of water injection. However, despite being capable of nudging past Mach 1 in a shallow dive, the GR.1 was optimised for subsonic flight at relatively low level. Stores could be carried on underwing pylons, with a maximum weight of about 5,000lb (2,267kg). Only a rolling take-off would be possible in this condition.

Weapons carried included free-fall bombs, BL755 cluster bombs, unguided rockets, or 30mm Aden Mk 4 cannon packs (each with 100 rounds) below the central fuselage section. Other underwing options included 100-gallon (454-litre) drop tanks or a daylight photo-reconnaissance pod. No forward radar system was carried by the GR.1, as this was deemed unnecessary at the time. Although VTOL was possible without external stores, it was soon accepted that short take-offs and vertical landings without stores would become the normal method of operation, allowing a combat radius of approximately 230 miles (370km). This might be considered rather unsatisfactory when compared to a conventional strike fighter, but the Harrier was intended for use from improvised forward sites and its range could be extended with in-flight refuelling, using an accessory probe. In total, sixty-one GR.1s and ten T.2s were built for the RAF, plus three two-seat prototypes used for development purposes.

Further improvements to the Pegasus engine led to the Mark 102, which provided 20,500lb (91.98kN) of thrust, followed by the extensively revised Pegasus 11 Mark 103, providing another 1,000lb (4.44kN) of thrust, improved reliability and easier maintenance. This led to the Harrier GR.3 and the T.4. One visible change to the

GR.3 was an elongated nose, using the Ferranti 106 laser target designation system. Harriers were now operating from RAF Wittering, RAF Wildenrath in West Germany and deployed later to RAF Gütersloh, also in West Germany. Their primary purpose was to provide close support to ground forces in the event of a European East-West conflict. Operations would be undertaken from improvised sites in forests, areas where metallic runways could be put down and autobahns or major roads. The first recorded active deployment of Harriers took place in the mid-1970s when the former British colony Belize was threatened by Guatamala and six Harriers from No 1 Squadron were moved there as a deterrent.

Meanwhile, the US Marine Corps had expressed a strong interest in acquiring the Harrier and this led to negotiations with the British government and the UK/US contractors who would be involved. The Marine Corps had fully evaluated the Kestrel at the Naval Air Test Center at Patuxent River, Maryland, after several of the TES aircraft had been passed to them and they were interested in acquiring an improved version. A direct purchase from the British was considered politically difficult, but it was agreed that if the deal went ahead, McDonnell Douglas would be licensed to build a version of the GR.1 known as the AV-8A. In addition, Pratt & Whitney would be contracted to build a version of the Pegasus engine under licence, which would become the P&W F402-RR.

An agreement was finally reached, although it was not quite as straightforward as planned. McDonnell Douglas was unable to build the aircraft for an affordable price, as it would have required a new production line. As a consequence, the required 110 aircraft ordered by the US Marine Corps were built largely in the UK and finished by McDonnell Douglas. A number of alterations were made at this point, with new avionics, radio equipment, cockpit instrument changes, a different ejector seat and larger drop tanks. Other modifications included rewiring for US weapons, including the Sidewinder AAM. That aside, the aircraft remained very similar in appearance to the GR.1, with the first US combat unit taking delivery of these aircraft in 1971.

This was followed by a small Spanish Navy order for AV-8As and TAV-8As in 1973. Supplied via the US for political reasons, the aircraft operated from the elderly carrier *Dedalo*, which was eventually replaced by the *Principe de Asturias*, a modern-design 16,700-ton (15,150 metric tonnes) vessel commissioned in 1988 and designed from the outset to handle Harriers and helicopters. In 1997, the Harriers sold to Spain were upgraded and the original aircraft sold to the Thai Navy. These would operate from their newly purchased light carrier *Chakri Naruebet*, which was similar to the *Principe de Asturias*, and also from a land base. Note that the Spanish carrier *Principe de Asturias* was decommissioned in Feb 2013 due to deep defence cuts.

The Sea Harrier and Combat Operations

ABOVE Sea Harriers 715 and 710 are prepared for flight.
Bill Rose

The P.1127 had proved its ability to function as a carrier-based aircraft, although there was some Admiralty opposition to the introduction of a new combat aircraft that lacked supersonic performance. Nevertheless, the Royal Navy finally decided to adopt a revised version of the VTOL strike fighter, with development beginning in the early 1970s. Subsequently, the P.1184, which became the Sea Harrier Fighter-Reconnaissance-Strike Mark 1 (FRS.1), made its

first flight on 20 August 1978. It was broadly similar to the GR.3, but featured a new nose and a redesigned cockpit, with improved visibility for the pilot. The engine was modified to cope with the more corrosive marine environment and alterations were made to the wingtip reaction control system. The FRS.1 was in many ways an improvement over the GR.3, undertaking a range of different roles including intercept missions. To achieve this, the FRS.1 carried two Sidewinder missiles and the Ferranti Blue Fox radar system.

The first production Sea Harrier entered Royal Navy service in June 1979 and subsequent aircraft, known to the pilots and crew as Shars, eventually became operational onboard HMS *Illustrious*, *Invincible* and Ark Royal. Enhancing the aircraft's capability significantly was a relatively simple deck modification invented by RN Lieutenant-Commander Douglas Taylor. He came up with the idea of a ski-jump that allowed a short take-off and greater payload. Surprisingly, there was some resistance to the idea, but it was finally adopted. HMS *Illustrious* and *Invincible* were initially fitted with 7° ski-jumps, later modified to a steeper angle of 13°. HMS *Ark Royal* was equipped with a 12° ski-jump when it was commissioned in 1985. The Spanish and Thai navies also adopted this system for their carriers.

In 1982, the British responded to an Argentinian invasion of the Falkland Islands by assembling a naval task force under the name Operation Corporate. This involved a fleet made up from various ships, headed by two aircraft carriers, HMS *Hermes* and HMS *Invincible*, carrying a total of 28 Harriers. In addition, 14 RAF GR.3 Harriers from No 1 Squadron flew from the UK to Ascension Island in the South Atlantic, taking nine hours and requiring five separate mid-air refuellings. Ten of these aircraft were transferred to container ships, while another four flew the remainder of the distance with in-flight refuelling. The GR.3s were not designed to undertake air combat, so each aircraft was rewired during the voyage to allow the carriage of Sidewinder missiles. The Sea Harriers also underwent last-minute modifications to allow the carriage of chaff/flare dispensers and some may have been equipped with an electronic countermeasures unit developed for use with the Tornado.

During the conflict Sea Harriers were primarily responsible for air defence, while the GR.3s attacked ground targets. On paper, the Sea Harriers were outclassed by the Argentine Dassault Mirage and IAI Dagger supersonic fighters. However, these aircraft were operating at maximum range, the Sea Harriers were armed with the latest AIM-9L Sidewinders and the British pilots were highly skilled. By the end of the conflict, Sea Harriers had shot down 21 enemy aircraft, of which 10 were supersonic fighters. No British aircraft were lost in aerial combat, but three GR.3s were shot down and one suffered an engine failure at Port San Carlos. Two Sea Harriers were also shot down, two more from HMS *Invincible* collided in mid-air, killing the pilots, and one rolled off the deck of HMS *Invincible* in very bad weather conditions. The pilot ejected and was rescued. On the same day, another Sea Harrier exploded shortly after take-off. The pilot was killed and the cause remains unknown. During this conflict, more than 2,000 Harrier sorties were flown and it seems fair to say that the Falklands would have remained under Argentine rule without the Harriers.

Soon after the Falklands War ended, India became interested in purchasing a small number of Sea Harriers for use with its extensively overhauled aircraft carrier INS *Vikrant* (originally HMS *Hercules*). A small initial batch of Sea Harriers and two-seat trainers were supplied to the Indian Navy, with a series of modifications, including a different radar system and the ability to carry the French Matra Magic AAM. India then purchased HMS *Hermes*, renaming it INS *Viraat* and purchased more Sea Harriers from the UK. This vessel remains in service, although it is due to be replaced by 2020 with one of two new larger carriers. Originally intended to carry the Sea Harrier, these will

now be equipped with the MiG-29K strike fighter and possibly the HAL Tejas.

The Falklands War had shown a number of deficiencies and shortcomings with the aircraft. For air-to-air combat, the Sea Harrier was inadequately armed, requiring four longer-range missiles, and a further issue was the Blue Fox radar system, which proved unsatisfactory. The Sea Harrier's range also remained a problem. These concerns led to a number of upgrades, which included additional pylons for missiles and larger drop tanks. Various other modifications were introduced and the Sea Eagle anti-ship missile soon became available, although this had been planned before the Falklands War.

Before moving away from the FRS.1 Shar, it is worth mentioning that Royal Navy FRS.1 Sea Harriers undertook patrols to enforce the UN's no-fly zone over Bosnia and Herzegovina during Operation Deny Flight (1993–1995). One aircraft from HMS *Ark Royal* was shot down by a shoulder-launched missile, with the pilot ejecting and being rescued by an SAS unit. At the end of 1995, the FRS.1 was withdrawn from service. A replacement aircraft was now in development known as the FRS.2, which featured a new Blue Vixen radar system with much improved performance and the ability to carry four AIM-120 Advanced Medium-Range Air-to-Air Missiles (AMRAAM). Other improvements included a range of cockpit upgrades and changes to the Pegasus engine. However, this was not exactly a new design and it was possible to upgrade 33 existing FRS.1 aircraft to FRS.2 specification, with the last of these entering RN service in 1997. Eight-brand new FRS.2 Shars and seven upgraded T.8 trainers were also supplied to the RN at the end of 1998, making these the last entirely British-built naval fighters. One other small change was the redesignation of the aircraft to Fighter-Attack, receiving the new designation FA.2. In 2005, the Indian Navy considered the option of buying a batch of surplus RN FA.2 aircraft, but finally decided they were too expensive, so upgraded its existing aircraft with the Israeli Elta EL/M-2032 multi-mode radar and Rafael missiles.

ABOVE The first production Sea Harrier (XZ450) is demonstrated at Farnborough by John Farley in September 1978. It was then set aside for weapons trials and equipped to carry the Sea Eagle anti-ship missile. At the start of the Falklands War, this aircraft was hastily pressed into service and shot down over Goose Green on 4 May 1982. The pilot, Lieutenant Nick Taylor, was killed. When the Argentines examined the wreckage of XZ450, they discovered the Sea Eagle control system and incorrectly deduced that all the British Sea Harriers were equipped to fire this missile. It is believed that this assumption was responsible for keeping the Argentine Navy in port during most of the conflict. *Bill Rose*

Harrier II

For some time prior to the Falklands War there had been a desire on both sides of the Atlantic to replace existing Harriers with a more advanced VTOL strike fighter. This initially took the form of a British supersonic derivative known as the P.1154, which came very close to being built, and some time later was followed by a series of supersonic proposals put forward by McDonnell Douglas. I will look at these separately in a later section.

British Aerospace and McDonnell Douglas produced an initial study for an improved Harrier in 1973, which received the designation AV-16A (or AV-8X), which would use an uprated Pegasus turbofan using plenum chamber burning (PCB). The intention was to produce a marginally supersonic strike fighter with double the range and payload of the existing AV-8A. However, there were problems with funding the proposed Pegasus 15 engine and as a result the project was put back on the shelf. Then McDonnell Douglas began to examine a more reserved update for the US Marine Corps, using a bigger composite wing. This led to two YAV-8Bs being produced, which were little more than existing AV-8As with the new wing. The first flight took place on 9 November 1978 and it was immediately apparent that this was a worthwhile upgrade. After some political manoeuvring, the RAF (which was already looking at Harrier upgrades) agreed to buy 60 new aircraft with the American wing, subject to various modifications. The British aircraft would differ in some respects from the American version, with production

for both variants being split between McDonnell Douglas and BAe. The first all-new prototype flew on 5 November 1981 and the first production AV-8B flew on 29 August 1983.

Although it was intended to be a relatively modest upgrade, the AV-8B became much more than a rewinged AV-8A, with the extensive use of weight-reducing composites and more underwing pylons able to carry a range of different stores. The US version was also equipped with a single 25mm cannon that replaced the two 30mm Aden cannons fitted to UK-built aircraft. The cockpit was extensively redesigned, utilising state-of-the-art controls, new display panels and providing good visibility for the pilot. A new avionics suite was installed, along with chaff/flare dispensers and the option of a jammer pod. In addition, the in-flight refuelling capability was improved with a fully retractable probe.

The engine used in the AV-8B was also a slightly tweaked version of the Pegasus 104, not surprisingly called the Pegasus 105. A US version built by Pratt & Whitney was designated as the F402-RR-406 and this turbofan had a maximum rated thrust of 22,000lb

BELOW US Marine Corps Harrier YAV-8B undertakes ski-jump trials at Naval Air Station Patuxent River, Maryland, in June 1979. Surprisingly, the Americans never adopted this system. *McDonnell Douglas*

LEFT Two US Marine Corps AV-8B Harriers from the VMF-214 Marine Squadron are fuelled aboard the Tarawa-class amphibious assault ship USS *Peleliu* (LHA-5) during Pacific Ocean operations in 2005. *US Navy*

RIGHT A US Marine Corps AV-8B+(R)-27-MC Harrier II Plus (BuNo 165597) from Marine attack squadron VMA-231 Ace of Spades at the EAA AirVenture Convention at Oshosh, Wisconsin, in 2003. *Paul Maritz*

(97.8kN), with digital engine management. In addition, it was decided to build a two-seat TAV-8B trainer version, which first flew on 21 November 1986. An additional minor US variant known as the AV-8B (NA) was optimised for night attack. It was equipped with an infrared imager, some revision to the instruments, increased chaff, flare and electronic countermeasures and a new engine. This was the Pegasus 11-61 (F402-RR-408), providing increased thrust and a further maintenance reduction. Unfortunately, there were some unexpected reliability issues requiring the blades to be changed from titanium to steel. The AV-8B (NA) entered service during September 1989.

Further modifications to the AV-8B, included the Hughes AN/APG-65 multi-mode radar, used by the F/A-18 Hornet, additional AAM launch rails and eventually a capability to carry the Rafael/Northrop Grumman Litening II and later Litening-ER (Extended Range) target acquisition and designation pod.

US AV-8Bs participated in the first Gulf War of 1991 and were responsible for an impressive 7.7% of the sorties flown during this campaign. Of the substantial number of AV-8Bs deployed, four were shot down in a period of just over one month: two by anti-aircraft fire and two by surface-to-air missiles. US Marine Corps AV-8Bs were also deployed to Afghanistan in late 2001. Operating from the assault ship USS *Peleliu*, they mainly conducted ground strikes in support of Special Forces. US and British Harriers were also amongst the first combat aircraft to attack Republican Guard strongholds during the US-led invasion of Iraq in 2003. A small number of AV-8B aircraft (designated EAV-8B) were purchased by the Spanish, with the first three being delivered in 1988, followed by a further eight AV-

8Bs and one trainer. These were then upgraded to the 'Plus' standard by CASA (now EADS-CASA) in Spain. The Spanish Navy already operated Harriers and these would equip its new aircraft carrier, the *Principe de Asturias*. Italy also purchased eighteen new Harriers from the Americans for its new light carrier, the *Giuseppe Garibaldi*. Following a small initial batch of aircraft, the remaining AV-8Bs were supplied as components and assembled in Italy by Alenia Aeronautica. Spain deployed land-based EAV-8Bs to enforce the UN's no-fly zone in the Balkans during Operation Deny Flight. There were no losses. Italian AV-8Bs also saw action in Libya during 2011, undertaking numerous raids against Gaddafi's forces from the aircraft carrier *Garibaldi*.

Britain's Harrier II Series

TOP RAF Harrier GR.7A (ZD431) photographed in 2006. *Adrian Pingstone*

ABOVE An RAF Harrier GR.9 during a combat patrol above Afghanistan on 12 December 2008. *Staff Sgt Aaron Allmon, USAF*

The UK version of the AV-8B was known as the GR.5, although it differed in a number of ways from the American aircraft. The RAF had insisted on substantial changes to the avionics, communications, various cockpit modifications and entirely different countermeasures. This included Bofors BOL chaff dispensers, a Plessey missile approach warning (MAW) unit and an advanced Marconi Zeus ECM system. Two newly designed 25mm Aden cannons were fitted, although these weapons proved unreliable and the source of continual problems.

The first GR.5 was test flown at Dunsfold in Surrey on 30 April 1985 and four years later the first batch of GR.5s began to replace existing RAF GR.3s. A total of 41 aircraft were supplied to the RAF and these were followed by 21 GR.5As, which were prepared to accept a series of upgrades that would bring them in line with the GR.7 when it became available. This aircraft was broadly similar to the American AV-8B (NA) version, but utilised British-built electronics. Like the GR.5, the GR.7 was fitted with a Rolls-Royce Pegasus 11-21/Mk

105 vectored-thrust turbofan, rated at 21,750lb (96.7kN) thrust, and in most respects the two variants were very similar.

The first GR.7 flew on 20 November 1989, with service entry for the first 34 aircraft beginning in 1990. Subsequently, the majority of GR.5s would be upgraded to GR.7 standard and short leading- edge root extensions (LERX) were added to improve handling at high angles of attack (AOA). During the mid-1990s, RAF GR.7s undertook air strikes against Serb military targets in the Balkans as part of the NATO campaign, with aircraft receiving further updates allowing the carriage of AGM-65 Maverick air-to-surface missiles and Enhanced Paveway bombs.

GR.7s were now able to operate from RN aircraft carriers, with Sea Harriers providing fighter cover. This method of operation became Joint Force Harrier in 2000, with the RAF formally working with the Royal Navy. In 2003, RAF GR.7s undertook ground-attack missions against Iraqi targets in Operation Telic. The majority of precision strikes were undertaken with Maverick missiles and Paveway II laser-guided bombs. No aircraft were lost during operations over Iraq. However, on 14 October 2005, two RAF GR.7As were hit by a Taliban rocket attack while parked on the tarmac at Kandahar Air Base in Afghanistan. One aircraft was destroyed and the other damaged, although it was later repaired. From this period onwards, GR.7As were deployed in larger numbers to Afghanistan, normally providing close air support for ground forces.

There was already a move to retire the remaining Sea Harriers and standardise on a single RAF and RN aircraft that would have further upgrades to its performance and capability. The new aircraft, known as the GR.9, was essentially a GR.7 with substantial avionics upgrades and improved weapon-handling capabilities. Aircraft rebuilt to the GR.9 specification became operational in Afghanistan during January 2007 as part of the NATO International Security Assistance Force (ISAF). A programme of engine upgrades now commenced, with GR.9s being equipped with the Pegasus 107 turbofan, providing a maximum thrust of 23,800lb (105.8kN) and adding further improvements to maintenance and reliability. The revised aircraft was now renamed GR.9A.

The Sea Harrier had been retired in 2006 and Britain now planned to replace the remaining Harrier IIs with F-35B Lightning II stealth strike fighters when they became available. These would operate from two new 65,000-ton Queen Elizabeth Class aircraft carriers.

Although the GR.9 was expected to remain in service until at least 2018, there was intense political pressure placed on the MoD in 2010 to save money. Various decisions were made after the October 2010 Strategic

Defence and Security Review, but it seems very likely that a plan to scrap the Harrier was conceived earlier in the year. After a major rearrangement of RAF Squadrons using this aircraft in spring 2010, all GR.7s had ceased operations by July 2010. On 19 October 2010, the GR.9s were taken out of service and HMS *Ark Royal* was scheduled for decommissioning. As a result of this, the Harrier made its last ever flight from HMS *Ark Royal* on 24 November 2010.

In June 2011, journalists uncovered a deal between the MoD and the US Marine Corps for the sale of Britain's entire Harrier fleet, spares and ground equipment, although there were immediate denials by UK officials. Nevertheless, the story was true and the Americans had secured an absolute bargain. Seventy-two aircraft were shipped to the US, which included GR.7, GR.9, GR.9A versions and nine trainers, plus a substantial quantity of spares and maintenance/

handling equipment, all for $180 million. This deal followed the completion of a major refit costing UK taxpayers hundreds of millions of pounds. Such was the sensitivity of what had taken place that the MoD secretly urged all government officials to stonewall any difficult questions put by the media. The UK government successfully diverted attention from the affair, although this sale would eventually generate considerable anger when the details became more widely known. At the time of writing many of the ex-British Harriers are stored by the Aerospace Maintenance and Regeneration Group at its open-air facility in Tucson, Arizona. However, it is understood that the US Marine Corps has put a number of British GR.9s into service, due to the excellent condition of these well-maintained aircraft. Just two Harrier GR.9s were retained for the Fleet Air Arm Museum at RNAS Yeovilton and the RAF Museum at RAF Cosford.

Harrier Special Projects

The name Skyhook has been applied to a number of specialised aviation projects, often of a secret or covert nature. The Harrier Skyhook Project was conceived at about the end of 1980 by Heinz Erwin Frick (1940–) who worked for BAe as a test pilot. BAe was undertaking a study of future options for the Sea Harrier and Frick came up with an idea that allowed deployment of the Harrier from small ships and allowed the aircraft's weight to be reduced, thus improving overall performance. Frick suggested the use of a crane-like apparatus that would handle the launch and retrieval of modified Sea Harrier at sea, indicating that it would actually be safer to use than a normal aircraft carrier deck in less than ideal conditions. The company were sufficiently impressed with his proposal to apply for a UK Patent in mid-1981 and a US Patent one year later.

Skyhook would allow a destroyer-sized vessel to normally operate four to six combat aircraft, without the need for a landing deck. There would be further advantages in the elimination of engine re-ingestion problems and aircraft would be able to refuel from the crane without coming aboard the vessel. Calculations indicated that it would be possible to transfer fuel at the rate of 1,000lb (453.5kg) per minute, making the operation relatively brief. A key feature of the design would be an advanced control system that fully compensated for the ship's movements and ensured stability in difficult conditions. The release and capture sequence would be largely automated, with improvements taking place as computer technology advanced. However, Skyhook would require a specially adapted Sea Harrier with a suitable docking unit directly positioned above the centre of gravity. The weight of the aircraft would be significantly reduced by

the elimination of an undercarriage, improving range and payload. In addition to two cranes, there would be the need for a hangar section to store aircraft, fuel, ordnance and maintenance equipment.

BAe now appointed engineer Dennis J. Mottram as Skyhook project manager and experiments were undertaken at Dunsfold Aerodrome using a large crane with a simulated coupling unit suspended from it. Four test pilots undertook hover trials directly underneath, with no obvious problems. The cost of developing this system is said to have been relatively modest and Mottram's team liaised with naval architects who envisaged no major problems with the scheme.

Skyhook remained under development throughout most of the 1980s, with proposals to use oil-drilling rigs as Harrier refuelling and rearming facilities in special circumstances. Another Skyhook concept involved the use of semi-submersible barges and, according to Mottram, the Skyhook system might even be used with some helicopters. Unfortunately for BAe's Skyhook team, the MoD showed relatively little interest in the idea and was unwilling to fund any further development. Mottram had also been considering the idea of using Skyhook for ship-to-ship and ship-to-shore transfer of cargo and fuel, which was the logical progression for this design. US Patents were filed and appeared in 1988/9, but this appears to be as far as the project progressed.

Another intriguing idea was the replacement of Harrier fuel tanks with pods designed to carry either a single passenger or

BELOW One of the more unusual Harrier proposals was Skyhook, developed by BAe, which would allow fighter aircraft to operate from smaller warships. Hover trials with a large rig were conducted at Dunsfold Aerodrome during the 1980s, but the project progressed no further. *US Patent Office/Bill Rose*

some highly specialised item of equipment. The origins
of this concept are somewhat unclear as *Popular
Mechanics* ran a story on the Harrier pod in its
September 1994 issue which stated that 'Using its own
money, the company (McDonnell Douglas) has spent a
year designing and building a people pod to hang from
the wing of an AV-8B Harrier jump jet.' This contradicts
almost every other available report, which indicates
that the pod was designed by a specialist defence
consultancy based in North West London called Avpro
Ltd. I would add that, despite making various enquiries,
it was not possible to clarify this situation prior to
publication. However, everything suggests that the pod
was designed in the UK and McDonnell Douglas
conducted a detailed review, which led to a design
known as the Ground Rescue Insertion Extraction
Resupply (GRIER) pod specifically designed for the AV-
8B. Whether any units were supplied to the US Marine
Corps for evaluation remains unknown.

In Britain, the Hunting Engineering Company
constructed several prototype units duri ng the late
1990s, which were known as Extraction & Insertion
(EXINT) pods. These were tested by the Defence
Evaluation and Research Agency at Boscombe Down
mounted on a Harrier GR.7 in 1998. Details
of the trials remain unknown, but there is
no reason to believe the EXINT pod was
adopted by the RAF or Royal Navy for use
with the Harrier. If the US Marine Corps
have any of these units, the details remain classified.

That aside, there would be serious problems
operating these composite pods with Harriers. Noise
close to the Pegasus engine can be literally
deafening and easily exceeds 140dB. Hot
exhaust also presents problems for
personnel prior to take-off or landing and
placing the pod on an outer pylon would

probably make the ride very unpleasant for a passenger
during any form of manoeuvring. The EXINT has been
suggested for use with the AH-64 Apache helicopter
and this seems like a more realistic proposition,
especially for Special Forces insertion and extraction.
Each unit is apparently able to carry up to 500lb
(226kg) and presumably, in addition to soundproofing,
each pod would be designed to resist small-arms fire.
There is no information available to indicate if the
EXINT pod entered production and, if so, how many are
in service.

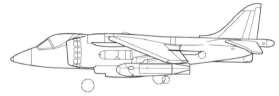

ABOVE A special one-person transportation pod designed
for use with the AV-8B Harrier, known in the UK as the
Extraction & Insertion (EXINT) pod and in the US as the
Ground Rescue Insertion Extraction Resupply (GRIER) pod.
It is understood that Hunting Engineering Company in the
UK constructed several prototype units during the late
1990s, although it seems unlikely that this equipment was
adopted for use with the Harrier. Bill Rose

France's Harrier

Michel Wibault's VTOL propulsion concept was
rejected by the French during the mid-1950s and
welcomed by the British, leading to the very successful
Pegasus series of engines that powered the Harrier.
Despite an initial lack of interest, France's biggest
aviation contractor Dassault Aviation monitored VTOL
developments in the UK with increasing interest and
during the late 1950s a design team was assigned to
undertake a detailed study of a strike fighter powered
by the Bristol BE.53/8 engine. Rather optimistically (at
that time), this engine was expected to provide a
maximum thrust of 19,000lb (84.5kN) and it utilised
two cold and two hot vectoring nozzles, allowing VTOL
and hover in addition to level flight. It is almost a
certainty that Dassault's designers contemplated the

use of a reaction control system during VTOL
operations.

This swept-wing, single-seat design was fairly similar
to the Harrier in overall appearance, receiving the
company name Cavalier and the reference MD 610. The
French were moving towards a test of their first nuclear
bomb (Gerboise Bleue – Blue Jerboa [Desert Rodent], a
65-kiloton plutonium device, which was airburst in the
Algerian Sahara on 13 February 1960), with the Cavalier
being considered as a possible future delivery system
for a single tactical nuclear weapon.

The aircraft was slightly longer than the British
Kestrel at 48.6ft (14.8m) and the wingspan was greater
at 28.9ft (8.8m), although both aircraft would have
weighed about the same empty. Dassault believed the

Cavalier would be capable of reaching Mach 1 at altitude, which seems to have been a reasonable estimate when allowing for weight and engine performance. The engine was located at the centre of the fuselage with air intakes on each side of the forward-positioned cockpit. In the nuclear strike role, the single free-fall bomb would be carried semi-recessed directly below the engine. The Cavalier's fully retractable undercarriage comprised a bicycle arrangement with each strut being fitted with a set of two wheels. Two skids would be extended from the fuselage to ensure lateral stability on the ground.

As part of the same study, Dassault also produced an alternative VTOL strike fighter powered by a different propulsion system. Known as the MD 620, this version of the Cavalier was broadly similar in appearance but featured a repositioned wing and a tricycle undercarriage. Propulsion was to be provided by a single Rolls-Royce RB.165 engine rated at 9,000lb (40kN) thrust and four vertically positioned Rolls-Royce RB.153 lift engines, each providing 3,500lb (15.5kN) of thrust. The MD 620 would also be capable of carrying a single free-fall nuclear weapon, which would be partly recessed in the lower central fuselage section. An STOL variant of the Dassault Cavalier called the MD 630 was also proposed and this strike fighter was

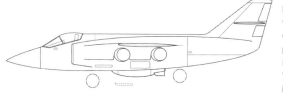

LEFT General appearance of the Dassault MD 610 Cavalier strike fighter powered by a Bristol BE.53/8 engine. This Mach 1 VTOL design was primarily intended to deliver a single nuclear weapon from an improvised site. *Bill Rose*

similar in appearance, size and horizontal performance to the other aircraft in this series. It was to be powered by two RB.165 engines, each rated at 9,000lb (40kN) thrust and two Rolls-Royce RB.162-31 turbojets located in upright slightly tilted positions behind the cockpit area. These would provide the additional lift required for short horizontal take-off, with each providing about 4,409lb (19.61kN) of thrust.

The Dassault Cavalier study was submitted to the *Armée de l'Air* at the start of 1960 and evaluated by the *Service Techniques de'Aéronautique* (STAé). On 5 June 1960, they rejected the proposal on the grounds that the Cavalier in all three forms was capable of reaching only Mach 1. However, this was not entirely bad news as there was now official support for development of the Mirage as a VTOL strike fighter. Dassault had been working on this proposal for several months and there was an official request for the company to begin joint development of a VTOL fighter based on the Mirage III in September 1960.

Supersonic Harriers

The idea of a supersonic Harrier stretches right back to the days of the P.1127, with Ralph Hooper's team producing an advanced concept given the designation P.1150 that received Hawker's approval for further development on 13 April 1961. This design had the appearance of a larger P.1127, but the main difference was that it had a more advanced version of the Pegasus engine, which used PCB for the forward nozzles, a system that worked rather like afterburning.

In August 1961, NATO issued NBMR-3 to all members calling for a VTOL strike fighter with a series of specific capabilities. Subsequently, Hawker submitted a further revision of its proposed supersonic VTOL fighter, now designated P.1154. It was virtually the same as the P.1150 but equipped with the very powerful Bristol Siddeley BS.100 vectored-thrust PCB turbofan that was in development. This was expected to provide a maximum thrust of at least 33,000lb (146kN).

Although the P.1154 was generally considered to be the best option for NBMR-3, the French were unwilling to accept the British design and continued to promote their Mirage supersonic VTOL entry, which won considerable favour. NBMR-3 eventually came to nothing, with participants failing to agree, although work on some of the projects continued without NATO support. However, the RAF and Royal Navy had both

expressed considerable interest in the P.1154 to replace the Hunter and Sea Vixen towards the end of the 1960s. As a consequence, the Ministry of Aviation issued Hawker with a request for further development in April 1962. There was just one problem. Both services required a new aircraft with very different capabilities. The RAF wanted the strike aircraft specified in NBMR-3 and the Royal Navy wanted a two-seat supersonic interceptor configured for carrier operations.

This would lead to major difficulties and rising costs as the designers began to work on two increasingly different variants. In August 1962, about

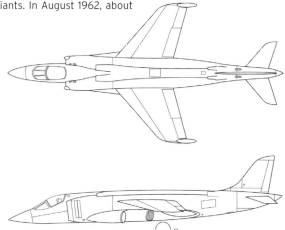

RIGHT The single-seat supersonic Harrier P.1154, specifically tailored to RAF requirements. Although placed on order during the 1960s, this project and its advanced BS.100 engine met with official cancellation in February 1965. *Bill Rose*

80% of the two designs were common, but by May 1963, there had been a major revision with only about 20% commonality remaining. To all intents and purposes, Hawker was now working on two completely different aircraft. The single-seat RAF strike fighter remained largely unchanged, but the two-seat naval version would be equipped with different air inlets to ensure Mach 2 performance, larger wings, an alternative undercarriage, a powerful radar system and extensive modifications for carrier use. A further complication to the P.1154 project was Rolls-Royce's suggestion to replace the BS.100 engine with tandem Spey engines using vectored thrust, which also received serious consideration.

Development of the RAF version continued at Kingston, with work starting on a full-sized mock-up. The aircraft would have supersonic performance, the ability to carry air-to-surface missiles, free-fall bombs and tactical nuclear weapons. Despite this, the Defence Research Policy Committee decided in June 1963 that a common version of the P.1154 needed to be produced for both services. The Royal Navy was unwilling to accept this recommendation and there are suggestions in various reference works that resistance to the P.1154 was substantial. The McDonnell F-4C Phantom had been the RN's preferred choice for some time and the following year it received approval to obtain a UK-modified version of the aircraft, powered by Spey engines. The RAF continued to support the P.1154, with the development continuing under the direction of John Fozard, assisted by former Blackburn Aircraft designer Barry P. Laight (1920-).

The project now moved forward quite quickly, with the RAF approving a slightly revised design and Hawker Siddeley tooling up to commence manufacture of parts for eight pre-production aircraft that would be produced at Kingston and Hamble. In mid-1964, Rolls-Royce received funding to continue with development of the BS.100 engine and the company planned to use an adapted Vulcan B.1A (XA896) as a test-bed. The RAF now decided that the P.1154 would be given the name Harrier (although this would be reassigned to the GR.1) and there would eventually be eight operational Harrier squadrons based in the UK, Germany, Middle and Far East.

The specification for the supersonic RAF Harrier was largely complete and the aircraft would have an overall length of 57.5ft (17.5m), a wingspan of 28.33ft (8.63m) and a wing area of 269ft² (25m²). Empty, the P.1154 would weigh 20,100lb (9,117kg), with a maximum high/low-level strike weight of 30,970lb (14,047kg). This would allow a maximum speed of Mach 1.3 at sea level and Mach 1.7 at altitude with a ceiling of about 52,500ft (16,000m). Estimates for the proposed Bristol Siddeley BS.100/8 turbofan engine indicated a maximum thrust of 33,900lb (150.7kN) with PCB.

Variable-geometry air inlets were located on each side of the fuselage just behind the cockpit.

Like every other VTOL fighter, there would be a serious penalty for using vertical take-off and to achieve a satisfactory range and payload capability the aircraft would normally make a short rolling take-off. This would allow a combat range of 466 miles (750km) with drop tanks and in-flight refuelling would be available. For training pilots a two-seater was contemplated and this would have been slightly longer to accommodate the larger cockpit, with an overall length of approximately 61ft (18.6m). As an interceptor, the P.1154 would carry four Red Top missiles and, in the strike role, various free-fall bombs, napalm canisters, SNEB rockets, the Martel AJ.168 ASM or a tactical nuclear weapon.

Much of the airframe would be built from aluminium and titanium alloy, with the engine being removed using a detachable ventral tray. A bicycle undercarriage layout similar to other Harriers was chosen for this version, with two stabilising outriggers carried in wingtip nacelles. Interestingly, the RAF's P.1154 Harrier was intended to be fully capable of operating from all Royal Navy carriers and the nose would fold to reduce length and assist with storage and deck lift space. The government finally approved the purchase of 157 P.1154 strike fighters and 25 trainers, with an overall cost of about £210 million. This received final approval in December 1964. Thousands of Hawker Siddeley personnel were now working on this project, the first airframe was being assembled and around £21 million of taxpayers' money had been spent on the programme. However, there was a change of government and the new Labour administration commenced a defence spending review, which pushed the RAF into choosing between the P.1154 Harrier or the TSR.2. As a result of this, the TSR.2 was selected, with the politicians claiming that the P.1154 would not be ready in time to replace the Hunter at the end of the 1960s. This appears to have been totally misleading as the RAF had actually planned to retain the Hunter until 1971/2.

However, it was decided to replace the RAF's P.1154 with the costly UK-adapted F-4 Phantom powered by Spey engines and to continue with development of the subsonic P.1127 Kestrel, using some of the technology developed for the P.1154. Both the P.1154 and BS.100 engine were officially cancelled on 2 February 1965 and this would become the country's last all-British fighter project. It is difficult to speculate on how the supersonic Harrier would have performed and there were still some substantial issues to resolve such as gas re-ingestion while using the PCB in VTOL mode near the ground. That said, it is possible that the aircraft would have proved successful, with the potential for overseas sales and future development.

Republic Fokker D-24 Alliance

Another design reliant on the advanced BS.100 vectored thrust engine was the Republic Fokker D-24 Alliance. This was a very ambitious multi-role, supersonic VTOL strike fighter, that was probably too advanced to have been a practical proposition at that time. The design originated with Republic Aviation in the US and had been developed to meet the USAF's SOR-183 request for an F-105 replacement, which was issued in June 1960. Known as the Tactical Fighter Experimental (TFX) programme, this was joined some months later by the US Navy's Fleet Air Defense Fighter (FADF) requirement seeking a future replacement for the F-4 Phantom. Most of the major US aviation contractors submitted proposals for the TFX contest, with the General Dynamics F-111 emerging as the winner in 1962.

Republic's TFX entry was an impressive variable-geometry design, which was built as a mock-up for official inspection. Exact details of the design are unclear, but the overall length was 75-80ft (22.8-24.3m) with an extended wingspan of approximately 46-50ft (14-15.2m). Propulsion was to be provided by two Pratt & Whitney TF30-P-100 turbofans, each providing a maximum thrust of 25,100lb (111.6kN) with afterburning. While the TFX programme was under way, Republic felt its design had sufficient potential to be re-engineered for the European market. So, in 1961, negotiations were opened with Fokker in the Netherlands to jointly develop an advanced VTOL strike fighter for NATO's NBMR-3 requirement. Central to this project was the advanced BS.100 vectored-thrust engine and having involved Bristol Siddeley, it was decided to open a Republic Fokker office at Schipol, with Republic's Alexander Wadkowsky taking charge as project manager.

Combining variable geometry with an experimental vectored-thrust PCB engine would push the boundaries of engineering, but a more compact VTOL version of their TFX design seemed capable of establishing the benchmark for combat aircraft if there were no insurmountable technical problems. The principal design for the project received the Republic reference RAC 758-1A30 and it would soon be called the D-24 Alliance. Capable of fulfilling the NBMR-3 strike-reconnaissance requirement, this all-weather aircraft would be suitable for high-altitude supersonic interception and carrier-based operations.

The (base model) Alliance was somewhat smaller than the TFX proposal, with an overall length of 63.5ft (19.35m), a fully extended wingspan of 32.66ft (9.95m) and a VTOL take-off weight of 30,000lb (13,607kg). This could be increased by 3,000lb (1,360kg) if STO was used. A single Bristol Siddeley BS.100/3 vectored-thrust PCB turbofan engine would provide power, with future versions expected to deliver a massive

maximum thrust of around 38,500lb (171kN). Air inlets for the engine were located on each side of the lower fuselage, alongside or directly behind the cockpit. Because of the variable-geometry wings, the engine would be dropped through a lower fuselage opening for major overhauls or replacement. Low-speed control during VTOL was handled by a reaction control system, the airframe was primarily built from titanium alloy and the aircraft was supported on the ground by a fully retractable tricycle undercarriage.

Early documentation suggested a maximum speed of Mach 1.25 at sea level with the wings fully swept to comply with the fixed 70° delta wing. This would ensure minimal gust response, providing a relatively smooth ride at very low altitudes. Should the aircraft's wings jam in the fully retracted position due to hydraulic failure or battle damage, the aircraft would still be capable of making a conventional runway landing. At 40,000ft (12,192m), Mach 2.5 was achievable, with the aircraft's ceiling set at 70,000ft (21,336m) but with the ability to make a zoom climb to 100,000ft (30,480m). It

TOP A full-sized mock-up of Republic's variable-geometry entry for the US TFX programme, which, although unsuccessful, would lead to the European D-24 Alliance multi-role, supersonic VTOL fighter. *Republic Aviation*

BOTTOM Early company artwork showing the Republic Fokker D-24 Alliance supersonic VTOL, with its wings in different positions. *Fokker*

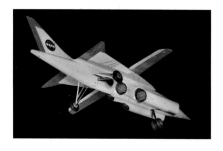

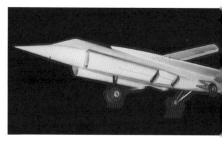

has not been possible to find a reliable quote for combat range, but in clean condition an estimate of 350 miles (563km) might be a reasonable starting point for a strike mission. External fuel tanks and in-flight refuelling would both be available and a 3,000-mile (4828km) ferry range was anticipated.

The D-24 was expected to carry a variety of different weapons and the internal bay was designed to accommodate a single 1,000lb (453kg) 'next-generation' tactical nuclear weapon or a photo-reconnaissance pack. External hardpoints would be located under the fuselage and the fixed delta- wing section, allowing the carriage of drop tanks, AAMs, ASMs or free-fall bombs. It seems unlikely that an internal cannon was planned for this aircraft. The design team at Schipol considered single- and two-seat versions of the Alliance. A number of D-24 scale models were built and wind tunnel tested by the NASA Langley Research Center. This led to various recommendations for aerodynamic changes to the wing and nose.

Estimates for inspections and maintenance compared favourably with those produced for the Mirage VTOL fighter and although the D-24 Alliance failed to reach the final selection for NBMR-3, it was offered to the Royal Navy and US Navy in a slightly revised form. However, despite its advanced nature, the

BELOW This drawing is based on an early proposal for the Republic Fokker D-24 Alliance multi-role VTOL combat aircraft. There were many variants of this design with relatively minor differences. *Bill Rose*

TOP LEFT This scale-sized model of the D-24 Alliance tested by NASA in the early 1960s would lead to a number of aerodynamic changes. Note the fixed wing trailing-edge control surfaces, with short extensions. *NASA*

TOP CENTRE This view of the superb scale-sized D-24 Alliance model tested by NASA Langley shows some detail of the normally hidden variable-geometry mechanism. *NASA*

TOP RIGHT NASA's scale-sized D-24 Alliance model, showing the engine exhaust outlets. *NASA*

D-24 was competing against the more straightforward supersonic Harrier and the VTOL Mirage and it seems that nobody was really certain how much the D-24 Alliance would cost to fully develop. In the end the project floundered, the BS.100 was cancelled and this interesting design was consigned to history.

Saab VTOL Strike Fighters

In 1944, the Finnish aircraft designer Aarne Lakomaa (1914-2001) went to work for the Swedish company Saab. From this point onwards, he was responsible for a string of well-known civil and military aircraft, including the JA 37 strike fighter. Development of this advanced combat aircraft began in the 1950s and it was initially intended to be a replacement for the Saab J 32 Lansen (Lance), although the JA 37's features were steadily extended until it became capable of also taking over from the Saab J 35 Draken (Dragon) fighter.

Lakomaa was set the task of designing a single-seat supersonic combat aircraft, with high reliability, low maintenance and good STOL performance. Furthermore, this was a lengthy development programme and it was clear from the outset that the JA 37 would have to remain effective as a combat aircraft until the end of the century, which meant a

rolling programme of upgrades. By the early 1960s, the design of the JA 37 was taking shape as a single-engined canard with Mach 2 performance that was able to operate in wartime conditions from suitable improvised sites and stretches of roadway. Having received official approval in 1962, work on the first prototype began in 1964 and the aircraft, now known as the Viggen (Thunderbolt), made its first test flight on 8 February 1967.

Prior to acceptance of the JA 37 for prototyping, Lakomaa's design team undertook a series of studies to evaluate the possibility of adding a VTOL capability to the fighter. The exact number of different designs considered is unclear and some are very similar in general appearance. However, the two most promising variants were the Saab 1562 from September 1961, and the Saab 1563 produced in October 1961. The 1562 was

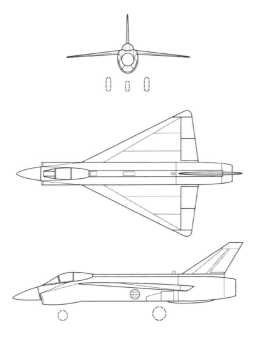

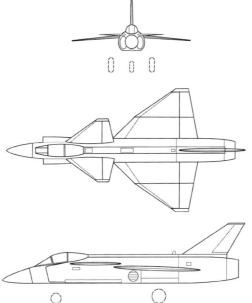

LEFT The Saab 1562 supersonic VTOL fighter concept produced in 1961. It was one of many different designs to emerge from this project that would lead to the Viggen (Thunderbolt). *Bill Rose, with assistance from Tony Buttler and Saab*

RIGHT Looking more like the later Viggen fighter, this advanced supersonic VTOL Saab design was produced in 1961 and received the company reference 1563. *Bill Rose, with assistance from Tony Buttler and Saab*

a tailless delta with a large chin-positioned air inlet for the engine and the 1563 was much closer to the Viggen in overall appearance with engine inlets on each side of the cockpit, a similar wing profile, elevons, a single tail fin with rudder and canards. Both aircraft were fitted with fully retracting tricycle undercarriages and carried similar weapons. The propulsion system considered for these (and several other) VTOL variants is thought to have been a modified three-nozzle version of the Rolls-Royce RB.168 Spey, although the specification is

unknown. Based on the JA 37's details, it seems probable that either fighter would have an overall length of 53-54ft (16-16.5m) and a wingspan in the region of 35ft (10.6m). Overall performance is unlikely to have matched the Viggen, although any of these VTOL designs would have been supersonic. It is hard to know how seriously these proposals were taken, although the expense of developing designs that were reliant on complex, largely unproven technology must have ruled them out fairly swiftly.

BAC Vickers Type 583V

Relatively little information is available for the BAC Type 583V variable-geometry VTOL multi-role fighter. In 1963, this single-seat aircraft proposal attracted attention from the UK Ministry of Aviation, which funded a brief study at Weybridge. Although broadly similar to the Kestrel in overall appearance, the Type 583V would be powered by two separate RB.168-32D (Spey) engines carried in the central fuselage section. Both would be equipped with vectored-thrust nozzles and the aircraft would remain flyable in the event of one failing. This was of particular interest to the Royal Navy, which sought increased reliability in a marine environment where ditching an aircraft carried significant risks. What appears to have been the definitive version of this aircraft was expected to have a fully extended wingspan, measuring 43ft (13.1m), with a leading edge sweep of 25°. This would reduce to 25ft (7.6m) when fully swept at 75°. The overall length would be 52ft (15.8m), with a maximum STO weight of 45,100lb (20,457kg). The exact engine performance is unclear, but the thrust for each engine would almost certainly be in excess of 15,000lb (66.7kN). This would

allow a maximum speed of about Mach 1.2 at sea level and Mach 2.5 at high altitude, with a ceiling of approximately 60,000ft+ (18,288m+). Range is unknown but would probably match the P.1154. The proposed armament was two or four Red Top AAMs and the option of various under-fuselage stores.

Weybridge was fairly confident that the Type 583V could be ready for service by 1971 and models may have been wind tunnel tested, but the design progressed no further. Conceivably, the aircraft was considered too complex, or it was rejected because there was already a substantial commitment to the HawkerSiddeley P.1154 Harrier.

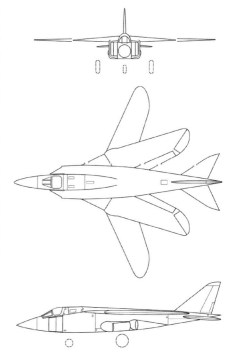

RIGHT The BAC Vickers, Weybridge-designed Type 583V supersonic variable-geometry VTOL fighter was designed in 1963 and proposed for RAF and Royal Navy service in the early 1970s. *Bill Rose*

McDonnell Douglas Supersonic Studies

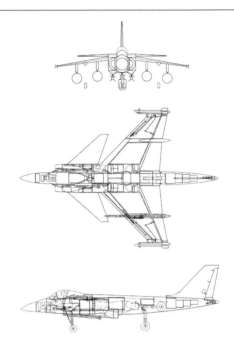

LEFT The first McDonnell Douglas design in a series of proposed supersonic replacements for the Harrier, which was given the company reference 279-1. *McDonnell Douglas*

RIGHT The single-seat McDonnell Douglas 279-3 supersonic multi-role VTOL fighter, intended to replace the AV-8B Harrier. Had this aircraft been built, it would have used many off-the-shelf components produced for the A-7, AV-8B, F-15 and F-18. *McDonnell Douglas/Bill Rose*

McDonnell Douglas had been working on advanced derivatives of the Harrier since the US Navy's SCS programme with a substantial joint US/UK study commencing in 1973 to produce an advanced subsonic Harrier known as the AV-16/HS.1184. The study came to an end the following year with no positive outcome, although there were proposals to develop a multi-role supersonic version of the aircraft using a Pegasus 15-13 turbofan with PCB. This version was known as the AV-16S/HS.1185 and it would have been 53ft (16.2m) long with a wingspan of 31ft (9.4m) and the ability to carry a wide range of underwing stores. Potential customers were the US Marine Corps, US Navy, Royal Navy, RAF and perhaps other international buyers.

It remains unclear why this project faltered, although further development may have simply been considered too expensive during a difficult economic period, with PCB technology proving significantly more difficult to master than first seemed apparent. Sometimes a military system that works in the laboratory fails to work properly when scaled up, or serious issues concerning use and reliability become evident. McDonnell Douglas continued to work on Harrier development, which would lead to the AV-8B, although the quest for a supersonic V/STOL strike fighter never diminished and there was what amounted to an ongoing US Navy requirement for this type of aircraft by the 1990s.

The company, in association with Rolls-Royce, was proposing an improved version of the AV-16S powered by the Pegasus 11F-35 vectored-thrust turbofan with PCB, which is sometimes referred to as fan stream burning (FSB) in the US. This VTOL aircraft, designated AV-16SX, would have an overall length of 55.6ft (16.9m),

a height of 11.33ft (3.45m), a wingspan of 30ft (9.1m) and a much bigger wing with an estimated area of about 300ft² (27.8m²). An alternative design was given the company reference 279-1 and utilised a canard layout with a large forward-positioned ventral air intake, with an overall length of 52.1ft (15.8m), a height of 14.8ft (4.5m) but the same wingspan and wing area as the more conventional proposal. Both aircraft would have a maximum VTO take-off weight of about 28,450lb (12,904kg) and a maximum engine thrust of 29,250lb (130kN). This would normally provide an adequate thrust-to-weight difference, although in practice the aircraft would make a short rolling take-off to improve range/payload performance. Both of these designs were tested as scale-sized models in the MCAIR Advanced Design Wind Tunnel (ADWT) at Western Michigan University and in larger form at NASA Ames.

Rolls-Royce in the UK was now heavily involved in the development of a new PCB Pegasus engine, with significant financial assistance from the MoD. By early 1983, it was using MoD facilities at Shoeburyness, Essex, to test a surplus Harrier airframe fitted with a fairly old re-engineered Pegasus 2A engine. This was suspended beneath a 140-ton gantry and its purpose was to explore issues of hot gas re-ingestion (HGR), airframe heating and the effects of ground erosion. PCB had been experimented with for many years, but there were various concerns that needed to be addressed before it could be considered for operational use with a new, primarily American fighter. Computer models were being used to aid development, but this was insufficient to resolve practical issues of water ingestion and intake distortion. Furthermore, the PCB units were becoming more complex as time passed and

there were serious concerns about the small gauge injectors, expected to create significant maintenance problems. In the meantime, McDonnell Douglas had moved forward from its initial designs, developing a new canard fighter with side-mounted half-axisymmetric air inlets for the engine. This new design was given the company reference 279-3. (It remains unclear if there was a Model 279-2.)

The single-seat 279-3 would weigh 19,808lb (8,985kg) empty and have a maximum STO weight of about 41,000lb (18,597kg). To ensure the lowest possible structural mass, graphite epoxy components would be used wherever possible, with remaining parts fabricated from various forms of aluminium, titanium or steel. In practice, it was intended to use many off-the-shelf components produced for the A-7, AV-8B, F-15 and F-18. In common with other designs based on the Harrier, the 279-3 would be equipped with a fully retractable bicycle undercarriage and outriggers carried in wing nacelles.

The wingspan was set at 35.8ft (10.9m) with a leading edge sweep of 45° and a wing area of 428.4ft^2 (39.8m^2). The canard area was 85.6ft^2 (7.95 m^2) and Model 279-3 was 56ft (17m) long, with a height of 17.34ft (5.28m). McDonnell Douglas designers intended to power the aircraft with a Pratt & Whitney Pegasus-based PCB turbofan with the reference STF561-C2, producing a maximum thrust of 34,316lb (152.6kN). Like most similar V/STOL designs, there would be an air-bleed three-axis reaction control system for low-speed handling and a sophisticated digital fly-by-wire control system, fully integrated with all airborne operations. In normal flight, the all-moving, coupled canard surfaces would control pitch and there would be elevons, flaps and a substantial rudder. Maximum anticipated speed was Mach 2 at altitude, with the ability to accelerate from Mach 0.8 to Mach 1.6 in 70 seconds at 35,000ft (10,668m). The estimated absolute ceiling was 62,000ft (19,050m) and the aircraft's combat radius would be dependent on a number of different factors, although a short rolling take-off was required. Typically, a Deck Launched Intercept (DLI) and supersonic dash while carrying four external AAMs

could allow a range in the region of 177 miles (285km) to 220 miles (354km), depending on the required altitude. In the strike role, with a 1,000lb (453kg) payload, two AAMs and drop tanks, the combat radius could be 1,035 miles (1,665km) and extended with in-flight refuelling.

The quoted ferry range with four underwing 600(US)-gallon (2,271-litre) fuel tanks would be 3,000 miles (4,828km). Armament for the 279-3 would provisionally consist of one internal 25mm cannon with 400 rounds, Sidewinder or AMRAAM AAMs, and air-to-surface missiles, free-fall/guided bombs or one tactical nuclear weapon. Various other options would include underwing reconnaissance, target designation or EW equipment. While Rolls-Royce was gearing up for engine trials at Shoeburyness, the wind tunnel testing of 279-3 models was under way at NASA's Ames Research Center in California. This was leading to fresh concerns about hot gas re-ingestion and ground effect issues, already expressed by Rolls-Royce, and suggestions that part of the solution might be to size-up the engine to reduce PCB temperature. Trials continued into the late 1980s, with British Aerospace Kingston (formerly Hawker Siddeley Aviation) undertaking studies for a comparable aircraft to the Model 279-3, with the reference P.1228.

A further McDonnell Douglas proposal in this series was the 279-4. Similar in appearance to the 279-3, but powered by two side-by-side Pegasus engines and equipped with F-15-style air inlets, this design was built as several highly detailed models, in one case fitted with a hot gas tunnel assembly to simulate the engines. McDonnell Douglas was aiming to secure official funding to construct a 279-3 prototype and probably hoped that a study being undertaken by the Defense Advanced Research Projects Agency (DARPA) to examine a supersonic follow-on to the AV-8B Harrier would favour its proposals.

DARPA's programme began in 1983 and was known as the Advanced Short Take-Off/Vertical Landing (ASTOVL) project. It would eventually involve the US DoD and the UK Ministry of Defence (MoD). DARPA had started out by looking at proposals for a fighter built

LEFT Company artwork, showing two McDonnell Douglas 279-3 supersonic VTOL canard fighters in flight. *McDonnell Douglas*

CENTRE This company illustration from the early 1980s shows a 279-3 fighter with engine nozzles directed downwards and undercarriage extended in US Navy markings. *McDonnell Douglas*

RIGHT NASA Ames engineer Don Durston checks a scale-sized model of the McDonnell Douglas 279-3 VTOL fighter in the 9ft x 7ft (2.7m x 2m) wind tunnel. *NASA*

around the Pegasus PCB turbofan, but it became increasingly apparent that the Pegasus technology was approaching its limits and something new was required. DARPA's starting point for a replacement was the high-performance Pratt & Whitney F119 engine, already in development, which would be shaft- or gas-coupled to a forward lift fan. By 1987, further development of the PCB Pegasus turbofan seemed to be over, along with McDonnell Douglas's 279-3/4 V/STOL strike fighter. The ASTOVL programme had effectively demonstrated the need to move on and DARPA now approached Lockheed's Skunk Works and NASA Ames to secretly study fighter designs to replace the Harrier. Although details of this work remain classified, it is believed that some of the research was utilised during development of the Joint Strike fighter (JSF), ultimately leading to the Lockheed Martin F-35B Lightning II.

British 1970/80 V/STOL Fighter Proposals

BELOW LEFT The Hawker Siddeley design team at Kingston produced this proposal for a supersonic VTOL fighter in the late 1970s and its general appearance suggests some level of co-operation with at least one American defence contractor. Given the reference HS.1205, there were aerodynamic problems that led to this design being abandoned in 1979. *Bill Rose*

BELOW RIGHT The unusual looking Hawker Siddeley P.1214 'X'-wing fighter created considerable interest, being described as the 'Star Wars' fighter, but this concept showed no real aerodynamic gains over a more conventional design and was abandoned in 1980. *Bill Rose*

Throughout the 1970s there was continued UK interest in the possibility of developing an improved supersonic Harrier, with several joint projects between Hawker Siddeley's team at Kingston and McDonnell Douglas. The most notable design was the AV-16S, powered by a Pegasus 15-13 turbofan with PCB. Produced as an alternative to the McDonnell Douglas Model 279-3, this project continued into the 1980s, leading to the supersonic P.1230, which retained the Harrier's appearance and was initially proposed as a joint UK/US alternative to the Model 279-3.

The Hawker Siddeley design team studied a number of different V/STOL fighter concepts that included the HS.1205, which looks like a P.1154 descendant blended with a General Dynamics F-16A. The principal aim was to produce a highly agile fighter, with the forward fuselage section being fitted with LERX and power provided by a four-nozzle PCB Pegasus engine. Armament was provisionally established as four wing-mounted Sidewinder missiles and one internal cannon. The HS.1205 study commenced during 1976 and this led to wind tunnel testing, which appears to have produced mixed results with concerns about gas ingestion caused by the engine's large ventral air intake. Further experiments took place using twin air intakes that were closer in design to the standard Harrier, but a combination of technical and aerodynamic difficulties would finally bring the HS.1205 study to an end in 1979. The next Kingston design of significance was the P.1212, which was a twin-tail-boom fighter using the proposed three-nozzle PCB Pegasus 11F-33 turbofan. This also met with problems during wind tunnel trials of scale models and the project was abandoned.

Attention now switched to a new series of increasingly unusual concepts. These began with the P.1214 'X'-wing fighter, with a short fuselage, a large chin-positioned air inlet for a three-nozzle PCB turbofan engine and forward/backward swept wings. Several different versions were considered, with the P.1214-4 being the only variant to have remaining documentation. This shows the aircraft with forward swept wings and small tail fins on booms. Although the aircraft generated considerable interest and was briefly described as the 'Star Wars' fighter, this design demonstrated no significant aerodynamic gains and was dropped in 1980.

It was already realised that the best way to counteract aerodynamic problems generated by high-performance PCB vectored-thrust engines was to eliminate the aircraft's tail completely and as a consequence the P.1214 evolved into a design called the P.1216. This was similar to the 'X'-wing fighter, but equipped with a conventional swept wing and lengthy booms with tailplanes and fins. In addition to supporting the rear wheels of the tricycle undercarriage, these booms would carry most of the aircraft's weapons. Each boom would be fitted with an internal forward-firing 27mm cannon and there would be attachment points for Sidewinder, ASRAAM or AMRAAM missiles, Sea Eagle ASMs, free-fall bombs, drop tanks, reconnaissance or target designation equipment. There would also be provision for two Sidewinder AAMs on wingtip launch rails. Constructionally, much of the aircraft would be built from titanium alloy, aluminium alloy or composites. The overall length of the P.1216 was

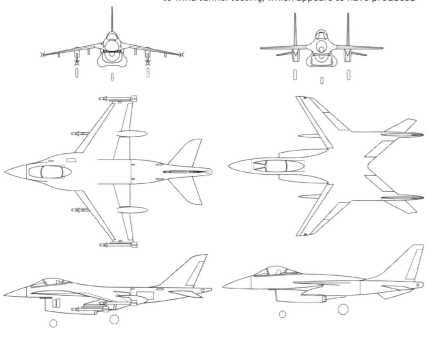

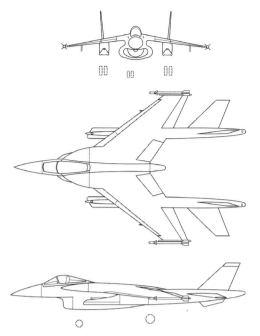

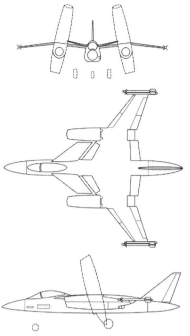

expected to be 55.9ft (17m), with a wingspan of 34.75ft (10.6m) and a wing area of 421ft^2 (39.11m^2). At low speeds a reaction control system would stabilise the aircraft. The engine chosen for the P.1216 was a three-nozzle PCB Rolls-Royce RB.422-60 turbofan with a dry rating of 31,400lb (139.6kN), rising to 44,600lb (198.3kN) with full PCB. Allowing for a typical STO weight of 31,000lb (14,061kg), this would provide a maximum speed of about Mach 1 at sea level and around Mach 1.8 at altitude, with a ceiling of 55,000ft (16,764m). Range would be totally dependent on the mission and payload, but a combat radius for a strike operation of about 350 miles (563kn) appears to be a reasonable estimate. Production aircraft would be provided with in-flight refuelling equipment.

Following Britain's success in the Falklands Campaign, there was renewed official interest in securing a supersonic replacement for the Harrier and the P.1216 attracted considerable attention, despite its rather unorthodox appearance. A naval variant was considered and this would have been configured as a two-seat interceptor. Wind tunnel tests of scale models were undertaken and a mock-up built, but by this time there was no hope of securing government funding to progress to prototyping.

An interesting strike fighter design to emerge from BAe at Warton in the late 1970s was produced by Dr Ivan Yates (1929–), who would later become the company's engineering director. Known as the P.103, this was not a V/STOL capable aircraft in the strictest sense, although it was fairly close in most respects. Propulsion would be provided by two underwing nacelles, each containing an RB.199 turbofan producing 9,100lb (40.5kN) of thrust dry and 16,400lb (72.95kN) with afterburner. These engines are normally associated with the Panavia Tornado and

may have been chosen for performance or simply availability. Each engine nacelle was hinged to tilt downwards during take-off and landing, possibly to allow near-vertical touchdowns. At the time it was recognised that a sophisticated computer control system would be required to make these procedures manageable and there can be little doubt that the failure of an engine during take-off or landing would have proved catastrophic.

This aircraft was a canard with a forward-positioned cockpit and a single vertical tail fin. The P.103 would be supported on the ground by a fully retractable tricycle undercarriage and it was decided that the aircraft would be provisionally armed with one 27mm cannon and wingtip-mounted Sidewinder air-to-air missiles. For strike missions, ordnance would be carried below the fuselage. The fighter was expected to have a gross take-off weight of about 36,000lb (16,329kg) and a maximum speed in the region of Mach 2 at altitude. The overall length is quoted as 42ft (12.8m), with a wingspan of 50ft (15.2m). BAe undertook wind tunnel tests of scale-size P.103 models, which provided sufficiently satisfactory results to build a full-sized mock-up. BAe envisaged the P.103 as a replacement for the Jaguar and the design was discussed with other European organisations in 1980 and Saudi Arabia in 1981. However, there were no customers for this concept and the project was finally scrapped.

In 1983, a meeting took place at Farnborough between various officials from the RAE, NASA, the US DoD and the MoD. The purpose of this gathering was to discuss the future of propulsion systems for VTOL or STOVL combat aircraft. Four different methods were under consideration at that time, which included an improved version of the Pegasus vectored-thrust engine using PCB, RALS, TF and the EL system. The following year BAe Warton in conjunction with Rolls-Royce were contracted by the MoD to produce detailed studies of suitable aircraft for the four different propulsion systems. The P.1230 remained the main aircraft in this set of proposals involving the Americans and the P.1216 seems to have been developed separately, with BAe considering the twin-boom arrangement superior in all respects. Kingston had been working on a RALS design known as P.1222, which was a canard, double-delta with an appearance much like an earlier DHC study that used an external augmentor lift system. This layout was adopted by Warton and was soon replaced by a new study called P.112.

In appearance P.112 had some similarity to the Agile Combat Aircraft (ACA) proposal, which was an early ancestor of the Eurofighter Typhoon. The P.112 using RALS would have supersonic performance, an armament of eight AAMs and in most respects it had the appearance of a conventional modern combat aircraft with a single tail exhaust. As far as it has been possible to establish, the design team working on this Warton project was headed by George Sully, Graham N. Freeman and Kenneth Ainscow.

This was followed by P.115 using the TF system, with a number of variants produced in single- and twin-engine configurations and the most noticeable visual difference being the engine's (or engines') air intake. Weight, performance and dimensions were similar to the P.112. The wing was a near-delta with a straight leading edge, swept to about 50°. Canards were fitted, although positioned well back, and short booms were fitted that extended from the rear of the fuselage, carrying tail fins with rudders. Large nozzles mounted in the forward section of the wing were designed to swivel through 90°. These were slightly flattened in appearance, becoming non-functional and flush with the surrounding surface during normal flight. The main exhaust outlet at the rear of the fuselage would be vectored downwards during VTOL or STOL.

In addition, there would be a reaction control system for low-speed handling. The aircraft was supported on the ground by a fully retractable tricycle undercarriage

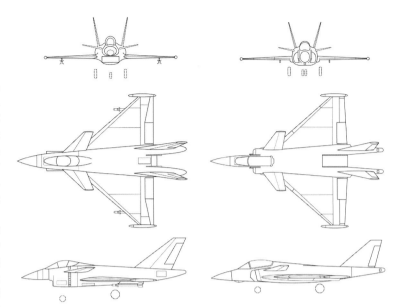

and armament would comprise of AMRAAM, ASRAAM or Sidewinder missiles, with various other options, perhaps including an internal cannon. The overall length of this proposed aircraft was in the region of 50ft (15.24m), with a wingspan of about 36ft (11m). These details are based on available documentation and remain unconfirmed. Capable of normal horizontal take-offs and landings, this supersonic VTOL fighter was designed primarily for naval use. A further Warton study considered the EL system and this led to the P.116 which differed quite a bit from the P.112 and P.115, having a centrally positioned swept wing and using four ejector augmentor units positioned forward and aft. Apparently, this system did not win too much support at Warton and the P.115 was considered the most promising way forward.

Further reviews led to a UK/US inter-government Memorandum of Understanding being signed in early 1986 and work continued for another year, but slowed and finally stopped. At the time of writing, little further information is available, although models were wind tunnel tested and some work to improve stealth characteristics was undertaken before these concepts were abandoned.

LEFT This drawing shows one of several BAe P.115 VTOL fighter proposals, which may have its origins at Kingston during the mid-1980s, but is attributed to Preston. *Bill Rose*

RIGHT This drawing shows the tandem fan version of the BAe P.115 VTOL fighter with engine inlets on each side of the cockpit. *Bill Rose*

Fighter VTOL Lift Units

In early 1981, a New York-based designer called August C. Sarrantonio completed his initial design for a VTOL platform intended to launch and retrieve a single conventional aircraft. In March 1981, Sarrantonio applied for a US patent, but finally decided to abandon the idea for reasons unknown. Five years later the invention reappeared and was patented, with the design being assigned to Grumman Aerospace. This minimalistic design could probably best be described as a flying framework that acted as a low-speed

mothership for a fighter aircraft. When the patent was published in July 1987 (Ref: 4,678141), drawings of the Aircraft Launcher & Retriever (ALR) showed what looked like an F-18A attached to this vehicle. Sarrantonio's VTOL carrier comprised an aerodynamic beam, with two engines at each end in swivelling nacelles. These would provide lift and forward flight. Alongside each engine unit was a fuel tank and on each side of this would be long struts with dampeners and a forward and rear wheel. In the centre of the beam was a cockpit-gondola providing an excellent forward view for the pilot and the fighter would be suspended directly below this unit. Both sets of engines would pivot in unison and aerodynamic control would be achieved by vanes in the jet exhaust and some form of reaction control method. It was suggested that this VTOL launch platform could be used to carry an aircraft with no landing gear, extending operational range.

A second VTOL platform called the Flying Multi-Purpose Aircraft Carrier (FMPAC) was patented in March 1991 (Ref: 5,000398) by Michael S. Rashev, also based in New York. There are some strange similarities between this and the Sarrantonio design which suggest a possible link. Both were based on uncompleted patent applications, both designers come from the same US state, both use similar references and both show their designs carrying F-18-style fighters. I was unable to find any direct connection between the two designs, although it is possible that something might surface with more research. The Rashev proposal differs in several ways, which are primarily the use of large rotors for lift and smaller rotors to stabilise the platform. There are also twin jet engines in nacelles, which are not explained properly. The central section is called a runway, although it is no more than the length of the aircraft being carried. Fuselage sections are attached to each side of the central runway, each fitted with a flush cockpit section. During carriage, the fighter would have its landing gear fully extended and locked to the runway section.

Grumman must have considered Sarrantonio's design potentially worthwhile and it is certainly the more promising of the two concepts. It remains unclear

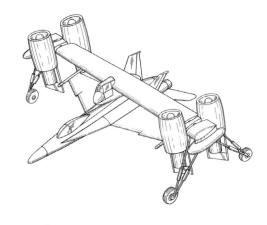

TOP Produced by New York designer August C. Sarrantonio, who assigned the design to Grumman Aerospace, this early 1980s proposal for a VTOL Aircraft Launcher & Retriever (ALR) was never built and the possible applications appear rather limited. *US Patent Office/Bill Rose*

CENTRE Forward view of the Grumman Aircraft Launcher & Retriever (ALR), carrying an F-18-sized fighter. *US Patent Office/Bill Rose*

BOTTOM This design for a VTOL aircraft launch platform was produced by Michael S. Rashev in the early 1990s. It progressed no further than the initial concept stage. *US Patent Office/Bill Rose*

if it intended to offer this to the US Navy or US Marine Corps and how it might be put to use. The Rashev proposal seems rather ill- considered and less likely to be workable. Both designs would present obvious operational problems and it seems these designs were soon forgotten.

Lockheed VTOL Fighter Designs

At the beginning of the 1970s, Lockheed's Skunk Works started work on a series of V/STOL strike fighters, which would be submitted to the US Navy and for alternative USAF requirements. Assigned the Lockheed designation CL-1292, at least seven different single-seat V/STOL supersonic combat aircraft were produced during this particular study, and perhaps more.

The first with the reference CL-1292-1, was of fairly conventional appearance. It was powered by a single unspecified afterburning turbofan (with downward directable exhaust for VTOL) rated at approximately 30,000lb (133kN) thrust, plus two vertically positioned, side-by-side lift engines directly behind the cockpit area, each expected to provide 10,000lb (44.5kN) of thrust. Another design, with the reference CL-1292-5, was a canard layout with the same overall dimensions powered by two engines in underwing nacelles and two vertical lift engines in the centre of the fuselage. Yet another variant was the CL-1292-6, looking rather like a

modified Gloster Javelin with two lift fans in the wing and one behind the cockpit. This was similar in overall size to other proposals in the series, but the delta wing provided a substantial increase in area. These concepts were all intended to provide supersonic performance in level flight and their armament would have comprised 25mm cannon, Sidewinder and/or Sparrow AAMs, with various options for ground attack missions.

Of particular interest in this large study was the CL-1292-2, which can best be described as a Harrier clone. The engine was a non-specific Pegasus vectored-thrust turbofan (or P&W derivative), presumably with PCB and drawing air through sizeable inlets on each side of the forward fuselage. Anticipated performance is unclear, but a supersonic capability was envisaged. The CL-1292-2 fighter was 52.33ft (16m) in length, with a wingspan of 30ft (9.14m), a wing area of 300ft² (27.8m²), a height of 16.33ft (4.96m) and a leading-edge sweep of 45°. The forward-positioned cockpit with bubble canopy

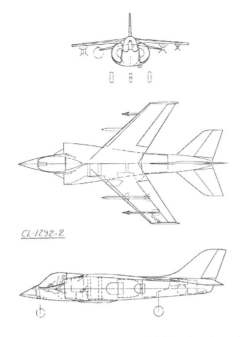

CL-1292-2

would have provided good visibility for the pilot. Weights are not specified, but a few calculations based on various other broadly similar concepts and designs suggests the aircraft would weigh about 19-20,000lb (8,600-9,070kg) and up to 32,000lb (14,500kg) with an intercept mission using a rolling take-off. However, please bear in mind that this is simply an estimate. Armament would comprise a single 25mm cannon in the lower left air intake housing. Four underwing hardpoints would be used to carry AIM-9 Sidewinder or AIM-7 Sparrow AAMs and it seems probable that two extra AIM-9 missiles could be carried on wingtip launch rails. In a strike role, the CL-1292-2 would be able to carry air-to-surface missiles, rockets or free-fall bombs. Drops tanks were also specified for this design and there would be provision in-flight refuelling. In addition to a reaction control system for low-speed handling, the aircraft would be equipped with control surfaces for

normal flight. An unspecified all-weather multi-mode radar system would be carried and, unlike the Harrier, Lockheed appears to have opted for tricycle landing gear with the main wheels retracting into the rear fuselage section. This design does not appear to have progressed beyond the conceptual stage and probably was not built as a wind tunnel model.

A number of designs utilising the Pegasus engine followed, with the CL-1563 study appearing in about 1972, although its origins were probably a little earlier. This series of concepts aimed to produce a rugged, subsonic V/STOL close-support aircraft. The CL-1563-1 was designed with a conventional fuselage and an offset upper wing supported by a large tail-fin. Lockheed described this arrangement as a box-wing configuration, although biplane might be equally suitable. The aircraft would have exceptional manoeuvring capability and be able to make very short take-offs without the assistance of vectored thrust. A simpler version of this design powered by a single turbofan engine was proposed, with the reference CL-1564-3, and there was at least one other completely conventional monoplane variant. Relatively few details of these proposals are available, although CL-1563-1 was intended to be 47.5ft (14.5m) long with an overall span of 25ft (7.62m). Armament would comprise a single 30mm cannon with 230 rounds carried in a ventral fairing, two wingtip-mounted AIM-9 Sidewinder missiles for self-defence and free-fall bombs or Hellfire air-to-surface missiles. The aircraft would be supported on the ground by a Harrier-style undercarriage with outriggers and the forward-positioned cockpit would provide the pilot with good visibility. It was anticipated that much of the aircraft would be constructed from composites, providing significant weight savings. There are no performance estimates available for any of the designs in this series. The CL-1563-1 was undoubtedly intended to meet the USAF's 1970 Attack Experimental (AX) programme, which would eventually lead to the Fairchild A-10A Warthog. It is known that Lockheed undertook wind tunnel testing of box-wing models up to supersonic speeds, but the unusual concept failed to win any official support and progressed no further.

Lockheed has produced numerous studies for VTOL combat and transport aircraft, but many of the details remain classified or are no longer available. One poor quality drawing of a supersonic VTOL fighter proposal known as CL-1618 survives from the early 1970s, with little documentation. The front end of this two-seater bears some resemblance to an F-4 Phantom, with rearward-positioned wing and short booms carrying tail fins. Two small canards are located below the engine air intakes alongside the cockpit area. The aircraft would be powered by a three-nozzle Pegasus PCB turbofan, with the forward nozzles visible only from the underside. Estimated maximum speed was Mach 1.6, with a

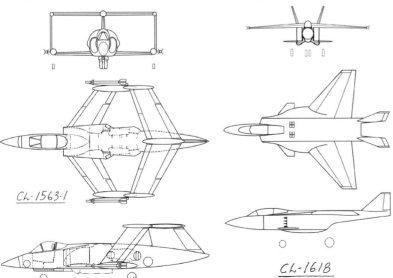

CL-1563-1

CL-1618

maximum STO weight of about 30,000lb (13,608kg). Nothing more is currently known about CL-1618, which was apparently intended for naval use.

During 1976, Lockheed's Skunk Works produced a new Pegasus-powered supersonic V/STOL strike fighter design to meet future US Navy requirements. With the company reference CL-1662, this was essentially a compact alternative to McDonnell Douglas's AV-16SX proposal, with a smaller wing area of 193ft^2 (17.93m^2). Lockheed designers considered this optimal for good manoeuvrability at speeds of about Mach 0.90 and a 30,000ft (9,144m) altitude. CL-1662 would be armed with various weapons on four underwing hardpoints and there would be provision for Sidewinder AAMs on wingtip launch rails and a single 20mm cannon carried in a ventral nacelle. The undercarriage design for this proposal would be a tricycle layout, with no outriggers and an offset forward wheel, positioned to clear the gun pack. Lockheed did not specify the engine for the CL-1662 in any detail, but it seems almost a certainty that it was considering the Rolls-Royce Pegasus 11F-35 vectored-thrust turbofan with PCB. As expected, there would be an air-bleed reaction control system. The CL-1662 would be equipped with a multi-mode radar system and an advanced fly-by-wire system. An operational radius, depending on mission requirements, would be 465 miles (748km) with a short rolling take-off and this could be extended with underwing drop tanks and/or in-flight refuelling. Composites would be used wherever possible in the construction of this aircraft, making the estimated STO weight 29,973lb (13,595kg). It seems probable that models were wind tunnel tested, but no details are currently available and CL-1662 progressed no further.

The next Lockheed VTOL supersonic fighter study to be included in this section took place in 1978 and it received the company reference CL-1626. Possibly funded by the US Navy, this concept was intended to replace the AV-8B and F/A-18, with the ability to operate in full VTOL mode from warships and larger, adapted commercial vessels. Power would be provided by a modified version of the Rolls-Royce three-nozzle PCB Pegasus 11F-33 turbofan. A fixed-geometry engine inlet was chosen to aid design simplicity, although it was acknowledged that this would limit the aircraft's maximum speed to about Mach 1.6 at altitude. Normal control surfaces would be used for conventional flight, with an air-bleed reaction control system for VTOL operations. All functions would be regulated by a sophisticated fly-by-wire system and the aircraft would be fitted with multi-mode radar and a full defensive countermeasures suite. One of the more unusual features was the installation of the aircraft's cannon in a special nacelle that formed part of the tail fin. Apparently, Lockheed's designers considered this necessary to avoid gas ingestion by the large ventral intake.

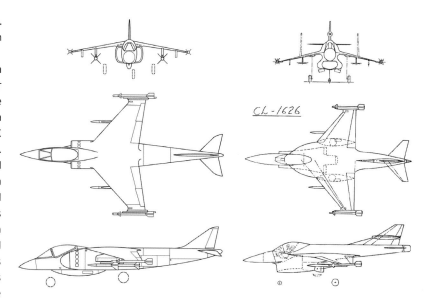

Intriguingly, this design is very similar to the Hawker Siddeley HS.1205. Both have the same general appearance, the same engine and the same estimated performance. It is almost impossible to avoid drawing the conclusion that these designs have a common origin. The dates for both projects coincide and there has often been technical information shared between US and UK defence companies in the past. So was the CL-1626 an original Lockheed concept, or could it have been adapted from work undertaken at Hawker Siddeley? Whatever the answer, this Lockheed design never progressed to the wind tunnel testing of models, although the HS.1205 was examined in considerable detail until 1979 when the project was dropped due to technical issues.

By the early 1980s, DARPA was pushing ahead with a detailed study into ways of improving engine systems for V/STOL combat aircraft. Research into new propulsion systems for STOVL and VTOL was under way on both sides of the Atlantic and DARPA encouraged a joint development agreement between the US Department of Defense (DoD) and the UK MoD, which was signed in January 1986. The objective of this research was to produce the means of powering a supersonic multi-role V/STOL fighter for service entry in the early 21st century. Organisations directly involved in this work included BAe, Rolls-Royce, several US aerospace contractors and NASA.

Four technologies were identified and this programme would last five years, hopefully leading to the construction and testing of a demonstrator by 1993. Designs under review were advanced versions of the Pegasus engine with PCB, the remote augmented lift system (RALS) that uses engine bypass air ducted to a forward combustion system and outlet to provide lift. The third method undergoing investigation by NASA was the EL system, pioneered by De Havilland Canada and the fourth used two widely separated shaft-coupled

LEFT The CL-1662 was a 1976 study produced by Lockheed's Skunk Works for a supersonic V/STOL strike fighter to meet future US Navy requirements. Power would have been provided by a Pegasus-derived PCB turbofan. *Bill Rose*

RIGHT Designed in 1978, the Lockheed CL-1626 may have been intended for use by the US Navy as a future replacement for the AV-8B and F/A-18. It is hard to ignore the similarity between this proposal and the Hawker Siddeley HS.1205, suggesting that information was shared between the two companies. *Lockheed/Bill Rose*

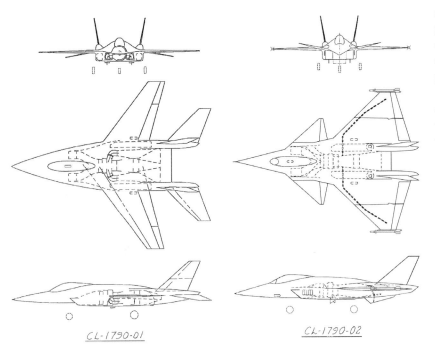

CL-1790-01

CL-1790-02

fan stages to provide lift.

Lockheed's Skunk Works appear to have been contracted by NASA Ames to examine a series of advanced supersonic V/STOL fighter designs for use with this engine development project under the company reference CL-1790. This was the first phase in a classified programme that would continue into the 1990s. The initial proposal (CL-1790-01) was given a slightly arrowhead-shaped fuselage with a centrally positioned engine, swept wing and short twin booms with upright and horizontal fins. Propulsion was provided by a single hybrid fan vectored thrust (HFVT) engine. A second design, with the reference CL-1790-02, utilised a canard configuration and the same HFVT system. The third design in this series, CL-1790-03, was similar in most respects to CL-1790-02, with the same overall length of 59.75ft (18.2m) and the same substantial wing area of 847ft^2 (78.68 m^2). The main difference with this variant was the turbine bypass engine (TBE), used in conjunction with RALS. No details of estimated weights or performance were released, although all three designs were expected to have a supersonic capability in normal flight. Each aircraft would be equipped with a reaction control system for use at low speeds, conventional tricycle landing gear and a weapons bay on each side of the engine. The CL-1790 designs were intended to be stealthy, with a low radar cross section (RCS) and it remains unknown if there were other variants in this series, which seem to have been primarily intended to demonstrate future propulsion possibilities.

Various US V/STOL proposals followed this engine research and there were numerous reviews examining the options for a future high-performance STOVL multi-role fighter. DARPA's original 1980s ASTOVL programme effectively continued to evolve during the early 1990s, either becoming or taking on board the Common Affordable Lightweight Fighter (CALF) programme, with Lockheed as the prime contractor, McDonnell Douglas in second place and Boeing eventually joining the endeavour. The revised objective was development of conventional and STOVL variants for all services, with high commonality of parts and the lowest possible production costs. One type of engine would be used, with the STOVL variant having an additional lift feature.

In March 1993, DARPA contracted Lockheed to develop a shaft-driven lift fan and McDonnell Douglas to study a gas-driven version. This approach was expected to eliminate most of the problems associated with hot gas re-ingestion. In 1994, Northrop Grumman became involved with the CALF project. It partnered McDonnell Douglas, along with the British aerospace contractor BAe. DARPA was now preparing to fund the construction of a prototype, having secured the designation X-32. Running in parallel to DARPA's project was the Joint Advanced Strike Technology (JAST) Programme operated by the USAF and USN, with participation by most of the same defence contractors. Eventually Congress exercised some common sense and in late 1994 both programmes were merged under the JAST name.

The objective remained largely unchanged, which was the development of three advanced strike fighter variants to replace a number of existing aircraft. These comprised a conventional fighter for the USAF and RAF, a carrier-based version for the US Navy and an STOVL model for the US Marine Corps and Royal Navy. Other NATO members were already expressing an interest in this programme and there was good export potential. Although under consideration for some time, the Pratt & Whitney F119 engine was officially selected in 1995 for the three different fighters proposed by participating contractors and General Electric received a request to study an alternative engine. By early 1996 this major programme had been renamed as the Joint Strike Fighter (JSF) project. At this time, Rear-Admiral Craig Steidle, who was acting as JSF project manager, placed considerable emphasis on affordability, suggesting that the future flyaway price of the conventional version would be no more than $28 million. This would be achieved by large production runs, advanced manufacturing methods and standardisation of components across all services. Some 15 years later, the aircraft that emerged from this programme had yet to enter service and the price had climbed to a breathtaking USAF estimate of at least $122 million per aircraft, with the figure expected to rise even further. This made it the most expensive defence programme in history.

Joint Strike Fighter

I have written about the Harrier in more detail than originally planned as this aircraft and its engine have been central to many of the designs in this book. On the other hand, the STOVL version of the JSF was part of a larger conventional fighter project, which is very well documented, and to delve deeply into this area would move too far from my general aim to discuss lesser-known, often previously secret vertical take-off fighter projects (even if relatively few have actually met the VTO requirement). However, the STOVL variant was developed as a Harrier replacement and therefore justifies some background detail. At the start of the JSF project the planned 'tri-service' family of combat aircraft would all use the same basic airframe. The most important version was the conventional take-off and landing (CTOL) fighter for the USAF. Its primary purpose was to replace the F-16 and the A-10. The second carrier variant (CV) would become the US Navy's stealth strike fighter, occupying the place originally intended for the advanced General Dynamics/ McDonnell Douglas A-12A Avenger II. The third STOVL design was primarily intended for the US Marine Corps and the Royal Navy as a Harrier replacement.

The requirement specified a single-seat CTOL, CV and STOVL strike fighter. The unit cost would be $28 million to $38 million, depending on the version, and all three aircraft would use the Pratt & Whitney F119-PW-100 turbofan developed for the Lockheed Martin F-22A Raptor. Empty weight was specified at 22,500lb (10,205kg) to 24,000lb (10,886kg) depending on the version, with 15-16,000lb (6,800-7,257kg) of fuel and a payload of up to 17,000lb (7,700kg). The overall length of all three aircraft was provisionally set at 45ft (13.7m) with a wingspan of 36ft (10.7m). All variants would be capable of supersonic speed with a range of at least 690 miles (1110km). In-flight refuelling would be a standard feature and there were classified requirements for stealth. However, it is known that that the STOVL variant was expected to have the same infrared signature as the CTOL and CV variants, providing a major improvement over the V/STOL Harrier. In mid-1996, the three separate design groups formally submitted their JSF proposals for the $2 billion concept demonstrator phase of the project. Two aircraft would be selected, with one receiving the X-32 designation and the other being known as the X-35.

Boeing's initial JSF design utilised a one-piece, predominantly thermoplastic, delta wing to maintain low production costs, a blended fuselage section, twin tail fins and a large ventral air inlet below the cockpit. It was originally intended to power the STOVL version with a tandem fan version of the P&W F119 engine but this was altered to a ducted direct-lift system with retractable forward nozzles and a directable main exhaust flow.

The entry from McDonnell Douglas (heavily supported by Northrop Grumman and British Aerospace) was partly based on the Northrop YF-23A stealth fighter, which lost out to the Lockheed Martin YF-22A in the USAF's Advanced Tactical Fighter (ATF) competition. Like the YF-23A, this aircraft would have no tail fin and just tailplanes with modest dihedral. This reduced drag, provided good low-speed handling and improved the aircraft's stealth characteristics.

As development progressed, the STOVL version of McDonnell Douglas's JSF proposal underwent a major propulsion revision with the gas-driven lift fan (located behind the cockpit area) being abandoned. This was replaced by a GE/Allison/RR GEA-FXL lift engine, producing an expected 16,000lb (71kN) of thrust. Northrop Grumman engineers were largely responsible for this change, aware that the substitute engine was lighter and the gas ducts were a problem, as they seriously interfered with the commonality of parts requirement for all JSF variants. However, from the outset this revision was opposed by the US Marine Corps who believed it would complicate maintenance and increase fuel consumption.

In addition to the forward lift engine, the main turbofan was fitted with retractable side nozzles for use at low speeds and the vectored main exhaust outlet was also usable for manoeuvrability enhancement. The CTOL and presumably the CV versions would be fitted with an additional fuel tank in place of the lift engine. A reaction control system would stabilise the STOVL aircraft at low speeds and in normal flight there were split outboard brake/rudder/aileron surfaces based on those used for the B-2.

Lockheed Martin's stealthy JSF proposal was considered the most conventional of the three designs and sometimes described as a single-engine F-22A Raptor 'Lite'. The STOVL version was fitted with a vertically positioned lift fan behind the cockpit area,

BELOW The McDonnell Douglas STOVL proposal for the JSF programme. Designed from the outset to have good stealth characteristics and high performance, this sleek aircraft had no upright tail fin. *McDonnell Douglas/Bill Rose*

LEFT The Boeing X-32B STOVL prototype flown by test pilot Dennis O'Donoghue touches down at Edwards AFB after completing its initial 50-minute flight from the company's facility at Palmdale, California, on 29 March 2001. *Dave Martin, USAF*

CENTRE Lockheed Martin's X-35B STOVL demonstrator hovers. *Lockheed Martin*

RIGHT The Lockheed Martin X-35B during a test flight, having undergone a change in colour scheme. *USAF*

which was shaft-driven by the P&W F119 engine. Dr Paul Bevilaqua originally designed (and patented) this system at the Skunk Works. It was the least complicated method of generating forward lift and effectively dealt with hot gas re-ingestion problems. Some bypass air would be ducted to nozzles on each side of the fuselage and a three-bearing nozzle would direct the main exhaust flow downwards during low-speed operations. This system is often associated with the Russian Yak-41 Freestyle STOVL fighter and Lockheed is known to have studied this aircraft in detail, purchasing development data from Yakovlev in the 1990s. Nevertheless, the idea goes back much further and during the early 1970s Pratt & Whitney experimented with a three-bearing downward-vectoring exhaust nozzle for the JTF22A-30A engine, which was intended to power several proposed VTOL fighters for the US Navy's SCS project. The conventional take-off and landing variants of the Lockheed Martin JSF would carry extra fuel in the space occupied by the lift fan.

On 16 November 1996, a decision was announced to award the construction of prototype aircraft to Boeing and Lockheed Martin. Each contractor would receive $750 million to build a conventional take-off and STOVL demonstrator. At the same time, the UK MoD launched its own formal project to replace the Harrier, which would result in the JSF being selected in January 2001. Rejection of the McDonnell Douglas design was not unexpected and the alteration to the propulsion system was largely to blame. Nevertheless, this proved very damaging to the company, which had been in difficulty since cancellation of the A-12A Avenger strike aircraft, a joint project with General Dynamics. It also experienced a fall-off in commercial aircraft sales, had entered into a badly judged business arrangement with the Chinese and made unrealistic attempts to develop the large MD-12 airliner. Subsequently, McDonnell Douglas became part of The Boeing Company in August 1997. Previous JSF partners, Northrop Grumman and British Aerospace, would now become involved with the Lockheed Martin proposal.

The Boeing JSF design was assigned the designation X-32 and Lockheed Martin's aircraft would be known as the X-35. The cost allowance for this 51-month project had now risen to $2.2 billion, including an additional contract to Pratt & Whitney for further engine development. Some eight months after the start of construction, the Navy requested a series of changes to the design, with major alterations to the tail section. These were considered essential to improve manoeuvrability and payload capability, although the proposed changes caused major problems for Boeing's engineers. On the other hand, it was too late to rebuild the prototypes and the Navy agreed that the X-32 would be adequate in existing form for demonstration purposes.

The X-32 was never going to be described as the most attractive aircraft ever built, although it was a functional machine with a high degree of commonality between the conventional and STOVL variants. It had a deep fuselage and a large forward-positioned air inlet, which would hinge downwards to improve engine performance at low speed on the STOVL version. The first test flight of the X-32A (CTOL version) was undertaken on 18 September 2000 by test pilot Fred Knox at Boeing's Palmdale plant in California. He then flew the aircraft to Edwards Air Force Base. This short flight was relatively uneventful, apart from a minor hydraulic leak, which Knox described as a 'non-event'. Taxiing trials of the STOVL X-32B began on 10 January 2001, with the first test flight taking place on 29 March 2001. With completion of flight-testing at Edwards AFB in May 2001, the X-35B flew across the United States to Patuxent River Naval Air Station for STOVL flight-testing. This came to an end in July 2001.

The Lockheed Martin X-35A first flew at Palmdale on 24 October 2000 with senior Skunk Works test pilot Tom Morgenfeld at the controls. On 18 November 2000, the X-35A was flown by the first British test pilot, RAF Squadron Leader Justin Paines. Four days later the X-35A trials concluded and the prototype was rebuilt as the X-35B. On 23 June 2001, the X-35B undertook its first vertical take off and vertical landing. Less than one month later the X-35B demonstrated its ability to take-off in less than 500ft (152m), reach supersonic speed and return to land vertically. The X-35C had already flown from Palmdale to Edwards AFB and on to Patuxent River, where flight-testing was completed by 11 March 2001. Once the JSF flight-testing phase was completed, the US Department of Defense began its formal evaluation of the two aircraft. Although the Boeing X-32 had a number of points in its favour, the Lockheed Martin design had consistently out-performed its rival and was considered the clear winner. This was announced on 26 October 2001. In 2005, the X-32A was transported to the National Museum of the USAF in Dayton, Ohio, for restoration and display. The X-32B ended up at the Patuxent River Naval Air Museum, Maryland.

On 19 February 2006, the first F-35A (AA-1) was rolled out at Fort Worth, Texas, and this was the start of a major defence programme with potential sales of this high-tech aircraft running into several thousand. A few months later the USAF officially assigned the name Lightning II to the aircraft. This was chosen in honour of the wartime Lockheed P-38 Lightning and the British supersonic Lightning fighter from the 1960s. In addition to the USA and UK, who are Level 1 partners, a number of other countries joined the F-35 programme. Italy and the Netherlands became Level 2 partners, making a substantial financial contribution, and Canada, Turkey, Australia, Norway and Denmark joined with a Level 3 involvement. Many other countries have shown a serious interest in buying the F-35, including Israel, Singapore and Japan. In the case of Israel, it expressed a wish to integrate its own electronic systems with the aircraft's built-in system, which was declined, although a compromise was reached which would permit the Israelis to use equipment in parallel, allowing the use of its own electronic warfare modules, air-to-air missiles and precision-guided weapons. Israel has also suggested it would be interested in working on the development of a two-seat version of the F-35.

For some time, there have been widespread calls to scrap the F-35B STOL version and reduce the numbers of F-35A and F-35C fighters on order. There can be little doubt that the ongoing economic crisis has made this a very tempting option for politicians, although the US Marine Corps has no alternative replacement for the AV-8B and has managed to keep the F-35B alive. In the case of foreign customers, Canada has expressed grave concerns about the long term cost of the F-35 programme and may drop out, while Japan has indicated that it is also worried about ever increasing costs. Nevertheless, the F-35 remains a very advanced combat aircraft that is claimed to be several times more effective than any existing fighter in air-to-air and air-to-ground combat situations. The pilot's situational awareness and ability to identify targets is fast and effective, with a high-tech cockpit environment that includes voice activation and a helmet-mounted display system (HMDS) used with all versions of the aircraft.

While no version of the F-35 can match the range or payload capability of the F-15, this new aircraft enjoys superior stealth characteristics that are only (currently) surpassed by the F-22 Raptor.

In the case of the STOVL F-35B, which is the aircraft of most interest to readers of this book, present estimates suggest a maximum take-off weight of 60,000lb (27,000kg), with a combat radius of 517 miles (832km). Maximum speed is Mach 1.67, with a ceiling of 60,000ft (18,288m). Supercruise is not a feature of the engine design (but is possible over a limited distance). The F-35B has a length of 51.3ft (15.6m), a wingspan of 35ft (10.7m) and a wing area of 460ft^2 (42.7m^2). A wide range of weapons will be available to this aircraft, although the GAU-12 25mm cannon (carried internally by the F-35A) is located in a 'stealthy' ventral pod with 220 rounds. The internal bays are able to carry two 1,000lb (453kg) JDAMs, or six small-diameter 250lb (113kg) bombs and two AMRAAMs on the inner doors. Hardpoints are also available for underwing stores,

ABOVE The first F-35B Lightning II STOVL fighter rolls off the Lockheed Martin production line at Fort Worth, Texas on 18 December 2007. *Lockheed Martin*

BELOW F-35B Lightning II STOVL fighter (BF-01), which undertook the first vertical landing of a production F-35 at NAS Patuxent River, Maryland, on 18 March 2010. The aircraft was flown by BAE Systems test pilot Graham Tomlinson. *US Navy*

although external carriage reduces the aircraft's stealth performance. Various configurations for AAMs are possible with internal and external AIM-120, AMRAAM and AIM-9s.

A number of different air-to-surface guided weapons can be carried, including the AGM-154 JSOW, AGM-158 Joint Air-to-Surface Stand-off Missile (JASSM) and Storm Shadow/SCALP. Other underwing options include 480 (US)-gallon (1,817-litre) and 600 (US)-gallon (2,271-litre) drop tanks and reconnaissance units. It is unclear if US F-35Bs will have the ability to deliver the B61 nuclear weapon. There is also a classified programme under way to develop a laser weapon for the conventional F-35 variants that occupies the area behind the cockpit. This would be powered with a generator shaft-driven by the engine in the same manner as the lift engine.

The F-35B is equipped with the Northrop Grumman Electronic Systems AN/APG-81 AESA radar and the Electro-Optical Targeting System (EOTS) produced by Lockheed Martin. A highly modified Boeing 737-300 has been used to develop and test all the F-35's electronic systems and the aircraft carries a complete F-35 cockpit.

In-flight refuelling tests began in March 2008 and supersonic speeds were achieved on 13 November 2008, with the first F-35A reaching Mach 1.05 at 30,000ft (9,144m). The first F-35B flew on 11 June 2008, with BAE Systems test pilot Graham Tomlinson at the controls. It was an uneventful conventional take-off and landing. However, testing of the STOVL lift system did not start until 7 January 2010. The first mid-air hover took place on 17 March 2010, and this aircraft achieved supersonic speed during a test flight on 10 June 2010. At the time of writing, the F-35 has yet to become fully operational, although the US Marine Corps Strike Fighter Squadron (All Weather)-121 (VMFA(AW)-121) based at Yuma, Arizona, became the first operational squadron to convert from the Boeing F/A-18 to the F-35B, with an official cerimony taking place on 20 November 2012. Sixteen F-35B aircraft are scheduled for delivery by September 2013, but their flight

envelope will remain limited and there are no immediate plans to clear them for combat operations. In 2014, VMA-211 will become the second US Marine Corps squadron to receive the F-35B, converting from Harriers.

Despite original intentions to have this fifth-generation, multi-role fighter in service with US forces by 2008. Development has been plagued by ever-increasing weight issues, steeply rising costs and a string of technical problems. The worst to date was the failure of a fueldraulic connection to the engine's swivelling exhaust nozzle on 18 January 2013, which was traced to a manufacturing fault. This was followed by the discovery of a potentially serious engine problem during a routine inspection on 19 February 2013 at Edwards AFB. Engineers found a fractured low pressure turbine blade and as a consequence, all versions of the F-35 were immediately grounded while Pratt & Whitney undertook laboratory tests.

Although the F-35 is way behind schedule and well over budget, this strike fighter is expected to continue in service until around 2050, perhaps becoming the last major manned combat aircraft programme to be undertaken before unmanned craft take over.

ABOVE Lockheed Martin F-35B Lightning II STOVL fighter (BF-02) was rolled out on 18 August 2008. Seen here demonstrating low-speed handling, this aircraft exceeded the speed of sound for the first time on 10 June 2010 during its thirtieth flight near NAS Patuxent River, Maryland. *US Navy*

Soviet Cold War Developments

Soviet interest in developing a VTOL fighter predates World War 2, although nothing of any real significance progressed beyond the drawing board until the mid-1950s. In eventual response to growing Western interest in military VTOL aircraft, the Yakovlev OKB was assigned the task of designing and building an equivalent to the Rolls-Royce Flying Bedstead for the development of VTOL control systems.

A design study managed by Professor A. N. Rafaelyantsa was started and this led to the construction of a four-legged steel-framed test platform, measuring

approximately 33ft (10m) square with a centrally located, upright Tumansky RD-9BL engine rated at 5,700lb (25.35kN). This turbojet was modified for vertical use and adapted to provide compressor-bleed air to a reaction control system, comprising four nozzles on arms positioned around the framework. Perhaps reflecting the cold weather climate, or issues with noise, the test rig featured an enclosed box-shaped cockpit. The maximum take-off weight was about 5,000lb (2,268kg) and two separate tanks each carried 44 gallons (200 litres) of fuel, allowing a maximum test period of about 10 minutes. This

unusual machine received the unofficial name 'Turboleta' and although the exact date when this project began is somewhat unclear, the first test flight is believed to have taken place in late 1956 or early 1957, with Yuri Garnayev at the controls. Initial trials were undoubtedly tethered, although no details are available at present. Tests involving the Yakovlev Turboleta are thought to have continued into the early 1960s and this research project led to the development of small vertical lift engines at the Kolesov OKB, resulting in the RD-36, with a rating of 5,200lb (23kN) thrust.

The next stage involved the adaptation of a MiG-21 to carry lift engines in the forward fuselage sections. The MiG OKB began work on this project at the beginning of the 1960s. It resulted in a standard MiG-21PFM being modified to accept two near-vertical, tandem-mounted RD-36-55 engines, covered with a large louvred door that was raised at low speed. Centrally positioned, this installation required an additional 4ft (1.2m) fuselage section, with air for the main engine being ducted around both turbojets. Exhaust from the two RD-36-35 engines exited directly under the fuselage and a fairly basic air-bleed reaction control system was added to improve low-speed handling. When completed, the aircraft was designated MiG-21PD, or more correctly Ye-7PD/23-31. It is possible that MiG designers set out with the intention of building a VTOL fighter, although engine power was insufficient to provide anything more than improved STOL performance. The well-known, highly decorated test pilot Pyotr Ostapenko (1928-2012) made the first flight on 16 June 1966 and the aircraft is reported to have handled very badly. Further flights took place, but there was little scope for improvement and the aircraft was finally grounded at the end of 1967.

During the 1960s, MiG was conducting a comprehensive study into replacing the MiG-21 and this led to the MiG-23PD, which was intended to provide good STOL performance with a maximum speed in excess of Mach 2. The initial prototype known as the MiG-23PD (23-01) was powered by a single afterburning R-27-30 turbojet for normal flight and two centrally positioned Kolesov RD-36-35 lift engines in a similar tandem configuration to the MiG-21PD. The MiG-23PD was fitted with a fixed delta wing based on the proven MiG-21 design, but slightly larger. In addition, blown flaps were used. A maximum speed in excess of Mach 2 was anticipated in normal flight and the aircraft's primary role would be an interceptor. Proposed armament comprised a single 23mm cannon and two AAMs.

Pyotr Ostapenko undertook the first test flight on 3 April 1967. Initial results were good, with the MiG able to take off in 640ft (195m) and land within 820ft (250m). Nevertheless, it was apparent that the extra engines and their fuel requirements introduced unacceptable weight and payload penalties. As a consequence the prototype was scrapped. At the same time, a second MiG-23 (23-11) prototype was built as a variable-geometry aircraft able to adjust its wing sweep from 16° to 72°. The first test flight took place on 10 June 1967 and this aircraft was immediately recognised as a more promising design, with approval being granted for mass-production during December 1967. An STOL reconnaissance version of the MiG-25, fitted with two additional lift engines, was also briefly considered. Perhaps not surprisingly, this seems to have progressed little further than the drawing board.

As part of the ongoing STOL fighter programme, Pavel Sukhoi's OKB was assigned the task of developing a suitable fighter, which resulted in a partial rebuild of the prototype T-58D-1 Mach 2 interceptor that first flew in May 1962. The T-58D-1 proved to have less than ideal take-off and landing performance due in part to the compact delta-wing design, so this aircraft was an ideal candidate for improvement. Externally, the most noticeable modification was a change to the wing, with

LEFT The MiG-23PD (23-01) was another attempt to utilise Kolesov RD-36-35 lift engines to improve short-take-off performance. Trials were disappointing and the project was soon abandoned. *Bill Rose collection*

RIGHT First flown in June 1966, the Sukhoi T-58VD-1 was another attempt to provide an existing Soviet fighter aircraft with a short-take-off capability, by means of additional lift jets. Some improvements were noted but the drawbacks were numerous and the project went no further. However, various engineering changes made to this prototype were adopted in future versions of the aircraft, which became the Su-15. *Bill Rose collection*

a new section being added outboard of the fence, which increased the overall span to 30.66ft (9.34m). This was followed by what appears to have been a modest change to the cockpit location and installation of a centrally located engine bay accommodating three vertically positioned Kolesov RD-36-35 lift engines. The engine inlets would be covered in normal flight by two ventral doors and the air ducting to the main engines required some re-engineering. The final result was a loss in fuel storage capacity and an unwelcome weight gain. The modified aircraft was assigned the designation VD, for Vertikalniye Dvigateli (vertical engines).

T-58VD-1 carried no radar or weapons and was simply regarded as an experimental aircraft. Yevgeny Solovyov made the first flight on 6 June 1966 and although take-off performance was superior to the original T-58, the aircraft showed little improvement when landing. No further STOL prototypes were built, but some features such as the modified wing found their way into production versions of these aircraft known as the Su-15. In July 1967, the two experimental MiG STOL fighters and the Sukhoi T-58VD were unveiled at the Domodedovo Air Show, although it was effectively the end of the road for all three of them.

Yakovlev VTOL Designs

From the time of the Turboleta, a new design section at the Yakovlev (OKB-115) began to study various proposals for future VTOL and STOL combat aircraft. Amongst the earliest Yakovlev VTOL concepts were a series of very ambitious designs, falling within the general designation Yak-33.

The broad aim was to develop a multi-role VTOL aircraft capable of performing as a Mach 3 interceptor, a fighter-bomber, reconnaissance aircraft and a high-performance low-level launch vehicle for an air-to-surface missile fitted with a thermonuclear warhead. The sleek, tailless interceptor would carry a crew of two in tandem. The two main afterburning turbojets were equipped with a form of vectored thrust for use during VTOL and there would be three lift jets positioned in tandem behind the cockpit area. The Yak-33 interceptor would have an anticipated maximum speed of Mach 3 with a suggested ceiling of about 70,000ft (21,336m) and armament was expected to comprise two or four external AAMs. Further versions would be equipped with canards and perhaps as many as six centrally located lift engines. Another canard version of the Yak-33 was powered by two main engines in wingtip nacelles. Each nacelle also carried two small vertically positioned lift engines in the forward section. To provide balance during VTOL, two additional lift engines were located behind the cockpit area and it is probable that Yakovlev engineers planned to use a

reaction control system for low-speed handling. The aircraft was to be built primarily from titanium and steel, with structural optimisation for low-level flight. Although this version appears to have been mainly intended for nuclear strike missions, the aircraft was expected to have a multi-role capability. Needless to say, these early 1960s designs were too advanced for this era and progressed no further.

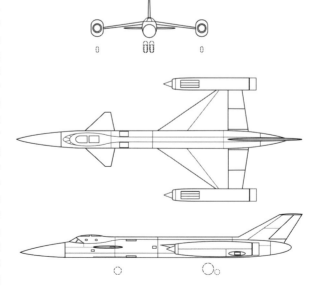

LEFT One of several supersonic VTOL combat aircraft designs produced during the Yak-33 programme, this concept utilised lift engines in the forward engine nacelles and behind the cockpit area. In level flight some versions were expected to have a maximum speed in excess of Mach 3. *Bill Rose*

Yak-36

While the Yak-33 was an interesting series of mainly paperwork concepts, OKB-115 had already been assigned the task of producing an aircraft that would rival the British Kestrel VTOL prototype. The Tumansky Design Bureau (OKB-300) was already working on a vectored-thrust engine, although what eventually emerged was a turbojet based on the R-27-300 with a single vectored exhaust. This non-afterburning design was known as the R-27V-300 and Yakovlev intended to use two of these engines side by side to power an experimental fighter-sized VTOL aircraft known as the Yak-36.

The Yak-36 was a very basic design with a rather ugly appearance, conceived by Stanislav G. Mordovin who headed the VTOL project. The two R-27V-300 engines were placed at the centre of gravity, with a large air intake at the nose. An air-bleed reaction control system stabilised the aircraft during VTOL operations, with nozzles in the wing, a long nose probe and at the rear of the fuselage. Each engine was rated at 11,680lb (51.95kN) thrust and fitted with a hydraulically controlled rotating nozzle positioned on each side of the lower fuselage. These were linked to move in unison. Alexander Yakovlev had initially hoped that Tumansky would develop an equivalent to the British Pegasus four-nozzle engine, but studies showed this would be technically challenging and costly, with an official decision being taken to opt for a simpler and ultimately rather unsatisfactory solution.

The airframe was built from aluminium alloy and steel, with short wings having a 37° sweep and 5° anhedral. The tail was of a conventional design, derived from the Yak-25, with two stabilising fins below the lower rear fuselage. On the ground the Yak-36 rested on a fully retractable bicycle undercarriage, with one forward wheel and two at the rear, plus stabilising outriggers, which would retract into wingtip nacelles during normal flight. There is some confusion about the exact number of Yak-36 prototypes built, although available documentation suggests that as many as 10 airframes could have been partly assembled, with only three being completed. The first (No 36) was used as a static test example and the other two (No 37 and 38) were completed for flight-testing.

Tethered trials with No 37 began in January 1963 and from the outset there were major problems with hot gas re-ingestion and difficulties with the reaction control system. After a series of modifications, the first untethered flight was made by Yuri Garnayev on 23 June 1963. Following a hard vertical landing that caused considerable damage, No 37 was taken out of service for repairs and the first conventional runway take-off and landing was made in No 38 by test pilot Valentin Mukhin on 27 July 1964. Mukhin also made the first vertical take-off and transition to horizontal flight on 7

February 1966. However, the design was flawed from the outset and the main problem of hot gas re-ingestion never appears to have been completely resolved. The design was an unsatisfactory compromise, with some serious potential problems such as the failure of an engine. This could cause the aircraft to flip over, with fatal consequences.

The Yak-36 was unveiled at the Domodedovo Air Show in July 1967, with No 37 and No 38 present. Dummy (or simply empty) underwing rocket launchers were fitted to suggest that the Yak-36 was fully functional as a ground-attack aircraft. NATO observers were certainly intrigued by the aircraft and assigned it the reporting name 'Freehand'. It is unclear exactly

TOP The Yak-36 (No 37) during early flight trials. *Bill Rose collection*

BOTTOM Rear view of Yak-36 (No 37) during flight-testing. Note the size of the large forward probe, used to position the forward nozzle of the reaction control system. *Bill Rose collection*

LEFT The static test example of the Yak-36 (No 36) undergoing wind tunnel trials in the T-101 Wind Tunnel at TsAGI during autumn 1962. *Bill Rose collection*

when the Yak-36 programme concluded and hard to judge how much was learnt from this research project. However, some testing continued into the early 1970s. The static test version (No 36) is currently an exhibit at Monino and No 37 appears to be in storage. The other Yak-36 (No 38) was written off in a landing accident.

Yakovlev had studied an improved version of the aircraft, configured for close-support, reconnaissance and possibly marine operations, with an effective operational range of about 100 miles (160km). This proposal was designated Yak-36MP, although the Soviet military was unimpressed. Yakovlev then took a major change in direction, with OKB-115 designers producing a re-engined concept that looked more like the British Harrier. In the early stages of the Yak-36 project there were designs produced for an aircraft that would use an engine similar to the British Pegasus

four-nozzle engine. The OKB-115 reference is unknown, but it was Yakovlev's preferred option and it seems that Tupolev was requested to study a competitor powered by the same engine.

The Tupolev VTOL fighter project was undertaken in the early 1960s and loosely resembles the Yak-36MP with a second set of engine nozzles. The study received the designation Tu-136, which rather confusingly is now associated with two completely different Tupolev programmes. Nevertheless, when Tumansky announced that development of a Pegasus engine was too demanding, all work on Yakovlev and Tupolev VTOL fighters using a four-nozzle engine came to an end. Intriguingly, the Yak-36MP design appears to have been dusted off in 1974, when it was decided to develop a supersonic replacement for the Yak-38. The new aircraft was fitted with an unspecified engine with a vectored exhaust and two forward lift engines. The nose air inlet was revised and the wings were fitted with strakes, presumably to improve manoeuvrability. The tailplane was repositioned on the rear fuselage and the landing gear became a tricycle arrangement with wheels housed in wing nacelles.

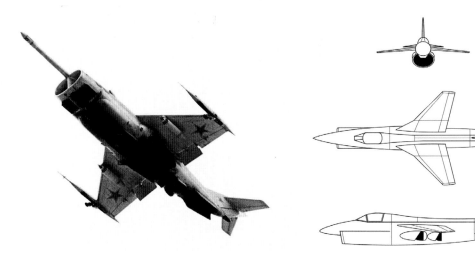

Yak-38

When development of the Yak-36 began it was decided not to use lift jets. A Pegasus-style engine was the initial choice, but it could not be produced in the short term so a simpler propulsion system using vectored thrust was selected to avoid the weight penalty of additional lift engines. After a combat-capable version of the Yak-36 had been rejected by the Soviet military, Mordovin's team re-examined its work with the intention of developing something better. A new design would use a single engine with vectored thrust, accompanied by two forward-located lift engines. This would be packaged into a more aerodynamic aircraft that was closer in appearance to the British Harrier. When these proposals for a new VTOL fighter were submitted to the Soviet Navy in 1967, it wasted little time in approving the construction of five prototypes, which included a two-seat version. A VTOL fighter with marginal supersonic performance would be ideal for Project 1143 (*Kiev* class aircraft carriers), scheduled to begin entering service during the second half of the 1970s.

The new fighter was initially designated as the Yak-36M and it would have a limited capability that included interception, anti-shipping and reconnaissance missions. The Yak-36M would be capable of VSTOL and was equipped with a parachute for normal runway landings. The improved Tumansky R27V-300 main engine was fitted with two linked swivelling exhaust outlets and there were two Kolesov RD-36-35FVR lift engines positioned in tandem, almost vertically, behind the cockpit area. A louvred door would cover the dorsal air inlets for these two engines during normal flight. Air inlets for the main engine were located on each side of the cockpit and air bleed from the main engine's compressor stage would feed

the reaction control system. In overall terms the aircraft was very close in size to the Sea Harrier, aside from being just over 3ft (0.90m) longer. Unlike the Harrier, the aircraft was supported on the ground by a fully retractable tricycle undercarriage with no outriggers. Most of the fuselage was built from newly developed Al-Li alloy, which is especially useful for a naval aircraft as it has superior corrosion resistance to aluminium. Avionics for the initial pre-production and early production aircraft were extremely basic. There was no radar, target-designation equipment or self-defence capability such as flares or chaff. However, the electronic engine management system was reportedly very sophisticated. Proposed weapons for the new VTOL fighter may have included a twin-barrelled GSh-23L 23mm cannon below the fuselage, although there is no indication that it was ever fitted. It appears that the Yak-36M was designed from the outset to carry its weapons on two wing pylons with four hardpoints. For air-to-air combat the aircraft would carry AA-8 Aphid AAMs and for ground-attack or anti-shipping operations there would be AS-10 Karen ASMs with a guidance pod. Other options included free-fall bombs and air-to-surface unguided

ABOVE An engine-equipped test fuselage for the new Yak-36M VTOL fighter is carried beneath an adapted Tu-16 bomber in 1970. *Bill Rose collection*

LEFT Yak-38 (41) performs a vertical take-off. *Bill Rose collection*

ABOVE This picture shows several Yak-38M VTOL fighters on board the Minsk aircraft carrier during the late 1970s. Aircraft No 46 is currently on display at the Ukraine State Aviation Museum, Kiev.
Bill Rose collection

rockets. Drop tanks could be fitted and the total payload capability is thought to have been about 1,325lb (600kg).

The test phase began in May 1969 with a specially built fuselage section being suspended below an adapted Tu-16 bomber. After several months of ground trials the fuselage, which contained engines, was flown beneath the Tu-16 and lowered from the bomb bay to test the systems. These trials continued for some time, while construction of the first prototype Yak-36M took place. Information gathered from the captive fuselage tests would result in a series of rolling improvements to the aircraft's design. The first Yak-36M prototype completed a brief initial hover flight on 22 September 1970 and made a conventional runway

take-off and landing on 2 December 1970. Work on the project was under routine observation by CIA spy satellites and NATO assigned the reporting name 'Forger A' to the aircraft.

However, progress remained slow and the first full VTOL flight did not take place until 25 February 1972. This was followed on 18 November 1972 with trials on board the Moskva helicopter cruiser. Modifications to the basic design continued on a regular basis, until the Soviet Navy was finally satisfied that the aircraft was suitable for service entry. The first production aircraft was completed in early 1975 and officially received in October 1976. This also led to a change of designation, with the fighter being renamed as the Yak-38. The ungainly two-seat version was also renamed as the Yak-38UM. Improvements continued with the addition of boundary layer splitter plates at the air inlets and modifications to the lift engine inlet cover. The Yak-38 had now earned an unenviable reputation as being unreliable, difficult to fly and potentially dangerous. The aircraft's range was limited to about 62 miles (100km) and the poor payload capability led carrier pilots to make rolling take-offs and landings, which encouraged the introduction of a safety barrier net.

Failure of components became routine and the forward lift engines had a life expectancy of little more than 20 hours. They could also be difficult to start in very hot conditions, leading to the eventual installation of an oxygen boost system. On return from the *Kiev's* first Mediterranean cruise in 1976, only one of the six Yak-38s remained flyable. Pilots were now in fear of this aircraft and accidents took place on a continual basis. In April 1980, four Yak-38s were deployed to a base near Shindand

LEFT Yak-38 (74) 'Forger' photographed with its wings folded on the deck of an unidentified Soviet aircraft in October 1985. *US Navy*

in Afghanistan for operational trials. This assessment lasted for 50 days and it received the official name ROMB-1. Two prototype Su-25s also operated alongside the Yaks. Twelve combat sorties were undertaken and a small number of bombs dropped, but whether any real targets were attacked remains unclear. The Su-25s performed well, but the Yaks were troublesome from the outset and performed badly in local conditions. As a warplane, the Yak-38 was unreliable, performed badly and crashes, which sometimes killed the pilot, were occurring on a regular basis.

The situation was so bad that a high-level decision was taken in late 1981 to prioritise the development of a new version of the VTOL fighter that would provide the level of reliability and performance currently lacking. The main issue was insufficient engine power, and a series of engineering improvements were immediately undertaken which resulted in an overall increase of about 10% thrust. Oxygen boost for the lift engines also became a standard feature, along with numerous other changes. The new model was known as the Yak-38M and the first example flew in 1982. From all accounts, it was a much better aircraft than its predecessors. There were also suggestions to upgrade the aircraft further with the installation of advanced radar, a larger wing area and increased fuel capacity, but these changes progressed no further.

During September 1983, a series of trials were conducted to ascertain if the Yak-38M could operate

BELOW This Yak-38M is understood to have been one of the last of these aircraft to roll off the production line. *Bill Rose collection*

from a large container ship. There can be little doubt that British Harrier operations during the Falklands War were responsible for encouraging this. Two merchant 'Ro-Ro' ships, the Agostino Neto and Nikolai Cherkasov, were fitted with heat-resistant sections of decking and this was followed by a series of exercises from dispersed land-based sites.

In excess of 200 Yak-38s were built and many were lost in accidents. The aircraft had been prematurely pressed into service as the Soviet's answer to the Harrier, but from the outset it was a third-rate piece of machinery, often feared by the pilots who flew it. Soon after the Soviet Union collapsed, all Yak-38s were taken out of service. As relations improved with the West a Yak-38U was shipped to the United States and flown by two US Navy pilots in 1992. Later that same year a Yak-38M was demonstrated at Farnborough. A number of surviving aircraft are on display or currently in storage.

ABOVE Partly buried in deep snow, this Yak-36M crashed on farmland near Moscow on 4 March 1976. The pilot had been accidentally ejected due to a system fault while the aircraft was in its transition phase. He landed in the freezing waters of the Volga and was rescued, while the aircraft continued to circle for 18 minutes before hitting the ground, having generated a major defence alert. *Bill Rose collection*

Yakovlev Yak-41 Freestyle

ABOVE A non-flying Yak-41 prototype (48) used for engine testing. *Bill Rose collection*

B y the early 1970s, Yakovlev had started design work on a third-generation VTOL fighter with supersonic performance, primarily intended for carrier-based operations. Some initial concepts seemed to be upgrades of much earlier designs, but the new aircraft steadily evolved into something that looked rather like a compact MiG-25 Foxbat from forward angles. On paper, the new fighter appeared to be a substantial improvement over the Yak-38 and would have superior performance to the British Harrier. This led to the project being given a green light in 1977, with funding provided for the construction of four prototypes.

The first aircraft (48-0) was to be used for static destructive testing and the second prototype (48-1) was for test-rig engine trials. The third and fourth aircraft (48-2 and 48-3, given the numbers 75 and 77) would undertake test flights. The new supersonic VTOL fighter had been designated Yak-41 and this was now revised to Yak-41M to reflect the fighter's multi-role capability. The main powerplant in the Yak-41M was a Kobchenko/ Soyuz R-79V-300 vectored-thrust turbofan, rated at

24,300lb (108kN) dry thrust and 34,170lb (152kN) with afterburning. To facilitate VTOL, an additional two Rybinsk (Kolesov) RD-41 lift jets were carried in vertical tandem positions directly behind the cockpit area. Each engine was rated at 9,039lb (40.2kN) thrust. This part of the propulsion system was fairly similar to the Yak-38, with a door covering the lift engine inlets and a cover over the exhausts. A forward flap also helped to reduce hot gas reingestion. The main engine was supplied with air from two rectangular inlets on each side of the fuselage with compressor air bleed for a reaction control system. Finally, the main exhaust could be directed downwards by 90° for VTOL and typically set at 65° for STO.

The fuselage was a significant departure from the Yak-38 and the aircraft utilised a larger area wing with a 45° sweep and twin booms with tail-fins. The forward-positioned pressurised cockpit provided good visibility and the aircraft was fitted with a straightforward fully retractable tricycle undercarriage. The avionics suite carried by the Yak-41M was a major improvement over the previous aircraft, with a digital fly-by-wire system and diagnostic flight control. This would prevent take-off in the event of a system malfunction and should a dramatic failure take place while the aircraft was in flight, the pilot would be automatically ejected. The aircraft carried an advanced navigation system, a similar radar system to the MiG-29, albeit with a smaller dish, and a digital fire control system connected to a helmet-mounted sight. Production aircraft would be equipped with self-defence countermeasures. Armament comprised an internal GSh-6-30 six-barrelled 30mm cannon with 120 rounds and four underwing pylons able to carry 2,204lb (1,000kg) in VTO mode and 5,732lb (2,600kg) with a short take-off. As an interceptor the Yak-41M could carry R-73 Archer, R-77 Adder or R-27 Alamo AAMs and, in the strike role, free-fall bombs, air-to-surface missiles, rockets or a tactical nuclear weapon. Drop tanks, target designation,

RIGHT Yak-41 (77) prototype displayed with air-to-air missiles. *Bill Rose collection*

TOP The Yak-41 during early trials. *Bill Rose collection*   **BOTTOM** The Yak-41 (77) prototype during a test flight. *Bill Rose collection*

reconnaissance and electronic warfare pods were other options.

The first conventional runway take-off using 48-2 (75) was made by Yakovlev's chief test pilot, Andrei A. Sinitsyn on 9 March 1987 at Zhukovsky, Moscow.

The first hover test was conducted by Sinitsyn on 29 December 1989, followed by a vertical take-off, transition to horizontal flight and vertical landing on 13 June 1990. Testing continued throughout 1991, with some trials involving the use of a ski-jump. Sinitsyn had now set 12 new flight records, but the aircraft and its designation Yak-41 were classified, so the Russians

altered the aircraft's reference to Yak-141 for submission to the International Aeronautical Federation. This would lead to a degree of confusion with the designation Yak-141 becoming accepted. Furthermore, when the aircraft were eventually repainted and unveiled, they received the numbers 141 in place of 75 and 77.

On 26 September 1991, Sinitsyn made a vertical landing on the aircraft carrier Admiral Gorshkov in 48-2. Testing of both Yak-41M prototypes continued until 5 October 1991, when test pilot Vladimir Yakimov made an exceptionally hard vertical landing on the carrier's deck in 48-3 (77). This seems to have resulted in a

broken landing leg being driven into a fuel tank, which immediately exploded due to fuel/vapour coming into contact with hot engine exhaust. After almost 30 seconds Yakimov ejected from the aircraft and was quickly recovered from the sea. The fire crew managed to extinguish the blaze and although the aircraft has often been reported as a write-off, the largely titanium airframe and major components survived and the Yak-41M was fully repaired. No 77 is currently on display at Yakovlev's museum. Soon after the accident it was announced that there would be no further official funding available for the Yak-41M project due to financial restraints.

Despite being an impressive aircraft that promised superior performance to the Harrier, the Russian Navy had decided that its future aircraft carrier needs could be met with modified versions of the MiG-29 and Su-27. There were attempts to attract international partners to fully develop the aircraft, but the early 1990s were difficult economic times and this never happened. However, Yakovlev and the engine manufacturer AMNTK Soyuz appear to have entered into technology transfer arrangements with Lockheed Martin, which was in the process of developing the STOVL version of the Joint Strike Fighter. Their development data must have proved extremely useful to the Americans.

ABOVE Yak-41 (141) demonstrates its ability to hover. *via Alexi Malinovsky*

Yakovlev Yak-43

During the early 1980s, Yakovlev's designers began to examine options for an advanced successor to the Yak-41. Although not generally publicised, it seems there was some effort made to reduce the radar signature, making the aircraft stealthier. The new design received the company designation Yak-43 and it would be powered by a single Kuznetsov NK-321 turbofan, used for the Tupolev Tu-160 supersonic bomber, and in this instance equipped with a vectoring exhaust outlet. The engine would provide a dry thrust of 30,900lb (137kN), increasing to 55,100lb (245kN) with afterburner. Two forward lift engines located behind the cockpit would be used for VTOL, possibly supplemented by a compressor air bleed to a forward outlet with some form of PCB system. The maximum speed would be in the region of Mach 2+, with a ceiling of about 60,000ft (18,288m) and a combat radius of 600 miles (965km). Quoted maximum VTO weight would be 34,833lb (15,800kg) and maximum STO weight would be 47,400lb (21,500kg). Other improvements would include an advanced radar system, state-of-the-art avionics, a comprehensive self-defence system, all-glass cockpit and the ability to carry a wide range of different weapons.

The Yak-43 was described as a lower cost, more effective alternative to the F-35B and there was the suggestion that it could be built as a conventional take-off aircraft offering greater range and payload capability. After the collapse of the Soviet economy, there was no money available for development of the Yak-43 and no international partners willing to invest.

However, from about 2010 onwards there have been suggestions that the Chinese are interested in acquiring a VTOL or STOVL fighter and this aircraft in updated form would be an obvious candidate.

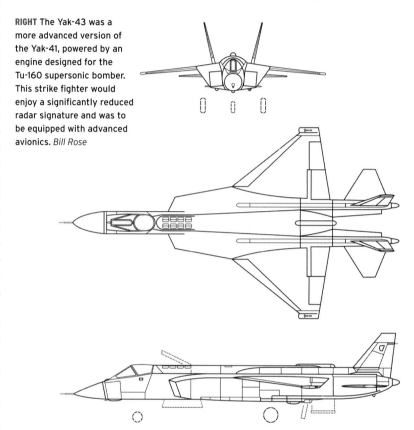

RIGHT The Yak-43 was a more advanced version of the Yak-41, powered by an engine designed for the Tu-160 supersonic bomber. This strike fighter would enjoy a significantly reduced radar signature and was to be equipped with advanced avionics. *Bill Rose*

Chapter Six: Aircraft Details

Hawker P.1127
Crew: 1
Wingspan: 24.33ft (7.41m)
Wing area: 185ft² (17.18m²)
Sweep (leading edge): N/A
Length: 41.16ft (12.54m)
Height: 10.75ft (3.27m)
Empty Weight: 10,200lb (4,626kg)
Loaded weight: 15,500lb (7,030kg)
Maximum Speed at Altitude: 715mph
  (1,150km/h)
Ceiling: 49,800ft (15,179m)
Powerplant (XP976): 1 x Bristol Siddeley
  Pegasus 3 vectored-thrust turbofan, rated
  at 13,500lb (60kN); the final aircraft
  (XP984) was fitted with the first Bristol
  Siddeley Pegasus 5 vectored-thrust
  turbofan, rated at 15,000lb (66.7kN) thrust
Armament: None

Kestrel FGA.1
Crew: 1
Wingspan: 22.9ft (6.97m)
Wing area: 186ft² (17.27m²)
Sweep (leading edge): N/A
Length: 42.5ft (12.95m)
Height: 10.75ft (3.28m)
Empty Weight: 9,800lb (4,445kg) approx
Loaded VTO Weight: 14,500lb (6,577kg)
Maximum STO Weight: 17,000lb (7,711kg)
  approx
Maximum Speed (sea level): 710mph
  (1,142km/h)
Maximum Speed (at altitude): 750mph
  (1,207km/h)
Ceiling: 50,000ft (15,240m) approx
Range: 1,245 miles (2,000km)
Rate of climb: 30,000ft/min (9,144m/min)
  approx
Thrust/weight: 1.04
Powerplant: 1 x Bristol Siddeley Pegasus 5
  vectored-thrust turbofan, rated at 15,000lb
  (66.7kN) maximum thrust
Armament: Underwing practice bombs
  carried during some trials

Harrier GR.3
Crew: 1
Wingspan: 25.25ft (7.7m)
Wing area: 201ft² (18.67m²)
Sweep (leading edge): 40°
Length: 46.83ft (14.27m)
Height: 11.9ft (3.63m)
Empty Weight: 13,535lb (6,139kg)
Loaded weight: 25,200lb (11,430kg)
Maximum Speed: 730mph (1,175km/h)
Ceiling: 55,000ft (16,764m)
Combat Radius: 415 miles (667km)
Powerplant: 1 x Pegasus 11 Mark 103
  vectored-thrust turbofan engine, rated at
  21,500lb (95.6kN) maximum thrust

Armament: 2 x 30mm Aden cannons in
  ventral pods, each carrying 100 rounds;
  free-fall bombs, Hunting Engineering BL755
  cluster bombs, air-to-ground unguided
  rockets; some aircraft were adapted to carry
  the Sidewinder AAM and Shrike AGM

Sea Harrier FRS.1
Crew: 1
Wingspan: 25.25ft (7.7m)
Wing area: 201ft² (18.67m²)
Sweep (leading edge): N/A
Length: 47.5ft (14.47m)
Height: 12.16ft (3.7m)
Empty Weight: 13,100lb (5,942kg)
Maximum Loaded weight: 26,200lb (11,884kg)
Maximum Speed: 740mph (1,190km/h)
Ceiling: 50,000ft (15,240m)
Operational radius: 465 miles (748km)
Powerplant: 1 x Pegasus 104 vectored-thrust
  turbofan engine, rated at 21,500lb (95.6kN)
Armament: 2 x 30mm Aden cannon in pods; 4
  x AIM-9 Sidewinder AAMs, Sea Eagle ASM,
  Harpoon ASM, free-fall bombs, rockets

AV-8B Harrier
Crew: 1; TAV-8B Trainer: 2
Wingspan: 30.33ft (9.25m)
Wing area: 230.7ft² (21.37m²)
Sweep (leading edge): 36°
Length AV-8B: 46.5ft (14.12m); TAV-8B:
  50.25ft (15.32m)
Height Overall: 11.66ft (3.55m)
Empty Weight: 13,968lb (6,336kg); TAV-8B:
  14,222lb (6,451kg)
Maximum Weight STO: 31,000lb (14,060kg)
Maximum Weight VTO: 18,950lb (8,595kg)
Maximum Vertical Landing Weight: 20,000lb
  (9072kg); TAV-8B: 19,550lb (8,867kg)
Maximum Speed: Mach 0.89 at sea level;
  Mach 0.98 at altitude
Ceiling: 50,000ft (15,240m)
Range (STO): Combat radius with full external
  load: 350 miles (563km); 683 miles
  (1099km) with 300 (US)-gallon (1,135-litre)
  drop tanks; ferry Range: 2,015 miles
  (3,243km); in-flight refuelling
Powerplant (AV-8B/TAV-8B): 1 x Rolls-Royce
  Pegasus F402-RR-406 turbofan engine
  rated at 20,280lb (90kN) maximum thrust;
  AV-8B (NA): 1 x Rolls-Royce Pegasus
  F402-RR-408A turbofan engine rated at
  22,200lb (98.75kN) thrust
Armament: 1 x 25mm cannon; 4 x AIM-9L/M
  Sidewinder AAMs or 6 x AIM-120 AMRAAM
  (Radar equipped AV-8B Plus); 6 x AGM-65
  Maverick ASM, or 2 x AGM-88 HARM, 2 x
  AGM-84 Harpoon; free-fall, JDAM and
  Paveway bombs, air-to-ground rockets or
  tactical nuclear weapons

Harrier GR.7
Crew: 1
Wingspan: 30.33ft (9.25m)
Wing area: 230.7ft² (21.37m²)
Sweep (leading edge): 36°
Length: 46.33ft (14.12m)
Height: 11.66ft (3.56m)
Empty Weight: 12,500lb (5,700kg)
Loaded weight: 15,703lb (7,123kg)
Maximum Take-off Weight: VTO 18,950lb
  (8,595kg); STO 31,000lb (14,061kg)
Maximum Speed: 662mph (1,065km/h)
Rate of climb: 14,715ft/min (4,485m/min)
Ceiling: 50,000ft (15,240m)
Combat Radius: 345 miles (555km)
Ferry Range: 2,015 miles (3,243km)
Powerplant: 1 x Rolls-Royce Pegasus Mk 105
  vectored-thrust turbofan rated at 21,750lb
  (96.7kN) maximum thrust
Armament: Initially 2 x 30mm Aden cannon
  pods under the fuselage; 6 x AIM-9
  Sidewinder AAMs or 4 x AGM-65 Maverick
  ASMs; 4 x LAU-5003 rocket pods (19 x CRV7
  70mm rockets per unit), or 4 x Matra rocket
  pods (18 x SNEB 68mm rockets per unit);
  Paveway/Enhanced and Paveway laser-
  guided bombs, free-fall bombs

Dassault Cavalier MD 610
Wingspan: 28.9ft (8.8m)
Wing area: N/A
Length: 48.6ft (14.8m)
Empty Weight: 10,097lb (4,580kg)
VTOL Weight: 16,535lb (7,500kg)
Power: 1 x Bristol BE 53-8 rated at 19,000lb
  (84.5kN) maximum thrust
Maximum Speed: Mach 1
Ceiling: 50,000ft (15,240m)
Range: N/A
Armament: 1 x internal cannon, possibly
  underwing stores; 1 x semi-recessed tactical
  nuclear weapon

Harrier P.1154 (RAF Version)
Crew: 1
Wingspan: 28.33ft (8.63m)
Wing area: 269ft² (25m²)
Sweep (leading edge): 41.2°
Length: 57.5ft (17.5m)
Height: 12.5ft (3.8m)
Empty Weight: 20,100lb (9,117kg)
Maximum Weight (High/Low-Level Strike):
  30,970lb (14,047kg)
Maximum Weight (Ferry): 40,050lb (18,166kg)
Maximum Speed: Mach 1.13 at sea level; Mach
  1.7 at altitude with PCB
Stressed to: 7.5g for combat
Ceiling: 52,500ft (16,000m)
Range: 322 miles (518km) at Mach 0.92
  cruise; with combat tanks: 466 miles
  (750km); in-flight refuelling available

Powerplant: 1 x Bristol Siddeley BS.100/8 vectored-thrust turbofan engine with PCB; maximum thrust with PCB 33,900lb (150.7kN)

Armament: 4 x Red Top AAMs; for strike missions: low-drag and retarded 1,000lb (453kg) bombs, cluster bombs, napalm tanks, SNEB rockets, Martel AJ.168 ASM or single tactical nuclear weapon

Republic Fokker D-24 Alliance
Details below apply to RAC 758-1A30 Proposal
Crew: 1 (other versions: 2)
Wingspan: Extended 32.66ft (11.17m); Stowed: 19ft (5.79m)
Wing area: N/A
Sweep: Extended 11°; Stowed 70°
Length: 63.5ft (19.35m)
Height: 14.4ft (4.38m)
Empty Weight: 20,500lb (9,299kg) approx
VTOL Gross Weight: 30,000lb (13,608kg)
STOL Gross Weight (500ft/152m runway): 33,000lb (14,968kg)
Maximum Speed: Mach 2.4 at altitude
Ceiling: 70,000ft (21,336m) estimated
Range: N/A
Ferry Range: 3,000 miles (4,828km)
Powerplant: 1 x Bristol Siddeley BS.100 vectored-thrust turbofan engine with PCB; quoted maximum thrust for this version was 38,500lb (171kN)
Armament: AAMs, ASMs, free-fall bombs or a single tactical nuclear weapon

D-24 Variations
RAC 758-1A25 - Length: 59.33ft (18m); VTOL Gross Weight: 25,280lb (11,466kg)
RAC 758-1A34 - Length: 67.75ft (20.65m); VTOL Gross Weight: 33,990lb (15,408kg)
RAC 758-1A37 - Length: 70.5ft (21.48m); VTOL Gross Weight: 37,500lb (17,009kg)
NASA Config 1 - Length: 61.6ft (18.87m); N/A
NASA Config 2 - Length: 65.8ft (20m); N/A

BAC Vickers Type 583V (8-1963)
Crew: 1
Wingspan (Fully Extended): 43ft (13.1m); Swept: 25ft (7.6m)
Wing Area (Swept): 250ft² (23.3m²)
Sweep (leading edge): Fully Extended: 25°; Swept: 75°
Length: 52ft (15.8m)
Height: N/A
Empty Weight: N/A
Gross Weight: 45,100lb (20,457kg)
Maximum Speed: Mach 1.2 at sea level; Mach 2.5 at altitude
Ceiling: 60,000ft+ (18,288m+)
Range: N/A
Powerplant: 2 x Rolls-Royce RB.168-32D Spey engines in tandem with vectored thrust; the engine performance is not entirely clear, but the thrust for each engine would be in

excess of 15,000lb (66.7kN)
Armament: 2 x Red Top AAMs, free-fall bombs or rockets

BAe P.1216
Wingspan: 34.75ft (10.6m)
Wing area: 421ft² (39.11m²)
Sweep (leading edge): N/A
Length: 55.9ft (17m)
Height: N/A
Empty Weight: N/A
Gross Weight: 31,000lb (14,061kg)
Maximum Speed: Mach 1 at sea level; Mach 1.8 at altitude
Ceiling: 55,000ft (16,764m) approx
Combat Radius (Strike Mission): 350 miles (563km) approx
Powerplant: 1 x three-nozzle PCB Rolls-Royce RB.422-60 turbofan with a dry rating of 31,400lb (139.6kN), rising to 44,600lb (198.3kN) with full PCB
Armament: 2 x 27mm cannon, AIM-9 Sidewinder AAMs, ASRAAM, AMRAAM, Sea Eagle, free-fall bombs, various other types of ordnance

McDonnell Douglas 279-1
Crew: 1
Wingspan: 30ft (9.1m)
Wing area: 300ft² (27.8m²)
Sweep (leading edge): N/A
Length: 52.1ft (15.8m)
Height: 14.8ft (4.5m)
Empty Weight: 17,950lb (8,142kg)
Gross Weight (VTO): 28,450lb (12,904kg)
Maximum Speed: Mach 2 at altitude
Ceiling: 60,000ft+ (18,288m+)
Range: N/A
Powerplant: 1 x Pegasus 11F-35 vectored-thrust turbofan with PCB, producing an estimated maximum thrust of 29,250lb (130kN)
Armament: 1 x 25mm cannon, AIM-9J, AMRAAM, free-fall bombs, various unspecified options

McDonnell Douglas 279-3
Crew: 1
Wingspan: 35.8ft (10.9m)
Wing area: 428.4ft² (39.8m²); Canard Area: 85.6ft² (7.95m²)
Sweep (leading edge): 45°; Canard: 50°
Length: 56ft (17m)
Height: 17.34ft (5.28m)
Empty Weight: 19,808lb (8,985kg)
Gross Weight (VTO): 29,840lb (13,535kg)
STO Gross Weight: 41,000lb+ (18,597kg+)
Maximum Speed: Mach 2
Ceiling: 62,000ft (19,050m)
Range: Supersonic intercept: 172 miles (276km); interdiction combat radius (with retained drop tanks): 1,035 miles (1,665km)
Ferry Range (with four 600 US-gal

(2,271-litre) drop tanks): 3,000 miles (4,828km)
Powerplant: 1 x P&W STF561-C2 vectored-thrust PCB turbofan rated at 34,316lb (152.6kN) thrust
Armament: 1 x 25mm cannon with 400 rounds; AIM-9J, AMRAAM, free-fall bombs, Mk82 LDGP, 11 weapons points

Lockheed CL-1292-2
Crew: 1
Wingspan: 30ft (9.14m)
Wing area: 300ft² (27.8m²)
Sweep (leading edge): 45°
Length: 52.33ft (16m)
Height: 16.33ft (4.96m)
Empty Weight: 19-20,000lb (8,600-9,070kg) approx
Gross Weight (STO): 29-32,000lb (13,100-14,500kg) approx
Maximum Speed: Mach 1.4 approx
Ceiling: 50,000ft (15,240m)
Range: N/A
Powerplant: 1 x unspecified Pegasus PCB turbofan engine
Armament: 1 x internal 25mm cannon; AIM-7 or AIM-9 AAMs, various other stores on four underwing hardpoints

Lockheed CL-1662
Crew: 1
Wingspan: 26.1ft (7.95m)
Wing area: 193ft² (17.93m²)
Sweep (leading edge): 42°
Length: 46.5ft (14.17m)
Height: 11ft (3.35m)
Empty Weight: 15,000lb (6,804kg)
Maximum Take-off Weight: 29,973lb (13,595kg) (355ft/102m STO)
Landing Weight: 19,560lb (8,872kg)
Maximum Speed: Mach 1.6+
Ceiling: 50,000ft+ (15,240m+)
Operational Radius: 465 miles (748km)
Powerplant: 1 x Pegasus 11F-35 vectored-thrust PCB turbofan rated at 29,250lb (130kN) maximum thrust
Armament: M61 20mm cannon in nacelle; AIM-9L Sidewinder AAMs; AIM-7F Sparrow AIM-54, AGM-84, Mk 83 bombs

Lockheed CL-1626
Crew: 1
Wingspan: 29ft (8.83m)
Wing area: 280ft² (26m²)
Sweep (leading edge): 33.5°
Length: 49.2ft (15m)
Height: 17.75ft (5.4m)
Empty Weight: N/A
Loaded weight: 28,630lb (12,986kg)
Gross Weight: 29,000lb (13,154kg)
Gross STO Weight: 37,000lb (16,783kg)
Maximum Speed: Mach 1.6
Ceiling: 55,000ft (16,764m) estimate

Radius of Action (depending on mission): 300 miles (482km)

Powerplant: 1 x Rolls-Royce Pegasus three-nozzle PCB Pegasus 11F-33 turbofan, rated at 30,000lb (133.4kN) thrust

Armament: 1 x 20mm cannon; 2 x Sidewinders, 2 x AIM-7 Sparrow, ASMs, free-fall, tactical nuclear weapon

Lockheed CL-1790-01/02/03

Crew: 1

Wingspan 01: 48.5ft (14.8m) 02/03: 43ft (13m)

Wing Area 01: 585ft² (54.34m²) 02/03: 847ft² (78.68 m²)

Sweep (leading edge) 01: 35° 02/03: 37°

Length 01: 62.9ft (19.2m) 02/03: 59.75ft (18.2m)

Height 01: 16.6ft (m) 02/03: 15.6ft (4.76m)

Empty Weight: N/A

Loaded weight: N/A

Maximum Speed: Supersonic

Ceiling: N/A

Powerplant: (01/02) 1 x HFVT engine; (03) 1 x TBE, in conjunction with a remote augmented lift system (RALS)

Armament: 2 x internal weapons bays; wingtip AIM-9 Sidewinder AAMs

Boeing X-32

Crew: 1

Wingspan: 36ft (10.97m)

Wing area: 590ft² (54.8m²)

Sweep (leading edge): 55°

Length: 45.01ft (13.72m)

Height: 17.33ft (5.28m)

Empty Weight: N/A

Maximum Take-off weight: 38,000lb (17,200kg)

Maximum Speed: Mach 1.6 at altitude

Ceiling: 60,000ft (18,288m)

Range: USAF mission profile: 980 miles (1,577km); US Navy mission profile: 860 miles (1,384km); USMC/RN mission profile: 690 miles (1,110km)

Powerplant: 1 x Pratt & Whitney F119 afterburning turbofan derivative, rated at 28,000lb (124.5kN) dry thrust and 43,000lb (191kN) with afterburner

Armament: 1 x 20mm M61A2 cannon or 27mm Mauser BK-27 cannon. Internal: 6 x AMRAAM air to air missiles or 2 x AMRAAM air to air missiles and 2 x 2,000lb (907kg) guided bombs. External: Up to 15,000lb (6,803kg) of full range of external stores including anti-radiation missiles, various air-to-surface weapons

Lockheed Martin F-35B

Crew: 1

Length: 51.3ft (15.6m)

Wingspan: 35ft (10.7m)

Height: 14.2ft (4.33m)

Wing area: 460ft² (42.7m²)

Empty Weight: 32,000lb (14,514kg)

Maximum Take-off Weight: 60,000lb (27,215kg)

Maximum Speed: Mach 1.67

Ceiling: 60,000ft (18,288m)

Combat Radius: 517 miles (832km)

Range: 1,035 miles (1,665km)

Powerplant: 1 x Pratt & Whitney F119 afterburning turbofan derivative, rated at 28,000lb (124.5kN) dry thrust and 43,000lb (191kN) with afterburner

Armament: 1 x 25mm GAU-22/A cannon in an external pod with 220 rounds; 6 x underwing pylons with a 15,000lb (6,804kg) capacity; 2 x internal bays with a 3,000lb (1,360kg) capacity. Weapons options: AIM-9X Sidewinder AAM, AIM-120 AAM, AMRAAM, AIM-132 ASRAAM, IRIS-T, Joint Dual Role Air Dominance Missile (JDRADM) (after 2020), AGM-154 JSOW, AGM-158 JASSM, Paveway laser-guided bombs, JDAM bombs, small diameter bomb (SDB)

Avionics: Northrop Grumman Electronic Systems AN/APG-81 AESA radar

MiG-21PD 23-31 Fishbed G*

Crew: 1

Wingspan: 25.4ft (7.76m)

Sweep (leading edge): 57°

Length (excluding boom): 58.1ft (17.72m)

Wing area: 285ft² (26.5m²)

T/O distance 650ft (200m) approx

Empty Weight: N/A

Gross Weight: N/A

Maximum Speed: Supersonic in normal flight

Powerplant: 1 x Tumansky R-27-300 turbojet providing 8,565lb (38.1kN) dry thrust and 12,656lb (56.3kN) with afterburner; 2 x Kolesov RD-36-35 lift engines, each rated at 5,200lb (23kN) thrust

Armament: 1 x GSh-23 23mm cannon, 2 x AAMs

MiG-23PD Faithless*

Crew: 1

Wingspan: 25.33ft (7.72m)

Wing area: 430.5ft² (40m²)

Length: 55ft (16.80m)

Height: 16.8ft (5.15m)

Empty Weight: 26,500lb (12,020kg)

Take-off Weight: 35,273lb (16,000kg)

Maximum Speed: Mach 2

Cruising Speed: Mach 0.83

Ceiling: N/A

Range: N/A

Take-off Distance: 590-650ft (180-200m)

Landing Distance, with parachute and braking: 820ft (250m)

Powerplant: 1 x Tumansky R-27-300 turbojet providing 8,565lb (38.1kN) dry thrust and 12,656lb (56.3kN) with afterburner; 2 x Kolesov RD-36-35 lift engines, each rated at 5,200lb (23kN) thrust

Armament: 1 x GSh-23 23mm cannon, 2 x R-23 AAMs

Sukhoi T-58VD Flagon B*

Crew: 1

Wingspan: 30.6ft (9.34m)

Wing area: 394ft² (36.60m²)

Sweep (leading edge): Primary 60°; Outer 45°

Length: 67.38ft (20.54m); with probe: 70.34ft (21.44m)

Height: 16.4ft (5m)

Empty Weight: N/A

Maximum Take-off Weight: N/A

Landing Weight: N/A

Maximum Speed: Mach 2

Ceiling: 55,000ft (16,750m)

Range: N/A

Powerplant: 2 x Tumansky R-27-300 turbojets, each rated at 8,565lb (38.1kN) dry thrust and 12,656lb (56.3kN) with afterburner; 3 x Kolesov RD-36-35 lift engines, each rated at 5,200lb (23kN) thrust

Armament: None for this prototype

Yak-33

Crew: 2 (pilot and navigator)

Length: 88.5ft (27m) approx

Wingspan: 36ft (11m) approx

Wing area: N/A

Height: N/A

Normal Take-off Weight (Strike): 70,547lb (32,000kg)

Maximum Take-off Weight (Strike): 88,184lb (40,000kg)

Maximum Speed: Đach 3.0

Cruise Speed: Mach 2.0

Ceiling: 70,000ft (21,336m)

Range: 2,485 miles (4,000km)

Powerplant: 2 x Kolesov RD-36-41 vectored-thrust turbojets, each rated at 15,500lb (69kN) dry thrust and 35,000lb (156kN) afterburning; 6 to 8 x Kolesov RD-36-35 lift engines, each rated at 5,200lb (23kN) thrust

Armament: 4 x AAMs (interceptor); 1 x Đ-22 or Đ-30 missile; 1 x free-fall nuclear weapon

Tupolev Tu-136 VTOL

Crew: 1

Wingspan: 16.8ft (5.12m)

Wing area: N/A

Sweep (leading edge): 60° and 45°

Length: 38.7ft (11.8m)

Height: 8.2ft (2.5m)

Maximum Speed: Subsonic

Ceiling: N/A

Range: N/A

Powerplant: 1 x Tumansky vectored-thrust turbofan (unbuilt)

Armament: N/A

Yakovlev Yak-36 Freehand*

Crew: 1

Wingspan: 34.4ft (10.5m)

Wing area: 172ft² (16m²)

Sweep (leading edge): 37°

Length (with probe): 55.8ft (17m)
Height: 14.8ft (4.5m)
Empty Weight: 11,684lb (5,300kg)
Maximum STO Weight: 19,625lb (8,900kg)
Maximum Speed: 620mph (1,000km/h)
Ceiling: 40,000ft (12,192m)
Operational Radius: 230 miles (370km)
Powerplant: 2 x Tumansky R-27V-300 vectoring turbojets, each rated at 11,680lb (51.95kN) thrust
Armament: None (although demonstrated in 1967 with underwing rocket pods)

Yakovlev Yak-38 Forger A*
Crew: 1
Wingspan: 24ft (7.32m)
Wing area: 199ft² (18.5m²)
Sweep (leading edge): 45°
Length: 50.85ft (15.5m)
Height: 14.4ft (4.4m)
Empty Weight: 16,500lb (7,484kg)
Maximum Take-off Weight: 25,794lb (11,700kg)
Maximum Speed: 680mph (1,100km/h)

Ceiling: 40,000ft (12,192m)
Operational Radius: 62 miles (100km)
Powerplant: 1 x Tumansky R-28V-300 turbojet rated at 15,000lb (66.7kN) thrust 2 x Kolesov RD-36-35FVR lift engines, each providing a maximum thrust of 6,400lb (28.4kN)
Armament: 1 x GSh-23L 23mm cannon in underwing pod; 2 x R-60 or R-60M AAMs, 2 x Kh-23 ASM (guidance pod required), free-fall bombs, air-to-surface rockets, tactical nuclear weapon

Yakovlev Yak-41M Freestyle*
Crew: 1
Wingspan: 33.1ft (10.1m)
Wing area: 341ft² (31.7 m²)
Sweep (leading edge): 45°
Length: 60ft (18.3m)
Height: 16.4ft (5m)
Empty Weight: 25,690lb (11,650kg)
Maximum VTO Weight: 34,833lb (15,800kg)
Maximum STO Take-off Weight: 43,000lb (19,500kg)

Maximum Speed: Mach 1.55 at altitude
Rate of Climb: 50,000ft/min (15,240m/min)
Ceiling: 50,850ft (15,500m)
Operational Radius: 870 miles (1,400km)
Maximum Range: 1,305 miles (2,100km)
Ferry Range: 1,865 miles (3,000km)
Powerplant: 1 x Soyuz/Kobchenko R-79V-300 vectored-thrust lift/cruise turbofan, rated at 23,148lb (103kN) dry thrust and 34,170lb (152kN) thrust with afterburning; 2 x Rybinsk/Kuznetsov RD-41 turbofan lift engines each rated at 9,039lb (40.2kN)
Armament: 1 x 30mm GSh-301 cannon with 120 rounds; hardpoints: 4 x underwing and 1 x fuselage hardpoints with 5,733lb (2,600kg) capacity of external stores; including R-73 Archer AAM, R-77 Adder AAM or R-27 Alamo AAM, free-fall bombs, air-to-surface missiles, rockets, tactical nuclear weapon

* NATO reporting name for Soviet military aircraft

Glossary

AAM: Air-to-Air Missile

AFB: Air Force Base

AGM: Air-to-Ground Missile, also sometimes referred to as ASM: Air-to-Surface Missile

AMRAAM: AIM-120 Advanced Medium-Range AAM

Armée de l'Air: French Air Force

ASRAAM: Advanced Short-Range AAM (US)

ASTOVL: Advanced Short Take-Off/Vertical Landing project undertaken by DARPA in the 1980s

Atar: *Atelier Technique Aéronautique Rickenbach* (jet engine manufacturer)

BAC: British Aircraft Corporation

BAe: British Aerospace

BMVg: *Bundesministerium der Verteidigung* (West Germany's Ministry of Defence)

BuAer: US Navy's Bureau of Aeronautics

BTZ: Bureau Technique Zborowski. An aircraft design organisation, operating in postwar France and headed by Dr Helmut von Zborowski

Convair: Consolidated Vultee Aircraft

CTOL: Conventional Take-Off Landing

DARPA: US Defense Advanced Research Projects Agency

DLI: Deck Launched Intercept

DoD: Department of Defense (US)

EL: Ejector Lift system, pioneered by De Havilland Canada

HFVT: Hybrid Fan Vectored-Thrust engine

Laser: Light amplification by stimulated emission of radiation - monochromatic visible/invisible light

LERX: Leading-edge root extensions, providing better handling at high angles of attack

Luftwaffe: German Air Force

MAI: *Moskovskiy Aviatsionniy Institut*

MoD: UK Ministry of Defence, 1964-present day

MoS: UK Ministry of Supply, 1939-1959

Mt: Megaton

MWDP: Mutual Weapons Development Programme; operated in Paris by NATO

NACA: National Advisory Committee for Aeronautics (NASA predecessor)

NASA: National Aeronautics and Space Administration

NATO: The North Atlantic Treaty Organization; an inter-governmental military alliance based on the North Atlantic Treaty that was signed on 4 April 1949.

NBMR-3: 1961 NATO Basic Military Requirement 3; contest for a VTOL strike aircraft

OKB: *Opytnoe Konstructorskoe Byuro* - Soviet Experimental Design Bureau

Payload: Normally cargo or equipment but can refer to military ordnance

PCB: Plenum Chamber Burning

RAE: Royal Aircraft Establishment

RALS: Remote Augmented Lift System

RATO: Rocket-Assisted Take-Off

RLM: *Reichsluftfahrtministerium* (Wartime German Air Ministry)

SCS: Sea Control Ships; a 1970s US Navy programme to develop a new class of small aircraft carriers, operating supersonic VTOL fighters

SFECMAS: *Société Française d'Etude et de Construction de Matériels Aéronautiques Spéciaux* (France)

Shar: Royal Navy slang term for the Sea Harrier aircraft (SeaHARrier)

SNCAN: *Société Nationale de Constructions Aéronautiques du Sud-est* (France)

SNECMA: *Société Nationale d'Études et de Construction de Moteurs d'Aviation* (France)

Stealth: Low-visibility technologies

STO: Short Take-Off

STOL: Short Take-Off and Landing

STOVL: Short Take-Off and Vertical Landing

TEMCO: Texas Engineering and Manufacturing Company

TF: Tandem Fan (Engine)

TsAGI (Central Aerohydrodynamic Institute - Russia's equivalent to NACA/NASA)

USAAF: United States Army Air Force

USAF: United States Air Force

VATOL: Vertical Attitude Take-off and Landing

VD (Sukhoi T-58 VD): Vertikalniye Dvigateli (vertical engines)

VTO: Vertical Take-Off

VTOL: Vertical Take-Off and Landing

VSTOL: Vertical/Short Take-Off and Landing

Warsaw Pact: A defence treaty between eight Eastern European Communist countries that existed during much of the Cold War

ZEL or ZELL: Zero-Length Launch

Directory of Aircraft

Significant People